Adv...
Moto...

HANDBOOK

A ROUTE AND PLANNING GUIDE

CHRIS SCOTT

TRAILBLAZER PUBLICATIONS

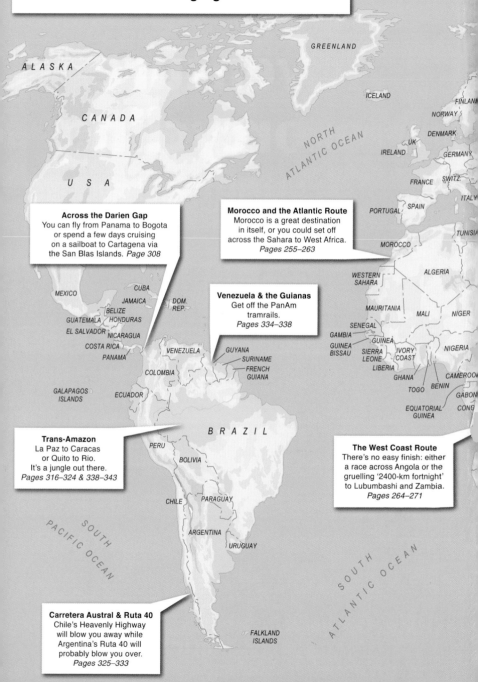

The Adventure Motorcycling Zone
Selected highlights

ARCTIC

GREENLAND

ALASKA

CANADA

ICELAND

FINLAND

NORWAY

NORTH ATLANTIC OCEAN

DENMARK

UK

IRELAND

GERMANY

USA

FRANCE

SWITZ.

ITALY

Across the Darien Gap
You can fly from Panama to Bogota
or spend a few days cruising
on a sailboat to Cartagena via
the San Blas Islands. *Page 308*

Morocco and the Atlantic Route
Morocco is a great destination
in itself, or you could set off
across the Sahara to West Africa.
Pages 255–263

PORTUGAL

SPAIN

TUNISIA

MOROCCO

MEXICO

CUBA

JAMAICA

DOM. REP.

BELIZE

GUATEMALA

HONDURAS

EL SALVADOR

NICARAGUA

COSTA RICA

PANAMA

VENEZUELA

GUYANA

SURINAME

FRENCH GUIANA

COLOMBIA

GALAPAGOS ISLANDS

ECUADOR

WESTERN SAHARA

ALGERIA

MAURITANIA

MALI

NIGER

SENEGAL

GAMBIA

GUINEA

GUINEA BISSAU

SIERRA LEONE

IVORY COAST

NIGERIA

LIBERIA

GHANA

TOGO

BENIN

CAMEROO

EQUATORIAL GUINEA

GABON

CONG

Venezuela & the Guianas
Get off the PanAm
tramrails.
Pages 334–338

Trans-Amazon
La Paz to Caracas
or Quito to Rio.
It's a jungle out there.
Pages 316–324 & 338–343

BRAZIL

PERU

BOLIVIA

The West Coast Route
There's no easy finish: either
a race across Angola or the
gruelling '2400-km fortnight'
to Lubumbashi and Zambia.
Pages 264–271

CHILE

PARAGUAY

SOUTH PACIFIC OCEAN

ARGENTINA

URUGUAY

SOUTH ATLANTIC OCEAN

Carretera Austral & Ruta 40
Chile's Heavenly Highway
will blow you away while
Argentina's Ruta 40 will
probably blow you over.
Pages 325–333

FALKLAND ISLANDS

Siberia Off Road
Swing off the Trans-Sib and strike out along the BAMsky Trakt for Yakutia and the Road of Bones. *Pages 229–235*

Mongolia
Still a raw wilderness of nomadic grasslands, mountain and desert. *Page 241*

India
Bite the bullet and ride an Enfield Bullet along the world's highest roads. *Pages 211–220*

Pakistan
The KKH and its offshoots are the highlight on the road to India and Nepal. *Pages 205–211*

The Nile Route
The classic ride from the Pyramids to the Serengeti. Spice it up via Lake Turkana if you have the range. *Pages 272–279*

CHRIS SCOTT's first motorcycle adventure got him halfway to Wales aboard a moped whereupon a long affair with bikes ensued. While working as a despatch rider in London on anything from IT250s to a 900SS (with one especially productive week on a nitrox XS650), most winters were spent exploring the Sahara on trail bikes. *Desert Travels* (available on Kindle) describes those adventures and misfortunes.

In the early 90s he wrote *Desert Biking, A Guide to Independent Motorcycling in the Sahara* (which evolved into *AMH*, see p6) while also working for Rough Guides, specifically their Australia title. With the advent of affordable mini DV cameras he then got into filming his rides in the Yukon, Sahara and the Australian outback (featured on National Geographic Channel and all on DVD). His other books for Trailblazer include *Sahara Overland*, *Overlanders' Handbook* and *Morocco Overland*. Apparently he's also working on an urban memoir of his early motorcycling years.

Adventure Motorcycling
HANDBOOK

A ROUTE & PLANNING GUIDE

CHRIS SCOTT

WITH
Enzo Elphick-Pooley, Mark Harfenist, Jamie Kenyon, Lois Pryce, Dr Paul Rowe, Charlie & Nina Weatherill

AND
Walter J Colebatch, Jacqui Furneaux, Duncan Hughes, Gaurav Jani, Grant Johnson, Jay Kannaiyan, Carla King, Andy Pag, Tony Pettie, Dawie Du Plessis, James & Cat Rix, Simon Roberts and Nick Taylor

ADDITIONAL MATERIAL BY
Hugh Bergin, Jeremy Bullard, Ken & Carol Duval, Bill Eakins, Bob Goggs, Chris & Chloe Granger, Darrin Johansen, Pat McCarthy, Sean Munro, Daniel Radford, Paul Randall, Ken Thomas, Richard Virr and Richard Wolters

ILLUSTRATIONS BY
Simon Roberts

TRAILBLAZER PUBLICATIONS

Adventure Motorcycling Handbook

Sixth edition: October 2012

Publisher
Trailblazer Publications – The Old Manse, Tower Rd, Hindhead, Surrey, GU26 6SU, UK
Fax (+44) 01428-607571 info@trailblazer-guides.com www.trailblazer-guides.com

British Library Cataloguing in Publication Data
A catalogue record for this book is available from the British Library

ISBN 978-1-905864-46-1

© Chris Scott 2001, 2005, 2012
Text, maps and photographs (unless otherwise credited)
The right of Chris Scott to be identified as the author of this work has been asserted
by him in accordance with the Copyright, Designs and Patents Act 1988

Editor: Nicky Slade
Series Editor: Bryn Thomas
Layout: Chris Scott
Proofreading: Nicky Slade
Cartography: Nick Hill
Graphics: Simon Roberts (www.sr-illustration.com)
Index: Patrick D. Hummingbird

Acknowledgements

Contributions from riders all around the world help make the *AMH* what it is, a collection of
guidelines for adventurous travel by motorcycle, in Asia, Africa and Latin America. Without them
AMH-6 would have been a pretty thin book, so a big thank you to the thirty-odd contributors listed
on the previous page as well as to credited photographers who supplied material for free or for
negligible fees. Some of their biogs appear on p367. Thanks also to the team at Trailblazer.

A request

The author and the publisher have tried to ensure that the information in this book is as up to date
as possible. Nevertheless, things are certain to change; even before the ink is dry. If you notice any
changes or omissions that you think should be included in the next edition or have any other feed-
back, please email the author at the website below or via Trailblazer (address above).

Warning

Global travel by motorcycle is unpredictable and can be dangerous.
Efforts have been made by the author, contributors and the publisher to ensure that the
information contained herein is as accurate as possible. However, they are unable to
accept responsibility for any inconvenience, loss or injury sustained by anyone as a result
of the advice and information given in this book – so be careful and check the latest news.

Updates and a whole lot more at:
www.adventure-motorcycling.com

Photos – Front cover: Bolivia, © Christopher Siewald
Frontispiece: La Mano del Desierto, Pan-Am Hwy, Chile, © Chris Granger
Page 8: Ted Simon's 1970s pannier © Andrew Harbron

Printed on chlorine-free paper by D'Print (☎ +65-6581 3832), Singapore

CONTENTS

PART 3: LIFE ON THE ROAD *(cont'd)*

LIST OF BOXED TEXT

PART 4: ASIA ROUTE OUTLINES

PART 5: AFRICA ROUTE OUTLINES

PART 6: LATIN AMERICA ROUTE OUTLINES

PART 7: TALES FROM THE SADDLE

APPENDIX

INDEX

HISTORY OF THE *ADVENTURE MOTORCYCLING HANDBOOK*

In the summer of 1991 I was dishwashing in a Mexican restaurant, recovering from a broken leg and another costly Saharan fiasco. The job was not too intellectually taxing so I thought I'd get into writing, having enjoyed describing my travels for bike magazines in the 1980s.

I decided to compose a short report on what I'd learned the hard way in the previous decade's biking in the Sahara. Many riders, myself included, had trouble-strewn first trips, partly on account of a lack of hard information on all aspects of what's now become known as 'adventure motorcycling'.

I bought myself an Amstrad, worked out how to turn it on and after a lot of wasted paper, dropped off a 30-page report entitled *Desert Biking: A Guide to Independent Motorcycling in the Sahara* at the Royal Geographical Society in London. For all I know the original is still tucked away in the Map Room's archives today.

Rather pleased with the end result, I figured the report might have some faint commercial value and proposed this idea to what was then the Travellers Bookshop off London's Charing Cross Road. It was good timing as they were considering publishing niche travel guides and an expanded version of *DB* fitted the bill.

I spent a couple of months padding out the RGS report into the 100-page first edition of *Desert Biking* which was eventually published in late 1993. It didn't exactly hit the bookshops. Instead, as word got around and demand trickled in, batches were Xeroxed and stapled in a copy shop in Notting Hill and then sent out.

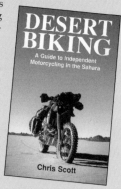

Following the moderate success of this hand-made version, a revised and suitably expanded paperback edition (right) was published in September 1995. The updated format included the addition of 'travellers' tales' in the back.

With nothing similar around in English and seeing promise in the concept, Compass Star picked up the idea and took it a big step further with the publication of the retitled *The Adventure Motorbiking Handbook* (*AMH*) in November 1997. It featured the practicalities and yarns of *Desert Biking* but brought in a network of two-wheeling contributors from around the globe to add expertise and help fill the gaps. It's a collaborative formula which helps make the *AMH* what it is today.

I created 🖥 **adventure-motorcycling.com** around the same time, which now features over a thousand of your trip reports as well as whatever else is going on.

Compass Star in turn passed the rights on to Trailblazer Guides which, 22 years down the line, brings us to the sixth edition of the *AMH*. Since the last yellow edition adventure motorcycling has boomed, evolving into the fastest growing sector of motorcycling in western markets. The range of gear, bikes, know-how and even tours is now greater than ever, but the fundamentals of trip planning and bike preparation remain much as they did in the original *Desert Biking* report.

Enjoy the ride.

INTRODUCTION

Welcome to edition six of the *AMH*, a handbook for planning, preparing and riding in the developing countries in Africa, Asia and Latin America. Out there you're beyond the safety net of conventional motorcycle touring closer to home and so the word 'adventure', with its associations of risk and uncertainty, is appropriate.

The adventure-motorcycling scene has exploded since the last edition, with new bikes, tours and magazines as well as a greater range of gear and services. The blogosphere, too, is packed with riders' accounts of their epic journeys. But prices have also climbed so the option to adapt your own gear remains, while political instability continues to jinx routes across parts of Africa and Asia.

We're in a golden age of global motorcycle travel, if for no other reason than it's become a less eccentric activity and many people have shown how easy – and yet how fulfilling – it can be. You don't need a huge bike or an array of sponsors, you just need the curiosity to ride out into the real world to see it for yourself.

A map, a bike and a road. What the picture doesn't show is the months of planning and bike preparation to get to that stage.

PLANNING & PREPARATION

Prepare. That's still the first word of the first chapter of this edition. The motorcycle adventure you're about to take on is going to be expensive, demanding and maybe even dangerous. Preparation doesn't mean running the most expensive bike dripping with all the latest adventure motorcycling accessories; it means having as good an understanding as possible of what you're taking on and being appropriately equipped to do it.

The decision to set off on a long motorcycle journey can germinate from a moment's inspiration, a decision to take on the 'Big Trip' after a succession of easier rides, or just the plain old desire to cut loose from the rat race and have a big adventure.

You may not think so yet, but within a few pages you'll appreciate the mushroom effect of taking on such a venture. Choosing and preparing your bike might take up the lion's share of your time and the budget, but realigning your initial itinerary with the reality of visa acquisition, open borders and regional security issues also takes a huge amount of research. The situation will have changed since this was written and that won't end once you're on the road, so the planning is never really over until you stop.

The more you learn the more there is to consider, until you get to a magical point where, however briefly, you're ahead of the game. If you're very lucky, that moment of overlanding nirvana will coincide with your departure.

The extent of preparation varies between individuals. Some will want a GPS waypoint for every fuel station, consulate and border post – that information is probably out there somewhere. Others will be satisfied with a good map, some guidebooks and a loose schedule for any visa applications that must be made en route. You need to reach a level of preparation that gives you enough confidence in a venture that'll always be unpredictable.

Acquiring the correct **paperwork and visas** and sorting out your **money** arrangements is tedious but essential. It's common to worry about carrying half a year's cash with you, acquiring visas on

Spontaneity is a wonderful thing but it's best saved for short-range route deviations once on the road.

the road and motor insurance at each new border, as well as trying to get by without a carnet (see p24). Without just one of the several documents listed in this section, your trip could eventually grind to a halt, but the two key items are and always will be a **passport** and the **vehicle ownership document**.

Spontaneity is a wonderful thing but it's best saved for short-range route deviations once on the road. There'll be enough unexpected dramas to handle without adding to them with inadequate planning. Do yourself a favour and set off knowing that, whatever happens, you've done all the preparation you intended to do. The more effort you put into planning, the smoother your trip is likely to be. But don't worry, it'll still be an adventure – you can count on that. No one's ever set off to ride around the world but given up because it was just too dang boring!

A plan

Before the preparation comes **a plan**, an outline of the regions and destinations you'd like to visit. It's not uncommon to initially come up with a certain romantic flow or theme: following the Silk Road to Beijing or following the Mediterranean coast counterclockwise from Casablanca to Istanbul. Or setting off on an old Triumph like your parents did before you came along. Then you discover there is no single 'Silk Road', the border between Morocco and Algeria has been closed for years (though see p255) and that these days an old Bonnie is better pampered than ridden for months on end.

This is just the start. If you make it past p26 your expertise in the whole business will have multiplied exponentially. A few edges may have been knocked off your starry-eyed dream too, but you'll be in much better shape to take on what lies ahead.

Once you've got over that possible disappointment there comes another shock that can be paraphrased from the Prussian military strategist Helmuth von Moltke's famous quote: 'no plan survives contact with the road'. It's hard to imagine not having some sort of outline before you leave, if only to avoid undesirable interruptions and expenses. But soon enough that **schedule** becomes derailed, in most cases before you even leave. Your big adventure is like a major civil engineering project: it will be late and over budget. It's rare to leave on your original departure date, so don't set this

Without necessarily adorning yourself with a headband and sandals, once on the road be ready to 'go with the flow'.

or what follows in stone. Without necessarily adorning yourself with a headband and sandals like Peter Fonda in *Easy Rider*, once on the road be ready to 'go with the flow'. Compared to the life you've probably been leading up to now, life on the road will be unpredictable and requires flexibility.

Be wary of **over-ambitious goals**, or anticipate them and be happy to return home having done much less than you planned but still satisfied. Even in the right season (see p12) most first-time overland riders greatly **underestimate** the time it takes to cover ground in parts of Asia and Africa, let alone the desirability of simply slowing down.

To want to try and **see it all** is understandable when you consider the cost and effort you're investing in the project, but once you're inching out of a Far Eastern container depot into the chaos of the city, or rolling off the end of a sealed highway into a remote area of tracks, reality bites.

Reality bites... Sitting at the sharp end of your adventure, it then runs around and jabs you in the butt and your spectacular, trans-continental expedition, unparalleled since the sweeping hordes of Genghis Khan, crumples like a paper cup.

PLANNING & PREPARATION

Sitting at the sharp end of your adventure, it then runs around and jabs you in the butt and your spectacular trans-continental expedition, unparalleled since the sweeping hordes of Genghis Khan, crumples like a paper cup. The good thing is: you're there. With a new-found humility you might whisper '*er... bring it on?*'.

WHICH CONTINENT?

Assuming that most of us come from the rich nations of the developed West – North America, Europe, Southern Africa and Australasia – certain **classic overland routes** present themselves. They're illustrated and described in more detail in each of the three Route Outline maps for **Africa** (pp258-9 & p280), **Asia** (pp194-5) and **Latin America** (pp296-7), with an overview map in the colour section (pp192-3).

It's worth comparing these three big continents in terms of difficulty. Without shipping your bike out or buying it overseas, **European departures**

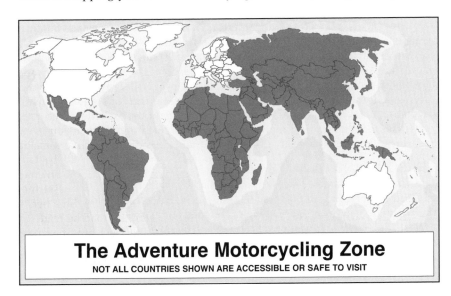

The Adventure Motorcycling Zone
NOT ALL COUNTRIES SHOWN ARE ACCESSIBLE OR SAFE TO VISIT

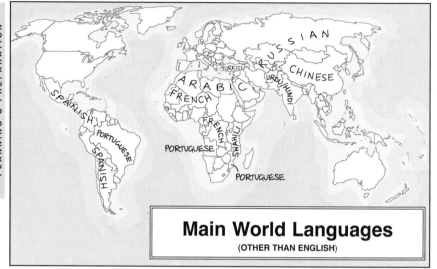

Main World Languages
(OTHER THAN ENGLISH)

offer the most options, with both Asia and Africa easily accessible. From Europe, the northern route across **Asia** goes as far as Far Eastern Russia. The southern route runs to India, requires a shipping detour to get round Burma, and then continues overland across Southeast Asia. China too is a special case – see p246. The southern route to India can be comfortably done on a road bike with as few as three visas.

Alternatively, departing from Europe you can head down the length of **Africa**, typically ending at the Cape of Good Hope. Although it's getting easier year by year, Africa south of the Sahara still represents the toughest challenge for a mainstream overland route from Europe, a real adventure both in terms of driving conditions, visa acquisition, security and even expense.

Many riders not from North America choose to start their transit of **Latin America** above the Arctic Circle in Alaska to end it some 25,000km (15,000 miles) later in Tierra del Fuego, just 1000km (600 miles) from the Antarctic mainland. Assuming you follow the line of least resistance, Latin America is the least challenging of the three big continental routes in terms of paperwork, driving conditions and language, while offering as impressive scenic and cultural attractions as anywhere, particularly in the Andean countries.

If you're intent on **ringing the globe**, shipping across the oceans that separate these continents is easily done from certain key ports described on p190.

SEASONS AND CLIMATE
The season and expected weather at certain key stages of your route must be factored in. Seasons and the climate can be anticipated (⌨ worldclimate.com); the weather cannot. In regions where the road infrastructure is not adequate to deal with extreme conditions, progress will be slow or briefly impossible. At other times, even if the riding is straightforward, extreme temperatures can make simple survival a challenge. The Sahara is a good example; it's no hotter

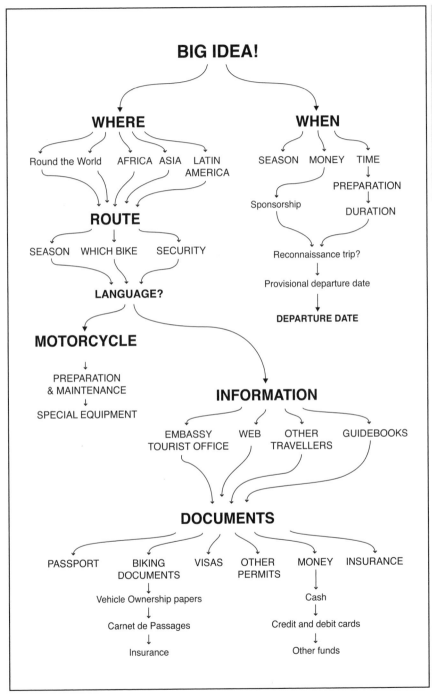

than the interior of Australia, Pakistan or Arizona in summer, but riding alone on anything other than the main trans-desert highways reduces your safety margin to the amount of water carried per person per day.

Seasons and the climate can be anticipated, the weather cannot.

To head blithely across northern Asia or into the Andes in winter, or the equatorial regions of the Amazon and in particular the Congo basin in the wet season, is also asking for trouble. Ironically, in Far Eastern Russia (as in northern Canada), some ice roads only exist in winter, following the courses of deeply frozen rivers able to support 20-ton trucks. Whether your heated vest can support you is another matter. At any other time traversing the sodden tundra or taiga requires much more effort.

By and large Himalayan passes over 4000m (13,100′) close around the end of October until late spring, while in the Congo Basin transportation takes to the rivers at the height of the rains and can be a fun interlude on a bike.

TIME AND BUDGET

Once the spark has been lit, assuming that you're beginning preparations while in full-time employment, organising a trans-continental journey for the first time requires about **a year**. If you're just taking an exploratory nibble into one continent, six months will do. Preparing to explore a wilderness region within your own country may only require a few weeks of planning and, as you'll soon learn, doing so as a test-trip prior to the Big Day is a very good idea.

Ask yourself how much of a commitment you want to make to your overland adventure. Do you have an urge to see some distant part of the planet, but still like the idea of returning to a job and house? Or are you ready to

Are you ready to throw the dice and take an entirely new direction in your life for several months or even years?

throw the dice and take an entirely new direction in your life for several months or even years? When heading into an unknown future, having enough money to deal with the predictably unpredictable events will of course help. If you're organised you ought to be able to **calculate an average daily expenditure** fairly closely: guidebooks and guidebook publishers' websites are invaluable for this. How precisely you need to plan your budget will depend on whether you've cut loose from life back home, whether you'll still have some sort of income while on the road – like rent or a pension for example – or if you've given yourself a set amount of money or time to undertake a journey.

Assess carefully if you have the will and opportunity to put the money together in the time you've given yourself – let alone to be on the road for months. To cross Africa expect to **budget** on at least £3500, €4000 or US$5600, in addition to the cost of your machine. The expense of the carnet and some visas apart (see p24 and p19), Asia can be cheaper. You could probably ride from Europe to India for around £2500, €3000 or $4000. To cross the length of

PLANNING & PREPARATION

the Americas costs at least as much as Africa, and a genuine round-the-world (RTW) trip is going to set you back around £10,000, €12,000 or $15,000, mostly in fuel and getting your motorcycle from one continent to the next. Some people will achieve the above for less, most will spend more, but these estimates account for at least some of the unplanned expenses that most trips encounter.

FUEL PRICES AROUND THE WORLD

Fuel prices vary staggeringly around the world, from a couple of cents a litre for diesel in Venezuela and Iran (a fraction of the price of the crude oil from which it is actually refined), to at least double the fuel's true value. Extreme subsidisation in a dozen or so countries and heavy taxation in many more is what explains this dramatic discrepancy.

At around $4 a US gallon, the **price of fuel in the US** can be considered average by international standards, neither amazingly cheap nor ridiculously expensive, including as it does a reasonable 12% in tax. Compared with the US, many countries in Africa with low GDPs tax fuel extremely highly, as does the UK, Ireland, Holland, Turkey and Norway.

This can have a big impact when the size of a country is taken into consideration. The **cost of fuel in a neighbouring country** has an impact too, especially where fuel is as much as ten times more expensive across the border as it is in Venezuela rather than Brazil, Algeria rather than Niger, and in Iran rather than Turkey.

Continent by continent

Things will change of course but excepting Venezuela, Bolivia and Ecuador, the US has among the cheapest fuel in the **Americas**, and Peru and Brazil the

priciest. In Central America fuel costs in Mexico are cheaper than the US but in Costa Rica they're nearly double US prices. South of the Darien Gap petrol is much more expensive in Brazil, Chile, Uruguay and French Guiana.

In **Africa**, South African prices fall about midway between the most expensive countries immediately to its northeast and the heavily subsidised fuel across North Africa in Algeria, Libya and Egypt. Although among the cheapest in the world, these three examples show how the price of fuel doesn't necessarily make them the cheapest places to visit. Egypt and Libya demand a carnet (see p24) and Algeria and probably Libya (by the time tourism resumes) require escorts when riding in the Sahara, which cost around €100 (£82) a day. So what you save on fuel you pay in other ways.

Riders setting off from Australia into **Asia** won't find petrol noticeably less expensive (mostly 20–30% pricier than in the US), with only a couple of Central Asian countries plus Jordan, Malaysia, Indonesia and of course Iran being cheaper. Turkey, a large and key gateway country, is somewhere you'd also want to spend more time exploring if it didn't have just about the priciest petrol in the world.

As you'll read on p202, Iran imposes certain fees on buying fuel that's otherwise cheaper than water. Taking the high route across Asia (see p196), Mongolia is another worthwhile but large country on the overlander's map where not only is fuel expensive but it's of a notoriously low quality. Fuel in any **remote location** is often very pricey.

Every November or so the German Gesellschaft für Technische Zusammenarbeit (GTZ) produces a very well presented and interesting document on **world fuel prices** collated the previous year. You can download it at 🖥 www.gtz.de/fuelprices, although on close scrutiny I've found the information is only correct in one in five cases, can be out in both directions by 50% – and of course, it's up to a year old. To help you budget on fuel costs see the Wikipedia page titled 'Gasoline and diesel usage and pricing'.

Getting information

You may well have a lot to learn, but particularly regarding information about routes and border regulations, this book was probably out of date long before the ink was dry. Here are the most likely sources of up-to-date information.

THE INTERNET
Everything you need to know (including the contents of this book rearranged and repeated to near infinity) is out there online. The trouble is that it's spread all over cyberspace like the Milky Way; the task is to track it all down sometime before the Milky Way implodes.

In recent years Grant and Susan Johnson's Horizons Unlimited Bulletin Board, aka the **HUBB** (🖥 www.horizonsunlimited.com/hubb), has become the premier motorcycle overlanders' resource in English. Its dozen **regional forums** (North Asia, South America, sub-Saharan Africa, etc) cover topics that relate to all travellers and a day or two spent acquainting yourself with your region or route on HU will answer many questions as well raise many you'd not thought of. Nothing else in English comes close to its truly global reach.

Lonely Planet's **Thorn Tree** (💻 www.thorntree.lonelyplanet.com) isn't vehicle-oriented, but has border and route details, and for a North American perspective the **Expedition Portal** (💻 www.expeditionportal.com/forum) is a good source of Latin American reports, but remains more useful for information and opinions on locally sourced cars and equipment. Also in the US, the **Adventure Rider Motorcycle Forum** (💻 advrider.com/forums) is especially good on trip reports with hits on popular ones running into the millions.

EMBASSIES AND TOURIST OFFICES
This may seem an obvious place to start but, particularly with embassies, is usually the last place you'll get anything useful, beyond a free map or brochure about mainstream holidaymaking. You may get some country information on a tourist board website, while a consular website ought to have visa types, fees, conditions and possibly a form to download. All state-based consular or tourist information sources tend to gloss over, or even deny, regional security issues, and neither place will be likely to advise you about the situation in remote locales or what facilities you might find when you get there.

GOVERNMENT OVERSEAS DEPARTMENTS
More useful than an embassy is the opinion of your country's foreign ministry. In the UK it's the Foreign & Commonwealth Office (FCO) Travel Advice Unit; in the US it's the Department of State; and the French Ministère des Affaires Étrangères is better than most for the Francophone countries of Africa. In Britain at least, the lazier end of the travel media has a habit of taking the FCO's advice as gospel rather than the *advice* that it is. While the FCO has in recent years got much better at acknowledging that distant or outdated threats need not write off a whole country, like all these agencies they're primarily concerned with avoiding international incidents involving their nationals, if not discouraging casual visits to countries with whom political relations may be strained. Take everything these advisories say with a pinch of salt and accept that politics and convenience inevitably colours their advice. Be warned though that many **travel insurance** providers (see p21) won't offer cover for countries deemed unsafe by the FCO or its equivalent. There is more on this subject in 'When Things Go Wrong' on p165.

NATIONAL MOTORING ORGANISATIONS
Again not a lot of help for the aspiring motorcycle adventurer, but sometimes useful on documentation and essential when it comes to coughing up for a Carnet de Passage. In the UK this, along with an International Driving Permit, is all the **RAC and AA** can do for you, though, to be fair, motorcycle overlanding is such a minority form of motoring, you can't expect them to devote any resources to it.

TRAVEL GUIDEBOOKS
Although users often grumble about their inaccuracies or opinions, for what it costs, a guidebook will repay you in advice and recommendations many,

many times over. Lonely Planet and Rough Guides are the two best-known series in English; the former covers just about every country on the planet, but both have their origins in the backpacker or independent traveller market, not motorcyclists. Because of this you'll find only the most general advice on riding, and accommodation offering secure parking is an example of a commonly overlooked detail.

ONCOMING TRAVELLERS

Don't dismiss the likelihood and usefulness of running into other overland travellers coming from where you're going. You couldn't ask for a more up-to-date source of information unless you're bitten by the horse's mouth itself. They'll be able to assuage your current anxieties about fuel prices, road conditions and the friendliness or otherwise of border officials, and, likely as not, will be as keen to hear your news too.

Travel documents

For any journey covering half a dozen countries or more, visas are something you'll need to address early on because they can take weeks and occasionally even months to arrange. With some visas starting from the date they're issued or only available in your home country, this sort of planning ahead is easier said than done.

PASSPORT

If you don't yet own a passport, get onto it straight away. If you already own one, make sure it's **valid for at least six months** after your anticipated journey's end, if not a year. Many countries won't issue visas for passports that have less than six months left to run. As ever, by ensuring that your passport has plenty of use left in it (as well as pages), you're one step ahead of some awkward border official. Once you get your passport, check all the details. Discrepancies between it and your other vital documents, even just the misspelling of one word or date, can be all the excuse someone needs to bring your day to a premature stop.

Many countries issue so-called **'diplomatic' passports** with up to double the number of pages for frequent overseas travellers. Visas acquired in advance tend to fill a whole page and anyone who's travelled in Africa will know how officials love to 'mark their territory' by slapping a blurred triangular stamp bang in the middle of a blank page. Count on each country that requires **a visa taking up two pages** in your passport. At this rate the 23 usable pages of a standard (non-diplomatic) British passport won't go so far on a round-the-world trip.

Although they don't exactly shout it from the rooftops of Whitehall, in Britain at least it's possible to get a **second passport**. The Passport Office will want a good reason; the most convincing is to explain you need to make protracted visa applications en route during which time you'll also need your other passport to cross borders. Better still is to somehow tie it in with your work. If your request is sound and you have documentary evidence, ideally from an employer, a second passport may be issued without a fuss. Dual nationality – passports in your name from two countries – is not the same thing but can be as useful. It's better never to declare to an immigration official that you're travelling with two passports, chances are it's not legal but as you'll soon learn, what is considered legal in one territory and what is actually useful or permitted don't always overlap.

VISAS

A visa is a temporary immigration permit allowing nationals of one country to visit another. Some countries (very often neighbouring) don't require a visa at all, others will issue one at the border allowing a stay up to a certain period, usually a month or 90 days. Some countries require visas to be secured **in advance** and it's these that'll make up the bulk of your bureaucratic headaches and can govern the pace and direction of your travels. Brits and Americans will have few visa hassles in Latin America, but across Africa or Central Asia anyone might end up paying hundreds in **visa fees**. Very often the onerous demands and associated delays are down to similar regulations imposed on that country by your country, or an antipathy towards your country that has its origins in colonial times; it's something that Brits and Americans experience more than, say, Canadians or Irish.

Applying for a visa

Some visas **start** from the day of issue, others require you to specify the exact date and place that you expect to arrive at a border – something hard to pinpoint when there's 1500 miles of desert, jungle and yeti-infested mountains between you and that place. Still others have no set entry date, just a certain amount of time before their validity expires. You need to understand the difference between this **validity** – say three months before you must begin using the visa by entering the county– and the **duration** of a visa, typically 30 days as mentioned. On some borders where a visa in advance is considered essential, just turning up may get you one issued right there or, if that border is remote, a pass to get one in the nearest city.

Don't expect to get all your visas nicely sorted out before you go. Instead, work out as closely as you can where you'll pass a consulate for your next country. (Very often the websites of previous overlanders will spell out the routine.) On a trans-continental trek this need to **apply for visas as you go** will be a game of careful timing and anticipated arrival dates that'll mould your itinerary. You may find yourself racing across a country or taking a thousand-mile detour just to be sure you can gain entry to your next destination. Crossing Africa down the west side, for example, once out of Nigeria (and depending on your nationality), the need to acquire a succession of visas across the western Congo basin will dominate the journey and, for some, will culminate in what can be just a five-day pass to get across Angola.

When applying back home, consider using a **visa agency**. Though pricey, these agencies earn their money by providing a speedy postal service as well as doing the queuing and applying for you. They can make getting visas from consulates not represented in your country much easier and they may also be clued up on tricks or procedures that can help facilitate a successful application. Even for relatively straightforward applications, an agency can save you valuable time if you're busy working or live far away from the capital, where consulates are usually located.

As a rule, avoid **business visas**: they're more expensive and risk awkward questions on arrival. Russia and post-revolution Libya are known exceptions. Stick to simple, innocuous **tourist visas**.

Before applying for any visa find out:

- What other documentation apart from your passport must you present on application? Besides a handful of passport photos, this might also include bank statements or other evidence of funds, letters of introduction or onward travel tickets.
- How to pay? Many consulates are very specific about the currency.
- How long do you have before you need to use the visa (typically from one month to a year)?
- Is the visa easily renewable or extendable, and if so for how long?
- Can you easily get a multiple-entry visa (which often have longer validities), enabling you to make excursions to neighbouring countries?

Visa problems

All you can do is give yourself plenty of time do deal with **problems**, expect those problems to crop up and have a Plan B to Z. Without experience it's hard to know this in advance, but don't underestimate your ability to deal with problems en route; it's one of the key lessons learned from adventure-travelling. Remember that countless others have succeeded in traversing the same route; they've all worked it out – by using their wits, being flexible and, as a last resort, offering an 'incentive'. So can you.

It must be remembered that having a visa will not guarantee you entry into that country; if they don't like you for whatever reason, the rules have changed or something is wrong with your paperwork, you'll be turned away. And being sent back to a country that's just officially wished you *bon voyage* can be tricky.

Although what appears above might seem like a rigid set of **rules** created to discourage international travel, these rules get a bit mushy once on the road: expired visas need not mean a firing squad at dawn (but could mean a fine). Not keeping WFO on the aforementioned five-day transit of Angola from DRC down to Namibia can cost you $70 or just a scowl.

Take visas seriously but recognise that once on the road, the further you are off the beaten track anything goes; this where the fluid interpretation of laws and regulations in the Adventure Motorcycling Zone (AMZ) can work in your favour. If you happen to stumble into a country via an **unmanned border**, present yourself at the nearest police station unless you're leaving soon in the same clandestine manner.

A word of warning: most of the countries in the AMZ are paranoid about their security and very often have tense relationships with their neighbours. Accusations of being 'a spy' might seem absurd, but might well be taken very seriously, especially if you happen to turn up in a country without proper documentation.

LOCAL PERMITS

Once you're on the road, **additional documentation** will be gleefully issued by local officials for any number of reasons (mainly to get more money out of you, or 'fine' you for not having it). Typical examples include registering with the police within so many days of arrival, photography and filming permits (although a camcorder is often immune to these), 'tourist registration cards', currency declaration forms (see p121), and permits to cross 'forbidden' areas such as China, Egypt's Western Desert or tribal homelands/reserves. As these are the sorts of places where police roadblocks are frequent, not getting one of the required permits may cost you more in the long run.

As much as following correct procedure, paperwork is a game of wits as well as an opportunity for corrupt officials to create difficulties that can only be solved with a **bribe**. In recent years the run down from the Mauritanian border to Dakar in Senegal became a slalom of cops every few kilometres demanding all the usual documents as well as a yellow fever certificate, two warning triangles, spare bulbs, a fire extinguisher and a boxed set of Jean-Claude Van Damme movies on Blu-Ray.

By at least starting your journey with proper documentation you'll have a good chance of getting well underway without unnecessary hassles until you learn the ropes and find out what you can and can't get away with.

TRAVEL AND MEDICAL INSURANCE

For what it costs, travel insurance covering you to an adequate level can set your mind at ease. Ordinary travel insurance that can come free with your credit card may offer 'package holiday' cover but is unlikely to cover a fraction of the cost of an evacuation from a Rajasthani village. Getting travel insurance for anything involving motorcycling is hard at the best of times so it's best to approach insurance companies who specialise in adventurous activities. A recent online quote from a UK specialist for a three-month trans-African trip including 'Level 1' activities came to £110. Including North America, the Caribbean and Japan would cost another £21.

Whoever you end up with, make sure they're in no doubt about the nature of your intended trip and where you'll be going. As well as covering you for all the mundane events like robbery, cancellation and lost baggage, travel insurance also includes **medical cover and repatriation** – realistically the most vital component. The worst-case scenario is getting yourself evacuated by air from some remote spot while requiring intensive medical care.

Along with admitting to any previous **medical history**, which the insurers may dig up anyway, it's vital to obtain travel insurance that's compatible with your **mode of travel** and the regions you'll visit. In the UK, many insurers will not offer cover for countries that are on the FCO 'black list' – countries where your government advises against all travel – or if they do it won't be valid. Right now on the FCO website that is a short list of just one country, which you can probably guess – Somalia. There follows, however, a very long list advising against all travel *to parts of* nearly half the countries in the world, all but four of which are covered in this book.

If you're a European in Africa, most medical emergencies involve **repatriation**, which is where the greater expense can lie. As a European or US national in Central or South America, the US might end up as your ultimate destination if you need urgent medical treatment. Anything involving repatriation to the US, even from neighbouring Mexico, could run into to six figures so it's vital that you have sufficient medical cover: £500,000 may sound like an astronomical sum but is just a starting point, £1m ($1.5m) is better. Make sure this figure covers *everything* to do with an accident, including medivac, ambulances, hospitalisation and possible surgery.

Remember too that to get an insurance claim underway you must first make that all-important phone call to the country where the policy was issued. When you receive your policy, find this **telephone number**, highlight it and write it clearly somewhere obvious and easy to get to; in your wallet or passport and somewhere on the bike. This way you can direct someone to ring the number if you can't do so yourself. For more on what to do in a dire emergency see p165.

Vehicle documents

Riding overland with your own vehicle might seem a fairly innocuous activity but unfortunately, just as with visas, a bureaucracy of **paperwork** developed early on in the history of motoring and these days in some places it's easier to import a gun. The explanation might be that in many developing countries a large-capacity motorcycle is a highly prized commodity the ownership of which is restricted by swingeing import taxes.

Of all the documentation required, the **carnet** presents the biggest burden in financial terms, while getting **third-party insurance** is simply not always possible and so not something to worry about unduly – until you have an accident, that is.

You'll accumulate a whole lot of **additional paperwork** at various borders, mostly to do with temporary vehicle importation or driving permits. Keep it all until you're in the next country, even if you don't know what half of it's about. Now is the time to invest in a wallet that expands like an accordion.

With all the documentation listed below you need to establish early on:
• Which papers you already have.
• What additional items are needed before departure.
• Which others you can get on the road.

You also need to know:
• How long it'll take to get what you don't have.
• How much it will all cost.

VEHICLE OWNERSHIP DOCUMENT
Your **vehicle ownership document** is much more important than a driver's licence and will be used and inspected so many times you may want to get it

laminated. In the UK it's called a 'logbook' or, officially, a vehicle registration document (VRD); the US has a state registration document as well as a 'title' or ownership document. In French it's a *carte grise*, in Hispanic Latin America it's a *titular* and in Russian it's your *svidelstvo* or *registratsja motocyklova*. The lingua franca is of course, 'Papers!', with or without a 'Halt!' beforehand.

Having a vehicle ownership document that's **not in your name** is not always a problem. All you need is a good story and official-looking letter from the owner in the local language(s) – official-looking stamps help too.

At many borders you'll need to present your passport and vehicle documents simultaneously. It's crucial that the details on the ownership/registration document, particularly **the chassis and engine numbers** (aka 'VIN') match those on your vehicle and carnet, if applicable. Outside Latin America, photocopies may not be good enough, but a duplicate is always handy. If your bike has had a replacement frame, check those numbers or risk losing all to some nit-picking official down the track.

The reason for these elaborate checks is to ensure you've not committed the cardinal crime against humanity of selling your motorcycle in the country concerned. Even slightly damaged engine or chassis numerals may be grounds for raising complications. To you the very idea of selling your dream machine is absurd, but because of punitive import taxes, rich locals will go to extreme lengths to acquire a desirable foreign-registered model using the right local papers. It explains why you see so many clapped-out bikes in some developing countries.

I also find that it helps to **highlight your Vehicle Identification Number** (VIN; usually the same as the chassis number) on your vehicle ownership document. This is what the customs guy will be looking for amongst all the other details, so it helps speed things up. It also doesn't hurt to sign your ownership document somewhere, even if you don't need to.

DRIVING LICENCE, IDP AND ICMV

Like your passport, your **driving licence** ought to show correct (or, at least, consistent) information with other documentation and be valid long after your trip expires. In the UK your driving licence lasts till you're 70, elsewhere in the world they're valid for as little as a year. If you expect to be on the road for longer than that and renewing it is not possible by post, making a good facsimile is a way round it.

If your licence doesn't show the bearer's **photograph**, it should be supplemented with an **International Driving Permit** (IDP) that does. These multilingual translations of your domestic driving licence can be picked up over the counter by presenting your driving licence plus a photo or two at your local motoring organisation's office. In the UK it costs just £5.50 and is issued by the RAC (🖳 www.rac.co.uk) who also do carnets.

Although IDPs are not mandatory, in Asia they're especially useful and in Latin America officials will often ask to see your driving licence, something that's rarely demanded in Africa. You may never have to show your IDP, but be on the safe side and get one. With their official-looking stamps they can double-up as another important document with which to dazzle a semiliterate official.

BACK-UP DOCUMENTS

With all these documents, keeping photocopies, duplicates, a list or even just photos of the vital details, makes replacement easier if they go missing. Stash paper **copies** somewhere secure or better still scan or photograph them and put the information onto an SD card or a USB stick plus a private webpage. You may also want to add travel insurance details, consular offices en route, your bike's main dealers in the countries you pass through – in fact your whole overlanding dossier. This way even if your bike and luggage are burned to a crisp or sink on the high seas, you'll be able to retrieve the details online.

Another good idea is to carry **duplicates** or 'spare' originals: ownership documents can be duplicated, either officially or by 'losing' the original and requesting a replacement (sometimes for a small fee).

There are two different IDPs. The '1949' version covers most of the world, except **Brazil, Burundi, Iraq, Nigeria and Somalia**; the '1926' version covers those five countries only. If you're including Brazil or Nigeria in your itinerary you'll need both versions; otherwise, unless you're a mercenary or have a terrible sense of direction, just the 1949 should do you.

An **International Certificate for Motor Vehicles** (ICMV) is to your vehicle registration document what an IDP is to your driving licence; a multilingual translation issued by motoring organisations (in the UK it's the RAC) for countries that don't recognise or can't read the original. It's especially useful in Russia and Mongolia.

CARNET DE PASSAGES EN DOUANE (CDP)

Many an overlander panics when they discover the need to **finance a carnet** (or 'CdP' as it's commonly abbreviated), something that could cost several thousand pounds. To summarise, a carnet is bit like a duty-dodging visa for your bike, being an internationally recognised temporary importation document that allows you to bring your bike into participating countries without having to deposit duties or fees with customs officials. In exchange for you having set aside or guaranteed a certain amount of money in your home country (as outlined below), it provides accredited security for the payment of any local duties and import taxes should the vehicle not be re-exported.

Not all countries require a CdP; a few issue their own while also accepting a worldwide version, while others, such as Egypt, offer their own version but may also require a large deposit. Most other countries will just be content to stamp your passport as having entered with a vehicle and may also issue a **temporary vehicle importation permit** (TVIP), which adds up to the same thing but without the financial cost of a CdP. You can go right through the Americas, northwest Africa and across northern Asia without a CdP.

Carnets are issued by certain accredited **national motoring organisations**, which are also a source of specific information on which countries require CdPs and how best to finance them. In the UK it's the RAC Motoring Services in Bristol (⌨ www.rac.co.uk). For Canadian *and* US-registered vehicles the Canadian Automobile Association in Ottawa does the job (⌨ www.national.caa.ca); in South Africa it's the AA of SA in Braamfontein (⌨ www.aa.co.za); and in Australia it's the AAA in Canberra (⌨ www.aaa.asn.au).

Carnets essentially guarantee your ability to cover **the cost** of the highest level of duty on your bike in the countries you expect to visit. For somewhere like Pakistan or India this can be **five times** your bike's estimated value, in Egypt it's 800%. This is not so bad for a little 125, but with a £15,000 BMW you could be looking at a £120,000 bond! Of course the **valuation** of your bike is open to interpretation and is something that, in Britain at least, the RAC treats with some flexibility.

You can **cover the bond** in one of three ways:

- Leave a sum with a bank in a locked account.
- Get your bank to cover the amount because of your collateral, usually property.
- Pay an insurance company to underwrite your carnet. This is the most common method where you can pay 10% of the total indemnity and get half of that back on discharging the carnet. With the above example of a BMW heading for India that means paying £7500 and getting £3750 back – still a hefty sum.

A carnet **lasts one year** and, if necessary, can be renewed or extended from the motoring organisation in the country where it's about to expire. (Make sure this extension is noted on every page and not just the front cover). There's a list (see p194 for Asia, p258 for Africa) of which countries require a carnet, but to cut a long story short they include: central, east and southern Africa plus Egypt, the Middle East, west Asia and the subcontinent; and it'll help in Australia.

How a carnet is used

Carnets come in a number of pages from five to twenty-five, each page is used for a country where this document is mandatory. A page is divided into three perforated sections, or **vouchers** a bit like a cheque book: an entry voucher (*volet d'entrée*), an exit voucher (*volet de sortie*), and a counterfoil (*souche*).

When you enter a country that requires a carnet, the customs official will stamp your counterfoil and exit voucher and tear off and keep the entry voucher. When you leave that country, the counterfoil will be stamped again and then the exit voucher will be retained. When your travels are complete you return the carnet to the issuing organisation for discharging. What they'll want to see is a bunch of double-stamped counterfoils and probably a few unused but intact pages.

Should you **sell your bike** and slip out of the country, your carnet will not be discharged and you'll eventually be liable for the duty in that country – remember, they could have your money. Should you have **missed a stamp** for whatever reason, all is not lost. On arrival back home get the customs in the port to inspect your bike's VIN and issue some sort of official notification that the vehicle as described in the carnet has returned.

THIRD-PARTY MOTOR INSURANCE

If you're boldly going where no one you know has gone before, don't expect to be able to get motor insurance from your domestic broker. In the UK you can get cover as far east as Turkey as well as Morocco and Tunisia although travellers on the Continent have long been able to get both motor insurance as well as vehicle recovery insurance to cover the Mediterranean rim, which includes such unlikely countries as Algeria and Libya.

Instead, **buy motor insurance as you go** but, again, don't expect to be able to buy it everywhere. You can often buy insurance at the border; if not, border officials may be able to advise where to get it. In the economic confederation of Francophone West Africa, around £3/$4.50 a day covers several adjacent countries; in Uzbekistan you pay a few pounds for two weeks' cover; in Colombia even less (see p310).

The dubious validity of motor insurance in the developing world or the impossibility of getting it at all underlines the fact that should you **cause an accident** such as killing someone's child or, worse still, a breadwinner, the complications may take years and large amounts of money to resolve. You may find yourself getting nailed for compensation even if you were not at fault.

Motor insurance is an unravellable quandary; rigorously enforced in your own country, out in the world it may be unattainable or of little actual value but a necessary part of your papers to present at checkpoints. Make an effort to buy it and if you can't then ride carefully and avoid doing so at night.

Money

Along with insurance, money and how to carry it is another thing that many riders worry about, although year by year it gets easier to get hold of cash, the most useful form of money. Any major trip is likely to cost you a few thousand on the road and carrying that sort of money through the insecure parts of Asia, Africa and Latin America is enough to make anyone nervous. For advice on changing money, bargaining and dealing with the black market, see pp121-3.

Best currencies

The **US dollar** is well known in the remote corners of the world where other hard currencies might cause incomprehension. Certainly, throughout South America and some parts of Asia this is the most readily convertible hard currency to carry. In Africa, especially the north, they're now more used to the **Euro**, though in East Africa it's still the US dollar. These two currencies are by far the best to carry; nothing else comes close any more. Avoid collecting too many US$100 or €100. They may save space but are rarely seen abroad and are often thought to be fakes so avoid street deals for $100 bills anywhere around Nigeria where they're printed by the roll. The €500 note was withdrawn in 2010.

TRAVELLERS' CHEQUES

Travellers' cheques may be safer than cash but are no more useful than cards. In developing countries don't rely on them, they date from a heyday of travel that preceded the credit card boom and may be as useful as a floppy disk when you most need them.

Furthermore, you may find that cashing them in gets a handful of local currency and at a dire official rate. Some countries even levy a tax on imported travellers' cheques. Short of cash, these days debit or credit cards are much more useful.

SPONSORSHIP

Thank you for your enquiry. We regret to inform you that as we have allocated our annual marketing budget/due to current economic conditions, we are unable to consider your request but do wish you the best with your exciting venture.　Marketing Department

For some travellers getting sponsorship is part of the challenge of their overlanding adventure. Some go out of their way to secure it or at least attract attention, often in the name of a good cause or charity. It's an idea many overlanders toy with, ostensibly for the very tangible appeal of getting free stuff, but as often, as a means of validating or – when it involves charitable causes – justifying the journey.

Thirty years ago in western countries it was fairly easy to get gear on a pretty thin premise. These days the field is much more competitive and while it's still possible to get free stuff for stickers, it takes a lot of work or good connections to get actual financial support, unless you're some kind of celebrity or take on an outlandish, record-breaking stunt.

Unless you're doing something truly extraordinary and original, there's a certain vanity in assuming your adventure deserves sponsorship. Applicants often get resentful when they receive replies like the one quoted above, or when replies aren't forthcoming or appear patronising, but you must remember that the most obvious targets are constantly hit by these sorts of requests.

The big question that must be addressed is: **what's in it for them?** What does Touratech have to gain by supplying you with the fruits of their catalogue so you can ride to Cape Town, as thousands have done before you? Even if a spirit of outdoor adventure helps sell Touratech products, they'd rather lavish their equipment on someone who's likely to get on telly on a Sunday evening.

Getting some

Sponsorship can broadly be divided into four categories:

- Being funded in return for some form of promotion.
- Receiving products or services for promotion.
- Doing it for charity, involving both the above as well as donations.
- A new ploy is simply asking for online donations; you become the 'good cause'. If your trip captures readers' imaginations it can work, but setting out with this plan is presumptuous.

The minimum you should offer a conventional sponsor is exposure of their product or service in the form of prominently positioned branding, just like on racing cars. If you can also promise to feature photos online, in magazines or on TV, a local business may be thrilled to support your big trip. An honest review of a product, warts and all, is what the public deserve but rarely get. That's the nature of what might be called selling out. I recently read a report by a well-sponsored rider who threw in rather clumsy approbations to his sponsors' gear, as if he'd nearly forgotten to mention them.

Sponsors are often eagerly offered all this, but it's not uncommon for the sponsored to lose interest and fail to deliver. Oddly enough I've also found supporters lose interest in acknowledging the publicity put their way. Nevertheless, whether they appreciate it or not, it's good form to notify sponsors of any publicity you secure. Invite them to any events you may give or attend, and try to make them feel as if their contribution was valued rather than exploited.

My experience is that having a genuinely great proposal or an appropriate background is not enough. Rewards are far more likely if you have a certain self-promotional acumen allied with thick-skinned persistence – or of course are happy to accept trivial, low-value items in exchange for stickerage and hotlinked website banners.

I know of a few genuinely noteworthy expeditions that put themselves hugely in debt, partly due to a lack of self-marketing nous but also a stubborn and refreshing resistance to exploiting their marketability, while other comparatively ordinary trips get better results. It's who you know of course, but also your ability to sell yourself – something that's all too commonly confused with persistence.

Overlanders typically overestimate the importance of their venture, but if approached in the right way or with good connections, sponsors can still be won over. I suspect it's something much more easily done in small, non-Anglo countries where it's easier to attract the attention both of local sponsors and the media, who like to trumpet a plucky local hero.

CREDIT AND DEBIT CARDS

Plastic cards are the most useful way of avoiding the need to carry rolls of cash. Although it may be a while before we see ATMs along the Ho Chi Minh Trail, a compact selection of debit and credit cards are essential items on a long overland journey. Take a few because, despite reassuringly familiar logos, there's a good chance one won't work with a certain bank's ATM somewhere, although it's hard to ascertain this for sure until you actually get there.

One day, somewhere, you're going to bless one of those little plastic rectangles for getting you out of a fix, most probably to cover shipping to the next place or just paying for a restful night in a plush hotel when you're out of cash. And across North America, Europe, Australasia and South Africa you need hardly ever use cash at all.

Contrary to the reasonable assumption that credit card companies hit you hard for overseas purchases, they actually offer the best rates of exchange for the day of your purchase (at least with Visa in Europe). Drawbacks include **service charges** when withdrawing from ATMs or banks abroad, and the possibility of **fraud** when paying for a service or goods like a night in a hotel.

There are many stories of credit card accounts getting hung out to dry – in fact it's surprising it doesn't happen more often. For this reason it's best to **withdraw cash from ATMs only and pay for everything in cash**. Resist using your card as liberally as you might at home, even if it's possible. By doing so you greatly reduce the chance of someone cloning your card details to make fraudulent withdrawals or purchases. Although there's a good chance any suspicious purchases will be refunded, before that's cleared up your card may get blocked until you contact the issuer and prove it hasn't been lost or stolen. Use cards to get cash, use cash to pay for things and check your statements carefully; these days it's easily done online or on the phone.

Keep tabs on how much you're spending on the card, and at the very least, get your **minimum monthly payment** sorted out (arrange a direct debit with your bank before you go, assuming you have a regular income or adequate funds in the bank to pay it off). Or simply load up your card before you leave.

With the prevalence of credit card fraud, it's not uncommon to find your **account frozen** when you try and withdraw cash in places like Khabarovsk or Kampala. Some companies do so automatically, others might try and call you at home to confirm a purchase. If your contact number is a mobile that happens to be on, you're in the clear but the way round this is to call your credit card company before you leave and explain where you may be using your card. It may be worth confirming it in writing as some travellers still get their accounts blocked. As with insurance, have the magic phone number and any passwords or other security information handy so you can call them and set about unlocking your card.

> **... it's best to withdraw cash from ATMs only and pay for everything in cash.**

A good travel guidebook should tell you which of the three main brands (Visa, American Express or MasterCard) are widely used in your destination, but with the negative connotation 'America' has in some countries or to some individuals, the more anonymous Visa or MasterCard are more reliable.

PLANNING & PREPARATION

Travelling companions

Most of us instinctively know whether we want to set off alone, with a partner sitting snugly behind them, their mate in the mirror, or in a group, perhaps as part of an organised tour. Nevertheless, below are some considerations to mull over when considering travelling companions.

Alone

The perils and rewards of **going solo** are clear cut. On the debit side there's no one to help you in times of difficulty and no friendly face with whom to share your experiences. There's no one to help fix the bike or guard it while you nip into a store in a dodgy neighbourhood. All this will make your trip harder and inevitably introspective. This may be because you don't know anyone who's got the nerve or commitment to set off on a trip such as yours, or you're independent-minded and like the idea of doing it alone.

Alone in Islamabad.

It all sounds miserable until you consider the rewards of solitary travel. Riding solo, your social exposure can be more acute; unless you're a real hardcore loner you're forced to commune with strangers who'll often make up the richest (and sometimes the most frustrating!) aspect of your trip; you have to look *out* at the world instead of being protected by the bubble of companionship. And unless you're going somewhere really outlandish, you're bound to meet up with other riders and in most cases be very glad to ride with them.

Tough overland stages like the Sahara, Far Eastern Russia and Patagonia, or intimidating regions in Africa, Central Asia and Central America are where overland riders often bind together, irrespective of their origins or mode of travel. Alone you can choose to join in the safety of a convoy, and when you feel like going your own way, you can split with no awkwardness. This **freedom** to be your own boss is the biggest attraction of riding solo. A romantic location to rest up for a while, or who knows, maybe even a promising romance, can be explored with no pressure that your companion wants to press on; it's this **disparity in pace** that often causes tensions in groups.

Overall, you'll get more of a raw experience alone while at times may have the option of companionship – this is the ideal scenario for most adventure riders. Be under no illusions that at times it will be utter misery and frustration, but this is all part of the adventure and typically your fortunes will swing the other way before long.

PLANNING & PREPARATION

ADVENTURE MOTORCYCLING MINDSET

As the plan takes shape trust your instincts and resist the pressure to be seen as a brave individual or get swept up as reluctant member of a team. Do what feels right for you which can be a lot easier if you don't make a big issue of it. You need some level of stability to face the countless trials that will be thrown at you daily. Without an optimistically fatalistic attitude your trip could develop into a litany of miseries.

My first trip on an XT500 was like this, blundering into the void and it was amazing I got as far as I did before events turned on me halfway across the Sahara (see *Desert Travels*). Turning back then was the right thing to do. Returning after just five weeks but a lot older, it wasn't an enjoyable trip but a depressing baptism of fire.

Many motorcyclists are attracted to the idea and romance of an overland journey without truly facing up to the gruelling practicalities of the commitment required. Your own trip is likely to be one of the major events of your life, give it your best chance. Don't bite off more than you can chew – a tour or rental (see opposite) will be much more fun as well as an educational test for the realities of undertaking your own trip.

Two's company

The advantage of travelling with a friend is that, psychologically and literally, the huge load of your undertaking is halved. Two people also tend to be **braver**; checking out a crowded market café or following a remote short-cut become shared adventures instead of missed opportunities if you're alone – even if behind it all is a mild competitiveness of 'sure, I'm n-not scared...'. There's no doubt about it, you can have a lot more fun if there are two of you and you get on.

One drawback to travelling in company is that you tend to remain rather exclusive to social interaction. There's no need to be outgoing because there's always someone to talk to, whine at or help you out. You can miss out on a lot that travel has to offer by hiding in the security of your **companionship**, because there's no need to meet others.

Another problem which won't surprise anybody is **getting on**. Alone you can indulge your moods which will swing from one extreme to another as days go by. In company you have to put on a brave or polite face when you might not feel like it; your partner thinks they're the problem, becomes resentful and the whole day becomes edgy as you wish the road would open up and swallow your buddy.

Having a united goal doesn't help, once the rot sets in your whole trip can become shrouded in tension. If it gets bad, there is only one solution: **split up**. It may well be that they want to take the high road and you the low road, but whatever it is, it's far better to accommodate differing personal wishes, even if they mean temporarily breaking up.

It's well known that such conflicts occur in the stress of expeditions which is effectively what you're undertaking; try and anticipate how you might deal with these sorts of problems and don't feel that separation down the road turns the trip into a failure. **Discuss** the possibility of this eventuality during the planning stage and always prepare yourself and your bike for **autonomy**.

With a group of two or more, one thing that may be obvious but ought to be mentioned is **choose the same bike**. This has countless advantages in fault diagnosis, quantity of spares and shared know-how.

Two-up on one bike? Well as long as the machine is spacious and stable enough it can of course **reduce costs**. It can also make life easier and more fun, especially with an intercom. The long-range **comfort** of the pillion really does need to be considered carefully. Don't set off on an unfamiliar machine and hope that just because it has an extra set of footrests it'll be fine. It helps of course if both parties can confidently ride the bike, though usually

Two up in the Atacama. © Grant Johnston

this isn't the case. And of course the weight of a passenger will for most rule out difficult off-road stages.

Big groups

Outside of tours, big groups are much less common than solo or twinned riders, if for no other reason than forming a group of like-minded individuals and keeping them together is a tricky proposition. Numbers will fluctuate during the planning stage and even on the road the chances of a bunch of riders staying together for the whole trip are slim. As in any group, the dynamics evolve as the trip moves on, although inevitably a leader will dominate from the start, alternately respected or despised by the others. Expect never to want to talk to certain members of your merry gang by the time you return!

With a large group there's usually a shared or even officially-established goal which itself can cause pressures. It may help with sponsorship, and the mutual support is enviable but, as you'll find on the road, most people are more comfortable alone or with one or two companions.

Road-based **tour groups** need not be as bad as they sound as you don't ride in convoy, day after day. Most riders set off at their own pace with a road book to meet up in the evening.

RENTALS AND ORGANISED TOURS

The opportunities for joining a tour or renting bikes all over the world are greater now than ever before. Don't be put off by the idea of joining a tour to a remote location or renting a bike abroad and doing your own thing. Both these options allow you to dip your toe into the adventure motorcycling pool with only a financial commitment.

For many it's a worthwhile endeavour. Without taking on a Big Trip from a standing start they can discover that this foreign travel malarkey is not so hard after all. I would say 20% of the people that have come on my Sahara tours (in 4WDs and on bikes) have gone on to pursue their own adventures, including packing it all in and going round the world.

You can even see a tour as a **reconnaissance trip** (something that's recommended, on p111, as a practical shakedown anyway). Only on this occasion you'll be testing yourself rather than your machine.

Some trips were never meant to happen but when you have the momentum that months of preparation engenders, your pride can be too great to call it off because you don't have enough confidence or even just money, so you decide to go ahead, despite the uncertainties. If it's a few weeks' overseas rental or a tour that's not turned out as expected, the commitment has been smaller, the disappointment is less galling and you'll have learned a lot about how to do it right next time.

2

BIKE CHOICE & PREPARATION

Riders have been around the world on everything from scooters to 2.3-litre cruisers, covering vast distances from a fortnight up to a lifetime. Any machine that starts, turns and stops will do the job, but ask yourself would you like to chug across the Bolivian altiplano flat out on a 125 while llamas trot past, struggle over the Grand Erg on a tourer weighing half a ton, or ride a bike they stopped making before you were born? Probably not.

The fact is it's more common for the bike to choose you, in as much as you know what you want – all you have to do is find the time, money and motivation to go somewhere. One of the factors mentioned below is 'image preference' and as adventure motorcycling becomes mainstream, riders are less led by what's conventional and are instead guided by what 'starts, brakes and turns'.

MOTORCYCLES FOR ADVENTURE

What is an adventure motorcycle? According to manufacturers keen to capitalise on the trend, it's a big trail bike and it's no secret that everyone's after a bit of BMW's flat-twin GS action, the bike most associate with 'adventure motorcycling'. But in a decade of dominance the GS has developed a refinement few can catch, so all competitors can manage is to try and outpower or out-gadget them. In 2012 Triumph released a 260kg, 140mph Explorer and Honda came out with the even heftier Crosstourer 1200, based on the old VFR1200F but with high bars and the all-important beak. At the same time Honda introduced the progressive NC700X; something you'll either 'get' or not.

DR Big from the 80s. A beak ahead of its time.

Doubtless these are brilliant tourers but the chances of seeing a Crosstourer passing an Explorer on the trans-Sib' are slim because what sells in the name of adventure to affluent middle-aged road riders and what's actually used out in the AMZ are, in most cases, different things.

Most riders accept that part of a real adventure will mean dealing with inadequate infrastructure which will include riding on broken highways, unsealed roads and gravel tracks. By the nature of their layout, weight and not least, tyres, some bikes handle such roads better than others. In fact tyres have a lot to do with it (see p74),

... what sells in the name of adventure to affluent middle-aged road riders and what actually gets used out in the AMZ are, in most cases, different things.

but the upright seating, wide bars, sump protection and long travel suspension of your GS, Suzuki DL or Honda XL-V will all work well on dirt roads at an appropriate speed, while on normal roads and fast highways you'll have a smooth, comfortable and fast machine. For those who like a lighter and potentially more agile motorcycle for off-highway riding, the big singles currently made by Yamaha, BMW, KTM and the air-cooled dinosaurs like the Honda XR650L, Kawasaki KLR650 and Suzuki DR650SE will fit the bill for most adventure riders, even if they're probably approaching their last days – in carb form, at least.

WHICH BIKE: FACTORS TO CONSIDER

The bikes listed above are the obvious choices. Here, in no particular order, are some factors to consider. They're then discussed in more detail on the following pages:

- What's available in your area at your budget
- Your itinerary
- Your marque and image preferences
- Weight
- Comfort
- Mechanical simplicity
- Build quality and reputation for reliability
- Fuel economy
- Parts availability and service know-how en route

And here's another thing to consider: the bike you eventually choose is going to be loaded with up to 40kg (88lbs) of gear, more if you're riding two-up. This weight will reduce the machine's agility and braking performance as well as accelerate wear on all components, especially tyres and drive chains. So whatever bike you settle on, consider the worst-case scenario: riding it fully-loaded on a muddy track in a downpour, falling over and then trying to pick it up.

If you're not concerned about making an outlandish statement on two wheels and just want a machine to ride, then settle for a **single or twin cylinder machine of around 600cc**. A 40hp engine of this capacity produces enough power to carry you and your gear through the worst conditions while not over-stressing the motor. It ought to also give reasonable performance and fuel economy of at least 50mpg (17.6kpl, 5.7l/100km or 41.5 miles per US gallon). Multi-cylinder engines may be smoother but are unnecessary and, in case you hadn't yet guessed, **four strokes** are far superior to two strokes on a long trip, despite the latter engine's power-to-weight advantage.

BIKE CHOICE & PREPARATION

Budget and availability

How much should you spend on an overlanding bike? Or perhaps it's better to ask: why do riders spend so much? Around £2000 (or about the same in dollars in the US) for a mid-weight or bigger machine is a good figure to start with. Double that could get you a suitable motorcycle that's just a year or two old. Don't forget you're likely to spend at least another £1000/$1600 or so equipping the machine.

Once you decide, don't make life too hard on yourself by coveting a machine that's not available in your market and is too expensive to import. As a rule the range of bikes in North America is a little different – and for some marques much reduced – to those found in Europe, South Africa and Australasia, and the latter two will also sell a bigger range of farm bikes too (see p43). It was not till 2011 that the US finally got their hands on the Yamaha Super Ténéré when in fact what many riders had wanted was the 660Z single. America also missed out on nearly all previous Ténérés and the Transalp and Africa Twin. But they do still have the old KLR650s, long gone in Europe, as well as the ancient XR650L which for what it cost at the time, we didn't regret importing into the UK from Australia one time for *Desert Riders*.

Your itinerary

Some continents are easier to cross or explore than others, while some riders actively seek out gravel back roads as part of their overland adventure. While 'adventure motorcycles' claim to offer some off-tarmac utility much as an SUV car does, you can actually see enough of this planet from a sedan or station wagon equivalent of a bike. All you have to do is appreciate its limits when it comes to dirt-road diversions. You could potentially ride all the way from London to Kathmandu or Cape Town, or down the length of the Americas on tarmac, and in doing so not feel you've missed out or had it easy.

Image preferences

For many, especially first timers, the motorcycle they choose is central to the whole endeavour. It may not be cool to admit it but our vanity and perceived self image has a lot more to do with what we ride than whether the valves are shim- or tappet-adjusted. A rugged-looking KTM, an alloy-clad GS or a matt-black Bonneville – all send out signals about how you'd like to be seen by others, even if to a Nepali peasant the V-Strom was the obvious choice.

You want to feel **inspired** by your adventure and what you choose to ride for the months ahead is a big part of that so you'll feel good about yourself. Some choose to make an ostentatious statement, be it goofy or over the top (possibly to assist with self promotion), while others, many experienced travellers among them, recognise that it's not about the bike anymore, and adopt a lower profile astride an ordinary machine.

Come on baby light my fire (and put the kettle on while you're at it). © J. Bullard

Whatever you decide on, remember it's your adventure and you'll probably only do it once. You may never need to use your trail bike's off-road ability, but until you found that out for yourself it was nice to know it was there. Tick off all the other sensible

It may not be cool to admit it, but our vanity and perceived self image has a lot to do with what we choose to ride...

factors listed here, but don't forget the value of a machine that, even after weeks on the road, still gives you a thrill to look at as you crawl out of your tent each morning.

Weight

Few adventure riders come back grumbling that their bike was too light, but the other extreme is a common complaint. When everything is going steadily, what can be 400kg (880lbs) of solo rider and loaded bike will have no issues. But add in some potholes, crazy traffic, muddy diversions, sinking sidestands, steps leading to safe overnight parking or airfreight priced by the kilogram – all part of the overland motorcycling scenario – and your big rig can become a handful. Is it even possible for a normal person to pick up a fuelled and loaded Triumph Explorer which clocks in at around 260kg (575lbs) and yet claims off-tarmac aspirations?

In a European or North American touring setting, such heavy bikes are in their element cruising pristine highways, but no matter how much you hope to keep it that way, one day somewhere out in the world you'll be steaming from your ears trying to control or right your sled. I first crossed the Sahara with a guy on a BMW R80. I made it; his bike ended up a burned out wreck halfway across. Even at less than walking pace, soft sand and especially mud are misery to ride on a heavy bike, as effectively bald tyres slither around to dump you again and again. Lighter bikes of 600cc or less will be more manageable, but anything over a litre can become near unrideable in tough off-road conditions.

The worst thing is that you'll get scared off taking even some mild off-highway detour because you've lost confidence in piloting your tank. Without confidence it's hard to summon up the assertiveness needed to blast through an obstacle like a sandy creek bed. And so, like the R80 guy, you keep falling over until you're not able to get up again. It's not all just the bike's weight but gear too, and here again it's common to take too much stuff. More about that later.

Comfort

*... and when you're on a long ride it's all about comfort... **Ken Duval***

You'll be riding your bike all day for weeks and months at a time. Loaded like a pit mule, the finer points of handling and throttle response promised in the brochure – things which magazine reviewers get so worked up about – will be lost. What you want is to get off the bike at the end of the day without feeling like you've had a bad day on the Dakar. This is where the big touring bikes pilloried just a paragraph ago have an advantage. Even loaded, they're supremely **comfortable and stable** over miles of highway, running fat tyres on small wheels and big torquey engines.

Comfort doesn't just mean the thickness of the saddle (more on p67). It adds up to quiet, vibration-free engines with smooth power delivery, supple suspension, powerful brakes and aerodynamic protection from the wind (p69). All this enables you to relax, deferring the inevitable fatigue. And when you're not tired, cramped, aching and deafened, you cope so much better with the 101 daily challenges long-distance riding throws up. Comfort also means the clothes you're wearing, and your state of mind: these latter two subjects are covered on p107 and p113. And comfort also means the space and power to travel with a pillion passenger for an extended period, if that's your plan.

If you expect to be using **electrically heated clothing** (more on p110) you need to consider your bike's electrical output as it's not something that can be easily uprated. Big touring bikes are typically well endowed with high wattage alternators which produce ample current to recharge the battery. As it is systems like ABS, suspension levelling and EFI all require more electrical power than older or smaller bikes which will be less able to cope. Running heated clothing at night at low engine speeds is not an unusual scenario in icy conditions, but one where the battery could discharge quicker than the alternator can replenish it. If you can forsee such a situation on your trip, ascertain that the bike you choose has the wattage you need.

OLD SCHOOL OVERLANDER – HALF A MILLION CLICKS ON A BMW R80 G/S

We decided to set out on our first RTW in 1987, but replacing our super-comfy CX650 was not easy. Research led to the R80G/S airhead – much easier to get parts. We bought a well worn 1981 model in 1988 with a 32-litre Dakar tank. Some 25 years later, we've sold up and are still on the road. The G/S isn't perfect but it was as close as we could get at the time. Two-up, its advantages surpassed the available Japanese big singles of the time, and the Africa Twin wasn't sold in Australia.

The engine's power is adequate because overlanders don't travel fast and we take it pretty easy these days. It's a long ride, not a fast one – put that in your book! The clutch is as tough as, and if the transmission is overhauled right it'll last too. We get big mileages between shaft/bevel drive overhauls.

The frame needs reinforcing for two-up riding and the suspension is OK with some mods. We could say the same for the brakes, lights (H3 spots added) and charging (a weak point on many bikes from this era). The seat required a substantial makeover for two-up riding too – no surprise there, BMW.

As for luggage we currently use Givi 41-litre Keyless – we prefer plastic to alloy. On the back there's a cheapo, 60-litre top box plus a tank bag on the front.

We change the oil every 5000km and the gearbox, shaft/bevel and filters every other time. Tappets and plugs get checked every 20km, with forks and pivots greased at 50km. The biggest issue is pulled barrel studs. Boy are we good at repairing these! Tyre life varies; we buy whatever we can get but the 18-inch rear helps.

The G/S's appeal is its simplicity and parts availability worldwide and this bike is tough; the easiest 'patch and ride' machine we've come across, and as you can imagine we know it very well now. The network of Beemer people around the world is extraordinary, help is everywhere. Owning this bike, you develop mechanical skills to cover its idiosyncracies and acquiring that knowledge becomes a passion.

KEN & CAROL DUVAL

Mechanical simplicity

This is particularly something which old school riders may agonise over. The bikes of their youth which they learned to maintain or fix by the roadside are no longer made. Home maintenance is now discouraged or impossible without special equipment – instead an official dealer has become a vital link in maintaining your machine's composure. That's all very well if you're living a conventional, ordered life as a commuter or a weekend rider; it's not so handy once you head out into the Adventure Motorcycling Zone where your bike's as exotic as a space ship.

... even though mechanical simplicity is desirable and water-cooling is another thing to go wrong, it's not a valid reason to avoid a water-cooled machine; just choose one where the radiator and water pump are not vulnerable to road crashes or can be securely protected.

For regular touring that's safely covered by recovery insurance, any flash bike will do and doubtless be great fun to ride – not least because you can be sure if anything goes wrong you're covered. But one definition of adventure motorcycling could be touring beyond the range of freephone vehicle recovery. You can always get recovered of course, but it'll require organising locally. So, the further you wander and the more challenging your route, the simpler your bike should be so that you, or local mechanics (to whom diagnostics is something to do with Ron Hubbard) are more easily able to fix it. It has to be said though that modern bikes are extremely reliable and the ones that aren't are well known. Very often that can be a new model with several 'teething problems'; a curse which can burden a bike's reputation for years.

Take **water-cooling**; it may not be essential but is now the norm on modern, big-engined bikes not because it's better, but because a water-cooled barrel expands and contracts less and so can be built with finer tolerances to enable higher performance. Water-cooling also greatly reduces engine noise which, along with cleaner emissions, is an important requirement. And there's no doubt that because the heat dissipation is more even, water-cooled engines last longer than air-cooled. But you have the additional risks of radiators and fans that get damaged or clog up with mud, fuel pumps that pack up, hoses that split or leak. Even though mechanical simplicity is desirable and water-cooling is another thing to go wrong, it's not a valid reason to avoid a water-cooled machine; just choose one where the radiator and water pump aren't too vulnerable to road crashes or can be securely protected.

Despite the impression, a machine with a water-cooled engine will **not run cooler** in extreme heat and it can certainly overheat if you're progressing slowly and revving high and the radiator fan can't cope (in soft desert sand for example). You'd think a water temperature gauge will warn you, but be aware that some competition-oriented bikes like KTM 450s don't have this. If you choose a water cooled bike make sure it has a water-temperature gauge or fit one yourself – see p59.

These days air-cooled engines are really only still used on some single-cylinder bikes – most modern multis have liquid-cooling of some sort, but as

BIKE CHOICE & PREPARATION

long as it's in good condition and well maintained, an **air-cooled** engine is no worse than a water-cooled equivalent and you have no radiator, fan, hose or water-pump worries. Choose a bike with a relatively **lowly-tuned** (low compression) engine, it'll make less heat and so be less prone to overheating in tough conditions or on bad fuel. One of the best ways of maintaining an air-cooled engine while on the road is by making regular changes with quality oil and making sure the air filter is clean.

We all managed without **ABS** for years too, but as long as you've the ability to disable it if you wish (more common on trail or dual sport bikes where poor traction can make it come on too early), most riders will learn to appreciate if not depend on it when engaged in the unpredictable traffic conditions on a long ride. Other electronically controlled wonders also include **traction control** on higher spec machines – something that could be useful to novice riders on the dirt. On the highways of India or Peru you're unlikely to be riding at the limit, but being able to detune your over-powerful adventure bike to 'rain' mode as you climb a slippery series of hairpins has a lot going for it.

Transmission and electric starts

Final transmission is either by shaft or chain, or in a few cases by rubber belt. Shaft drive is heaviest, more expensive, absorbs a little power and can make for a clunky gear change, but these drawbacks are balanced by much less frequent maintenance – a chain and sprockets can require replacement in 10,000 miles. A lot will depend on **how you ride**; if you're an aggressive rider shaft may not be for you and at any time off road a rock can kick up and smash through the final drive housing. Shaft drive benefits from a smooth riding style which bigger, heavier and less sporty bikes that feature it encourage anyway.

Chains and sprockets are said to be very efficient when correctly tensioned and oiled and are a light and inexpensive means of transmitting power from an engine to a back wheel. Although they're exposed to the elements, modern 'o'-, 'x'- or lately x-y-z-ring chains can now last for thousands of miles with just a bit of cleaning. So when it comes to transmission, settle for shaft drive on a heavier machine or use a chain-driven bike with **top quality chain and sprockets**. There's more on chains on p61.

And if you happen to be deliberating over a kickstart or **electric start** only model: go for the button. Some 125s may still have kick-starters but one hot day, when your bowels are in freefall and you stall on a hill in Lima with traffic blaring, you'll bless that button in getting the engine running again. Having a kickstart *as well* is a handy back-up, but rare these days. If the starter motor fails any bike can be push- or jump-started (see Troubleshooting on p170), though doing that on a muddy trench in the Amazon with a full load of gear is not so easy.

Switchable electronic ignition

On a bike controlled with an ECU and in most cases fuel injection, **switchable ignition mapping** – either literally a switch on the bike or done by replacing an electronic component or reprogramming the ECU chip from a computer – can be a very useful feature. Most bikes are reviewed on their performance figures, not how they ride, yet these are not key attributes for non-competitive adventure motorcycle touring. And even domestic riders will have days when they just want to ride normally. In the AM Zone as mapped on p11 where few local bikes exceed 125cc, chances are you'll be top dog in terms of raw motorcycle performance and ought to have nothing to prove.

Originally, in the late 1990s, something like the KTM Adventure simply had plugs you switched around to retard the timing on electronic ignition and so enable the engine to cope with low octane fuel. Low octane fuel, as found out in the sticks, can cause harmful **detonation** (also known as 'pink-

Get 20% more miles per gallon at the flick of a switch on an XT1200Z.

ing') especially on lean-running or high-compression engines. Go back another thirty years and you could alter your ignition timing with a screwdriver, but then you needed to as it was always going off. Now, as you'd expect, ECUs have become exponentially smarter and the ignition 'map' can be switched between 'sport' or 'touring/rain' or 'birthday' modes (there's more on p57). The good thing is that bikes are getting cleverer and at the very least, a simple lower power/better fuel consumption mode (pictured above) suits the knee-sliding weekend warrior back home, or you on the long road to Mongolia. Benefitting from the gentler setting something like the 109hp XT1200Z will be more than adequate, use less fuel and reduce tyre wear.

Carbs or EFI

Electronic fuel injection (EFI) has become the norm on bigger motorcycles because it offers smoother and more consistent fuelling and superior economy even at high levels of tune, as well as cleaner emissions. Don't think fuel injection is new fangled – automotive diesel engines have been fuel injected for decades, only now it's electronic, like most petrol engines. EFI is also maintenance-free, something that carb-balancing BMW Boxer owners will be pleased to hear. A fuel injector does what a crude carb tries to do: fire a fine jet of fuel on time and at high pressure so it atomises instantly and so mixes with the air and burns more completely in the combustion chamber. A fuel injector's nozzle is much finer than any carb jet and so you'd think would be prone to blocking, especially with the dirty fuel you'll find on the road. In fact this is a rare occurrence with bike engines because filtration systems are up to the job, and when they're getting blocked a warning light will probably come on.

Injectors seem to be trouble free; it's the EFI management system that's more prone to problems. Early examples of some BMW and Yamaha singles (and doubtless other bikes too) were notorious for lumpy or inconsistent fuel delivery at lower speeds, but this got dialled out on subsequent models and it's no more unusual than other teething problems exposed by online opinions. The engine's electronic management computer (ECU or EMU) is constantly measuring various parameters in the engine (air and engine temperatures, throttle position, road speed and so on) to deliver an optimum fuel charge to the combustion chamber and this alone puts it miles ahead of any carburettor – once well described as 'a brick with holes in it'. Think of all the

BIKE CHOICE & PREPARATION

BIKE CHOICE & PREPARATION

DON'T LEAVE BEFORE THE BIKE!

I made a big mistake leaving Nairobi two hours before my bike. I was planning to end my trip by riding back to London from Rome rather than just arriving at dreary Heathrow.

When I got to Rome the local agent knew nothing of my shipment and the airway bill didn't register at all. I called my cousin who luckily lived in Nairobi. The freight manager, knowing I'd already left, had decided he wanted a bribe so he stopped my bike leaving. When Anne contacted him he said I'd been quoted the wrong rate and that it had now doubled. It took another three days to arrange for it to be shipped by another airline and I ended up sending it directly to Heathrow. But it was still nice to visit Rome. JEREMY BULLARD

YIPS, YOPS and YAKS induction tricks they've tried over years to smooth out carburation, especially on lumpy singles – well EFI fixes them in one go. Ride an old carb'd BMW Funduro alongside a 650GS and you'll feel the difference.

Another advantage of EFI is that it's much less affected by **altitude** (see p174) – the system compensates for the lack of oxygen by feeding less fuel; soon you'll be running up and down between Chile and Bolivia just for fun. There's nothing wrong with carbs and of course they can be taken apart and cleaned, unlike an injector, and like water-cooling, EFI on motorbikes may appear an unnecessary complication, but it's a real step forward and has brought a new lease of life to a lot of ropey old engine designs.

Catalytic converters

Many EFI bikes now also feature **catalytic converters** (or 'cats') built into their silencers to clean up emissions. Normally these must be fed unleaded fuel which isn't always available in the sticks. This is despite the confident claims of the maps featured on the UN Environment Programme website (🖥 www.unep.org/pcfv) which, since 2006, has claimed that leaded petrol is no longer available in Africa because the entire continent magically got together and agreed to ban it.

It's not quite so rosy but you can run a cat on leaded fuel for 'a few months' before the lead neutralises the fine matrix inside coated in precious metals. When this happens it won't alter your bike's performance, but it will affect its ability to reduce emissions which may see you fail your next road-worthy test. Over-sensitive **electronic sensors** may have their own ideas though and could flip out on leaded fuel; removing Lambda sensors can help.

On any bikes fitted with a cat, you can replace the stock silencer/cat with a regular aftermarket pipe. The bike's electronic emission sensor ought to adjust the fuel injection accordingly, meaning the machine should run fine.

Build quality and reliability

Anyone who's been riding for decades will recognise that the build quality of many modern motorcycles (and much else besides) has gone down while at the same time they're more reliable and perform better than ever. 'Built-in obsolescence' used to be the cynical explanation to why new things wear out early, but it's as much to do with what were once excessive manufacturing costs being trimmed, while more attention is paid to designing a superficially good-looking machine with as many electronic gizmos as the ECU can manage. Such a product is easy to sell and wins positive reviews, even if once you look below the surface you find cheap components and a rough finish.

It's a situation that's going to get worse until the current global financial crisis is worked through; just about all brands now have models which suffer from premature wear of cheap components. So while your modern bike is unlikely to be handed down to your descendants, as long as it runs it will do so as reliably as any machine ever made, particularly once you've replaced possibly cheap original equipment (OE) such as chains and suspension.

Nowadays more than ever it's possible to get abreast of a particular model's foibles with the mass of information to be found online. Owner-enthusiasts' forums and wikis will minutely dissect the beta on their machines, suggesting which upgrades and accessories work best. Horizons Unlimited has forums for all the major brands focussing on the most used models for overlanding.

TRAIL BIKES AND ENDURO BIKES

If you come from a dirt biking or trail biking background – a trailie (or 'dual sport' in the US) or an enduro bike might seem like the best choice. A trail bike is **versatile**. There's nowhere you can't go on your trailie and the whole thrilling realm of unsealed roads (or no roads at all) becomes open to you.

Trail bikes have genuinely useful features, such as folding foot controls, bigger than average front wheels to roll over bumps and holes better, long travel suspension to absorb those bumps and more ground clearance than aver-age when the sus-pension runs out. And, to a certain extent, they're designed to be dropped without suf-fering critical damage. But there are also **compromises**, with drawbacks including:

- High seats.
- Less sure-footed on the road due to long travel suspension, seating position, 21" front wheels, trail-pattern tyres and 'wind-catching' front mudguards.
- Narrow saddles give poor comfort, especially for passengers.

Enduro racers

If weight is such an important factor (it's the one thing that adventure motorcycling riders complain about most often), a light, powerful

four-stroke enduro like a KTM, Honda XR or Yamaha WR must make a great adventure bike, no? Well, they could be if your adven-ture is purely off-road. While it's true that, unloaded, these bikes are much more func-tional off-road than trail bikes, they differ in some key ways. The engines can consume more fuel and require more atten-tion due to their higher state of tune. And because they're designed for regular mainte-nance, the **engine oil capacity** of these machines is very small. That's fine if you change it after every few hours engine running time, as you're supposed to, but left for a couple of thousand miles is not so good for enduro engine longevity.

This no-frills nature also extends to **basic lighting** and a **narrow seat**, designed for standing up and shifting body weight rather than day-long support. **Rear subframes** are also a weak point; they were never meant to carry a load greater than a racing plate. Sure, you may be able to buy a long-range 'rally' tank but the truth is a machine like this would be all but wasted on a long touring trip. You must remember that by the time any bike is loaded up, **most traces of nim-bleness will be largely eradicated** so think twice unless you're committed to off road-ing, or like your enduro bike too much.

Fuel economy and parts availability

Even with the current range of fuel-injected engines, advances in **fuel economy** haven't quite kept up with cars, partly because to most users in rich countries, motorcycles are used to blow away the cobwebs on a weekend rather than as a functional, day-to-day means of transport. Fuel injection does provide economy as well as power: the BMW F-GS parallel twins are as good an anything in their class. But plain old carb bikes can be nearly as fuel efficient at the cost of capacity and so power. Bikes like a Yamaha TTR250 will return up to 80mpg, a Suzuki GS500 will get over 60mpg at normal speeds. Neither bike will necessarily tear the skin off a well cooked rice pudding, but how often are you likely to need to do that? They can sit on 60 all day which is enough.

Parts availability is a quandary, but the best attitude to take is that out in the AMZ there won't be any specialised parts to be found, especially in Africa north of the Zambezi. The richer countries of South America may be better off, with much of Asia falling somewhere in between. And what you do find out there in terms of tyres and chains will be of a lot lower quality than stuff back home, and often not of a size that fits big bikes.

Plan for the worst, **leave with new consumables** (tyres, chains, brakes), some key spares and maybe send some stuff on. Just recognise that your adventure includes unpredictable events which will require resourceful solutions. If something can't be fixed or diagnosed locally despite all your efforts, then consider DHL and the like, having someone fly out what you need or even flying to a nearby country where the component can be bought. Remember, with DHL you can often get bogged down with customs clearance which can drag on for weeks. And depending on where you are, that wait may well exceed the cost of simply flying somewhere and getting the part.

'Two wheels and an engine'

Over the page there's a closer look at ten overland-suited bikes that tick most of the boxes most of the time for most people, or that are otherwise worth considering for the big trip. It's followed by a pick and mix of other machines. Hopefully yours is in there somewhere but in the end anything that has the above two characteristics could be the star of your biking adventure. It's possible to get fixated on the ten bikes and their alternatives, and think that anything else will be less good. That is not a good idea.

Only across Africa might the need for off-road utility be desirable, but even then such stages are becoming shorter by the year. Unless you're purposely seeking off-road challenges (and so you should, it's a big part of their adventure!) for trans-Asia or the Americas any **road bike** will be fine just about all the time. You'll find that dual-purpose rather than full on motocross knobbly tyres will make your road bike more stable on dirt roads while still keeping it steerable on the highway – though it's amazing what you can ride with knobblies. In fact the main adventure bikes – not least the big GS BMWs – are becoming so obvious that more and more riders are going out of their way to be different and you hear of big trips taken on step-thrus and other scooters which, like regular bikes, have come on in recent years.

If you're new to this game sticking to the well-known or popular machines initially makes things a lot easier. You know you have a proven set-up, plus

AG BIKES FOR OVERLAND – MILKING THE POTENTIAL

In South Africa, Australasia and a few other markets, you can still buy yourself a basic Japanese branded 'ag' or 'agricultural' bike.

With barely a go-faster acronym between them, these are cheap, no-frills, functional farmers' hacks usually around 200cc. Using technology that was cutting edge in the 1970s, it's notable that nothing much has changed in this category since the last *AMH* edition in 2005; not something you can say for adventure touring bikes.

Your average farmer's sled is a parts bin special not unlike the BMW Basic/Kalahari (itself a bit of an 'ag' some might say). Old production lines have been quite literally farmed out to overseas factories where labour is cheap so that development of next year's crotch rocket is not disturbed.

The Honda **CTX 200 Bushlander** is one good example, costing 32,000 rand or around AUD5000. For that you get what looks like an old XR200 with electric start and a backup kick. They don't waste alloy on ag bikes; rims and swingarm, bars and racks are strictly ferrous for extra ballast. The CTX is heavy at over 130kg (290lbs) – an XR400 weighs 117kg, but then again it costs nearly double and is probably twice as good.

Crude handlebar lever protectors come as standard, part of a frontal rack which is matched by a similar 'sheep rack' on the back. There are also rudimentary engine protection bars and a tinny bashplate; tyres are 18- and 21 inchers. Along with the weight,

© Martin Wielecki

oversized mudguards and 9:1 compression help keep the speed down, and what other bike comes with a clutch lock for those sudden stops and *two* side stands: with a couple of rocks or a ditch you've got a centre stand!

Downsides (besides the whole idea altogether!) include a rear drum brake and the small tank with a range of 200km. Cruising speed is in the original Enfield Bullet category but without the roadside repairs.

Yamaha produce the broadly similar **AG 200E** (electric/kickstart, 10-litres, all-drum, enclosed chain, 119kg/262lbs and Suzuki have a **DR200SE**; same weight but with a 13-litre tank and an oil cooler, no less.

All of these bikes make a rugged, low maintenance, crashable ride, best suited to Indochina, Central Africa, the Darien Gap and other low-speed, short-range, low altitude environments where transportation along or across rivers will be an option.

BIKE CHOICE & PREPARATION

know-how and equipment will be easier to come by. If you like to be different or have experience and know that the following selection is rather conservative and self-perpetuating, then the only limit is your imagination, your budget and Newton's Three Laws of Motion.

Still agonising? Then think about **buying a bike abroad**; it may help narrow down your choices. For example at current prices (early 2012) you can buy a Suzuki V-Strom 650 in the US for 12% less than in Australia. Still in the US, less fashionable bikes like KLR650s or XR650Ls are incredible bargains by European standards and with plenty of kit and know-how available there too. In Brazil you can pick up a snazzy Honda XRE 300 (with a full beak), or a similar Yamaha 250 Ténéré for under R$13,000 (though check you can leave the country with it first).

If you're European and wanting to ride the Americas or start your RTW there, it makes sense to buy there, saving a whole lot on shipping costs. Check out the HU **bike sales and swap forum** too. Many riders are looking to sell their bike or buy yours in South America, or are willing to swap anywhere.

BMW G650GS

Manufactured from 2000-2008 and 2011 onwards

Engine 652cc water-cooled single

Kerb weight 192kg/423lb

Fuel capacity 14 ltr/3.7 US gal (17 ltr on F models)

Max range 400km/250 miles @ 23kpl/56.5mpg US

Riders like Great economy, smooth EFI engine, comfy seat

Don't like Weight, old surging and stalling issues, water pump leaks

© TOM BIERMA

After seven good years, in 2007 the original and proven EFI Rotax 650s were dropped, presumably to push the new 800cc twins or the X-series singles. Though there was nothing very wrong with them, the lightweight X series was a flop in most places and the similarly named F650GS and F800GS twins got off to an inauspicious start. And so the 650 singles returned to the fold in 2011 with a road-oriented G650GS model with cast wheels (19" front), and a few months later the original F650 'Dakar' was reborn as the snazzy 'Sertão' with 20% more suspension travel, spoked wheels (21" front) and switchable ABS and heated grips as standard. Though heavy for a single (what isn't these days), all the BMW 650 singles are ergonomically sorted and comfy, with a 400w alternator although fairly high 11.5:1 compression which requires 91 octane fuel. The tank is smaller and it could be premature to give the thumbs up, but it does look like it's the same bike which is no bad thing.

The first generation had enduring issues with **surging** and **stalling** but software updates and new injectors have surely fixed that by now. The underseat tank may be 17 litres but that's equivalent to at least a 20-litre 'carb' tank and is big enough. The plastic bashplate is another sign of the times; alloy works best to protect the hoses and water pump (some leaked). You'll find a mass of detail (if not so much on overland preparation) on the Chain Gang

© ANTOINE DE ST BRADOIS

website: 🖳 **www.f650.com**, although they gave up on the FAQs in 2007 so the new singles are not being covered there, it seems. Try 🖳 www.ukgser.com

Alternatives Don't write off the old models pictured here. Just be ready to deal with leaking water pumps and worn head bearings. Otherwise it's the usual suspects from Japan.

HONDA XL700V TRANSALP

Manufactured from 2008 (original 600cc model from 1987)

Engine 680cc water-cooled inline V-twin

Kerb weight 218kg/480lb

Fuel capacity 17.5 ltr/3.85 US gal

Max range 370km/230 miles @ 21.2kpl/50mpg US

Riders like Reliable, smooth V-twin power

Don't like MoR image, a bit plasticky, not that economical

The current 700cc incarnation of the venerable 'TA' was always in the shadow of the much-loved 'AT' Africa Twin which they stopped making way back in 2002. Originally based loosely on the Dakar-winning V-twins of the late 1980s, the XL-V is a bike with a great engine but a poor image among its adventure motorcycling competitors, for no better reason than that it might be seen as a bit Honda-bland. When it became a 700 it got a smaller 19" front wheel, a catalyser and best of all, ABS. The one-litre Valadero which followed in the AT's tyre tracks faired even worse in the AM fashion stakes, although the way things are going issues about its weight are no longer valid. Nothing doing in North America as usual, but over there you do get the same engine in the NT700V which in most cases would do the job as well.

By far the most common praise for the Transalp is the mind-numbing reliability marred only with little niggles, not something that could be said for the far more trendy BMWs. A taller screen may be needed and engine/radiator protection bars are a good idea, and there are non-cat pipes to slip on. The tank may not be huge but you can squeeze 350kg out of it if you need to; most people overestimate the need for huge tanks. Check out the UK-based 🖳 **www.xrv.org.uk** where they still lament the long-gone AT but will talk Transalp if you ask nicely.

Alternatives Suzuki's V-Strom might be considered the main competitor, same weight, bigger tank, not all with ABS but it beats the Honda on price. Or consider the older 650 model with a bigger front wheel, carbs and no cat pipe. Or if you don't mind parallel barrels then there's BMW's 800cc twins or the Triumph Tiger 800 triples. No one calls them bland.

BIKE CHOICE & PREPARATION

BMW F800 / 650 (700) GS

Manufactured from 2008

Engine 798cc water-cooled parallel twin

Kerb weight 207kg/460lbs (199kg/440lbs)

Fuel capacity 16 ltr/4.22 US gal

Max range 385km/240 miles @ 24kpl/56.5mpg US

Riders like Class-leading economy, weight, it's a BM

Don't like Early issues, 800's engine characteristics, it's a BM

For those who've never bought into the GS Boxer cult, the parallel twin F-GSs were a breath of fresh air. One initially inoffensively plain and dubbed a '650' in a clever twist of marketing back-projection, the other a snazzy evocation of the Paralever bumble bee.

Weighing in at around 200kg wet, here were a pair of Bavarians without the beer gut, although the twins got off to a bad start with other health issues. The modern malady of great design masking cheaply sourced components and inconsistent assembly saw some early adopters pulling their hair out and may well have led to BMW re-introducing the 650 singles. It's all on the web, just remember, 'the squeaky door gets all the oil'; many riders of early models experienced no problems in tens of thousands of miles.

Most will be drawn to the flashier 800, but in practical terms the '650' is a better bike for overlanding. At 71hp, it's 18% less than the 800 but is only 10% down on torque which also peaks 1250rpm lower. The result is a much more pleasant engine, marginally better economy as well as road manners from the single-disc, 19-inch front end. The seat is lower and cast wheels run on tubeless tyres – a huge benefit. And even at 12:1 compression it runs on 91 octane. In 2012 they brought out a better-equipped 'SE' 650 version (see AM website test), soon followed by a much-revised F700GS. All models need a bashplate, radiator protection and can be remapped to run on low octane fuel. The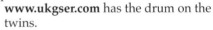

www.ukgser.com has the drum on the twins.

Alternatives The KTM V-twin will outride but also outguzzle an 800 on the dirt, but it's not a race so other contenders include a Transalp or even the NC700X, a V-Strom or Triumph's similar but heavier, smoother and much more powerful Tiger 800s.

SUZUKI GS500E OR SIMILAR

Manufactured from time immemorial

Engine mid-weight parallel twin

Dry weight Around 180kg/400lb

Fuel capacity Up to 20 ltr/5.3 US gal

Max range Potentially 420km/260 miles @ 21kpl/50mpg US

Riders like Cheap to buy and run, low seat, tried and tested

Don't like 17" tyres, it's not flash like those other GSs

This is really a tip for any generic, ordinary mid-sized road bike – a cheap and cheerful UJM that learners buy once they pass their test, although not the sort of thing you might expect to pull on. For most adventure riders the bike is central to the trip and being on it can be the very motivation. But once you get over all that there's a lot to be said for low-profile transportation, a commuter runabout with adequate speed, comfort and range that can cost less than an alloy luggage system.

The GS500E is a good example, well known round the world, you could buy it new in Europe as late as 2010. On a long ride, replacing 17-inch tyres in Africa and Asia might be a pain, but it's the same for many bikes with 17-inch rears. Converting to 18s or even 19s means new wheels with all sorts of brake and final drive complications, but once that's done ,you might just have yourself an AM steed with a bit of clearance and what they used to call a 'cooking' engine that will keep on keeping on. Check the website's 'Project Bikes' to see how mine turned out. The web is waist-deep in GS owners forums.

Alternatives A Honda CB500 is near identical to the GS, but with a water-cooled motor and probably better build quality. It also runs on 17s plus they stopped making them in 2003. Kawasaki's version, the watercooled ER-5 never had a great reputation in the UK, although that motor survived in the Transalp-like KLE 500 (right) which became the 650 Versys in 2008, popular in the US. But at this level there are other, conventional overland contenders.

Stick to the cheap-but-sound category, a Bandit 600 could fit the bill, with plenty of after-market accessories (including free tats). If you want to be different or save money, here's your chance.

BIKE CHOICE & PREPARATION

BMW OILHEAD AND HEXHEAD GS BOXERS

Manufactured 1100 from 1995–'98; 1150 '99–'05; 1200 since 2004

Engine 1085/1130/1170cc oil/air-cooled four-valve flat twin

Kerb weight from 229kg/505lb to 256kg/564lb

Fuel capacity From 20 ltr/5.3 US gal

Max range At least 400km/250 miles @ 21kpl/50mpg US

Riders like Image, poise, fuel consumption, ready for RTW

Don't like Weight, ubiquity, some component reliability issues

© MARGUS SOOTLA

Who would dare skip the fuel-injected Telelevers and risk book burnings? Right off the bat the 1100 was a hit, but the heavier 1150 was a whole lot better and the 1200GS better still, managing to lose 30kg (regained on the Adventure model). The 1200s are 'hexhead' engines: smoother, more powerful and managed by CAN bus electronics.

The 'Adventure' versions in 1150 and 1200 feature a lower first gear, switchable ignition for poor fuel, a 30-litre tank, a little more suspension travel plus hand guards, crash bars and other protective features as well as OE luggage which may not be up to the job. Commonly chosen for two-up tours and loaded down like a yak on market day, even custom-tuned Ohlins shocks get cooked and have been known to fail – Hyperpro seems the way to go but even then it's as well to remember what one rear shock can be putting up with. The telelever dive-free forks are trouble free. Final drives wear out, the notorious 'ring antenna' can fail and immobilise you ('05–'09 models; part number ending with '247' is good), as can a fuel pump controller and, less drastically, the fuel level sensor strip. To sum it up, despite their daunting bulk the giant GS is amazingly easy to handle loaded up, even on gravel roads.

Alternatives Ever since the GS sales became a runaway bestseller (helped by

© C SIEWALD

the LWR TV show), competitors have been trying to catch the quarter-ton adventure tourer and pick up the few who have it in for BMW or want to be different. Triumph's shaft-driven Explorer 1200 seems to fit best, or Yamaha's XT1200Z. Only the automatic Honda V4 Crosstourer offers something original in the battle of the heavyweights.

YAMAHA TTR250

Manufactured from 1993

Engine 249cc air-cooled single

Dry weight 122kg/269lb

Fuel capacity 10 ltr/2.4 US gal

Max range 265km/165 miles @ 26.5kpl/62.4 mpg US

Riders like A tough little number

Don't like Terrible seat, still a bit tall but can be lowered, needs a tank

© LOIS PRYCE

Still available new in Australia, for the smaller rider who doesn't seek to cruise at 80mph, the TT-R is among the pick of the crop of small trail bikes. The ancient air-cooled engine will run and run and reliably return 70mpg UK, sit on 50 all day plus the bike won't need a passer-by to help you lift it up when it falls. A Raid version comes with a larger tank and a huge headlight, but is otherwise lower spec'd and the XT250 still sold in the US and South Africa is a heavier and slower dual sport. The TT has the edge as an overlander without going too far with something like a WR. Lois Pryce reckons her trans-African TTR was just that bit tougher than a Serow she used across the Americas, those extra 25cc make all the difference and there's a rare 22-litre Acerbis tank available though Honda XR tanks can be made to fit.

Like an ag bike (see p43), a 120kg TTR or something like it, would also be a choice if you've a particularly gnarly and challenging ride in mind across energy sapping terrain that may involve manhandling bikes.

Downsides are that short folk find TTRs taller than a Serow, but you can fit a lowering rear suspension link which reduces seat height by an inch, as well as the other tricks including sliding the forks up, winding off the suspension and remoulding the seat which, as on so many trails bikes, is terrible. Consider a sheepskin as pictured above. On the web, it's 🖳 **www.ttr250.com**.

Alternatives In the air-cooled range there's the 225cc Yamaha Serow, several Honda XL-based 250s or the Suzuki DR350s. Remember, once you start getting into the water-cooled enduro bikes like WRs and CRFs you're erring too far in the other extreme for what counts out on the road. Stick with air-cooled trail or dual sports bikes.

BIKE CHOICE & PREPARATION

YAMAHA TÉNÉRÉ XT660Z

Manufactured from 2008

Engine 660cc water-cooled single

Kerb weight 206kg/454lb

Fuel capacity 23 ltr/6.1 US gal

Max range 577km/360 miles @ 25.1kpl/60mpg US

Riders like smooth EFI, fuel consumption, looks, heritage

Don't like Weight, height, build quality, steep price rise

Now entering its fourth decade and fifth iteration, the Ténéré is back after a nine-year hiatus and arguably it's the best ever. All you have to accept is that this is how the Japanese build some bikes these days: good looks covering cheap components and all the mandatory emissions claptrap. For the minority of owners who'll take it to Kathmandu via Timbuktu, it's one of the best platforms in its category on which to build an overlander. The EFI motor derived from the XT660R/X trail-bike/supermoto was not new, but Yamaha finally nailed low-speed fuelling issues – a common complaint with many bikes at that time.

When the bike came out in 2008 it was going for around £4500 in the UK, but you could tell they didn't put much effort into making it light or using quality components – a common ploy to get a new model off to a good start. As far as the chunky chassis goes, that's actually a good thing, but the mufflers are high and way out back marring the centre of gravity, and the double-disc front end weighs a ton; one big SM disc and caliper could do the job. The OE screen is a bit low for six-footers and they say cush drives wear out (a common complaint on big singles; stuff them with inner tubes). A low compression ratio of 10:1 means it will live with low octane fuel and you'll need a better bash plate, but apart from a rack and luggage, you're good to go.

Alternatives In the XT660Z's home markets of Europe and Australia there's not much in injected, faired and big-tanked singles, unless Suzuki and Honda get in on the game. Of the old air-cooled XTZs, choose the twin-lamp 3AJ or a younger XT-E which will need 'Ténérising'. Avoid the five-valve, water-cooled XTZ660 they made in the 90s. Or take a high jump and go for a KTM 640 Adventure.

KTM ADVENTURE 640R

Manufactured from 1997–2004

Engine 625cc water-cooled single

Dry weight 154kg / 340lb

Fuel capacity 28 ltr / 7.4 US gal

Max range 530km / 355 miles @ 19kpl / 45mpg US

Riders like Suspension, power, big tank, build quality, light weight

Don't like Vibration, seat pre-2003, engine reliability, not made anymore

Only eight years in production, but the Adventure R remains in a class of its own; a hardcore off-the-shelf overlander appealing to uncompromising riders who value the KTM's hard-edged design and focussed image. Build-quality, some components and attention to detail set the 640R apart, with a tough frame and class suspension.

© NOAH MALTZ

BIKE CHOICE & PREPARATION

But high compression accentuates vibration through the notorious seat. Get used to it, fit bar weights off a Duke plus foam grips and check regularly for vibration-induced issues like loose bolts. Oil leaks can be either unbearable or tolerable and reports of unreliability (a run of cheap Eastern European head / gearbox / main bearings, and broken electrical wires) also vary. Learn to live with engine noises too but, where fitted, check sidestand welds, fit *steel* sprockets, replace control cables and consider a second fan. From 2001 Mikuni CV carb'ed models were better and got switchable CDI to run on low octane fuel. Or better still go for post 2003 when it got an engine oil level sight glass, hydraulic clutch and a faster engine as well as twin front discs.

Alternatives Why no 690 Adventure version? Most probably because, despite its high profile the 640R was actually a low-sales, low-profit niche machine and at the time the V-twins needed a boost. But while not as reliable as a BMW Rotax or a Jap thumper, the injected 690 motor is a lot smoother than the 640, both literally and in power delivery, despite early fuelling issues. Don't wait for KTM: there are outfits in the UK, US, SA and Australia who'll supply the tank, seat and fairing job for you. Or consider the BMW XChallenge (see p55); solid motor and suspension to adapt; that's the way to do it.

© JEROME BULLARD

SUZUKI DL650 V-STROM

Manufactured From 2004

Engine 645cc, water-cooled, 90° V-twin

Dry weight 220kg/490lb

Fuel capacity 22 ltr/5.8 US gal

Max range 500km/310 miles @ 23kpl/54mpg US

Riders like Price, engine, fuel consumption, overall comfort

Don't like Not much at all, a bit low but top heavy perhaps

Equipped with a great engine that has been around since 1999 in the road-oriented SV650 (now a Gladius), like the SV, the inexpensive V-Strom is nothing more than a great all-rounder. It's the smooth engine that makes it much more popular than the bigger, one-litre DL, and as with any bike in this category, a good engine that you can ride all day is the key while suspension is far easier to tune in or adapt according to your weight, payload and riding preferences. A good fuel range and comfort come next and the DL delivers there too. Some find it a bit plasticky and say it's top heavy, but at least you can get alternative seats and bash plates.

Wheels are 17-inch and 19-inch, the bigger front implying that the bike is suited to off-tarmac scenarios, but tyre tread will have a lot more impact than wheel size. Bash plates to protect the vulnerable front pipe are readily made and ABS became an option in 2006.

In 2011 the V-Strom received a makeover with better looks, a more refined and economical engine based on the SVF Gladius, some firmer suspension and even a few kilos were lost on the way. At the same time they released the 650X version with a lot of the accessories you'd fit anyway, but not necessarily what will work best out on the road.

Alternatives The obvious comparison is the less popular Transalp from Honda; not quite as comfy or long ranging even if it might have the edge on dirt roads. There's the more obscure (for overlanding at least) Kawasaki Versys with a harder revving engine that's less suited to prolonged touring, or of course the 800cc F650GS from BMW.

KAWASAKI KLR650

Manufactured From 1987 – significant upgrade 2008

Engine 651cc water-cooled single

Kerb weight 195kg / 432lb (2012 model)

Fuel capacity 23 ltr / 6.1 US gal

Max range 480km / 300 miles @ 21kpl / 50mpg US

Riders like Know-how and aftermarket goodies, price

Don't like Seat, cam chain tension issues

© Tom Grenon

At least 25 years old and still going strong in the US and Australia. Banged out in Thailand, up until 2008 all they did was change the colours each year. Then came a significant if more road-oriented upgrade: chunkier spokes and forks (at last), more power, a new look with better brakes and firmer seat plus revised suspension and an alternator with bigger output .

KLR650s are the Ténérés North America never got and have been refined by enthusiasts and small-time engineering outfits who've fixed every last crease that Kawasaki didn't or wouldn't iron out. With a 9.8:1 compression ratio, it laughs off low octane fuel and on a run can easily top 21kpl (50mp USg) on its old-fangled carb. If only your butt could outlast the tank. Other seats and roadside rest areas are available – and it's hardly unique to KLRs.

The big tank, small fairing and the 650cc water-cooled engine gets the KLR off to a great start, but pre-2008, unless you like steering with oars, brace the front forks. Balancer chain tension is a weak point and it's said the 2008 upgrade saw a lame fix to the spring, so fit a 'doohickey' (google it). Another problem on old models was the stock idler shaft adjustment lever, but you can buy a re-engineered replacement for just $40. And disconnect the sidestand and clutch cut-out switches before they do it themselves. Any other questions? 🖥 **www.klr650.net** at your service.

Alternatives KLR users are mostly from North America where true alternatives are few. The unchanging air-cooled Honda XR650L is similarly well known there, a more dirt-oriented machine that needs a tank and fiddling with the jetting to run right. A Suzuki DR650SE is also an option, but all these carb'd big singles could be reaching the end of the line.

(side margin, vertical text) BIKE CHOICE & PREPARATION

YAMAHA XTW250 RYOKU – A CLOSER LOOK

At the 2011 Tokyo Motor Show Yamaha displayed an interesting concept bike; the **XTW 250 Ryoko**, seemingly based on the ancient XT250 but with TW200 wheels and featuring the fuel-injected motor from the Brazilian-made Lander or XT250Z Ténéré.

Its hard to know if the XTW was a bit of playdough fun which got out of hand, or a serious exercise, but for the overlander it displayed many genuinely useful features.

The looks won't appeal to all and some scoffed at the 250cc engine or that it's just a gimmick-clad designer ag bike, but clued-in adventure riders know what counts. If it can sit on 100kph, carry a load in comfort and with range then it's worth a look. Just note, this assessment is based on scrutiny of photos; Yamaha's press office didn't respond.

Assuming it's a Lander engine then 100mpgUK (35.4kpl) might be possible, so even a 12-litre tank would cover the 95% of

© TAUFIK N

AM stages of 400km or less. The fat tyres and thin forks may be suited to a 250, but you get the all-round discs off the XT trail bike.

On the back there's an LED light and an extra wide mudguard. The 'sheep rack' is set low, with hinged side platforms. They're set a bit too far back, but as long as they can take the weight, that's a great way for supporting luggage. There's a handpump there too.

There's no main stand but you get ag-style twin side stands and a detachable shovel head for a bash plate. Again, a bit gimmicky; a proper dural item is needed. There are also yellow 'bashrings' on the engine sides. The embossed panel logo on the footbrake side suggests a tyre compressor or just a hose? And next to that is a compact Li-Ion battery compartment. There are little extractor fans by the cylinder head for static ops or slow, revvy slogs through dunes or mud.

On the other side is an AC100V power supply through car-type PTOs. The front end gets tank- and headlight protector bars as well as a perspex light guard, hand guards and a fold-up screen. Notice the clearance on the front mudguard too; no clogging up with wet clay there. It's a shame there's no enclosed chain case, but if that's the biggest visible flaw, you must admit Yamaha have, perhaps unintentionally, conceived a great little overlander that addresses the functional versatility of a Unimog rather than adding a beak and high bars to a sports tourer.

12,000 MILES ON A YAMAHA TTR250

I'm 5' 4" and for us shorter folk, finding the right bike can often prove tricky as the seat heights and fully-loaded weights of the traditional overlanding machines can be intimidating. I used a XT225 Serow for my ride from Alaska to Argentina; a sturdy little trail bike but it did suffer at the higher altitudes. A few years later for London to Cape Town I decided I was ready for a bit more power so I went up an extra 25cc to a Yamaha TTR250.

TTR Good

The TTR is that little bit tougher than the Serow and because it's not a 'grey import' in the UK there are more parts like bash plates and tanks available. But it is taller so I fitted a Kuba lowering link and wound down the

suspension a touch so I could get my toes on the ground. My TTR took a serious beating crossing the Sahara and the churned up swamps and wrecked roads of the Congo and Angola. But it never failed me.

I didn't have a single mechanical problem except for dust getting in the switches. I changed the oil every 2000 miles and washed the air filter but that was about it for maintenance. Before I left I replaced the chain, sprocket, cables, bearings and brake pads with original Yamaha parts and I'm sure this played a large part in the reliability of the bike and believe it or not, I didn't even have to adjust the chain tension until the day before I reached Cape Town!

BMW G650 XCHALLENGE – WHY IT'S A GREAT ADVENTURE BIKE

The XC can go for miles without having to touch the engine and it can cruise at 80 mph. At 144kg dry, it can do single track and is easy to pick up. It has a comfortable seating position and the proven engine from the original F650 that runs on 76 octane and up at 5000 metres. It goes for 6000 miles before oil and filter changes; valves rarely need adjustment.

EFI and water cooling make it much more reliable and fuel-efficient than older air-cooled and carb'd engines and compared to an XT660Z it's some 30kg lighter, 15% more economical and more powerful. It has an *18-inch* rear wheel (with a 21-inch front), more suspension travel, clearance and water-fording depth. Compared to KTM's 690 Enduro it's about 20-25% more fuel efficient, is much more comfortable for touring, is more stable, with a more reliable engine and one that needs a fraction of the servicing.

You can get racks, proper seats, fuel tanks, bashplates and fairings. The suspension can be easily upgraded too. As with most bikes it's much easier to make a Xchallenge handle better than to improve engine performance and to me an 'adventurised' Xchallenge is arguably the finest adventure bike in the world! Reliable, light, economical, extremely capable and versatile. This is a bike that won't leave you crying in Mongolia because it's too heavy to handle off-road, and won't put your back out on the Road of Bones trying to pick it up.

... and why it's not

In 2008 the three G650X models replaced the (since-revived) F650 singles in favour of the parallel twins. Lighter singles – bigger twins, it should have worked but it didn't and the Xs were dropped. The XC 'hard enduro' model was perceived as too heavy for a dirt bike and the Xcountry 'street scrambler' and Xmoto supermoto were street bikes, so the Xchallenge didn't fit any niches; it was neither a KLR/Ténéré nor a KTM.

The stock suspension is poor – the rear uses an air sprung shock like the HP2. The seat is terrible and the fuel capacity is inadequate. All this can be fixed to make the XC into a fantastic adventure bike, but out of the box it's far from it, and the cost of those mods can get expensive unless you manage to find a cheap one – which is actually not so hard.

WALTER COLEBATCH
💻 www.sibirskyextreme.com

BIKE CHOICE & PREPARATION

12,000 MILES ... CONTINUED

I had an Acerbis 22 litre tank which gave a range of up to 400 miles, depending on the terrain. The TTR is a trusty friend and is still going strong. It's got enough oomph to get you out of most situations, is light enough for me to pick up, will cruise at 60mph and in my experience, is utterly dependable.

TTR Bad

The worst thing about the TTR250 is its agonising seat. Like most trail bikes it's fine for an occasional weekend ride but not for long-distance. I had my seat remodelled by 💻 www.motorbike-seats.co.uk then added the trusty sheepskin. Result! No more John Wayne impressions.

The 250cc engine was mostly fine, although a couple of times in very deep sand I had to push alongside. Because I had lowered the suspension, and due to the fact that majority of the riding in Africa was not on tarmac roads, when I got the bike back to the UK I discovered that all that bashing up and down over rocks, bomb-holes and in and out of wadis had worn away the front of the swingarm. It could probably have carried on fine but I got another swingarm on Ebay for £150 and the TTR continues to be my regular, if slightly battle-scarred, ride around town.

LOIS PRYCE
Lois' TTR book: *Red Tape and White Knuckles*

Bike preparation

There's a difference between going on a touring holiday and setting off across Asia, Africa or Latin America. Assuming that most users of this book don't live in these places, it can be summed up as 'exposure'. Among other things we'll get to later, you're going to be a long way from the traditional support networks of motorcycle dealers, warranty claims, insurance, vehicle recovery and repair. Of course recovery, repair and maybe occasionally a dealer can all be tracked down or arranged, but you may still be in a place where you don't speak the language and with only a limited time span on your visa.

Because ordinary problems can become complications, you want to simplify things as well as be ready for the worst. You'll need a certain level of autonomy and preparedness for when things go wrong because you have more to lose and the risk is greater. Money's no help because a trouble-free ride is not guaranteed by buying the most expensive adventure motorcycle and festooning it with the most expensive kit. What counts is some experience running the bike with as fool-proof a set-up as you can manage, and then the ability to deal with the issues as they come up. Whether you're buying at home or abroad, **thorough preparation** of your machine is just about the best insurance you can get to guarantee yourself a mechanically trouble-free trip. And because long-range adventuring will require modifications, the more time you spend riding your modified machine before you leave the better.

> You'll need a certain level of autonomy and preparedness for when things go wrong because you have more to lose and the risk is greater.

The great thing is that in the past few years, just as with bikes, the range of equipment for motorcycle overlanding has expanded greatly. There have been few actual innovations and all are quite understandably capitalising on the current trend. What counts hasn't changed and *what follows is what works for most people, backed up by experience; it is not a tablet brought down from the mountainside.* You may well have your own creative solutions which are part of the big adventure too.

Testing, testing

If you're heading overseas with a brand new set up like metal boxes, racks and modified suspension, a short **test run** to see how the whole rig handles is very worthwhile. The fewer surprises you encounter in the nerve-racking early days of the actual big trip the better, because you'll have enough on your plate without finding that with your alloy luggage suite fully packed, the suspension bottoms out and the tyre rubs on the slightest bump.

Try and do as much of the work as possible yourself, or under close guidance so that when something gives trouble, you have a clue how it all went together. Complex things like engine rebuilds, fabricating or welding have to be left to competent mechanics (which could include you), but basic repairs and maintenance tasks like fixing punctures and changing tyres and oil, or cleaning an air filter are things you must be able to do before you go.

> **... basic repairs and maintenance tasks like fixing punctures and changing tyres and oil... are things you must be able to do before you go.**

As a rule, if you doubt whether any consumable component will last the entire length of your planned trip, **renew it** and finish off the partially-worn item later or take it as a spare. This applies especially to things like tyres, chains and sprockets and brakes which wear faster on fully-laden bikes ridden on bad roads, but it can also include wheel bearings, cables and other consumables. If you're buying a **new bike**, get it well in advance of your departure so that any teething problems can be sorted out. And lastly, bear in mind that **modifications other than those recommended here** may be necessary or useful on the machine of your choice.

ABOUT FUEL

In 2006 the United Nations Environmental Program (UNEP) announced that leaded fuel had been eradicated from Africa. From Casablanca and Cairo via the Congo to the Cape, every fuel station was selling unleaded petrol which the modern bikes require. I thought this claim was rather far fetched at the time, and years later there are still plenty of places in the back country of central Africa and Asia where you won't find a green-handled petrol pump.

Leaded fuel, octane ratings and compression ratios

A petrol engine works by compressing a fuel-air mixture, igniting it at the right moment and allowed the resulting explosion to turn a crank, much like an old steam engine. The problem is pressure and heat can cause as-yet-unburned gases on the far side of the combustion chamber to spontaneously ignite, something known as **detonation**, 'knocking' or 'pinking'. Signs of knocking are a light tapping from the cylinder head, worst in higher gears or under heavy throttle loads. The fuel charge is igniting in two places; one caused by the spark, the other because low octane fuel has caused unburned gases to ignite. It won't ruin your engine the way much more damaging **pre-ignition** can, but it's certainly inefficient and results in power loss.

About a century ago they discovered that adding **lead** (or tetra-ethyl lead* to be precise) to petrol reduced knocking – it effectively increased the fuel's **octane** or anti-knocking properties. This is what 'four star', 'premium' or 'super' refers to in fuel; all translate to an octane rating of 95 RON (Research Octane Number) which as we know costs a bit more than 'two star' '*normale*', or 'regular' where the octane can drop below 90 – in outback Mongolia you'll be lucky to find anything above 90 RON. It took about half a century and the exponential increase in motor vehicle use to recognise that the lead contained in the exhaust emissions was a serious health hazard. It's been banned for road use in the much of the West for decades.

***

* A bi-product of tetra-ethyl lead in fuel included the lubrication of the valve seats in the combustion chamber. For 30 years or more, petrol has had other additives as manufacturers have designed engines which won't prematurely wear out their valves seats on unleaded fuel.

So while combustion chamber design has a lot to do with it, in general a high-compression engine – say anything with a CR of over 11:1 – is more prone to knock on low octane fuel which you'll find in poorer or rural regions of the world, places where emissions standards are less a priority than keeping the road open and an old banger running. A Suzuki GS500 runs 9:1, an XR650R is 10:1 while the 800cc BMW twins are 12:1. It's also true to say that a **lean-running** engine is more prone to detonation, and lean mixtures – more air, less fuel – are the norm these days because they burn hotter, encourage complete combustion and so lower emissions, more of which below.

At the cost of longevity and smoothness, increasing the compression ratio is an easy way of getting more power and also ensuring more complete combustion – it's one reason why diesel engines are more efficient; they use a much higher CR to 'auto-ignite' the charge without a spark which then burns more completely (an 18:1 CR also explains why diesels have to be more heavily built when compared to a similar petrol engine).

To reduce pollution, in recent decades increasingly strict **emissions standards** (Euro 5, Euro 6 and so on) have been imposed on vehicle manufacturers, including motorcycles. It's partly the reason **fuel injection** has replaced carbs on bikes, while parallel advances in computer technology have made electronic fuel injection (EFI) much more precise and efficient. Meanwhile, on the hot side of the cylinder head, **catalytic converters** featuring a matrix coated with precious metals, have become incorporated into exhaust systems as a way to further reduce toxic emissions.

The problem is the world is not equal. The three continents which add up to what I call the AMZ are poorer than the other two or three continents from which most AM riders set off on their moto adventures. In many of these poor places the fuel available might be leaded and/or of a lower octane, while the vehicles sold in that country come with less refined engines suited to running on this kind of fuel (the ethanol-based petrol made and sold in Brazil is another issue, see p313). So we have sophisticated bikes primarily sold in rich countries running on the crude fuel found in developing countries.

In the old days the way to avoid knocking on low octane fuel was to add base gaskets under the barrel to reduce compression permanently; retard the ignition by hand; or use octane booster, a fuel additive which contains tetraethyl lead. Today sophisticated electronics and ignition software is switchable or flexible enough to make many modern engines run fine on low octane fuel.

You could say we're are currently in an 'analogue-to-digital' transition period. As technology evolves and filters into the mainstream, manufacturers are discovering ways of making their ECU-managed engines more adaptable and flexible, so that for example, they don't shut down or go into 'limp-home mode' just because a light bulb has blown. At the same time, although probably unsanctioned by manufacturers, an industry is developing in 'chipping' or reprogramming an ECU using a laptop or even a smartphone married to a gadget like a MegaSquirt (🖳 www.megasquirt.info). In most cases an increase in performance is the goal, but there's no reason why detuning for low octane fuel or more economy can't also be done. In a few years doing this may become as normal as jetting a carb or meddling with the points was in the old days, but we're not there just yet.

ENGINE TEMPERATURE

With the prevalence of water-cooled engines and more sophisticated cooling, the old school dodge of fitting an **oil cooler** is less frequently necessary. If you do decide to fit a cooler, **dry sump engines** – that is those with separate oil tanks – lend themselves more easily to this modification as any of the external oil lines can be cut and a cooler spliced in with extra hosing.

Fitting an oil cooler reduces the oil pressure and increases the capacity a little. However, having an oil cooler (or water-cooling for that matter) doesn't mean that important things like oil level, valve clearances and fuelling (where adjustable) can be neglected if the bike is to run well in hot and demanding conditions. Mount an oil cooler up high and in front of the engine: under the head lamp or cut into your fairing are ideal places. If you move into a colder climatic zone cover the oil cooler (or part of a radiator). An over-cooled engine wears quickly and runs inefficiently.

If a water-cooled engine is **overheating** there's something wrong with the cooling system or quite simply the conditions are too hot: most likely in desert sand where you're revving the engine hard at low ground speeds with a tail wind creating a minimal flow through the radiator. In this case **stop but don't switch off and park into the wind** to let the running motor cool down. Unless it's running and parked into the wind, when a bike stops moving the lack of airflow over the motor or through the radiator causes the temperature to rise a little. Turning the engine off at this point causes the temperature to rise dramatically which could send it over the edge. By keeping the engine running during brief stops on hot days the oil (and water) continue to be pumped around, cooling the engine. Should your radiator boil over, refill it a little at a time; pouring cold water into the baking barrel could crack something.

Although most water-temperature gauges are pessimistic you shouldn't get into the habit of running close to the red zone unless you can face changing a blown cylinder head gasket. On air-cooled bikes it's also good to know your normal engine temperature. You can buy **oil temperature gauges** for some bikes which screw in in place of the cap/dipstick, in the frame in front of the tank. These gadgets are a handy way of gauging the *relative* temperature of your engine.

Better still is a proper oil temperature gauge. Touratech and others make a sender that replaces the sump

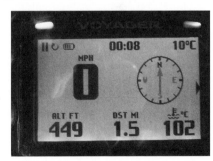

Spark plug temperature reading bottom right; it may not mean much but it's all relative.

drain plug on many bikes and which wires into a Touratech IMO or Voyager computer. I once wired it to a regular oil gauge but the results were not so legible. But because it's all relative it doesn't have to be the true oil temperature; a sensor attached to a spark plug will give you a reading that'll also have a normal operating level. Being able to see how much above normal the reading might get is useful in that it shows how hot your engine might be getting and when it might be an idea to back off or let it cool down.

BIKE CHOICE & PREPARATION

FUEL FILTERS AND VAPOUR LOCK (CARB ENGINES)

Whatever time of year you expect to be riding, it's a good idea to fit an **in-line fuel filter** into the fuel line(s) of your carb-engined bike. The inexpensive

Clean as a whistle, honest! © Trui Hanoulle

translucent, crinkled-paper element type (left, inset) work better than fine gauze items, which most bikes already have inside the tank as part of the fuel tap assembly. Make sure you fit it in the right direction of flow – there should be an arrow moulded into the filter body. These filters can be easily cleaned by simply flushing in a reverse direction with fuel from the tank. In desert areas dust is always present in the air and even in the fuel, and in Iran or Pakistan it's common for roadside fuel to be dished out from a drum with a ladle. The fact that they pour it through an old rag is little compensation.

In hot conditions in-line filters can create **vapour lock**: the evaporation of fuel in the filter body before it flows to the carburettor which leads to fuel starvation. When the engine dies and cools down, the fuel will eventually recondense and run into the carb again and the bike will run until it gets hot again. Vapour lock is worse when your tank fuel level is low and the filter body itself gets hot – we're talking temperatures of over 35°C here. To get round it, top up your tank and pour water over the fuel filter – you should see it fill up with fuel instantly. Wrap it in a damp cloth and think about some more permanent insulation. I had vapour lock on a Funduro in Libya once and taped a piece of cardboard alongside the barrel to keep the heat off the in-line filter. It worked fine for the rest of the trip, even when the temperatures got more extreme.

Fuel-injected engines require a very clean mixture and so have sophisticated and effective fuel pressurisation and filtration units built into the tank which can't be cleaned and rarely need it. They're also immune to vapour lock and adding an inline fuel filter may disrupt the sensitive fuel induction process, so unless you know better it's best to leave things standard.

Air filter

Carb or EFI, an air filter may require daily cleaning during high winds, sand-storms or if travelling behind a dusty convoy. The **reusable multi-layered oiled-foam types** such as those by Twin-Air, Multi Air or Uni Filter are best. It can help to carry a ready-oiled spare in a plastic bag that can be slipped in as necessary while the other gets cleaned later when you get a chance. Make sure the airbox lid seals correctly too.

Greasing all surfaces inside the airbox is messy but catches more airborne particles and keeps the surface of the air filter cleaner for longer; a stocking over the filter is another way of extending the maintenance periods. If you're *pushing* your turned off bike through deep water, put a plastic bag around the filter and then refit it to keep water out of the engine.

Dust riding in groups can clog filters. Paper elements work better but oiled foam can be cleaned.

A freshly-oiled foam filter. Disposable latex or thick rubber gloves are handy.

Some bikes have poorly positioned air intakes that will cake the filter in one sandy day. Check your bike's snorkel/air intake and which way it's pointing. After modifying the seat on an XR650L I found that sand spinning off the back tyre would have got shovelled straight into the airbox – an alloy baffle plate and some duct tape kept it out. You can rinse a re-usable foam filter with petrol and then soak it with engine oil, but proper **air filter oil** does the job much better, remaining sticky and not draining under gravity and drying, as engine oil does. But if you run out, engine oil is better than nothing.

CHAIN AND SPROCKETS

Enclosed from the elements, **shaft drives** are virtually maintenance free – at the very worst the final drive bearing on a hexhead BMW might require changing at 30,000 miles. In this respect shaft drives are ideal for overlanding, though they're usually fitted to heavier, machines which can bring about their own problems on rough terrain.

Sealed chains – making them last

Most bikes are fitted with roller **chains and sprockets** which are more efficient than a shaft when correctly oiled and tensioned. Cost and weight is also the main reason they're used. **Belt drives** are slowly migrating from mopeds, lumbering cruisers and camshaft drives onto the back end of sports bikes and could be the next big thing on all motorcycles. Lighter, quieter, lubrication free, transmission cushioning and very long wearing, they're even beginning to exceed the breaking strain of comparable chains. Their only drawback is that they're slightly less efficient (the cushioning effect), need a relatively large and wide, space-consuming sprocket to wrap around, and altering the gearing (as explained below) may be less easy. For the moment though we're just about all using chains or shafts.

O-ring chains have grease between the outer rollers and inner pins, sealed with tiny rubber rings between the rollers and side plates. Only when these rubber seals begin to wear out after many thousands of miles will the chain begin to wear out like an ordinary chain. Manufacturers have since come out with somewhat gimmicky 'X-' and 'W-' ring chains (effectively, multiple seals), some of which are guaranteed for 12,000 miles. For *Desert Riders* we were testing various systems; the other two guys fitted DID 'gold plate' x-rings while I tried out a similarly-priced RK 'XW' ring, also made in Japan. Result: the DIDs barely needed adjusting while my OK RK needed about three or four adjustments in 5000km. I've used DIDs before which lasted incredibly so, to cut a long story short, fit DID gold plate sealed chains, or whatever brand is said to be as good.

Chain tension and maintenance
Your bike's manual will give exact instructions, but in most cases a chain should be adjusted to provide **40mm** (1.5") **of slack** measured midway along the bottom run of the chain *without you on the bike*. On most trail bikes with long-travel suspension, this will give an impression of an overly slack chain when the machine is unloaded and at rest, but this slack will be taken up once the suspension is compressed to the correct level when the bike is on the move. I've found you can expect a certain amount of tightening and polishing of the chain towards the end of a hot day; this will slacken off to the correct tension as the chain cools overnight. Make sure you adjust it correctly: remember, an over-loose chain is less bad than an over-tight one, but correct adjustment is best. Realistically, with a quality chainset and moderate riding habits, you can expect to have to make adjustments every couple thousand miles.

Chains are obviously exposed and external lubrication will attract grit and so accelerate the wear faster than an Maico 450 with a jammed throttle. Automatic chain oilers (like the well-known Scott unit) are ideal for long road rides, but in sandy conditions should be disconnected. I've found sealed o-ring chains cope very well with minimal oiling. If you don't use aerosol chain lube (bulky and messy to carry), a bottle with a small nozzle full of non-synthetic gearbox oil or proper pushbike chain lube is more efficient. Lubricate at the end of the day when the chain is hot: start the engine, put the bike on the centre stand or push and support the bike on the sidestand with a stick or box, click into first, wipe clean with a toothbrush or rag if necessary then run oil along the inside of rollers. For the chain it's like sipping an ice cold in Alex. See p170.

Although **enclosed chain cases** are a much better idea, as far as I know only old-time MZ ever managed to make a sufficiently robust item; ag bikes (see p43) feature tinny, pressed steel cases. If anyone still makes them, aftermarket versions are only up to urban riding; on rough roads they'll eventually fall apart as well as make wheel changes horribly messy. That's why it's best to give your chain an oiling after each long day's ride.

'Highway' sprocket zip-tied to the frame for the ride home (which never happened...).

A cheap chain ruined this sprocket in just 4000 miles – stick to the well-known brands.

Sprockets

Good quality **steel sprockets** are the best way to get long service life from an o-ring chain. Avoid lighter alloy versions – they won't last as long no matter how hard they say they are. And beware of buying cheaper, pattern 'chain and sprocket kits' from some mail order suppliers who sell obscure brands of chains and inferior steel sprockets.

Original equipment (OE) sprockets matched up with a good chain should give you at least 10,000 miles of trouble-free riding on a 600cc bike, and probably double that with regular oiling and road riding. Both items are worth the extra expense for a longer service life.

Final drive ratio

The good thing with chains is you can easily alter the final drive ratio; in general bikes are often too highly geared. For a long highway run you'll want high gearing, but when the going gets tough on most bikes it's easy to swap the front sprocket with one that's one-tooth smaller so lowering the gearing. You'll gain better control on rocks as well as better response from the lower gears when you most need it. Remember, as already mentioned, more racy bikes have close internal gearbox ratios to keep them in the power range and improve acceleration. And on road-geared bikes with off-road potential, like BMW's F650GS or 1200GS (shaft) first gear is too high for steady off roading.

CARRYING EXTRA FUEL

Without fuel you're going nowhere but first ask yourself, does your motorcycle really need a **larger tank**? There are few places in the world where a fuel range of more than 300km or nearly 200 miles is needed on a sealed highway, and that translates to just 15.4 litres or just over 4 US gallons if riding at 19.5kpl (55 mpg; 45.8 mpg US or 5.13ltr/100km; there's a fuel mileage conversion table on the website). In fact that fuel consumption figure is pretty conservative when you think of today's fuel injected bikes and was close to the *lowest* I recorded on an XT660Z a few years ago while riding into a day-long gale in southern Morocco. The *average* over 5000 miles with that XTZ was 35% higher. A range of about **400km or 250 miles** is plenty and that adds up to just over 20 litres or 5.3 USg at the above mentioned consumption levels. Most of the ten bikes listed earlier have tanks that big.

Besides the expense (some special tanks from Germany went for over €2000!), think about the extra weight of carrying 45 litres or nearly 12 USg; the maximum practical capacity for most bikes. On *Desert Riders* we were able to source relatively inexpensive '40'-litre XR600 tanks for our XRLs but they made the bikes very unstable in some off-road situations even though we actually needed that range and a whole lot more (we set up fuel dumps in advance).

Buying a bike like a KLR650 or a DL650 or a big GS Adventure with

There's a KTM buried under there somewhere.

good-sized tanks in the first place is one reason why these machines are so popular; it's one less thing that you need to adapt or spend money on, and on the odd occasion where you might need extra fuel, a **plastic fuel can or bag of up to 10 litres** will see you through, and weigh next to nothing at other times.

There's another time where you might want to fill up a huge tank and that's when crossing from somewhere like Venezuela to Brazil, from Iran to Turkey or from Algeria to Niger. In these neighbouring countries the price of fuel has among the biggest disparity in the world, costing up to ten times more. In a diesel truck it may be worth filling an oil drum – I've done it myself – but on a bike the savings are not so spectacular.

Big plastic or alloy tanks

Although a major expense, if you want it, a bigger tank holding up to 30 litres is a practical limit. **Plastic tanks** combine the best in strength, lightness and durability, as well as providing resistance to vibration damage and, if necessary, being easily repairable with glue. Alloy may look nicer but needs to be thick to be strong and so ends up being heavier than you think.

The good thing about a big tank is that it places the heavy weight of fuel close to the machine's centre of gravity where it has a less pronounced effect on the balance of the machine – though you won't be thinking that when you first ride off with a full tank.

Acerbis still makes a number of large plastic tanks in the 20-25 litre range, but they're mostly to fit popular enduro and dual-sporters like XRs, DRs and WRs. IMS, Clarke and Safari take up the slack in the US and Australia, but cater for the same sort of machines at the same sizes, although IMS brought out a 9 gallon US (34 litre) tank for both KLR650s. Clarke make a 3.7 US universal tank and a 4.7 US tank (17.8 litres) for a Honda XR650L for just $200.

It's becoming less unusual for bikes to have **underseat tanks**. They're a good idea in that they lower the centre of gravity but as you can imagine, enlarging this is not a task which Acerbis or IMS are jumping over themselves to address. The BMW G650GS single (and its predecessors, see p44) is one such bike with a 14-litre underseat tank which will still give you a reliable 300km. Moulded **side tanks** are a solution here, coming at around 10 litres a side, but as with plastic tanks, they're more commonly found for enduro bikes which are being converted to rallying. They're also expensive for what they are and

A 33-litre tank on an oilhead GS Adventure. Fits a regular GS too but will cost hundreds.

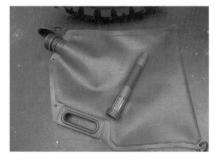

Liquid Containment 7L bladder. Another 100 miles for little expense, volume and weight.

fitting them is not so simple, though they don't both have to be used for fuel of course – one can be a water tank.

Jerricans used to be the old way of doing it; sold used from military surplus outlets from £10, the price is unbeatable. They make reliable and robust fuel containers but are of course heavy and awkward to stash when you don't need them, which is most of the time. A more modern solution is tough, plastic **fuel bladders** such as those made by Liquid Containment in Australia, and doubtless other places too. Think of it as a camelbak for your bike's drinking requirements. Their 7-litre PU bladder is an ideal size to extend a bike's range by a hundred miles and costs just AUD70, with a 20 litre bag going for another 30 dollars.

Remember, with all sealed fuel

A good way of keeping an eye on your **throttle's position**, and so your fuel consumption, is to inscribe a mark on the throttle housing on the left along with an adjacent mark on the twist grip; one with the throttle closed, one halfway as above (on bikes like XT600s this point engages the second carb), and one wide open.

On dual-bodied carbs like on an XT and especially with smaller-engined bikes, riding into a head wind or up a long incline, you'll find yourself inadvertently winding the throttle right open. It doesn't make you go any faster but it sure wastes fuel.

containers of any sort, heat and shaking will create **pressure** in the container; this is why fuel tanks have breathers. Hammering across an Iranian track in July with a pair of two-litre fizzy drink bottles full of petrol strapped to the back of your seat may see them leak or burst within minutes. Even with a fuel bladder, leave an **air gap** to allow for fuel expansion (proper jerricans have this built into the design). Remember too, that assuming the seal has held, that fuel may well be under pressure when you come to using it, so it's not the time to have a roll-up drooping from your lower lip.

There's not much you can do about shaking if you're on a rough track, but keeping a fuel bladder or a **temporary container** out of direct sunlight or draped in a wet rag will reduce expansion or stress on seams or the cap. It's not recommended of course, because some plastics are softened by petrol, but if you find yourself having to use a wine bladder or a plastic bottle to cover a lean stretch of road or track, decant that fuel into the main tank before it disintegrates and decants itself; it could be a matter of hours before that happens.

DAMAGE PROTECTION

The longer your planned ride the better it is to protect your motorcycle from small tumbles, loose rocks and bottoming out. Many trail bikes feature sump guards or bash plates from the factory, but some of these are not worthy of the name; the plastic items on BMW 650s, V-Stroms and Transalps spring to mind and yet the Dominator, 750 Super Ténéré and Africa Twin all had excellent OE bashplates. Especially if you expect to be riding off-road, but a good idea anyway, an **alloy plate of at least 4mm** is advisable. These can be easily fabricated or modified from other machines. On one desert trip two bikes sustained cracks

Only a week old and already you can see how this plate has taken the hits for the TTR250.

All the protection an airhead BMW sump needs. Note recessed location bolts.

to the engine from kicked-up rocks; one XT even had a good, broad plate. Make sure yours covers the width of the engine, including possible frontal impacts to water pumps and hoses as well as oil filters and low coolers. On BMW Boxers the cylinders and downpipes are fairly immune to low-flying hits although, as on any bike, the sump certainly needs protection – a suspension-bottoming bounce onto a rock will easily punch a hole in the sump, though on a BM this might be easier to repair than a vertically split crankcase of a typical Japanese bike. In the field I've fixed cracks with Liquid or Chemical Metal hardening paste – it's worth carrying some with you.

Hand and lever protectors are another good idea on any bike – a broken lever mount can ruin your day. Again don't rely on OE plastic items which won't help much when a fully-loaded overlander tips onto a kerb. Thick alloy bars which clamp solidly onto your handlebars are one less thing to worry about. Around these bars, plastic wind deflectors can be fitted to keep the weather off your hands. If the deflectors are rather skimpy and the weather is terrible, it's easy to extend the protection with plastic bottles splayed out, or even make rain-proof muffs with a pair of five-litre plastic containers; the sort of rubbish you can find anywhere and is good to recycle. Your bike won't win any beauty contests but if it means retaining feeling in your fingers it's worth it. Without protection, keep your lever mounts a little **loose** on the bars; that way the mounts may twist rather than snap when you fall off.

Lever protectors – you may need to saw the lever ends off. Hook is handy for shopping.

Engine bars. One less thing to worry about when the inevitable happens.

Engine crash bars are another worthwhile fitting; it all means you can relax a little, knowing that if you do have a prang the fragile alloy engine casings need not get mashed. Engine bars can also act as useful attachment points or front racks, or something to grab as you haul your bike out of a ditch.

Radiators, water pumps and hoses, and oil coolers are also especially vulnerable, as are damaged foot levers and protecting these items (as well as carrying radiator sealant and a spare gear-change lever) is a good idea. Some riders do get carried away with protecting their machine from all possible damage, though usually it'll be your luggage and handlebars

Carry a tube of Chemical Metal or similar hardening putty. Just make sure that when that 'rainy day' comes, it's not a tube that's been sat in your toolbox for 15 years or more and gone off.
A good wrap-around bashplate (as far left), would have avoided an expensive recovery off the side of this mountain.

which take the brunt of a fall, which is why metal boxes are preferred.

SEATS AND SCREENS

After protecting your bike you want to lavish some protection on yourself too, not least your butt and your back. One of the biggest complaints riders have about their machines are seats which become uncomfortable after just a couple of hours. We've all been there; shuffling off one side of the seat to the other, trying to ease the pain and get some circulation. Trail bikes are notorious in this respect and pukka enduro bikes are even worse. In the latter case it's partly because these bikes have high-compression single-cylinder engines and were not designed to cross continents, or at least not while seated.

Part of the reason could be that a truly comfortable, well-designed saddle would ruin the look of something like an F800GS (which needs it), or more likely cost too much. Regular saddles are hit and miss because everyone's different and what suits a skinny Laurel may not suit a more rotund Hardy. It's possible your butt can get used to a saddle over several weeks, and also that some days might be worse than others. The answer is to get off every two hours and if you can be bothered, do some stretching. Hopefully before the Big Day, a couple of day-long rides will have established whether your saddle is a friend or foe.

Improving your saddle

Traditionally, what feels soft and compliant in the showroom may not reflect your experience at the end of a 400-mile day. It's common to assume that the discomfort is caused by a saddle being too hard but, excepting some enduro bikes, it's more common to find that, when sat on all day the cheap foam is actually **too soft** to give day-long support before you sink down onto the seat base. Most manufacturers will use ordinary grade, open cell polyurethane foam that'll do the job, but not for a heavier rider on a long, rough ride.

The other cause of discomfort is that a saddle is **too narrow**; after all would you expect to spend a day at work sitting on an 8-inch wide piece of

BIKE CHOICE & PREPARATION

Sit on this. © S. Courrier

vinyl-covered foam? Just remember, a dual sport bike includes the need to stand up and grip the tank/seat area with your knees; that's why they're narrow. Both the foam's density, the seat's profile and possibly the type of covering can all be modified by a motorcycle seat specialist, and in the US a whole industry exists in uprating or manufacturing replacement saddles for the domestic touring market.

A narrow seat will have its limitations, but the key to back-end bliss on any seat is to **spread the load**. It allows the blood to circulate to reduce numbness and pain. It's also about breathability or **air circulation**. Much of the shuffling described earlier is about getting some fresh air to your backside as much as relieving pressure. Sitting all day against an impermeable layer of vinyl doesn't add up, but a bike seat needs to be weatherproof.

Sitting securely counts too. The **dishing** you see in some seat designs is not so much about increasing the contact area as stopping you sliding around, another cause of discomfort, especially sliding forward on a sloping seat. This depends partly on the fabric of your trousers, but for touring as opposed to any form of racing, the more planted you are the better.

Airseats, sheepskins and gel pads

Height permitting, adding a layer of something onto the original saddle is the simplest way of improving comfort. Airhawk pads are well known among bikers, making use of air's compressibility, but as with an air-bed, you don't want to pump it right up. Inflate it just enough to spread the load, otherwise you'll be wobbling around like an electrocuted Space Hopper which does the handling no good at all.

A little springiness and circulation is also the idea behind a **sheepskin** (below); although if permanently fitted they can take a while to dry if left in the rain. It's hard to think how a **gel pad** can improve a motorcycle saddle, but different solutions suit different people. Used as a thin pad with no other cushioning element, it may work on a road racer, but gel doesn't compress like open-cell foam or air, it merely squidges or displaces, rather like human tissue. And just because it resembles human tissue (as some gel pads boast) that does-

n't mean it's a comfortable medium for sitting on, unless you find sitting on other people agreeable.

Some other tricks I've heard of but not tried include wearing skin-tight lycra cycling shorts, though as a pushbike rider I'd think the main appeal here is the relief in taking them off at the end of the day.

Bottom line, no matter what you ride you'll be doing a lot of it for weeks at a time, and even if most over-landers won't be engaged in a 1000-mile day Iron Butt epics, addressing the age-old motorcyclist's complaint of saddle soreness is crucial. The dynamic elements of the bike you choose – power, braking, handling and looks – will appeal to a broad range of users, but a seat cannot be expected to do this. Because comfort is such a subjective matter only a few guidelines and principles have been given here. If you think you need a better seat, don't

Roadside emergency foam; I could not face the ride home without it.

hold back from investing in something you'll depend on every second you're riding. As mentioned elsewhere, **rider comfort is critical** because when you're fatigued you can make mistakes or be slower to react to hazards.

Windscreens

Sore butts are one complaint, sore backs and necks are another. I suspect one reason that giant adventure bikes have caught on with riders not necessarily seeking out the ends of the earth is that these bikes have the horsepower and macho profile of a sports bike, but are as comfortable as a tourer, something they'd not chose to be seen on for another 20 years at least.

However small or slow your bike, consider fitting some sort of wind shield. It doesn't have to be the all-enveloping barn door of whatever the latest flat-six Gold Wing is clad with. Just something in front of the bars a foot high and as wide will greatly help reduce wind pressure as well as take the edge off pelting rain. See what current bikes are using and notice that they're a lot more upright than the old Windjammer days. A smaller upright screen is as effective as a larger streamlined one because it pushes away more air while saving weight. But it does so at the risk of turbulence which affects riders differently; it needs some curvature.

As with seats not being able to suit all, taller riders can find the standard screen heights on their chosen bike inadequate. Some might be adjustable and some can be replaced with taller OE items. If not, then Touratech make a clip-on screen extension which worked well for me on my Ténéré, but has a rather ungainly mounting device; you could fabricate or experiment with something similar yourself.

Windshields which mount on the handlebars can crack when the bike falls and bars flex a little. Mounting on the frame is best, despite the fact that the screen doesn't turn with you in a bend. At road speeds the turn of your bars is minimal, anyway.

This shapely and adjustable little number is made by Givi. © Carla King

BIKE CHOICE & PREPARATION

EQUIPMENT CHECKLIST

It's unlikely that you'll take just these items, but consider this as part of a useful checklist to give you ideas on essentials you may have overlooked.

Documentation
- Passport
- Vehicle registration document
- Carnet
- Cash in hard currency
- Debit and credit cards
- Travel tickets
- Travel insurance
- Green Card and/or Third Party Insurance
- Driver's licence (including IDP)
- Several spare passport photos
- Address book (paper or digital and online)
- Photocopies and online images of all important documents

Clothing
- Helmet
- Boots and light shoes
- Socks and underpants
- Thermal underwear
- T-shirts or shirts
- Shorts
- Fleece
- Riding jacket
- One-piece waterproof riding suit
- Gloves, plus spare pair
- Trousers or riding pants, plus spare pair
- Balaclava or sun hat
- Handkerchief or bandana
- Sun glasses

Camping and sleeping
- Tent or self-supporting mozzie net
- Sleeping mat
- Sleeping bag
- Collapsible stool or chair (see p143)
- Ear plugs
- Head torch plus a back-up light source.

Cooking
- Stove and fuel (if not petrol) plus spares
- Tea towel and pan scrubber
- Lighter or other reliable fire source
- Spoon and fork
- Cooking pot(s) with lid and pot gripper
- Swiss Army knife or multitool
- Mug
- Ten-litre water bag
- Basic food items like salt, pepper, oil, sugar/sweetener (more compact)

Toiletries
- Soap and towel
- Toothbrush and toothpaste
- Toilet paper
- Skin moisturiser and insect repellent
- Universal basin plug
- Needle and thread
- First-aid kit (see p151)

Navigation and orientation
- Paper maps
- GPS or Satnav with relevant maps loaded
- Pocket compass
- Guidebook(s)
- Useful waypoints (online or on a device)

Miscellaneous
- Smart phone with GPS feature
- Basic mobile phone
- Laptop, tablet or iPod
- Camera and memory cards
- Spare batteries for everything
- Cables/adapter plugs to recharge gadgets
- Adapter wall plug for your regions
- Waterproof bags
- String or cord
- Elastic bands

FIT NEW – KEEP SPARES

It has been said already but get familiar with your bike by fitting good-quality new consumable items like tyres, brakes, batteries and chain and sprockets and keep the part-used-but-still-serviceable items as spares.

Taking new spares is not the same because anyone who's worked on their own bike will be familiar with the discovery that the replacement oil filter you spent half the morning tracking down and carried halfway across Africa doesn't fit. It's something better found out on a quiet Sunday morning on your drive with a steaming mug to hand, than by the roadside on the outskirts of Istanbul on a Friday evening. Fit new stuff now, keep the used item as a backup so you'll know for sure it will fit.

SPARES AND MAINTENANCE PARTS LIST

This list: is a start. Special tools and spares for your bike will be as essential.

Tools
- Allen or Torx keys
- Junior hacksaw with spare blades
- Multimeter, electric
- Oil filter removing tool
- Pliers with wire cutters
- Screwdrivers, selection
- Spanners and mini socket set to suit every fitting on your bike
- Tyre levers, pressure gauge and mini compressor
- Puncture-repair kit & inner tubes (see p81)
- ECU diagnostic tool (requires smartphone or laptop)

Spares
- Bolts, nuts, washers & self-tapping screws
- Spare bulbs
- Electrical connections, fuses, wire
- Old bulb in a socket with wire (for continuity testing
- Filters: fuel, oil

- Mini jump leads
- Keys, spare
- Pipes: fuel (rubber), siphoning (clear plastic)
- Spark plugs
- Tyre(s)
- Air filter, pre-oiled in a plastic bag

Sundries
- Cable (zip) ties, wire, duct tape
- Grease
- Jubilee (hose) clips
- Radiator sealant
- Epoxy glue and metal repair paste
- Instant gasket
- Thread-locking cement (Loctite)
- WD40/GT85 or similar
- Connecting link(s) for chain
- Control levers and cables (run cables alongside current ones)
- Diaphragm for CV carbs
- Spare bungees, straps and inner tube strips
- Spoke key
- Top-up oil and rag
- Thin wire and wire coathanger

BIKE CHOICE & PREPARATION

Some tools: From the top, bulb on a wire for circuit testing (bulb is in the film cannister), hose clips. Next includes back wheel spanner, mini sockets and zip ties, all in a nifty Kriega tool roll.

WHEELS

Here's a factoid for you. On any wheeled vehicle the mass of a wheel has a disproportionate influence on acceleration. Because these rotating masses need to overcome their own inertia to get moving, the lighter the wheel (and tyre/tube for that matter) the quicker the machine accelerates and brakes, which evokes the cycle frame-builder's maxim: "an ounce [saved] on the wheel equals a pound on the frame".

With motorcycle magazines and the like comparing acceleration times down to the nearest hundredth of a second, you can see why super sport bikes have super light cast wheels. The type of bike you'll probably be riding ought to have more robust items. 'Unsprung weight' – the part of the wheel and suspension assembly that moves up and down – is another motivation for light wheels, although again this is more critical on hard-running dirt racers.

Modern dual sport machines are built with spoked wheels on alloy rims to limit unsprung weight and improve road performance, but it's as much to do with looks: spokes = dirt bike. Once a bike has an overlanding load some rims may not be up to the continuous heavy beating they'll encounter over potholed tarmac and corrugated tracks. Rear wheels carry maximum loads and are especially prone to damage. With wire wheels carry a snug-fitting **spoke key** and check spoke tension after rough stages: tap for a clear 'ding'. The more frequently you do this, the less likely a rim gets too far out of true. If it does, make small changes in tension and as a rule, to pull a deflection back into alignment, tighten the spoke on the opposite side (left or right) of the rim.

Cast or wire, many motorcycles are produced with cheap components to support a low purchase price. Something like the Triumph Bonneville series is a good example; a great-looking bike that's fine for most intended users. Should you choose to take it overlanding it may require a close look at the wheels. If you're not convinced the spoked wheels on any machine are up to it, fit **heavy-duty spokes** or better still, uprate your wheels altogether with

quality rims from Akront, Excel or DID. The benefit of having this work done is the difference between having to check and tension your standard wheels regularly or largely ignoring the strengthened items.

Most overlanders shy away from **cast wheels**, believing they're not suited to rough roads, but like everything else, cast wheel technology has improved in recent years and cracking rims under *normal* use seems to be a thing of the past. It's certainly true that the in-built flex of spoked rims is better at absorbing dirt impacts, but I suspect there's also something of an image about spoked being seen as more 'adventuresome'. So it is that the snazzy BMW F800GS or GS Adventure

A kitchen conversion of spoked wheels on a Ténéré to run the tyres without tubes. Mastic was applied onto the spoke nipples to make them airtight. It worked until I dinged the front rim on the same evening I cracked an engine case (see p67). At the time neither full bashplates nor Tubliss inserts (which do the same thing differently) were available in Ténéré wheel sizes. Details on the website.

gets spokes while the plainer 650/700 or 1200 version gets cast wheels. The best thing about cast wheels is that they take **tubeless tyres** without any spoke complications. And as you're about to read, tubeless tyres are better.

Wheel sizes can be misleading. Trail bikes traditionally have 21-inch front wheels because a bigger diameter wheel rolls over bumps more readily than a smaller wheel, and narrower tyres cut through the dirt better than wider ones. But on any bike it will be

> It will be the wheel size that determines what locally available tyres will fit your bike. On a long trip this is a more important consideration, especially on a powerful, heavy bike which may get through tyres in 5000 miles or less.

the **tread pattern** that really dictates how well a machine performs on different surfaces, while it will be the wheel size that determines what **locally available tyres** will fit your bike. On a long trip this is a more important consideration, especially on a powerful, heavy bike which may get through tyres in 5000 miles or less. Just as with petrol quality mentioned earlier, tyre availability is unpredictable abroad for the same reason as what we can buy and ride in rich countries is not the same as what gets sold and used in the poorer lands of the AMZ.

Seventeen-inch wheels

Most modern road bikes over 600cc run 17-inch wheels front and back. Some in the adventure motorcycle category might have a 19-incher up front to pander to dirt road pretensions or for the 'bigger rolls over better' reason given above. I can't say I've noticed but we're told that once you start pushing the limits on the road, the dynamic attributes of a pair of fat 17s work best. The thing is, out in the world most poor locals don't ride ZZR1100s in full leathers, they ride four-up on handed down versions of Honda CG125s or similar which will run 18 or even 19-inch tyres, and even those will be on the slim side for the likes of a big BMW. It may well change over the years as wealth spreads to some in the developing world, but traditionally, 17-inch tyres are notoriously hard to come by in outback Asia, Africa and the poorer Andean countries. That is why you see round-the-worlders setting forth with a pair of spare tyres slung over the bike (see next page).

Changing 17-inch cast wheels for 18s or 19s is quite an expensive and complicated undertaking. Spoked wheels are much more easily modified with alternative rims because you can retain the all-important original hub. As mentioned on p102, in the US it's common to radically adapt a bike with an engine you like so as to run longer suspension, and in this way fitting the entire **front end** (triple clamps, forks, brakes and wheel) in whatever wheel size you like (usually bigger) is easier than finding a bigger cast wheel to fit your forks.

When I came to converting my GS500 project bike (see the website), I chose to replace the original 17-inch cast wheels with a DR650 front end and *identical* 19-inch spoked rims and tyres front and rear. The rationale here was that if either tyre got damaged beyond repair – it can happen – the single spare carried would fit both ends, and in Indian sub-continent there was a chance of finding a 19-inch replacement.

BIKE CHOICE & PREPARATION

TYRES

No other item gets prospective adventure riders in such a stew. And quite right too because having the wrong tyres is at the very least, tiresome, and at worst, downright dangerous. Rain or shine, they're out there on the front line, rolling over whatever surface you're riding on while supporting 3-500kg and translating whatever input you give to speed up, slow down or turn. We ask a lot of our tyres because the consequence of them not performing when it comes to traction, longevity and durability can be grave, and yet choices can often be governed initially by looks or later down the road, by what fits.

Choosing tyres

Punctures will probably be the most common breakdown you'll have to deal with on the road; the tread pattern or compound may be the most likely reason for you sliding off; and worrying about finding replacements may be the most frequent service item, short of where to fill up next with fuel. Choosing the right tyre won't have you dancing from the rooftops, but buying a sub-optimal tyre could be galling for all the above reasons.

For motorcycle overlanding tyre choice boils down to long wear, secure road manners but poor dirt grip from **street-oriented tyres** which includes the 'adventure tyres' mentioned later – or more **dirt-biased road legal tyres** with more aggressive tread which still work OK on highways, but will wear faster and certainly won't grip and corner so well in the rain.

Avoid tyres that have less than **three plies**; they're designed for light unsprung weight and won't be resistant to punctures on the potholed roads you'll encounter. Keep a regular check on your **tyre pressures** and the condition of the sidewalls. Stay well within the top speeds of the load index ratings listed opposite, especially in hot and fast conditions when your machine may effectively (if momentarily) exceed these limits on badly paved roads.

Above all recognise that whatever works for someone in one situation, they believe that's the best tyre for them – even if the experience of others is to the contrary. There are no bad tyres produced by the main manufacturers listed below, just tyres that are inappropriately fitted, used or maintained. This whole Bridgestone 'Death Wing' online urban myth is, as far as I can tell,

If you find a tyre you like that you can't buy locally, send them ahead. These K60s are on the way from the port to the post office.
© Margus Sootla

without foundation – or if it is, it could be relevant to any number of other tyres which come as original equipment. In some markets there are over twenty different types of Trail Wings. The TW301/2s I've used worked as expected; an average, road-oriented trail tyre that does neither job that well, especially on more powerful twins. Let those online wags ride off on the 'nylon' Pneumants that came with MZ in the 1970s. 'Cause of Death: Pneumania' we could have called them. The Heidenau K60 Scout is another tyre that gets people worked

TYRE SPEED RATINGS (LETTERS) AND LOAD INDEX CODES (NUMBERS)

Speed symbol	K	L	M	N	P	Q	R	S	T	U	H
Speed (kph)	110	120	130	140	150	160	170	180	190	200	210
Speed (mph)	68	75	81	87	93	99	106	112	118	124	130

Index	lbs	kg	Index	lbs	kg	Index	lbs	kg
36	181.7	125	50	276.2	190	64	407	280
37	186.1	128	51	283.5	195	65	421.5	290
38	191.9	132	52	290.7	200	66	436.1	300
39	197.7	136	53	299.4	206	67	446.3	307
40	203.5	140	54	308.2	212	68	457.9	315
41	210.8	145	55	316.9	218	69	472.4	325
42	218	150	56	325.6	224	70	487	335
43	225.3	155	57	334.3	230	71	501.5	345
44	232.6	160	58	343	236	72	516	355
45	239.8	165	59	353.2	243	73	530.6	365
46	247.1	170	60	363.4	250	74	545.1	375
47	254.4	175	61	373.6	257	75	562.5	387
48	261.6	180	62	385.2	265	76	581.4	400
49	268.9	185	63	395.4	272	77	598.9	412

All road-legal tyres are speed- and load-rated by the manufacturer: a tyre branded with '58P' will be designed to work at maximum speeds of 150kph while carrying a load of 236kg. Travelling two-up will probably put your machine near such a tyre's design limit.

Tyre sizes With a 140/80 R17 tyre that fits a BMW G650GS, the 140 refers to the notional width of the tyre in millimetres, the '80' refers to the equally notional height of the tyre as a percentage of the width, so in this case that will be 112mm, the 'R' refers to radial construction (see box p77) and the 17 refers to the diameter of your wheel. Just remember a 140/80 from one Metzeler may not be identical in size to a Michelin, but it will be very close. You can also tell the **age of your tyre** by deciphering a four-figure stamp which should be something like '2613' which means it was made in the 26th week of 2013. This can be useful to know if buying used tyres; anything more than five years old may be getting past its use-by date for heavy adventure touring.

BIKE CHOICE & PREPARATION

up. It's the way it is with tyre talk. I found them brilliant on an F650. Where you may run into problems is fitting some unknown Asian brand at some stage of your travels; a tyre that was probably never intended for bigger machines. This is why riders choose to post dependable tyres onward (left) or carry them with them for months, despite the inconvenience.

Tyre performance depends on your route, your riding style, your bike's power and weight, and your priorities, although conservative road riding and alert and responsive riding off-highways (especially in rocky terrain) will mean fewer punctures, less wear and less grey hair.

In the end of course anything **black and round** that keeps your rims from clattering over the bitumen will do the job, and across parts of the Adventure Motorcycling Zone (AMZ) you may have little choice but to buy brands you've never heard of. So at the outset, do yourself a favour by choosing an established **quality brand**: for motorcycles that adds up to tyres made by Avon, Bridgestone, Continental, Dunlop, Metzeler, Michelin and Pirelli and remember to take any excessively strong opinions with a pinch of salt.

Tread patterns and compounds

Despite tyre manufacturers' proclamations about cunning, computer-designed knobs, sipes and grooves, to their marketing departments a tyre's appearance or form is as important as its actual function. A cool-looking tread may sell better, but may be no more functional than a vintage-looking Dunlop K70 from the 1970s. What really matters in a tyre – the **compound** and the **construction** of its carcass – is impossible to evaluate just by looking at it, or even by doing some research.

Biking lore recognises that a tyre with a soft compound grips well wet or dry but doesn't last, while a long-lasting, hard-compound tyre may be skittish on wet roads, as will any tyre with a knobbly tread pattern. Construction technology has evolved greatly to control flex, as has mixing compounds, load indexes and lighter weight, but realistically tread patterns have not. A tractor tyre looks the same as it did 85 years ago because it works, and on any bike slicks would work best on smooth, dry, paved roads. Back in the real world **tread** is needed to cut through and expel surface rainwater on which a slick would aquaplane. Meanwhile on soft dirt, deep, widely-spaced knobs dig in for longitudinal and lateral traction, just like a spiked running shoe. Broadly speaking, it's as simple as that.

Heat, pressure and traction

Harsh braking and acceleration take their toll, but it's **heat** in the body of the tyre that will create wear during normal riding. Each rotation of a tyre causes the sidewall to flex a little as it's pressed down against the road and then rebound as the weight is released – much like each step you take compresses your feet momentarily, except at 60mph (100kph) a tyre is doing this about 30 times a second. These days clued-up sports bike riders will warm up their high performance tyres before going for it on their 1198 SP, but once any tyre gets too hot it will soften dramatically, become more puncture prone,

[keep tyre pressures] as high as possible, as low as necessary

wear more quickly – and at high speed it may even disintegrate.

So under-inflation is clearly bad for longevity, but **low pressures** can actually aid grip on loose, low traction surfaces like sand and mud. In this part-deflated state the contact patch or 'footprint' of a tyre lengthens dramatically and works like a tank track. Even a regular road tyre will grip better and feel more secure, but the tyre will get much hotter so you have to balance any pressure drop with the gross weight of your machine, keep your speed down and reinflate as soon as possible.

Over-inflation just 'to be on the safe side' or to keep your tyres cool will not make your tyre last longer and possibly quite the opposite. An over-inflated tyre centre bulges away from the rim, the contact patch is reduced (affecting traction), and the smaller area will wear quicker. This is why closely managing your tyre pressures will respond with much greater mileage. Increase pressure if your payload increases dramatically (for example, an unexpected passenger or a huge fuel load), and consider reducing it a bit on tracks (along with your speed) to gain better traction. As high as possible, as low as necessary, is the maxim.

TUBELESS TYRES AND RADIAL CONSTRUCTION

The trend for tubeless tyres and radial construction are both real steps forward for motorcycles. Especially on a bigger machine, if you can use these sorts of tyres, so much the better. Just be aware that the tubeless and radial revolution may not have extended into the outer edges of the AMZ where you may be forced to turn back to conventional tubed or bias-belted tyres. For my DIY **tubeless spoked-rim experiment**, see the website.

Lacking an inflated inner tube rubbing against the inside of the tyre as it flexes, tubeless tyres **run cooler** and so last longer than tubed. Furthermore, when a tubeless tyre punctures, it deflates gradually as the air leaks out through the tiny hole in the carcass. The tyre usually stays on the rim too, which gives you a chance to bring the bike to a standstill safely. When an inner tube is punctured it effectively bursts – a blow out which usually means a crash if it happens at speed.

Problems can arise when making your own **roadside repairs** with tubeless tyres but assuming the tyre is still on the rim, you just plug the hole from the outside with a ramming spike tool fitted with a rubber bung covered in glue. This is illegal in some countries where you must get the inside of the tyre vulcanised at a tyre shop. Ram-plugging is unbelievably easy compared to messing around with inner tubes, and in my experience reliable, even off-road, providing a rim is undamaged. If there's a slight ding it's easy to knock out, and if not, it's possible to fit an inner tube in a tubeless tyre until you can make a proper wheel repair.

The bead of a tubeless tyre seals by being located in a **groove** in the rim (see diagram). To remove a tyre you need a lot of force to 'break the bead', and then some fast and high air pressure to remount it. A tyre coming off a safety/tubeless rim is rare, but this will always be in the back of your mind if you have a puncture: can you remount such a tyre by hand by the side of the road?

The secret is to use a bike's sidestand to press down on the tyre wall and break the bead (right), and then the 'fast/high pressure' blast from a CO_2 cartridge or an electric pump plus some lube to remount it. **Practice at home** so you know what to do in the unlikely event of having to remount a tubeless or safety-rimmed tyre by the roadside.

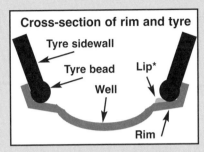

Cross-section of rim and tyre

Tyre sidewall

Tyre bead

Lip*

Well

Rim

*Lip and locating groove on tubeless or 'safety' rims, found even on tubed wheels.

Constructed with parallel rather than cross plies, a **radial tyre** has more flexible sidewalls than a cross ply or bias belted tyre. This enables the tyre to deform as you lean and so maintain a larger contact patch without generating the heat friction of crossed plies. More contact means grip; less heat means longevity. Many adventure tyres are radials now, such as the Metzeler Tourance EXP (or '0° steel belt' as they call it), and the similar Michelin Anakee, while the regular Tourance is bias belted. The Metzeler Karoo is a radial in some sizes, the Karoo T is bias belt.

Things may change, but you won't get a 21-inch radial tyre. Radials are more expensive, so are aimed at the more powerful and heavier adventure bikes whose front wheel is usually no bigger than 19 inches while the rears are pretty much all 17 inchers.

There may be something to be said for the stiffer sidewalls of a bias belted tyre being more suited to off-road riding where rocks can damage an otherwise thin sidewall, but assuming you've bought a quality tyre and watch your pressures or speed in rocks, that shouldn't happen.

BIKE CHOICE & PREPARATION

You can't have it both ways

For most adventure riders, a typical unsealed road would be a gravel or sand track, either graded smooth or corrugated into a 'washboard' surface by the passing of heavy vehicles. Riding at sensible speeds in a straight line your tread pattern will not come into play much; any tyre will do as steady traction is propelling you forward.

It's on **loose surface bends** and in the soft ruts carved by passing traffic where tread really comes into play and tyres without pronounced edge knobs skitter about just like a street tyre on a sports bike. Learning to ride a heavily loaded bike on this sort of surface will be part of your adventure and you'll be surprised what even a regular touring bike can manage – the only price being the fatigue in the early days as you learn to feel for and correct minor slides.

With a dirt tyre, the gnarly knobs that bite into unconsolidated surfaces so effectively are the same knobs that will flex, squirm and eventually let go as you lean into a bend at too high speed on the road. Furthermore, over many road miles those knobs will wear as the leading edge deforms under braking forces on the front tyre and acceleration on the rear (sometimes referred to as 'cupping'). This'll reduce traction still more on the highway, as well as creating vibration and noise. In dry conditions on hard but loose tracks a road tyre will work, but things can change when it **rains** or when any track becomes very sandy. Depending on your skill and experience as well as the bike's weight and dynamics, motorcycles with street-oriented 'adventure' tyres can become a handful in mud, clay or soft sand.

Adventure tyres

As with the many bike marques, some tyre makers have responded to the current AM trend by reclassifying dual-purpose tyres as 'adventure tyres' to suit the ever-faster and heavier adventure tourers like XT1200Zs, big GSs and Triumph Explorers. When new, these bikes must be sold with a tyre that looks the part, but for safety reasons, a 135hp, 260kg Explorer must run tyres that match its performance potential on the highway where it's likely to spend most of the time. Putting a set of Dunlop 980RRs on a KTM 990 Adventure R will make it great in the sand, but quite a handful on a wet Andean pass.

Adventure tyres from the left: on the gravel what looks like a Tourance on the front of a BMW 1200GS would be no better than a road tyre in terms of grip; next, the Metzeler Enduro 3 and Michelin T66 offer a little more bite, especially at lowered pressures, while (right) the Continental TKC 80 (or a similar Pirelli MT21) is secure in the dirt – while it lasts.

Tyres like the Avon Distanzia or Gripster, Bridgestone Battle Wing, Conti Trail Attack, Dunlop Trailmax, Metzeler Enduro 1, 2 and Tourance, Michelin Anakee or Siracs, Mitas E-07 or -08 and Pirelli MT60s purport to be dual-purpose tyres, but in some cases probably just a road touring tyre with a more blocky looking 'adventure' tread. On dirt roads they'll be barely better than a regular touring tyre and on the highway be marginally worse; the rider's skill is likely to be the deciding factor, not the tread.

This is an important distinction to understand. Instead of any of the above, you may well be better off with a **regular, hard-wearing road touring tyre**, even if it doesn't look sexy. On gravel roads the above tyres will be nothing special, and in sand or mud no better than a road tyre.

Dirt-biased dual-purpose tyres

With dirt-biased road tyres the places you can confidently explore are greatly multiplied. One day on your big adventure you'll come to a junction: left takes you to your destination via the highway, right is a 100-km long dirt road through the mountains. Even if it's shorter it may well take you longer, but on that day that's not what your adventure is about. Along that road you may come to a breathtaking panorama, spend the night in a friendly village that rarely sees tourists, or camp overnight in total solitude under the stars. You can do this on a highway too, but the chances of having memorable adventures are greatly increased by taking the road less travelled. You don't want to think 'Well, it looks interesting but my bike handles like a dog on gravel so I won't risk it'.

If you see highways as just a convenient way of linking one track with another, get yourself something that works in the dirt, rather than claims it might. Names may change and new tyres may come out by the time you read this, but the Continental TKC80 (pictured below left) is a well-respected tyre in this category. There is nothing flash or ground-breaking about it, just the usual spread of square knobs that are *less deep* than a full-on motocross tyre so your big GS won't squirm around as tall knobs distort on fast highway bends. TKCs are designated as 70/30 percent for road/dirt use but while that's pretty accurate, don't compare such precise descriptions between other brands.

A TKC run tubeless after about 4500 miles on a Ténéré, including rocky Moroccan trails. About 30% of the tread depth remains, but legally they may have less than 1000 miles.

Three years later this Heidenau K60 did the same Morocco trip on an F650GS, performed as well as the TKC and was not even a third worn. Full review on the website.

Similar tyres that appear designed to genuinely perform as well include Dunlop D606, 603 or 605 in increasing order of road-bias, their less dirt-worthy K550 and the similar Bridgestone Trail Wing 301/302. Available as a radial Metzeler's Karoo is another good one, as is the Michelin 'Desert' pattern T63, Mitas E-09 or -10 and another well known classic in this category, the Pirelli MT21 and a newcomer, the Heidenau K60 which may well be the best of this lot. A number of these tyres have been around for many years. They don't change just because adventure motorcycling has become fashionable, they merely deliver predictable off-road manners at the cost of longevity.

One exception in **longevity** is the Mitas E-09 which resembles a TKC but with taller knobs and stiffer sidewalls. The GS1100 pictured on p74 managed to get two-up from Namibia back to Europe with tread to spare on the rear with one of these, a distance of over 10,000kms. Up till then they were getting similar mileages from the less aggressive Heidenau K60.

Remember, the bigger and more powerful your bike, the less high knobs you want; typically around half an inch (12mm) or less, even if the tyre wears out more quickly. Yes they may last longer, but bigger knobs suited to a KX450 a third of the weight of a loaded GS will squirm, get hot and break off. While they last, knobs half-an-inch deep will make all the difference on the dirt and there will be a reason why some manufacturers specifically don't make some tyres to fit one wheel or the other of a big adventure bike.

... there'll be a reason why manufacturers don't make some tyres to fit a big adventure bike.

A word on **mixing road tyres and knobblies**; if you're going to do so, most put the knobbly up front. On the dirt the back end can spin and slide a little, but the steering and braking ought to be secure. Plus the fact a front tyre wears more slowly and so can afford to be a knobbly. Just don't forget to pack some Valium for those wet mountain hairpins.

PUNCTURES

You need to be confident you can fix punctures. **Practice before you leave** so when the inevitable occurs you can be sure that the operation can be accomplished relatively smoothly. Any emergency repair undertaken in a remote location can be unnerving; the better prepared you are the less likely you'll make absent-minded mistakes like forgetting to align the chain or leaving your tools by the roadside (or one time, somehow managing to leave a tyre lever *inside* the tyre...).

Avoid labour-saving aerosols which are messy, unreliable and usually explode in your panniers anyway. **Puncture-sealing fluids** like *Slime* or *Ultraseal* (in the UK) are said to do an amazing job of plugging small pricks, as well as balancing and cooling both tubed or tubeless tyres. Pour it in through the valve stem; whenever you get a puncture the pressure and centrifugal force squeezes the fluid out of the hole where it solidifies and seals.

If that stuff doesn't work for you, the best way to repair a puncture is to plug a tubeless tyre or fit a new tube without pinching it, though with some tyre and rim combinations this is easier said than done. Electric or manual, protect your pump from dust and loss; it could be vital.

If you can't repair a puncture, try stuffing the tyre with clothes or anything else that comes to hand to vaguely regain its profile. If you do a good job, you can carry on without too much difficulty, but if the tyre is damaged or starts to disintegrate and tear you're better off dumping it and continuing on the rim.

Puncture-repair kit

Assemble the items you need, listed below, into something like a small lunch box. Depending on the terrain and the sturdiness of your tyres, carry up to two spare inner tubes per wheel. Get a **mini electric compressor** but run the engine if you use it for more than a few seconds. Carry a **mini hand pump** too.

Taking into account the variables of personal preference, in my experience a good **tyre lever** is a blade no more than 20mm wide, up to 5mm thick and 200mm long. The crude wide, flat-ended types of bars with flattened 'spoon' ends are too wide and make lifting the bead harder which can lead to pinching a tube. The ideal blade has a slender curved lip at each end which readily hooks under the bead of a tyre to lift it, but without pushing in too far and pressing against the tube. Whatever lever you use, take care in the last stages of tyre mounting (photo 12, next page); avoid brute force.

Puncture kit
• One spare tube per tyre and two or three tyre levers
• Electric compressor, mini hand pump and air pressure gauge
• Patches and rubber solution, plus spare self adhesive patches
• Sandpaper or grater and a valve extractor if not on the valve cap
• (Tubeless plugs, reamer and valves and CO_2 cartridges for emergencies)
• Talc for lubing and to 'dust' the gluey patch on a tube

BIKE CHOICE & PREPARATION

(From top left): 12-volt compressor with a valve extractor tool on top, digital and aneroid pressure gauges, levers, hand pump, tubeless repair plugs with reamer and roller/grating tool on the right, and tube patches in the middle. Some talc in a film canister is also handy for tube repairs.

1. If it's a cold day, ride around so the tyre becomes pliable. Find a flat place away from the road. With no centre stand, use a pannier or rock opposite the sidestand, or just lay the bike down. Use a sheet plus a bowl for loose fittings.

2. Remove the valve cap and valve base nut and loosen the security bolt or rim screws if present. Unscrew the valve core, releasing any remaining air and push the valve and security bolt into the tyre as far as they'll go.

5. Getting the second lever in is hard until you release the first lever a little; hook the second one in then pull them both up in close succession. Note how the disc rotor holds one lever.

6. Keep working round the tyre until one side is outside the rim. Now stand the tyre up, push the valve into the tyre and drag the tube out.

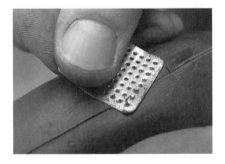

9. Release the air, place the tube on a firm surface and roughen the area around the hole with sandpaper or a grater. The rubber should have a scratched, matt appearance.

10. Clean off the rubber dust with a petrol rag, apply a thin film of adhesive over a broad area and let it dry to the touch. Apply the patch, foil-side down. Or use a self-adhesive patch, as pictured. Press the patch down firmly with a tyre lever and sprinkle with talc.

3. Stand on the tyre, jumping up and down if necessary to push the bead off the rim – or do sidestand trick (see p77) if another bike is present. Check again that security bolts are pushed into the tyre so they're not getting in the way.

4. Standing or kneeling on the tyre to keep the bead pushed into the well, ease in the first lever on the opposite side to hook under the tyre's bead.

7. Examine the outer tyre and pass your fingers over the inner surface to feel for any thorns, nails or whatever. It may be necessary to take the tyre right off to do this properly.

8. Inflate the tube to find the hole. If you can't hear a hiss, pass the tube over wet lips to feel for a cold jet of air. Or submerge the tube in water and look for bubbles. You may have more than one puncture.

11. Stand the wheel up, push the tube into the tyre by first pushing the valve through and fitting the 12mm nut. With stiff tyres, lever up the other side to make room for your fingers to work the valve in.

12. Standing or kneeling, position levers at 10- and 2 o'clock and start levering them towards 12 o'clock. As you lever kick at the tyre to make sure it's in the well to give you the necessary slack for the final satisfying 'pop'.

(Continued on next page)

BIKE CHOICE & PREPARATION

Now re-inflate the tyre and watch the bead remount the rim evenly. If it doesn't, keep inflating and deflating while adding soap or talc and levering if necessary, but don't worry too much if it doesn't remount perfectly. Once ridden about a bit it'll work its way on.

Check the pressure isn't dropping. If it is, start over. Otherwise, tighten up the security bolt (if present), fit the valve cap and refit the wheel. Make sure all the nuts are tight, then pack up the tools. Recheck tyre pressure, pump up the disc brake and off you go.

TYRE CREEP

Riding at the low pressures necessary for traction in deep sand or mud can cause an under-pressurised tyre to get pulled around the rim, especially on the rear wheel of torquey engines (frontal tyre creep from hard braking can also occur). Slippage is not a problem with tubeless tyres, but when an inner tube get dragged along with the turning tyre, the valve may eventually get ripped out, destroying the tube.

Therefore, for low-pressure use (typically, sandy deserts), it's essential to have **security bolts** (aka: rim locks) fitted to both rims, but definitely the rear, to limit excessive tyre creep. Security bolts clamp the bead of the tyre to the rim and, if not already there, require a hole to be drilled into the rim: an easy job. A slightly larger than necessary hole in the rim makes tyre fitting easier.

An alternative to security bolts which don't always work are **self-tapping screws** drilled into the rim so they just bite into the tyre bead and limit slippage. Two each side of the rim set at 90° intervals should keep the tyre in place. They make refitting a tyre easier, though not everyone will feel good about drilling holes through their rim. If you take this route carry some spare self-tappers as they can easily get lost.

In the early days when running low pressures keep an eye on your valves. If they begin to 'tilt over' as pictured below, it means your security bolt may need tightening or your tyre repositioning (some creep can occur even with rim locks). Always keep the 12mm nut at the base of your valve **loose**, or do not use it at all. They're only useful as an aid to refitting tubes.

If you're running tubes at low pressure, keep an eye on your valves. If they begin to lean it means the tyre is creeping.

Rim locks; they ought to be fitted as original equipment to most trail or enduro bikes running tubed tyres.

Load carrying

As the Nicholson character in *A Few Good Men* might have snarled: not making a bike looking like a Saharan *gros porteur* (right) requires *discipline*. A long ride needs a lot of stuff, right? That's what you may think, but one of the surprises of two-wheel overlanding is realising how little you actually need. **Overloading is by far the most common mistake**. You can take my word for it now or learn from experience. Second time around, everyone takes less stuff.

Riding or even just getting on an overweight bike can be demoralising, and yet we're still talking about a tiny amount of gear – in volume it adds up to the typical total allowance for an international flight – and all this to sustain yourself for months on the road. We all have different needs but with a full tank and a 40kg/90lb payload your machine may handle like a piano and be impossible to pick up alone.

Still in the early days of his big RTW, by the time I found this photo Simon had already substantially reduced his load. My first departure was the same; it's common to over-estimate your needs initially as you head into what you think is the void. © Simon Courrier.

BIKE CHOICE & PREPARATION

LUGGAGE SYSTEMS

On a motorcycle there's not much choice about where your baggage can go: behind you and alongside the back wheel with a tank bag or tank panniers in front and a small backpack on your back. The most basic level of motorcycle baggage is a **rucksack** or kit bag strapped across the back seat – something that many a young, cash-starved motorcycle traveller has tried – and interestingly what some worldly purists return to after many trips. It may not be secure in both a thieving and a fitting sense, but short of a pair of carrier bags, is as cheap as it gets and can easily be carried when off the bike.

Einstein's Theory of Relative Space states that no matter how capacious your luggage, it will be filled to bursting point. Keep it small and you'll take little; use big containers and you'll have a lot of stuff. It's tempting to assume that the former method is more evolved but the fact is, just as some riders like skimpy machines and have baggage strategies verging on OCD, others prefer a massive machine clad in an elephantine mass. Each to his own but few riders come back saying they wish they'd ridden a heavier motorcycle.

General principles

Soft, hard or firm, whatever you choose, convenience of access, ease of removal, robustness and security are the key considerations – see the table opposite. Visualise how your system will stack up in a day-long downpour, a shunt or an opportunist theft, but recognise that making it survive a heavy crash or resist a determined thief is not always possible.

Compartmentalisation aids organisation and access. Regularly used 'day' items should be close at hand, overnight stuff put elsewhere while back up items and spares are buried and valuable items are kept on your person. While securely mounted, it also it helps if whatever you use is **easily removable**.

After a few months on the road your system gets refined for access and convenience. Notice too how the soft bags which replaced fragile Zega boxes are further forward on the rack; handling was greatly improved, which on a KTM 640 is especially worthwhile. © Jerome Bullard

LUGGAGE CHOICE – SOME FACTORS

For	Against

SOFT FABRIC BAGS

For	Against
• Light and relatively inexpensive	• Can tear, burn and sag
• Light rack sufficient, or useable without	• May not be weatherproof without a liner
• Contents immunised from vibration	• Can get grubby; hard to clean
• Absorb crash impacts, sparing the subframe	• Where present, zips will fail eventually
• Less risk of leg injuries	• Less secure against ransacking or theft
• Can be easy to mend	• Fragile contents can get crushed in a fall

FIRM PLASTIC CASES

For	Against
• Robust, weatherproof, abrasion resistant	• Large cases are heavy for what they are
• Don't dent or deform like alloy	• Hinges/seal weak points on sideloaders
• Some top loaders have wheels & handles	• Not actually designed for motorcycles
• Some brands claim a lifetime guarantee	• Require a solid rack and mounting
• Inexpensive clones available	• Sideloaders spill out when opened on bike
• Rounded corners and edges, unlike alloy	• Unlocked latches may fail on impact

HARD ALLOY BOXES

For	Against
• More secure, depending on locks	• Can be heavy, wide and expensive
• Best examples are very robust	• Require a solid rack and mounting
• Weatherproof (until lid edge deformed)	• Not suited to hard, off-highway riding
• Can act as rear 'crash bars'	• Hard edges and corners can injure in a fall
• Easy to paint, sticker (and sit on if q/d)	• Hard to straighten once badly deformed
• Easy to bolt on external mounts & holders	• Tough boxes transfer stress to subframe

BIKE CHOICE & PREPARATION

When it comes to strapping things on the outside of your containers or on to your bike, don't rely solely on elasticated bungees – use **adjustable straps** and carry spares; they're easily lost, damaged or pilfered and have many uses.

Distribute the load as **low and centrally as possible**. It's the same principle as 'mass centralisation' which became an element of Honda's design philosophy a few years back; a centralised mass in motion is more agile than a dispersed one, be it a motorcycle, pushbike or a plane. On a bike it's easy to keep piling it all on the back until you look like a mobile eclipse, but the rider who packs thoughtfully will reap real benefits in the balance of their machine, especially the steering and, when fully loaded, off the highway.

A loaded bike's centre of gravity with you on it is more or less where the injectors or carb usually sit. Heavy weights want to be as close to this notional point as possible, while light things like clothes, sleeping bags or empty containers can go out on the back of the seat or even in front of the headlight.

How much volume? At least **30 litres** each side with the rest on the back. Factor in some **expansion capacity** as there'll be days when you'll need more.

Hard, firm or soft

Often the debate is simplified to 'hard or soft' while overlooking the nuances of what I call 'firm', but it's never one or the other, most bikers will use combinations of all three in their set up. Beginners are often drawn to alloy boxes for the same reasons most of us live in brick houses with cupboards, not tents with bags. A solid box looks weatherproof and can be locked securely to itself and the bike. The bigger the bike the harder the luggage tends to be and for all these good reasons alloy boxes have become 'the look'.

On *Desert Riders* we tried out alloy boxes from Touratech and Tesch on custom racks. At times off-piste on barely rideable terrain, even before it was over we agreed they were a mistake. The convenience was handy but they were too wide on narrow mountain tracks, and the hard edges and sharp corners were intimidating. For that trip away from cities and no chance of rain, a light rack with soft bags would have been better. But most overland rides aren't like that, they follow roads between towns and cities through all weathers where the benefits of solid luggage are appreciated daily.

HARD LUGGAGE

The first thing to acknowledge is that regular proprietary touring hard cases as well as whatever may be on the official accessory list of your new mega-adventurer may not be up to the actual demands of overlanding: bad roads, dust, vibration, occasional overloading, as well as shock loads, shunts and spills. What works for Mr & Mrs in their matching riding suits as they pull up outside an Andalucian parador on their gleaming tourer to be handed an aperitif, may not survive the rugged ride from Lahore to Kathmandu via Srinagar.

Adventure motorcycling is not like more predictable touring and slick, clip-on mounting arrangements like the Krausers of old may have to be modified or replaced if they're to deal with dust, vibration and hard use. One Africa Twin rider summed up his Givis hard luggage as 'panniers brilliant, racks dreadful' and some Givi 34-litre side cases are only rated to 10kg.

Alloy boxes

Aluminium boxes were originally handmade by riders until outfits in Germany like Därrs, Hepco & Becker and Tesch started producing them. Now the idea has caught on globally with people like Touratech, Metal Mule in the UK and Jesse Luggage in the US among the best known. But with prices up to a staggering £500 for 30-litre-plus box, close copies and all-out knock-offs have hit the booming market.

For hard use it does appear you get what you pay for: cheaper boxes suit those wanting the look; pricier items are the real thing that should be expected to last. Along with BMW OE kit, Jesse Luggage's Odyssey II system is about the most expensive out there but the engineering and attention to detail – including slimness – is sound. In the UK Metal Mule has a similar reputation

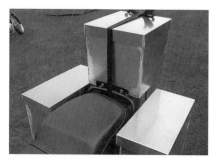

Home welded alloy luggage; fairly easy with the skills and tools, but with fittings and powder coating you may not save so much.

Sawn-off jerry; cheap but a bit small, especially when using Touratech 'disc' mounts which take up inner space. © Robin Webb

for bomb-proof cases. Buying a set of either may cost 15% of a new GSA1200 or XT1200Z, but you'll be relying on them daily for months.

What's a box?

At the very simplest level you get a six-sided rectilinear box and lid in **1.5 or 2mm** gauge that's either **welded** or **riveted** (or a bit of both). On a heavy bike with a long ride ahead, thicker is best. Riveting may look cheap but can be stronger than a plain, welded 1.5mm box – on the better items we're talking blind rivets as used on aircraft, not hobbyists' pop rivets. Any curves or bevels increase costs, but are well worth it as they add substantial rigidity and so resistance to deformation in a crash (as does a box section edge around the top where the lid closes). Any rigid vessel with a curved or multifaceted cross-section is more robust than a plain square one. There's a lot to be said for not having a pointy corner on the forward outer edge to dig in as a falling bike slides. The payoff for bevelling is a less efficient packing space.

All alloy boxes are top-loading; not so handy for access but you can get round this by using lift-out trays or bags inside. Most alloy box makers (as well as Kriega or Hein Gericke) offer a full-size **lift-out holdall** for their box so you can whip them out and carry them into a hotel room without having to remove the clanky, dirty box. A stout shopping bag or cheapo sports bag does the same job. Don't even think about it, get a pair. Something is needed if the inside of your box is not anodised, powder coated or painted. Otherwise you'll get a smeary residue on anything that rubs. A thick layer of powder coating is best.

The way these lids open, clamp down, **lock** and **seal** is another thing to inspect closely. It's not too much to expect your alloy cases to be watertight to the point of submersion and have clamps that can't be prised open by a 12-year old with a big screwdriver. Any sort of bent wire hasp that levers down on a thin, curled up tab – whether locked with a key or with a padlock as below – won't take much to prise off or whack open, but many box makers still use these cheap clasps. The peace of mind offered by a secure lid that discourages opportunists should be the main reason for investing in an alloy box.

Jesse use chunky locking clamps that would be hard to prise off; Touratech Zega clamps are notoriously flimsy and have been that way for at least ten years, although the later Zega Pros have better clamps which hinge up either forward or back as well as lift right off. Lift off lids can fall off if untethered;

Clamp close-up, left to right: BMW Motorrad side case integrated lock – similar to Zega Pro; another key clamp on a Hepco & Becker case; never mind that padlock, the tab riveted to the lid could get bent open with a rock; Jesse clasp and padlock rings; no one's getting in there easily.

BIKE CHOICE & PREPARATION

Jesse outfit with toast racks. Jesses are notable for trying to stay close in but big. Odyssey IIs slide back for pillion space.

Hepco & Becker (near identical to pricier Krausers). Top box takes a full face lid, but that can be U-locked anywhere on a bike.

most prefer those that hinge out sideways to make a level platform which – providing the hinge or a stay are up to it – becomes handy when you're digging around for stuff.

On any case lid, some strap rings are a good idea for additional top loading, as is a smooth top with a recessed handle (where present; as on Metal Mules), so you can use the case as a comfortable campsite seat, once removed.

Firm 'plastic' cases

An alternative to the blinding sheen of the alloy box are cases made from either rotomoulded polyethylene (like a rental kayak or canoe), or from denser and heavier injection-moulded polycarbonate resin. Both materials are tough and very resistant to abrasion and knocks. As such they're well suited to moto-overlanding, unlike more brittle touring cases made of thinner ABS plastic. Moulding these sorts of polymers enables complex shapes, including rounded corners and ribs to help make the structure more rigid, just as bevels do on metal boxes. The **weight** compares with the toughest alloy box.

On the side of a motorcycle, this stuff slides down the road a lot better than thin alloy or most fabric bags. Cases like those made by Peli come in all sorts of sizes and are well known for their suitability to rugged applications. For use

Peli cases in a variety of shapes and sizes are well suited to AM touring. The Storm range has more user-friendly latches but the original Peli clamps may be tougher in a crash.

on a bike, the Peli 1550 and the slightly lighter Peli Storm iM2600 give an ideal 35 litres of volume but weigh over 5.5kg (12lbs). Nanuk's 940 is about the same size but lighter, and Seahorse is another brand.

Caribou in the US were among the first to capitalise on converting firm cases for motorcycling, adding keyed lid locks and lanyards as well as retention straps for only around 20% more than the cost of a plain Peli . The keyed mounting system that Caribou use for their own racks looks as solid as the best of the rest and spreads the load

Caribou cases – adapting tough, ready made
waterproof resin cases for motorcycle use.
© Nate Sammons

H&B Gobis (once branded for KTMs). A
tough case but double skin adds width and
the single mounting clamp is not up to it.

better than some proprietary 'touring' mountings for which they also make kits. Just remember, in dusty conditions key locks for lids or mounts at the back of a bike are prone to jamming with dust. Stick a bit of tape over them if conditions require.

The **lids** on cases like this open outwards like a suitcase on its side which can be handy or a nuisance, especially when the bike's leaning on its side-stand. Load retaining straps can get around that up to a point, but lately Caribou's Case Liners suggest that this is the real solution.

The lid itself **seals** with an o-ring in a groove that can be easily repaired or replaced, although it's more exposed than an alloy lid. Another drawback is that the lids and their hinges take the impact when a bike hits the deck. Caribou claim the Peli guarantee is for life which is reassuring, but you wonder how many times a big, heavy bike can fall onto its sidecases. Probably more than the tinniest alloys, but if you're not convinced then the ribbed and **top-loading Peli 1440** might be a better choice. Also around 34 litres, it weighs a hefty 7.5kg (16.5lbs) and is a foot wide, but comes with wheels and a handle.

As well as the usual range of alloy boxes Hepco & Becker make the double-skinned, rotomoulded 37-litre, top-loading **Gobi** which came as an option on the original KTM 950 Adventure. A moulded back spreads its weight into an H&B rack, but if the single mounting latch lets go the whole thing goes tumbling; for off roading a back-up strap is a good idea. Gobis incorporate a not-so-usable 3.5 litre water reservoir but at 30cm that just makes them extra wide. The cost matches the best from Jesse and Metal Mule.

Rack mounting hard cases

Bolting a box or case permanently to the rack ought to be solid as long as the back is up to it, but isn't so convenient when you want to remove the rear wheel or wheel the bike into a Turkish hotel courtyard for safe parking. A

Sawn-off 30-litre water can. All rigidity is lost so a basket rack is needed – handy but makes the bike permanently wide. © Stuart Holding

strong, reliable and easy-to-use **quickly detachable** (or 'q/d') **system** is much more useful. Besides these examples, the ability to easily remove your box to sit on or use as a table, cooking wind break or bike stand is also very handy.

Whichever you choose, bear in mind that thin aluminium is soft and any load-bearing mountings can get damaged in a crash, or even just on a particularly rough road after which they may loosen or no longer locate properly. And aluminium alloy just a couple of millimetres thick is not so resilient to high frequency vibration, something that's exacerbated when a huge alloy box loaded with 20kg (44lbs) of gear takes all the typical vertical shearing forces through the mounts bolted onto the back plate. Payload, speed, suspension quality and the terrain have a lot to do with it which is why those who like to travel fast and light on the dirt choose soft baggage.

It's all about **spreading the load**. Something that might last years of domestic touring, like the parador scenario given earlier, may well end up lashed on with belts and ropes by the time you get to the far end of Ruta 40 in Patagonia. In my opinion the most bomb-proof and fastest (if not the lightest) q/d set up is to have the weight of a box **sitting on a tray or platform**, because the load is taken through the base of the case. This tray need not be the full width of the case. With a rigid-edged alloy box just a couple of inches of load-bearing 'shelf' will be enough to take the constant vertical shock loads as well as to contain the less extreme lateral forces when riding. The mounting points then become much less critical because the **vertical shock loads are separated from the mounts** – all those have to do is locate the box securely. The advantage of this system is that if the box or its mountings get mangled, you'll always be able to hammer the rack straight and lash the box back onto that tray: the tray ought to take the weight. As mentioned elsewhere, it's anticipating and devising systems to work round these kinds of meltdown scenarios which are part of planning for a long trip. There's more on platform racks below and on the website under 'Gear'.

The thing is no moto luggage maker that I know of takes this approach these days and all cases, plastic or metal, are hung on their back plates with q/d mounts of some kind. Again the key here is to spread the load over a large area such as a bar, not a single point, and if metal then using a vibration-proof block

Left, Touratech: lower mounts take the weight, upper tabs swivel to secure behind the frame – in a crash it all breaks off, ideally. Right, a tougher Metal Mule case with no metal-to-metal contact with the frame – always better. Location locking lever is held down by the lid. © Dan Ward

such as the polyethylene you get in kitchen chopping boards. It's unlikely that four clip-on pins, as found on some boxes, will be up to the job of overlanding unless your load is really light – and who takes hard cases to carry light loads?

As for securing the panniers against theft, broadly speaking there are two ways of doing it. A q/d system deployed **inside** the case which is protected by the locking lid – such as Touratech's spin-on wheels or Jesse's systems, including the elegant Quick Click (which may need additional support points) – or something external with a lock or, as in Metal Mule's case, an arm that levers down into place as the lid is closed; easy to use but potentially vulnerable. Touratech have a retrofitting Rapid-Trap clamp for their Zegas to remove the case without opening the lid while still retaining or relying on the handwheel mounts as a backup.

> **Mounting hard cases on motorcycles is not an exact science the way crumple zones and airbags are on cars [because] falling off can be just tipping over ... or a highside flip ... trying to calculate for all this reliably is not like the inertia lock on a car seat belt.**

Securing from inside may mean you have to take stuff out to remove the box, but it also means one less exterior lock to get clogged up or attract thieves – and so it makes a solid **lid lock** all the more important. External key locks can suffer from vibration as well as dust, so in the latter case keep a can of WD40 handy in case they gum up.

Crash proofing

Finally, consider how this solid mass clamped to your bike will deal with a crash. Mounting hard cases on motorcycles is not an exact science the way crumple zones and airbags are on cars. A fall can be just tipping over at a standstill, the result of a collision, a harmless lowside slide or a potentially more damaging highside flip. A heavy load on a rack clamped to a motorcycle subframe designed mainly for suspension-damped vertical loads cannot account for sudden side loads. To mitigate this, some box mounts are designed to break off before the force is transferred and does greater damage to the rack or subframe but as you can imagine, trying to calculate for this is not like the inertia lock on a car seat belt. One rider complained his Metal Mules demounted at the slightest tumble and required tedious refitting, while I bet I'm not the only one to mangle some Zegas without having them break off first.

Using a very solid mount means shock loads can get transferred to a rack – a common source of problems at the best of times – or even the motorcycle's subframe. A little distortion won't ruin a subframe but too much of that can't be sustained. Some bikes, especially enduros and old airhead BMWs, have notoriously skimpy subframes, whereas I got the impression that part of the weight in my old XT660Z Ténéré was quite rightly in the subframe where such a bike wants it. The problem of heavy, solid loads hung out on a beam is why soft baggage can be preferable. If you plan to rough it, that's the way to go.

Overall, a hard box mounting built to cope with rough roads and crashes is a priority over a theft-proof one (that job goes to the lid lock). There'll be many more opportunities for your side cases to get crash-damaged or fall right

BIKE CHOICE & PREPARATION

off on the move than for someone to try and steal them. Key-off bags are certainly handy and no fuss to use, but are more suited to undemanding touring.

SOFT BAGS

Soft baggage usually means some kind of fabric pannier as well as a duffle bag or kit bag across the back. The range of materials and designs has improved greatly over the years. And as previously said it doesn't have to be one or the other; there's no reason why you can't run soft panniers and an alloy or plastic lockable topbox, or hard cases and a light duffle over the back.

Materials and closures

Panniers and other bags usually come in Cordura nylon. Cordura is actually a brand of DuPont who manufacture many types of synthetic cloth, but most understand Cordura to be a chunky, canvas-like nylon fabric. Note that 'canvas' is a type of heavy stiff cloth that is *not necessarily* cotton-based. The importance of this will be addressed shortly. Another material, ballistic nylon, sounds flash and has better abrasion resistance than classic Cordura, but it won't actually stop a bullet.

None of the above fabrics are waterproof unless coated, and even then they will leak at sewn seams unless they are laboriously sealed. 'Vinyl' is a vague word but in our context refers to a PVC or similar urethane-coated nylon or polyester fabric. The strength of the underlying fabric weave, as well as the thickness and pliability of the vinyl coating, creates the stiffness and durability of the final fabric at a given weight. This stuff is waterproof and better still, panels are joined with high-frequency welding, or just heat welding, not stitching, ensuring that 'seams' don't become a weak point for water ingress.

Setting off on an long overland ride is not like a weekend away or even domestic touring where the nuisance of wet gear can be endured in the short term. Putting your stuff inside a drybag or worse still, having to fit your side bag with a giant 'shower cap', because it's not waterproof, is not a sustainable solution. Be it rain from above or spray from river crossings; if you're going to get soft panniers or indeed any soft baggage, go for a **roll-top PVC** or unwaterproof Cordura with a PVC liner. Both are easily repairable if holed, can be

Textbook setup for a trans-Asia ride: Ortlieb Rack Packs sit on a rigid platform rack giving up to 98 litres capacity; fuel and water underneath, day box on the back, © Sean Flanagan

hosed down and can even be used as a laundry tub or basin at a base camp. **Zips** are convenient but unless you clean them, never overfill your bag and take care never to yank at them when in a strop at a tropical border, they'll eventually jam or break and repair can be tricky.

Roll top is a simple, zip-free closure as used in kayaking dry bags. Despite the suggestion it's not actually submersion proof, though on a bike that's rarely necessary. If you roll the closure up tightly and without creases and then cinch it down, it certainly won't take in much if underwater for a few minutes and anyway it's too buoy-ant to sink. Only a day of pelting rain may work its way through, even with several rolls. The other good thing with roll tops as side bags or across the back rack is that they're only as full as they are; a half empty bag will roll down smaller unlike a rattly box.

> **Putting your stuff inside a drybag or worse still, having to fit your side bag with a giant 'shower cap' ... is not a sustainable solution.**

Use a rack

Fabrics being what they are, bags will sag under their own weight (like the Zegaflex bags pictured overleaf) and many riders will have had a synthetic fabric pannier melting on a pipe or canvas panniers catching fire. High speed (hot pipes), rough riding or just hasty packing has seen my bikes burn or melt their soft bags on at least four occasions. A plastic side panel – even one coated inside with aluminium foil and flame-proof material – is not enough to keep a fully loaded, jiggling pannier from pressing down and something melting. Nor I suspect are rubber back panels on the back of panniers. Bike designs differ and some may be immune to a throwover set up, but the only way to ensure that your bag doesn't melt is to **keep it away from silencers** by mounting it on or against a rack.

This may be contrary to the inexpensive and lightweight approach of going soft, but a rack doesn't have to be the hefty structure fit to hold an alloy pannier. Even a single, well-shaped **bar** will help keep throwovers off a high pipe as well as being something to attach them to, although mounting bags securely to a rack is the best solution. Granted a rack might be another thing to bend in a crash, but soft bags (and their contents...) absorb some of the impact rather than transfer it to a rack and subframe, so this is a less-likely-than-usual scenario. The rack mounts will also be much less prone to vibration from hard boxes and so as mentioned, don't need to be so heavy duty.

Soft bag selection

Let's start with the well-known Ortlieb brand. Their **Side Bag** in QL2 is a 28-litre soft baggage classic that clips onto the rectangle in a regular 'hanging rack', but for some possibly significant reason only fits 16mm tube when 18mm

BIKE CHOICE & PREPARATION

There's low and there's subterranean. These huge ex-army rucksacks were cheap and come with integral frames. © Austin Vince

1986: light but still learning: tank bag too big, no rack (canvas bag caught fire later). Bash plate tool pouch: good idea, badly executed.

Wolfman – waterproof PVC, no zips and solid mount, but at 19 litres the sidebags are small.

Roll-top 30-litre Enduristan Monsoons over a rack. Cordura lowers, PVC upper and liner.

is the norm. I've used similar but smaller QL bags for cycling in the Himalaya and at the end of a weary day, the ease of lifting them off without any faff is a huge relief. Ortlieb also do a 26-litre roll-top throwover **Saddle Bag** which can be adapted to fit a rack, or at least lashed to it, but this capacity is really a minimum. Without getting too wide or too long, the bigger the better on the side as that's where the weight wants to be, with little or nothing over the tail light.

Also from Switzerland, Enduristan make the 30-litre **Monsoon** throwovers. They differ significantly from Ortlieb's Saddle Bag by using a Cordura outer (onto which you can sew or rivet) and a sewn-in PVC liner, thereby cleverly separating the task of resisting abrasion from waterproofing. The capacity is nearly in the ballpark but I found them too wide on my bike.

The US Wolfman brand have lately turned to PVC and currently produce the **Expedition** Dry Saddle Bags in reliable and thick PVC which strap down solidly with buckles and straps onto their own racks, but a little too fussily for regular access. The problem is that at just 19 litres that's a pretty small expedition. The solid lashing system is perhaps more suited to hard and fast weekend dirt rides on your KTM 450 than continental crossings. One thing PVC bags lack are outside pockets – perhaps the heat welding can't manage it securely.

Other zip-free throwovers include Australian-made Andy Strapz **Expedition Pannierz** (pictured p49) and the similar but much more usefully sized Steel Pony Gascoynes giving a potential volume of 37 litres plus a pair of outer pockets. Both are merely 'water-resistant' so will require PVC liners (tougher than flimsy PU-coated 'stuff sacks'). Their fabric, described as '12-13oz reinforced canvas' should not be mistaken for Cordura or indeed melt-proof cotton canvas, as I've found to my cost when using Pannierz without a rack.

Kreiga's **Overlander** system securely mounts up to four 15-litre packs onto a pair of chunky CDPE 'platforms' (strictly speaking, a plate) a little like

THROWOVERS OR THROWBACKS?

In my opinion **throwovers** are better suited to pack animals than most modern machines. Now that the traditional slab-sided side panel and twin shock is less common, some sort of **rack** or just a bar is required to keep the bag from flapping into the chain guard and off a low pipe. No matter what they put on the back panel of throwover panniers, it ought to be kept well off an exposed high pipe if for no other reason than modern exhaust systems with catalytic converters run much hotter. At the very least put a grill over the silencer.

Aussie-made Steel Pony Gascoynes. Up to 37 litres plus two outer pockets. Zip-free but need a waterproof liner. © Dan

An Adventure-spec Magadan bag on the way to... Magadan. © W. Colebatch

Wolfmans and possibly for the same type of intended use. Each side weighs from 2.4kg empty, and the plate in turn q/d clips to any 18mm rack. Some riders may take to the modularity of four small bags, but a single 30-35 litre pannier more suited to overland travel could be in the works by the time you read this.

In the UK Adventure Spec produce 35-litre **Magadan** throwovers, developed by Siberian specialist Walter Colebatch. They're based on the Steel Pony's Gascoyne (above) but use a much tougher slash-proof fabric as well as the all-important *removable* waterproof liner, not sewn in like Monsoons. Other features make them less prone to theft and though they're throwovers with long velcro straps, Magadans are intended to be used with racks. Read Walter C's design statement on 🖥 adventure-spec.com; you can see he's thought it through.

Many of the listed bags here are reviewed in more detail **on the website** (see back cover).

On the back

If not using a lockable top box, across the back of your seat or the rack itself a soft duffle bag or holdall does the job. Longways or sideways the roll-top **Ortlieb Rack Pack** in the 49-litre size (pictured below) is just the right sized bag for the job. The key is top loading: it's easy to stow your tent, mat and sleeping

bag each morning. It can rain all day on a Rack Pack and if done up right it'll take longer to seep in. Bags opening at the end like a tube of Pringles are less useful, and drybags that open at *both* ends is a solution without a problem.

In the UK, Lomo or OverBoard are cheaper. And if you're engaged on an outlandish Siberian wet-fest I recommend the US **Watershed** brand as genuinely tough PU fabric, submersion-proof bags. At 30 litres the Chattooga model will take a tent, bag and a mat.

TT Zegaflex on a rack: not waterproof, many zips. Above it, a classic Ortlieb Rack Pack.

This is how it usually starts when throwovers press on a pipe, but things can escalate...

"My plate survived, TFFT!" You can use a rack or you can call the Pompiers. © Austin Vince

RACKS FOR SOFT OR HARD LUGGAGE

Soft or hard, for a long overland ride you'll need a **strong rack** to support your baggage. If you happen to possess unusual self-restraint you might get away with using soft luggage without a rack, as with the old Ténéré on p95. But even with just a 10-litre jerrican sat on the back seat the rear subframe on that bike flexed, inducing a weave over 50mph/80kph on loose surfaces, especially with those tyres. If your baggage is much heavier or the roads rough, subframes can bend or crack – and as illustrated above, bags pressing on pipes can have even graver consequences.

These days just about all alloy and plastic pannier sellers offer racks for all popular adventure bikes. You'd assume they're built to take the hammering, but don't count on it. Just as with AM bikes, the kit has become fashionable too. You'll still read reports of proprietary racks breaking out in the field which is why people get their own made to suit their exact needs.

Building a rack

As already said, mounting heavy racks and boxes on bike subframes is not an exact science, partly because each bike is different; the alloy subframe of an old KLR or XR650R is weaker than a new Ténéré or 650 Sertao. Mounting a heavy rack onto the unsupported beam or cantilever that is a motorcycle subframe

A and B are the key points. Anywhere between, including the pillion mounts, make up the other points. The less of a straight line they're all in, the better. © Longsong Motor Co

may just see the whole thing droop before you even load it. Slapping on metal willy nilly is not over-engineering, it's bad engineering.

Stronger rear subframe

A subframe is more or less a right angle triangle with the 90° angle under the seat reaching down to the footrests and back at the tail light. Loading the back end stresses the diagonal leading to the footrest, or the unsupported beam when this triangle is partial, as illustrated left. In this instance you can see the unsupported rear spars have

This is your standard hanging rack these days: 16/18mm tubes, 3 attachment points and the all-important crossbar on the back

Home-made 4-point platform rack for a DR650. Cut back corners don't dig in or snap at your shins. © Sean Flanagan

been curved so they can be gusseted with plates to add rigidity for little weight. Gusseting and bracing may be necessary on your frame too even before you start thinking about a rack – but doing this intuitively can make things worse. Few people really know what they're doing here, how can they without expensive testing? When meddling with a subframe design that may be more sophisticated than it looks it's not impossible to amplify stresses or simply transfer them elsewhere.

The rack

With the subframe attended to, by adding a rack you're augmenting the triangle with a notional spar running from A to B on the subframe picture opposite. This transfers compression down to the 'A' mount – a key area of stress, at its height when your suspension bottoms out, (a good reason to fit an uprated spring). A tail light-to-footrest spar may keep your throwover from flapping around like an untended fire hose, but it won't support the bag.

The frames shown above are doing the same in a less obvious way by using **three or more** mounts and a more practical **rectangle** between A and B to which you can more easily mount boxes or cases. As already stated, **separating the mounting from the load is a good idea** which is how the platform rack top right works, even if just about everyone these days makes or buys 'hanging racks', as above left.

Left: Subframes have a hard time when loaded; ideally a rack should add strength. (Disconnect the battery *completely* when welding on a bike; sensitive electrics can get fried. © Trui Hanoulle. **Right**: A light rack made of heat-bent PVC sheet; keeps throwovers out of the chain. © A. Jowlett.

Left: DIY-ers can buy the central rectangle in 18mm tube (Touratech p#: 01-051-0300-0).
Right: Bent strips on this XR650R are easy to fabricate and weld but are much less rigid than tube and not much lighter. Think carefully where racks attach – especially those with alloy frames.

Here are some other points to consider when building a rack. Most off-the-shelf racks are **too far back** and too high too; here's your chance to do it right.

- Use easily re-weldable and sourced **steel**, not aluminium.
- **Round tube** is stronger than same-sized square section but square is less work to weld. Minimise curved sections in either.
- **Bolt** the rack in three or more places per side. Don't weld it on.
- Where applicable, make sure there's **enough room** for wheel removal, chain adjustment, suspension compression and the swing of a kickstart.
- In most cases a **brace across the back** is vital to stop inward flexing and creating a more rigid 'cube'. Straight or 'V', the lower the better. If necessary this brace can be unboltable to aid wheel removal.
- Don't simply crush, drill and bolt tube ends as some frame makers do. Weld on a **tab** and drill that as this point is often prone to failure.
- Use **same sized bolts** for all mounts and check in the early days or after tough stages. Carry spares in case they shear.
- Don't expect total rigidity. Fully loaded, steel and mounts will **flex** as energy is absorbed. Better that than bending or snapping.

Because of the complex forces going on here, forces from all directions which were not necessarily anticipated when the bike was designed, the simplest way to ensure a rack – home-made or otherwise – doesn't lead to frame problems is to **keep your payload light**. This subject is discussed further in a series of illustrated articles **on the website** as I set about getting a platform rack made for my bike.

Other baggage

That's your main baggage covered but there are additional ways and means of stashing your nick-nacks and now more than ever there are scores of outfitters offering cunning solutions that would have Batman flitting back to the cave with a roll of Cordura and a handful of clips. These baggage accessories all help you reach the goal of **compartmentalisation** which adds up to speed and convenience of access, same as a well-organised work station. Just remember that even if it isn't your first time, you'll still find it takes a few weeks on the road to optimise your system for access, security and weather-proofness. I find

Left: A tankbag this big was a bad idea. Take something that's easy to carry around away from the bike; that's the point. **Right**: This 1150 has some sort of used RPG cannister on the crash bars, while, **far right**, on the back there's a discreet black box behind the number plate.

a jacket with a zillion big pockets suits me best, and maybe a backpack or a waist pack, because depending where you ride, more stuff lashed to the bike is more stuff to fall off, get damaged or get pinched.

Tank bags are a tried and tested way of keeping frequently used and high value gear handy and in view. Much of course will depend on your bike's tank (or area where tanks used to be) offering a broad and stable base, although cut foam pads can get around this. Just don't make the mistake of using a huge tank bag. It can get in the way of seeing your instruments, including accessories like GPS, and anyway you want a bag you can remove and carry easily when it comes to leaving the bike and going for a wander. Some tank bags can convert into backpacks and all should include a shoulder strap.

The tank can also be a place to sling over a pair of **tank panniers** (see p94) providing there's enough room for them in front of your knees, not inside them. In this position they do offer a bit of protection as well as handy access.

Kreiga, Touratech and others make all sorts of handy **pods and pouches** you can attach to the outside of your hard boxes; at the very least it's useful to have an external container for engine oil or a water bottle where they can leak harmlessly (see the KTM on p86). After that it's up to you to freestyle your baggage needs, as the 1150 pictured above has done. If there's room on your bike to stuff or hide spares and maybe a back-up phone plus a set of keys then so much the better. That way you can forget about it until you need it and it makes more room in your main baggage. You'll never have enough of that.

Testing your baggage system

When all that's done, take your fully-loaded bike for a test ride. Sitting a friend on the back and getting them to jump up and down is not the same thing. Riding in this state for the first time will be alarming, and the first time in the dirt will be even worse. As you wobble down the street you'll wonder how you're ever going to ride from Anchorage to Brazzaville.

While loaded up, lay the bike over and try to **pick it up**; if you can't it's too heavy, and unless you're certain there'll always be someone around to help you, consider reducing the weight or repositioning the baggage. This may be your last chance before lift off. Many first time riders send stuff home in the early days of a big trip.

BIKE CHOICE & PREPARATION

BUILDING YOUR OWN BIKE

Despite the decline of motorcycling in rich western countries, the latest adventure touring motorcycles are at least keeping sales figures from falling. Unfortunately, the machines produced these days are not necessarily what most of us would choose to ride in or around the real world, while less complex and expensive old machines are just getting too old to be worth investing in.

It was widely acknowledged that in the early 1980s the motorcycling world was not crying out for an allegedly 15hp, 200cc twin with a foot of suspension travel. But I went ahead and built one anyway and rode it to the Sahara (see website; Project Bikes). And as I write this my latest BYO project is nearing completion to hopefully be less of a turkey than the 1984 effort, pictured below.

Why bother, you may ask? Well, it's fun and for just a couple of thousand pounds you can get exactly what you want; a machine that owes you not much at all and can take the knocks of overlanding without depreciating.

The frankenplan

For most people the plan is to get a street bike with a nice, smooth **engine** and fit it with **longer suspension** and bigger diameter wheels. Doing it the other way round, you need to have a pretty good reason to go through the complications of fitting and aligning an engine into an alien frame. As with many such builds, the motivation is most probably because you happen to have the components lying around or cheap to access, rather than a crystal clear vision of the direction adventure bikes should be taking.

Any number of UJM motors make a good basis for a frankenbike project; the more common they are the less they'll cost to buy, run and repair; all the likely spares you might need like alternators, regulators and

all the rest are waiting for you in the junk yards of the world. In the US the K-series BMW 'brick' is commonly 'GS'd' as inevitably we're talking pre-CAN bus era motorcycles where a simple mechanical rearrangement won't put it in a spin. But give it a few years and we'll get around the complexities of modern electronics, too. The simpler the better, because it may well be your meddling that gives problems down the road, so test thoroughly.

If you're serious about overlanding and not just raising eyebrows at bike rallies, it makes sense to start with an economical engine or at least a big fuel tank; fabricating your own tank gets expensive or ends up messy. If choosing a sports bike, think about the viability of rearset footrest positions too, once you fit some high and wide 'bars.

Assuming there's space, changing rims on wire wheels is easy; a 19-inch front rim is a good compromise for dirt road touring. But hubs can be a pain to match up, so better to locate a complete front end: triple clamps, stem, forks, brakes and wheel. Then adapt the stem or fabricate a new one to fit the frame's steering head; bearings come in all shapes and sizes.

Don't overlook safety issues; a DR650 front disc won't hold back a galloping FJ12 motor. You may get in hot water with insurance and licensing authorities too, but out in the world it's doubtful anyone's bothered as long as the numbers match.

For inspiration and the occasional bout of insanity as pictured below, check out the Some Assembly Required forum on 🖳 advrider.com, in particular thread #330726 with over half a million views.

MX apehanger, anyone? © Marcin Olkowicz

A question of quads

In 2011 **Jamie Kenyon** *and* **Kristopher Davant** *were among three riders who completed a world-record 58,000-kilometre quad ride through 38 countries. So you'd think they'd have the drum on overlanding with quads.*

Why don't bikers like the idea of quads?
Most bikers attempting a journey of more than 5000km would think of quads as a poor choice as they are too slow, not adventurous enough and with four wheels you may as well be in a car. In many respects they are correct, but under ideal conditions I'd ride nothing but a quad. Try to cross 300km of sand dunes in the Sahara or 1500km of mud roads in Tanzania or Mozambique on a 1200cc adventure tourer and say you enjoy that. Very difficult on a big, loaded bike but on a similarly equipped quad it's an absolute pleasure and a lot of fun.

Knowing what you do now, what sort of quad is best for what you did?
As a team we rode for 14 months across Europe, Africa and Australia. We tested our quads on all roads and tracks imaginable: sand, gravel, dirt, mud, snow, ice, motorway, back roads. Firstly I'd suggest a quad that's produced by a manufacturer known for quality. We rode Yamaha quads as I was aware of Yamaha's Dakar Rally history.

Secondly a quad isn't suited to long continuous journeys on highways or tracks. If you're choosing a quad, pick one with enough power and capacity to reduce routine maintenance. As I know now, with a 1200GS you may need to service it once a month; we would be servicing the quads every few days after long stages. It's also worth adding that as with bikes, top end quads have sensors and other electronics that help them perform optimally. This can create problems if these components play up in remote locations, although we didn't experience this on our journey.

What are the important features to look for?
From the outset I'd look for a **large capacity engine**. Often larger means more heavily engineered. For example, some smaller quads have a single rear disc with fixed rear suspension. This is a poor comparison to the 700cc Yamaha we rode which had four wheel independent rear suspension with brake disks on all wheels, just like a car. With larger models you also get a greater payload, more robust suspension, plus a wider quad that will be more stable on harder surfaces at speed, or in corners. I'd also suggest a model with **power steering** for added comfort in slower conditions.

What typical adaptations are needed?
Essentially not many. Our quads were stock out of the showroom. What you need to change are your expectations of how they perform on a long journey. Speed is your first issue. A quad bike is designed to move stock around a field or tow small trailers at low speed and with a day-in day-out reliability. This is

BIKE CHOICE & PREPARATION

700cc Yamaha Grizzly. © quadsquad.org

entirely different to riding thousands of kilometres. The **low gearing** on a quad provides a lot of torque but has the same acceleration and top speed as a 100cc scooter. On the road we averaged 50-70kph (30-45mph). Any faster and you're reaching the redline in top so will have to expect your servicing to be even more frequent. So on many sections where 100kph would have been fine, like the gravel roads of Namibia, we kept it down to about 65kph. This adds considerably to riding time, so keep this in mind. I would focus on a journey of 5000km of tough terrain where the stability and traction of a quad is utilised to the full, rather than thousands of kilometres on open roads.

I notice you had radios. What sort?
We used Motorola hand-held two-way radios in conjunction with microphones and earpieces sold by Sonic in the UK. It worked well in all conditions even in the rain. A helmet comms system is essential for long group journeys, to alert other riders to hazards on the road, experience the scenery together or just for making plans. Just stopping on the side of the road to change clothing can be unsafe if your companion thinks you need to stop with real urgency. A radio will reduce that danger. In retrospect, I'd have chosen a radio that's hard wired to the battery, as with the correct antenna these models have a range of roughly 15km rather than one or two. Also continually charging batteries for hand-held radios was a challenge.

How long do tyres last?
Correct tyre choice is essential. We used Carlisle tyres from the US. They were a sponsor of ours but I will say I have no bias as I've seen their product pushed to the limits. In 58,000km we had no punctures other than piercing a tyre accidentally when bashing rims back into shape after a rough section. For best results try the Carlisle All-Trail; it has a flatter profile that's much more suited to harder surfaces so you'll get much less roll than a rounder dirt tyre. It has significantly more tread that will last longer and a tread pattern that's useful on road, sand and mud. I thought tyres would be our biggest concern but in terms of performance they weren't at all; the issue was shipping as such tyres are impossible to find in almost all parts of Africa. They should last around 12,000km on the front, 20,000km on the rear. Be aware of pressures, wheel alignment and also getting the wheels balanced to extend the life and reduce vibration.

Does the CVT overheat in slow, hot conditions?
We never had overheating issues with our 700cc quads and that includes the CVT. The hottest conditions we tested in were in southern Sudan where it was around 48°C. We always let the fan stop running before turning the engine off. Our Yamaha Grizzly quads have a great cooling system which meant that the engine just did not overheat.

BIKE CHOICE & PREPARATION

Was 4WD useful?
Certainly. We rarely used it in conditions where you were able to ride above 40kph as it increased fuel consumption. However in tighter trails and in sand it's a real asset, especially on inclines. A good 4WD off-road quad will perform better than almost anything else.

On deep rutted tracks was the quad's narrow wheel track a problem?
It certainly made these sort of roads exciting! The best thing to do was reduce speed. Amending your riding style depending on the surface was also important. In sand you can ride with one set of quad wheels in the rut, and by leaning away you can avoid it becoming unstable. However with hard-baked and deep mud tracks you must be much more careful as it's possible to be thrown from the quad.

How did the fuel consumption work out?
We maintained a consistent consumption of around 10kpl (30mpg, 25mpgUS); as thirsty as a 4x4. It also means with a 20-litre fuel tank our range would be only 200km. We had 35-litre auxiliary tanks that extended our range up to 550km, and this rear tank takes up a considerable amount of space.

What mechanical problems did you have?
We had a few mechanical issues and they were primarily due to the fact that a quad is not designed to ride long distance for extended periods. We initially serviced them every 10,000 km, as you would a motorbike. CVT belts need to be checked and changed frequently as they wear faster at high speed. The air filter must be cleaned or changed frequently too. It's best to check over your quad and do a full service every 2-3000 kilometres.

Can a foreign registered quad be ridden in countries where quads are not road legal, like US and Australia?
In some African countries quads are not road legal but we didn't have a problem as they were road legal in another country. However in Australia it was a different story. We had to gain approval from police, road authorities and government bodies to ride on the roads in Australia. They were initially extremely reluctant to let us ride on the roads in Australia. We were only able to make it possible as one rider, Valerio De Simoni, was killed on our journey and we were riding across Australia and home to Sydney in his honour. I have heard that the US government is even more difficult with the issue of quads on highways than in Australia, but it's hard to see how this is possible. We were approved to ride on the roads in Australia but were still pulled over almost daily by police in residential areas. I can only imagine what it would be like in many different states of America.

What was the reaction from locals, if any?
The reaction was often warm and welcoming. 'Is it a bike? Is it a car?' was a typical statement. The uniqueness of the quad certainly gained interest from local people in each country we travelled through; it worked in our favour and strangers never seemed threatened by our mode of transport, which was one of our initial concerns. You don't want to look like a special services high mobility unit while riding through places like Libya, Sudan or northern Kenya.

BIKE CHOICE & PREPARATION

Quad country, east Africa. © quadsquad.org

BIKE CHOICE & PREPARATION

Any extra border hassle on a quad?

Some less ethical border officers assumed we had more money than a biker and would hold us longer in attempt to extort a bribe. Because quads are a grey area in many countries road legislation you must be very careful with insurance too. If you have an accident and hurt or damage someone's property you may not be covered by the insurance you've paid for (though in some places that may often be the case with regular vehicles too). Insurance is often bought at a border crossing, a place you're keen to leave. However, examining an insurance policy then or before you go to the country could save you some money or even worse, time in prison.

What is a typical highway cruising speed?

Terrible. Being used to two-wheel cruising at 110kph, sitting on a motorway at 65-70 can be irritating and sometimes feel unsafe. We always travelled as two or three quads together which made us more visible. As well as having radios we alerted each other of big hazards like big trucks. Ironically in some ways, 'safer' first world countries were often more dangerous. In Africa cars and trucks are often old or overloaded so drive more slowly. We rode on the German autobahns with cars passing at over 200kph. Quite a frightening experience on a quad bike!

Do you feel safe on the road as quads feel less agile than a bike?

As discussed above, road use can be more difficult than a motorcycle. However I felt safe riding a quad. Would you get into a motorhome and drive into a tight corner at 100kph? No. Just because you can do it on a motorcycle or a car doesn't mean you can do so on a quad. You need to know a quad's limitations. This applies to off-road riding as well. In some conditions I'd feel safer on a quad at speed than on two wheels, but as with motos, slower is better as the conditions become more technical.

Overall, is this an ideal global adventure quad or a short range off-road pleasure machine?

There is no global adventure quad yet. Fuel consumption, frequent servicing, slow cruising speeds, gear capacity taken by extra parts or fuel; all this does not add up to a global tourer. A quad has the same appeal as a large farm tractor but we successfully completed our journey with some extreme endurance. Life on the road in Africa or South America or even Europe is pleasurable and challenging enough without these added difficulties.

However, for short range adventuring a quad is ideal. It'll attempt to cross any terrain where a car is too heavy and a bike gets unstable. Put a quad on a trailer and take it to the Sahara for a month, I might see you there!

Visit 🖥 quadsquad.org to read about more the journey, view images on 🖥 Facebook.com/expquadsquad and find out about the upcoming book and documentary.

Clothing for the long ride

As much as any of the advice given in this book, clothing is a matter of **personal taste** but, whatever image you decide to cultivate, you'll need to protect yourself from wind, sun, heat, cold, dust, rain, stones and crashing; it's a lot to ask of your clothes when on the road for months at a stretch. **Comfort**, **lightness**, **utility** and **quality of construction** are all important features to consider as you'll probably end up wearing the same kit most of the time.

Forget about taking excessive amounts of spare clothing and instead make do with one change. Wash what you wear every few days until it wears out, then replace it. Save space by opting for multi-functional items that are light and quick-drying, and resist the temptation to pack a smart outfit 'just in case'. In the unlikely event of an invitation to an embassy soirée, you'll create much more of a stir in your weather-beaten leathers than crammed into a crumpled shirt and tie.

Jackets

Any jacket wants to seal up snugly around your neck, wrists and waist for cold days, while being adjustable with zips and air vents as days or climates warm up. A **waist drawcord**, velcro or belt is particularly useful as it seals off your torso, so keeping the core of your body warm on a cool morning, while being easy to release on the move. A good jacket wants to have all the qualities mentioned above and also have enough good-sized pockets to carry valuables. Overland biking being what it is, keeping these items on your person is the best way of ensuring they stay with you, so look for **big zipped pockets**, at least one of which is internal. Make sure the ones on your chest are not so high up that you can't easily get your hand in, side entry often makes for a bigger pocket to hold a map or documents.

Probably the best jacket to fill all the above criteria most of the time is a **Cordura touring jacket**. Cordura is a tough woven nylon that's light, looks

BIKE CHOICE & PREPARATION

BREATHABLE FABRICS

The efficacy of breathable membranes like Gore-Tex is much discussed when applied to motorcycling. The micropore film sandwiched in the layers of your jacket (or lately, in a separate liner) releases the condensation vapour formed by sweat, while miraculously resisting the ingress of water (aka, rain).

Thing is, for such fabrics to work a certain amount of 'thermodynamic pressure' and heat must build up inside the jacket for the vapour to be purged. This heat can be easily generated climbing Nanga Parbat, less so when sat on a motorcycle at 70mph.

Some condensation is not so bad and can be deal with by vents, but a garment failing to keep rain out is a real drag.

Breathable membrane garments need to be washed regularly in special soaps and then re-coated or even cured in a hot dryer with a solution called DWR to help rainwater bead and run off the jacket, rather than soak in. Such maintenance is easily done with your weekend hiking cag and helps maintain breathability, but out in Lubumbashi, Olapoque or Krasny Ogurek, getting hold of that sort of stuff will not be so easy.

Left: Ancient Rukka PVC one-piece oversuit. This or something like it is the best way to keep dry in full-on downpours. **Right**: BMW gear costs but lasts. Whatever you rate, not all will agree.

good, abrades well as you slide down the road, is easy to clean and forms a tough shell for a Gore-Tex liner. Hein Gericke, Klim, Dainese, Lindstroms, Stadler and Rukka are among those making jackets from light but strong synthetic materials. You need to spend around £250/$400 to get something to do the job well, but you can pay four times that amount.

Elements of a good touring jacket

What you choose will partly depend on where you're going. Most of us who put up with winters in the northern hemisphere are looking to go riding somewhere warmer like Africa or Central America. But as we know, it's always colder than you think on a bike.

Comfort and fit With the internet it's easy to be lazy and buy something that looks cool, has great online reviews and is 35% off in a sale. Doing so with clothing is a gamble, so unless they do returns your best bet of trying it all under one roof is at a motorcycling show where you'll have a full range from Z-brand cheapies to outfits costing well over £1000. Sit on a bike in the jacket if you get a chance, to find out how it actually feels.

Waterproof/breathable As mentioned on p107, don't be too hopeful that breathable fabrics will also stay waterproof forever. Many bike jackets now come with a removable breathable liner, rather than having the membrane as part of the jacket shell. It may sound like the best of both worlds but is probably a cost saving measure, allowing the shell to be designed just so with an off-the-peg liner thrown in. Membrane in the shell is best while it lasts, but when it's absolutely pelting a PVC waterproof, one-piece or pull-over top with no front zip gives an added layer of impermeable protection. A thick, PVC fisherman or farmer's smock will do the job until it rips and even then can be fixed with glue or duct tape. Anything coated, like nylon, will wear and leak at the seams.

Ventilation is an admission that breathable membranes don't work so well, although for 'passive' motorcycling this is well known. Zipped vents appear on the chest or under the arms, with an associated exhaust vent across the back; they're a way of keeping the jacket in position so it doesn't flap around with the front open – that is the best vent of all. You'll welcome vents in any tropical country, but when hot riding gets technical any jacket will be too warm. Ventilation is worthwhile as it encourages you to always wear your jacket with all its storage capacity and protective qualities, but don't expect miracles.

Quality zips Zips have a hard time, being stressed, folded, caked in filth, ill-maintained and yanked upon. Do yourself a favour and make sure your jacket is fitted with chunky, quality items. A regular zip is not waterproof. The so-called water-resistant zips that appear on some jackets and Ortlieb bags are, as far as I can tell, merely fine-toothed and therefore less robust zips which bind a rubbery plastic edging together as they zip up to seal out rain. That may work for hill walking, but belting along at 70 into a storm, such a closure can't be expected to resist water. A regular robust zip with a *double* storm flap is the best protection against oncoming rain.

A while back Gore-Tex introduced something called a Lockout, a rubber railed closure that resembles a Ziplock freezer bag or indeed the seal on Watershed bags mentioned on p97. Almost certainly waterproof, they soon they found their way onto moto clothing, but the results up to now have not been promising: breakages, the seal bursting apart and people complaining that the closure needed lubricating (true of any such closure if it's to work well, and true of zips too). For the moment stick with zips and storm flaps.

Impact and wear protection has got much cleverer over the years and now includes plastics like 3DO or APS which are soft and malleable in normal use, but with molecules which manage to lock hard under impact – perfect for moto applications. You'll want it on the elbows, shoulders and maybe the back, and points of high wear like elbows can also benefit from a thicker or second layer of Cordura or kevlar. When it comes to choosing a jacket, look out for the 'CE' logo – a European Union standard that relates to many safety features like armour. A similar logo indicating 'China Export' is not the same thing.

Trousers – alternatives to jeans

With trousers the accent is on comfort and protection, pockets are not that important as sat down in a bike what's in them will get in the way. Here a good pair of **leather trousers** is an advantage: they're hard-wearing and still look good when dirty. Avoid cheap thin leather; look for soft supple cowhide and one piece legs (no seam across the knees) – a factor which jacks the price up. Bear in mind that leather trousers are heavy and will sag and stretch over the months, you'll need strong braces to avoid the crotch eventually splitting in the countless times you swing your leg over your bike.

Leather trousers are obviously less suited to tropical climates or regions with plenty of river crossings. Wearing nylon in humid conditions is not ideal either, but a pair of **motocross pants** is still a good all-round choice, offering proper dirt-biking protection, padding and durability, while being light and quick to dry. Fit **knee protectors** which slip into inside pockets on most brands. Even if you don't crash in them, it makes kneeling on the ground when working on the bike a whole lot more comfortable. Your choice of sober colour schemes will be limited of course, you'll need to flick through a few catalogues to find something that won't frighten the horses. Get a quality pair of pants fit for riding into the ground.

Getting back to jeans, it is of course possible to buy a pair with kevlar linings or patches as well as pockets for knee pads. Whatever you buy, just remember you'll be wearing it constantly so think about durability, wear and comfort in a range of climates. As a rule it's easier to cool off than warm up.

BIKE CHOICE & PREPARATION

Boots, gloves and helmet

Invest in a tough pair of **boots** that will last the trip and protect your feet and ankles in the frequent low-speed tumbles. The better you're prepared for these small accidents, the more you'll be able to enjoy your riding without fear of injury. Depending on where you plan to ride, full-on MX boots can be over the top and heavy; choose something that offers protection while still being suited to walking around the ruins of Machu Picchu or a spot of shopping.

Gloves are important not just for crashing but for grip and carting luggage around, so take **two pairs** as they're easily mislaid; thick ones for cold days and a thinner pair when it warms up or for lower speeds. If you can operate your camera through the thin pair, it saves a lot of faffing in order to grab a good shot. You'll get the usual claims from waterproof membranes; better to leave bad weather to either some muffs, hand guards or the screen. Waterproof mitts may have fewer seams but are more suited to ice climbing than motorcycling where you need fingers.

As for **helmets**, take your pick with full face, flip-ups, 'adventure' style like the well known Arai Tour X and its many copies, open face or the versatile modular style with a big visor and a removable chin piece such as a Nolan N43 Air or X-Lite X402GT (reviewed on the AMH website). Looking cool is important but above all you want comfort, quietness and good visibility and ventilation which the above models offer. Think too about visor maintenance and getting spares on the road. Minimise rain swipes with gritty gloves and wash visors gently with a soapy hand under running water.

COLD-WEATHER CLOTHING

Year-round bikers outside the tropics are familiar with the misery of riding in cold weather wearing inadequate gear. Little wonder most of us head south or east towards the sun. But some perverse individuals still choose to head in the opposite direction, while round-the-worlders will eventually run into a cold season or high altitude.

You want to face riding in freezing temperatures with optimism rather than dread; retaining and **maintaining body heat** is what counts. Fairings, **windshields** and handlebar muffs – temporarily bodged from available materials if necessary – are the first stage in keeping reducing heat loss and are a good idea in any climate. Maintaining body heat also means regular stops for **exercise** and refuelling with **hot food** and drinks.

Insulation is the next step as it's the trapped, still air heated by your body that keeps you warm, not bulky materials per se. Choose a thick fleece or even a compact down vest under a windproof outer shell. Seal off the points where heat will be lost like cuffs, the waist and neck, and wear a neck tube and a balaclava.

One-piece under-garments and outer shells (like the Aerostich Roadcrafter suit) are more efficient and also very comfortable to wear because they eliminate the gap or compressed waistbands in the kidney area where vital core body heat is easily lost. Plus they avoid that 'Michelin man' feeling when wearing several layers. The drawback with one-piece clothing comes in the palaver needed to get it off, when things warm up or when nature rings the bell.

Your engine produces electrical power so using **heated grips** and **electrically-heated clothing** is eminently sensible. As your body cools blood is drawn from the limbs to the core to sustain vital organs; by externally warming your trunk, blood can then be spared on frigid limbs. Many modern adventure bikes now have alternators powerful enough to run electrical accessories. Check out the gear from Symtec, exo2 or Aerostich.

If you get caught out, converting your water bag into a **hot water bottle** and stuffing newspapers in your clothes will help conserve warmth while giving you something to read once you've dug a snow hole.

LIFE ON THE ROAD

3

The Big Day arrives and the Sky News chopper is buzzing the neighbourhood while colourful street-bunting flutters in the breeze. Or more likely, some friends and family are buzzing around and the fluttering is in your stomach because one thing's fairly certain, you'll be nervous. If you've had the chance to prepare thoroughly and get everything sorted and packed, pat yourself on the back. Chances are though, like most mortals, you'll have overlooked some small thing, or will be dealing with a last-minute cockup. This seems to be normal, another test thrown down from the gods of the overland. Expect it.

One great way of avoiding a last-minute panic is to pack the bike days before you leave, or gather everything you need in a safe space like a garage. Assembling all the gear, at this time you're not yet chewing your lip over tomorrow's imminent departure, but instead have a quiet few days to thoughtfully check the bike and tick off a checklist. There'll still be eleventh-hour things to buy or do, but this way should the handlebars come away in your hands there'll be enough time to bolt them back on and stay on schedule.

SHAKEDOWN TRIP

Many of us will have travelled abroad in one way or another before setting off on our big motorcycle adventure. For the rest with less experience the best way of reducing the shock of hitting the road on the big one is to hit the road on a small one. A **shakedown trip** of a week or two to somewhere as far as you dare will be an invaluable dress rehearsal. When the real thing comes along it won't feel so daunting, just another, a bit further this time.

On a test run you'll have a chance to refine your set up without unnecessary pressure. Some flaw may also manifest itself – a wobble from low tyre pressures, overheating, or the

The Big Day. © Sean Flanagan

... it's better to find all this out by wading out from the shallow end than diving in at the deep end with a backpack.

suspension bottoming out because of overloading. Better to know this now when there's still a chance to do something about it.

From western Europe, somewhere like Morocco, Turkey or even just eastern Europe can be enough to give you an idea of what it's like to be in a significantly foreign country on the frontier of the overland zone. From North America it's obviously going to be Mexico and Central America, while South Africans can roam far north into their continent, taking on progressively more challenging countries as they go. For those I've missed out, you get the picture.

A short test run or an **organised tour** can be used to find out if you even like the very idea of a long-haul trip of your own. You may acknowledge that a short trip is as much as you want to take on at this stage of your life. It's nice to go camping on your well set-up bike for a couple of weeks, but hauling yourself all the way to Vladivostok or Ushuaia might be too much of a commitment as things stand. Again, it's better to find all this out by wading out from the shallow end than diving in at the deep end with a full backpack.

SETTING OFF

So here it is. You climb aboard, start the engine, heave the bike off the stand (don't forget to flick it up!), clunk into first and wobble off down the road, appalled at the weight of your rig. Once out on the open road you wind it up and allow some faint optimism to creep in to your multiplying anxieties as passing motorists glance at you with what you hope is envy.

Finally on the move after months if not years of preparation, the urge is to keep moving, especially if you're heading out across a cold continent. Recognise this restlessness for what it is: an inability to relax for fear that something bad is going to happen. It's all part of the acclimatisation process as your life takes on a whole new direction.

Try to resist covering excessive mileages in the early days. Racing through unfamiliar countries with perplexing road signs and 'wrong-side' driving can lead to an accident. If an estimated three-quarters of all overlanders achieve hospitalisation through accidents, rather than commonly-dreaded diseases or banditry, you can imagine what that figure is for motorcyclists. In many cases this happens very early in the trip. It may be intensely galling, but if things don't feel right or get off to a bad start and you have a chance to correct them, turn back. If you didn't make a big splash no one need know.

To help give yourself a good chance of not needing to do that, don't make any **crazy deadlines** to quit work and catch a ferry the next morning, or pick up a visa three countries away in less than a week. Instead, after a couple of days on the road make a conscious effort to park up somewhere warm and sunny, or visit friends, so as to catch your breath. Spread out for a while, tinker with the bike and just get used to being away from home but not up to your neck just yet. If you're a bit shaky about the whole enterprise it can make a real difference to your mood. And on your own, **managing your moods** is as important as keeping on the correct side of the road.

THE SHOCK OF THE NEW

Alone on your first big trip into foreign lands it's normal to feel self conscious, intimidated, if not a little paranoid. This is because you've just expelled yourself from your comfort zone and are entering the thrill of an adventure. 'Adventure travel' has become a tourism marketing term to distinguish active holidays from basting by a pool, but an 'adventure' is what it sounds like: indulging in an activity with an uncertain or dangerous outcome.

The less glamorous aspect of all this is the **stress** involved in dealing with strange people, languages, customs, places and food. Stress is usually what you're looking to get away from, but it's not necessarily a bad thing. Leaping into the air off the end of an elastic cord is stressful, so is standing up to give a speech or even taking a long-haul flight. To a certain extent it's an emotional response to losing control, and can also be classified as excitement. Your senses are sharpened and your imagination is stimulated, but with this comes irritability and possibly an exaggerated wariness of strange situations.

Having probably lived and worked in a secure environment for years, for better or for worse setting off overland can be just about the most stressful and exciting thing you'll have done for a long time. **Fears** of getting robbed, having a nasty accident, getting in trouble with the police or breaking down are all the more acute when you're on your own with everything you possess for the next few months in arm's reach. This situation is not improved by the way overseas news is presented in the media: one atrocity or tragedy after another. Who'd want to go to places like these? Paul Randall's anecdote below strikes a chord: bike problems, pressing deadlines and hyper-anxiety can look trivial in retrospect, but they all conspired to shorten a bigger trip.

CRACKING UP IN RUSSIA

... I realise that things have been far too easy travelling around to Lithuania, needless to say Russia put an end to all of that. I was nervous about visa headaches, no bike insurance, red tape – but I got in OK and stayed at Pskov. Back then in 2003 I had to get to St Petersburg to register otherwise there'd be trouble, and had to do it in three days.

Russia for me was tough – it's all very well knowing how to say 'Hello, my name is Paul – kak paniemajesh?' But that's not exactly a full vocabulary. I found the people very cold and felt too intimidated to buy food. Looking back I feel a bit daft but that's how it was – and I was in a rush so skipping meals seemed OK.

I got to St P cold, wet and miserable and found a suitably grotty hotel where I had to bribe the security bloke to make sure my bike was 'safe' at night. I tried to out-tough him but I've watched too many movies – it didn't work. Next day I went to collect my passport from reception but it had gone missing; the receptionist looked everywhere but couldn't find it. I guessed the security bloke had nicked it for another bribe. I was starting to panic but the receptionist told me they did not have it – I must have it, check your money belt Mr Paul – so I did and there was my passport! What a plonker! Anyway I got very upset, I could not say sorry in Russian, so I just left feeling very small.

I went to register but my bike wouldn't start. I managed to get it going somehow but it kept breaking down. I'd not eaten for a few days and I started to lose the plot a bit...

Looking back I think I was having a bit of a nervous breakdown fuelled by lack of food. At this point an American guy said 'Hello'. We chatted, I told him what I was doing and he offered me a luxury flat for the night with free secure parking for my broken bike and dinner with his family. After that I got the bike going and got registered and spent a few good days in the city.

PAUL RANDALL

LIFE ON THE ROAD

STREETWISE MANIFESTO

- Don't ride yourself ragged; rest often.
- Don't ride at night unless unavoidable.
- Wild camp out of sight of the road or stay in the security of settlements.
- Keep a low profile in hostile areas or just avoid them altogether.
- In towns and cities park off the street overnight where possible. Many hotels will let you put the bike inside.

- Keep your valuables on you at all times, but have a back-up stash.
- Trust your instincts – if a situation or a place doesn't feel good, move on or be prepared to leave quickly.
- Avoid exposing cash or valuables in crowded places.
- Learn and use the local language – you'll be amazed at the positive response.

A crucial part of the acclimatisation to life on the road is learning to see the world for what it actually is: regular people getting on with their ordinary lives; just like back home. In the collection of over a thousand trip reports on the AMH website the most common reply to the question: 'Biggest surprise?' is 'Friendliness of the people'. Many experienced overlanders come to recognise that when all's said and done, it's the good people they meet on their travels who count for more than the list of countries they visited or the gnarly roads they rode. It's hard to think so when you've spent months and a small fortune equipping the all-important machine while keeping tabs on the latest uprising, but without expecting to teach the world to sing in perfect harmony, it's perhaps the single biggest lesson to learn from travelling.

... when all's said and done, it's the good people they meet on their travels who count for more than the list of countries they visited or the gnarly roads they rode.

One of the most frustrating scenarios is when you realise you've been rude to someone who was only trying to help or be friendly. This can be understandable when you've been pestered for days by hustlers urging 'Meester, psst'. Distinguishing one from the other comes with experience; very often the most genuine encounters happen in rural areas where people are more 'normal', those with a proclivity for hustling having migrated to the richer pickings in cities and resorts.

It's common to see all journeys as a series of hops from one congested, hassle-ridden city to the next, and often it's a bureaucratic requirement as with the visa registering case in the box on p113 (city strategies are on p117 and p167). But out in the country pressures are less acute and locals indifferent, so make the most of roadside cafés for tea breaks, meals and rests. They're great places to mix with local people without feeling like you're on stage. The owners and customers will be regulars used to passing travellers and may well treat you like any other customer. Very often, that's all you want.

Riding abroad

Experienced motorcyclists will be well versed in the need to ride defensively, position themselves conspicuously and to **expect the unexpected**. Chances are, out in the AMZ the local driving standards will not be what you're used to back home. Very often the **horn** is used in place of the steering wheel or brakes or, as one overland blog put it, to say: 'out of the way/thanks for letting me pass/don't

overtake/cool bike, bro'. What's missing is the respect we have back home for road rules and other road users (or the fear of sanctions if we transgress).

Even if you're riding with all the due care and attention you can muster, the ante is upped further by a possible absence of driver training, licensing, roadworthiness testing and motor insurance. You'll be sharing roads with underpaid, overworked and amphetamine-fuelled truck drivers, as well as ageing bangers which, if it weren't for stringent local import regulations, would have been melted down into cheap cutlery many years ago. Mixing with these unroadworthy crates are the imported, blacked-out limos of local criminals, businessmen and politicians; stray domestic and wild animals; and dozy pedestrians who were never taught to 'look left, look right, and left again'. Throw in too much alcohol, some Latino/Arabic/Indian machismo, donkey carts, bad roads, unlit vehicles and unsigned diversions, plus some grossly overloaded vehicles, and you've arrived in the crazy world of riding in the AMZ where anything goes. All this can require an intense period of adjustment as you shudder past another pile of impossibly mangled wreckage being hosed off the road.

What's needed is **alertness** and a moderate dose of **assertiveness** that doesn't extend to aggression. This can be difficult to control when, because you're clearly a foreigner, you feel you're being singled out by local young men who regard being overtaken by you as a slap in the face. A good way of rationalising this is to acknowledge that among the hundreds of drivers you pass in a day you might generally encounter only one dickhead. Don't always take tailgating personally: there's a different concept of personal space out in the world (both on the road and in daily life). In fact, after a while this new uninhibited style of riding can be quite liberating; what counts is that all road users are on a similar wavelength, and this now includes you.

LOCAL DRIVING CUSTOMS

It's said that in Mexico, and certainly in many other places, a vehicle in front that you wish to pass will **signal** on the off side if it's safe to pass and to the near side (the kerb) if it's not safe. This is the opposite of what's done in Europe and North Africa, where a slow vehicle will indicate to the near side – 'pulling over' – that it's safe to pass. Misunderstanding this could be disastrous so it's best not to be rushed in such situations. Use your own judgement and visibility when performing such manoeuvres, not other people's.

Back home **flashing headlights** usually means the person you're flashing can go ahead; it can also mean 'Warning, speed trap / cops ahead!' when done to oncoming vehicles. In parts of North Africa flashing seems to be used by oncoming vehicles to ask 'Have you seen me? Please respond immediately!', except that just about every oncoming vehicle whose lights work seems to require this affirmation on a flat, perfectly clear road. If you don't flash back they'll flash again urgently. It can also be a message indicating 'Hey dumbass, you've got your lights on in broad daylight!', but it's rarely pointing out something you don't know, such as a condor is making a nest on your panniers.

Other local aspects of **driving etiquette** are detailed in the Continental Route Outlines (from p193). They might be addressed in more detail, along with other driving information, in the better travel guides for a given country or region.

THE WRONG SIDE OF THE ROAD

Although it's less of a problem on a bike than a car, if you've never ridden in a country where they drive on the other side of the road it's natural to be anxious about dealing with things like **roundabouts**. Riding fresh out of a foreign port, or crossing a border where driving sides change (as when crossing the northern borders of Pakistan, Angola or Kenya), you're usually hyper-alert.

Roundabouts, or traffic circles to some, are a good example. They seem to be proliferating across the highways of the world as a traffic-signal free way of controlling traffic at a crossroads. In the UK you give way to traffic already negotiating the roundabout, elsewhere you're supposed to give priority to those entering the roundabout, but I bet I'm not the only one to have ridden in countries where drivers will do it both ways on two adjacent roundabouts. The answer is to slow down, make eye contact and go for it when safe.

PINPOINTING A LOCATION ON GOOGLE MAPS

Sat-navs (see p130) may not always have adequate mapping for all the cities in the AMZ and you may not be using one anyway, but a **GPS waypoint** can be nearly as useful. It takes a bit of messing around as well as internet access, but by comparing a guidebook map against Google Maps you can find a spot. By right clicking on either 'Directions from here', 'To here', 'What's here' or 'Go to' you'll get a waypoint like this: 0.380334, 9.451659 and below it the more useful format: +0° 22' 50.05", +9° 27' 5.91" which many will recognise as the beachside Le Meridien Hotel in Libreville, Gabon. Or, enable the LatLng Tool Tip or Marker in the 'Maps Labs' section bottom left.

Key that into a GPS unit and at least you'll know how far away the hotel is when you're riding in circles round the slums. Even though you'll get there in the end, this sort of preparation can save stressful hours of pannier bashing through city traffic.

In my experience you commonly get the side of the road wrong when either you've been on tracks with little traffic for days, or you pull off the highway in a rural area for a lazy lunch. On returning to the road, the lack of any roadside infrastructure or momentary passing traffic sees you instinctively do what you've done all your riding years and head off down what's the wrong side of the road. Hopefully someone will point this out before something terrible happens and luckily such mistakes are usually made on quiet roads.

The other time you might blow it is when you've been riding for 20 hours non-stop, chomping Nescafé straight out of the jar. In a moment of frazzled panic you don't know if right is wrong or left is right. This confusion can mess you up even if you're in a country where they drive on the side that you're used to back home. As a Brit for example, you assume anything 'abroad' must equal driving on the other side of the road. Not if it's Kenya or Thailand or crazy India, where left is right, right is wrong and might is right anyway. One trick that helps me is visualising a memorable street scene back home. To a Brit, Australasian or southern African, most of the world is on the other side; remember the homely scene and get on the other side, quick (except when you shouldn't).

CITY STRATEGIES

Cairo, Quito, Dakar, Delhi; it's a good thing they're all so far apart, but like it or not your ride will be punctuated by visits to cities like these where dealing with congestion, noise and pollution comes on top of security issues and the expense of staying there. You need to go to these places for spares or repairs, to check email, get visas and, who knows, maybe even to stroll around the national museum or admire the Old Town.

If you have the choice, try to arrange visits to big cities on your terms. Above all, in a big, unfamiliar city it helps to **know where you're heading**, as opposed to blundering around looking for a cheap hotel in the old quarter. If you're having trouble finding the place you fixed on, hire a taxi driver or a kid on a moped to lead you there.

Initially it can be less stressful to camp or stay at a small hotel on the **outskirts** and bus in to see the sights or do the errands on foot, happy that you're not paying a fortune in a downtown hotel and that your bike is secure. Some places like Islamabad and cities in East Africa have centrally located camping parks (sometimes guarded), which solve the issue of location and expense, and of course these are great places to meet other travellers too. Many cities have guarded parking compounds, but as these are usually a piece of waste ground that has yet to be developed they're not necessarily good spots to leave a bike. Ask and you'll find that many small hotels will have a courtyard or even a storage lock-up where they'll be happy to put your bike, while others will allow you to ride it right into reception overnight.

A single, en suite.

Borders and checkpoints

No two ways about it, border crossings will be the most predictably intimidating episodes on your journey. Expect to encounter crowds of pushy locals, signs you can't read and instructions you can't understand, as well as hustlers looking to make a tip, and officials struck down with narcolepsy at the very sight of a starry-eyed foreigner waving a passport.

On top of all this is the worry that your papers aren't up to scratch or that a search will reveal something restricted such as a GPS or alcohol. The learning curve can be so steep you feel you need an ice axe and crampons as your passport disappears in one direction and your vehicle documents in another.

Borders

Notorious crossings include entering western Russia, mostly due to the language and forms; Egypt, especially at Aswan coming up from Sudan; the Mauritanian–Senegalese border at Rosso; and some Central American crossings, where $5 handed out here and there keeps things moving. If you get through any of these in less than an hour and for free you've done well.

Elsewhere, where an alphabet or numerals are unfamiliar to you – notably Arabic – local 'helpers' in league with the officials may try and overcharge you on genuine mandatory expenses like insurance or other permits. The main Iran–Turkey border at Bazargan is known for this so learn your **Arabic numerals**; it's not hard – see p254.

Remember you're not the first person to put up with this and at the very worst your naivety or momentary weakness may cost a few dollars. As with the rude staff you often have to deal with at consulates, look at these bottlenecks as the small price you pay for the freedom of being out on the road.

Border strategies

Over the weeks and months border procedures get easier to decipher as you learn the drill and the right levels of assertiveness required to slip through. Here are some guidelines; you'll soon develop your own tricks and strategies:

- Remain polite and smile a lot. They're stuck here day in, day out and don't get paid any more for being efficient.
- Impatience is usually counter-productive. Settle in for the long haul and have food and water on hand.
- Accept delays, queues and sudden 'lunch breaks' taken by the officials.
- Obey all the instructions for searches, however onerous.
- Resist confrontations; bite your lip in the face of provocation.
- But don't put up with people pushing in, outright theft, or 'This for me, yes?' attempts at petty extortion.

Stoicism and good humour can defuse a tense situation. Try to remember that the glamorous benefits of an ill-fitting uniform and an old machine gun soon pale when you're living in a tin shed far from your family and haven't been paid for six months. Recognise that if there's something wrong with your paperwork they have a legitimate excuse to follow their rules. Read the situation. If there's an opportunity to make a gift to cover a genuine transgression, pay up if you want to get moving.

The great thing about the comparatively slack attitude to rules and regulations in the AMZ is that it can work in your favour. An expired visa or other irregularity is not always the inflexible 'rules-are-rules' situation in Europe or North America that would see you locked up or on the next plane out. A small consideration and a promise to get it fixed is all that is needed to keep going.

Bribes

It's important to recognise that **bribes** aren't exclusively the unceasing daylight robbery of gullible foreigners, but are a way of life in the countries you'll visit. You may resent this custom but that's just what it is, a custom that oils the wheels. A few dollars or euros can save hours, and these payments are usually tiny in the overall scheme of things. You'll know when you're expected to pay – accept it as part of travelling, but don't assume you have to pay your way through every border or checkpoint just because your foreign number plate reads like a string of dollar signs.

Border procedures

Paperwork featuring impressive stamps is much admired out in the world and you'll amass a fair bit of locally issued documentation once you start crossing borders. One traveller described the paperwork collected at an Egyptian border as a 'folder that resembles a post-grad dissertation'.

To give you an idea of what to expect, the most common requirements are listed below. Apart from

visas, unless otherwise stated all these **documents** are obtained at the relevant border or office. Some border officials may want to see vaccination certificates and in some countries there may be further procedures like the need to register with the police elsewhere within a given number of days. It may also help not to display any controversial or flashy gadgets like satnavs or sat phones too prominently. On arrival take a deep breath and proceed as follows:

- Track down and fill out an immigration card.
- Take the card and get your passport stamped.
- Complete a form to temporarily import your bike (your vehicle ownership document will be needed).
- Or get your carnet stamped.
- Fill out a currency declaration form, which may include 'valuables'.
- Declare any restricted items or hide them well.
- Show vaccination certificates.
- Change money.
- Rent local number plates (Libya, Egypt, China, among others).
- Buy motor insurance, if possible or necessary.

Roadside checkpoints

Highway checkpoints are imposed by many countries to control or monitor the movement of the local population, very often on the main road into and out of a big town. They also crop up near borders to catch illegal immigrants and smugglers and where you may also have to present your recently acquired papers if you've just entered the country. Very often you'll be recognised as a harmless tourist and waved through, but no matter how many times this has happened before, **always slow down** and make eye contact with the soldier – even if they happen to be quickly zipping up their pants – before riding on. And in countries where assassins or suicide bombers use bikes, proper checkpoint etiquette is vital.

Some checkpoints alongside strategic installations or disputed areas such as eastern Turkey will have elaborate arrangements of spikes, oil drums and single-lane barricades to slow you down. There'll be a 'Stop' sign set up a short distance from the actual checkpoint and possibly a guy with a gun up a tower too. At night these places may require you to turn off your lights. Wait at the 'Stop' sign until you're waved on, especially if there's already a vehicle up ahead.

As in the Moroccan-occupied part of Western Sahara, checkpoints may be required to take your personal and vehicle details, which is usually written by hand into an ageing ledger. You can speed things up for both you and them by having this information pre-printed on a form to hand out. You can download and if necessary, adapt a French–English **checkpoint form** in Word at 🖥 www.morocco-overland.com/fiche. These forms can also be handed over to hotel receptionists at check-in. At a checkpoint (or a hotel), resist giving your passport away to anyone other than men in hats, and even then be wary in suspicious situations.

Sometimes you'll be pulled over just because you're a foreigner on a flash bike and the cops are curious or bored. This curiosity can extend to hospitality, or it can go the other way and they can try it on, making up some bogus infringement, as they often do in western Russia. As always, the old trick of playing dumb and pretending not to understand them or any shared Earthly language can encourage them to lose interest. But, as with all such encounters it's best to flip up the visor look them in the eye and kick off with a local greeting and a smile, as well as accede to all reasonable requests.

A working knowledge of the current composition of the **Manchester United** football team (🖥 www.manutd.com) can also help break the ice. In the 1970s many overlanders crossed Africa without delay by merely shouting 'Bobi Sharlton' at every official they met. 'Vaiyn Rouni' might do the trick these days, but unfortunately you're at their mercy and predatory types can read if you're nervous.

A lot depends on how you respond to each other, which is why **a greeting and a smile** is a good way to start, even if it's ignored. They may expect you to have a disrespectful attitude of a cocky foreigner that's in need of taking down a peg or two. You may pull over for the nth time that day with a scowl, thinking this is another roadside scam and this time you're not going to stand for it, but learning how to slip through checkpoints like a well-lubed eel is all part of the game.

Changing money and bargaining

As mentioned early on, the best form of money is cash drawn from ATMs. The best hard currencies are **euros** in North and West Africa and parts of the Middle East, and **US dollars** everywhere else, best brought from home or withdrawn from an ATM.

© Darrin Johansen

Once you're on the road you'll find some borders have currency-changing kiosks with posted rates, while others will have a guy walking around with a satchel full of local cash and a calculator. Otherwise, the nearest town will have a bank, ideally with a cashpoint, which is the simplest way to obtain local currency without getting diddled. If there's a good network of them you need withdraw only a little cash at a time. This way you won't get stuck trying to change a weak local currency back into something useful. Even if that's possible, it'll be at such a bad rate that it's often hardly worth it.

If ATMs are unknown or they don't take your cards, it may be possible to buy the local currency in the preceding country. Otherwise, changing money officially can take hours in some banks, going from one counter to another. **Currency-exchange kiosks** in the centre of large towns won't necessarily be as dodgy as they look, can save hours and might even offer a slightly better rate than a bank. And in some countries you can simply pay your hotel bills or whatever in foreign currency.

'Sorry, no change' is something you're bound to hear when paying for a local service with a high-denomination note. When you've got nothing else there's no way round it, so learn to hoard **low-denomination notes**: they're useful for tips.

Currency Declaration Forms

Some countries try and undermine currency black markets by using Currency Declaration Forms (CDF). On it you fill out all the foreign currency you're bringing into a country, and possibly other sellable valuables like cameras. Any further official exchange transactions you make in that country must match receipts or entries on the CDF, so that when you leave the cash you brought in equals what you're taking out, less what you officially exchanged.

Half the time these forms aren't even checked when you leave, but don't count on it. Any hard currency you don't declare on the form must obviously not be discovered on departure, but having a **stash of undeclared money** is a good way to cover unexpected costs or do a quick black-market deal.

LIFE ON THE ROAD

BLACK MARKET

Using the black market to change foreign currency into local at an advantageous rate is an accepted, if now less common, part of travel. It's also a popular way of fleecing naive travellers and by its very nature is illegal, leaving you liable to fines, confiscation of funds and even imprisonment.

Use the black market by all means (sometimes there is no choice and some banks will even encourage it to save work for themselves), but keep your eyes open and your wits about you. If you're a beginner, here are some guidelines:

- Establish exactly how many 'dogons' you're being offered for a dollar (for example). Repeat to them: 'So you are offering me 400 dogons for one dollar?' and if they agree then spell out the total amount you want to exchange: 'So you will give me 6000 dogons for 15 dollars?'
- Ask to see the currency offered and check that the notes have the right number of zeros. It's helpful to learn to read the nine cardinal Arabic numerals if heading that way – see p254.
- If there's room for negotiation, go ahead. A wily black-marketeer is going to offer as little as he can for your valuable currency.
- Deal one-to-one and don't get rushed or drawn into any shady corners.

Watch out for **sleight of hand**. I'm sure I was caught out with what I call the 'Romanian Hand Trick' near the Libyan border once. There is some ploy where they count out the money offered, then give it to you to count, which you do and find everything in order. They take it back to check, and even though you're staring intently at their hands, something happens and you later you realise you got less than you counted. If this 'you count then hand back' scenario happens, be on high alert, try and resist it or count it all again.

The black market can represent a major boost to your funds in some places such as Venezuela, but don't stick your neck out for a measly 10%. While you should never take them for granted, you'll soon get the hang of these useful if illegal street deals. And if you're ever unsure, trust your instincts and walk away.

© S. Lord

BARGAINING

Whether bargaining for souvenirs or negotiating for services, the first step is to appraise the object of your desire or your service needs and ask yourself **what you are prepared to pay** for it. Even if it's over the odds, once you've established this in your mind you should have no reason to feel cheated once you pay that amount.

When it comes to souvenirs, all the time-worn tricks will be tried to make you spend more: free shipping, two for the price of one plus a free pendant, but stick to your price for what you want unless you want the object at any cost. You may well be asked to 'give me your best price', but remember that if you do name a price, bargaining etiquette deems that you're obliged to pay it, so don't let any figure pass your lips that you're not prepared to pay. Bide your time, because this – along with that wad in your pocket – is your greatest asset. If you have the chance, look around for a few days and get to know the vendors and what they have (often it's all from the same source). If you find it hard to simply walk away, say you might come back tomorrow. Try not to allow yourself to be intimidated, however charming the vendor. In Islamic lands be wary of being drawn in by a carpet seller to have tea unless you're confident you can handle the extreme pressure that may be put on you. In Morocco these vendors are notorious and can get aggressive to the point of virtually robbing you.

Negotiating a price for other services like mechanical repairs, guides or food is less customary. There's usually a **set price** for such commodities. Despite the market scene in *The Life of Brian*, locals don't go to the souk every day and engage in protracted negotiations for the same bunch of coriander they bought last week, unless it's a seasonal commodity or the quality has varied. But if you feel you're being overcharged, most likely because of your origins, give it a go or ask the price in advance. In some cases, not to barter is seen as weak and not playing the game. It's all part of the travel experience, with market encounters one of the few occasions you get to interact with locals as normal people. Enjoy it.

Keeping in touch

NICK TAYLOR

Having reliable communications is essential, not least when something goes wrong. We're lucky to live in an age where **mobile communications** are well within an our budget.

GSM/mobile phones

Assuming you have a **GSM phone** (known in various countries as a 'mobile', 'cell' or 'handy'), you'll probably be aware that they're both expensive to use outside of your home country, and need to be less than 40km (23 miles) from the nearest GSM mast in line of sight. They can be ideal for short calls or text messages to co-ordinate a rendezvous with others, and are especially useful if you get split up while riding with others. In remote rural or wilderness areas there probably won't be a signal, although in an emergency getting to high ground is always worth a go.

Per capita usage of mobiles in some African and Asian countries is much higher than in the West. The market is huge, especially among the young, with

LIFE ON THE ROAD

DO-IT-ALL SMART PHONES

Smart phones are now becoming so clever there's a temptation to use them to do it all: comms, GPS navigation, text/music storage and still/video images. Soon enough they'll be measuring your blood pressure levels, too.

It sounds like a brilliant do-it-all tool until it gets lost, stolen or broken – then you lose it all. Better to see all the functions just listed as a handy **back up** if your separate sat nav, tablet or camera pack up.

Calling International Rescue.

mobile phone boutiques and advertising everywhere. In some countries private investment has seen the network leapfrog a land line system that was never that good in the first place, and per-minute charges are **much less** than we're used to back home, especially for calls abroad.

Providing your own handset is **unlocked** to accept alternative providers (something easily done in any phone boutique), buying a **local SIM card** is a cheap way to stay in touch. If you can't unlock your phone, the cheapest Nokia handset (pictured above) does nothing but voice and texts and costs as little as $25. With your local SIM card just make sure you're joining a network that'll cover you on your intended travels; a little research online may help. India for example has several **regional providers** who might as well be in adjacent countries; what works in one state won't work elsewhere. Otherwise, to save you buying card after card, international roaming SIM cards are available from many providers, offering a good discount over your domestic provider when calling from abroad.

For a link back home there are a number of options. GSM phones are obviously the most convenient. Even without a local SIM card, the odd text message or a brief urgent call is usually cheap or important enough to be worthwhile. Failing that, if you want to have a good natter with those back home, **international phone cards** to use from a phone box or land line will be widely available.

Internet access

Increasingly we're travelling with our own laptops, tablets or smart phones, connecting them to a café's ethernet connection or picking up a **wi-fi** signal anywhere, either secure or unencrypted. While some parts of the world seem to be connected to the internet by a frayed washing line, in terms of price per bit, getting a quick email out can't be beaten. Remember, if you get a good enough connection, voice and even video calling is possible through Skype or one of the other voice over internet protocol (VoIP) services. All will be far cheaper than using your GSM phone. Using internet cafés is also an ideal way to upload larger amounts of data to a website, especially photos and video.

The downside of **internet cafés** is their computers, complete with Fanta-stained mouse-mats, baffling keyboard layouts and who-knows-what sort of software installed – a key-logger recording your online banking password, perhaps? So it's best never to risk such activity on publicly used computers.

If you're using a smart phone or tablet, then connecting via the internet (rather than using the expensive GSM network) is another great option. You can compose offline and it'll all be sent automatically when you connect to the internet. Typically, you'll need a wireless network connection, but as with GSM mobiles, that's now becoming the rule rather than the exception. You can also install apps like **Skype** and benefit from cheap calls over the web.

SATELLITE COMMS

Once the preserve of large corporations and government agencies, the cost of satellite communication has now dropped dramatically. It's the only option when you're way out of GSM range and miles from the nearest internet café. You may never use it, but if you're planning riding in remote areas, sat comms can be a good back up if things go wrong.

Old model Thuraya (with email ability) makes a new friend.

Satellite phones

There are two principal **satellite phones** to choose from: Thuraya and Iridium. **Iridium** is the only company that offers truly global coverage, but if your travels exclude the Americas, Dubai-based **Thuraya** offers coverage from Ireland down to Australia and from Angola across to Mongolia. In other words, everywhere on land except Siberia, southern Africa and, as mentioned, the Americas. Charges per minute are up to $1.50 with Thuraya and at least $1.50 with Iridium, often cheaper than your GSM's roaming charge.

At around £400 used in the UK, the latest handsets for either network are comparatively expensive but are as small and sophisticated as a mobile from several years ago. But as a result of the wars in Iraq and Afghanistan, larger first-generation Thuraya handsets from Ascom and Hughes can still be found on ebay for $200. They have pitiful batteries but all supported SMS and satellite email as well as GSM usage (see below). Not all current Thuraya handsets like the SO-2510 can do this.

Both Iridium and Thuraya offer **data connections** of up to 9.6kbps (Iridium needs additional software, otherwise it's a miserable 2.4 kbps). With an enabled handset, short **emails** can be sent, and they'll probably be as short as an SMS as you'll be typing them on the telephone keypad.

Sat phones may also accept your regular mobile's SIM card to work in GSM mode, should you be in range and the charges cheaper. This can be handy if your GSM phone packs up, but in practical terms it's better to have a separate GSM phone as well as a sat phone. Some handsets, notably Thuraya, can also pick up a GPS position after a few minutes, which can be easily forwarded as an SMS, but this feature can't really be used for navigation.

Just like a GPS, a sat phone also needs to be out in the open to get a good signal. With Thuraya handsets, it helps to point the retractable antenna towards Somalia, above which their geo-stationary satellite is positioned.

Potential legal issues

Once outside of the developed world, radios and other communications equipment including sat phones are generally **prohibited for civilian use**. In practice, the question is rarely asked when crossing borders, and the worst thing likely to happen is a sat phone might be confiscated – though if you're currently rotting in some awful, sub-Saharan prison, remember that the decision to take equipment like this into the country solely rests with you!

LIFE ON THE ROAD

EMERGENCIES – EPIRB VERSUS SPOT

It's a mistake to confuse a 'fun' Spot device with something like a PRB – a personal rescuer beacon, also known as Emergency Position Indicating Radio Beacons, ELB or PLB (locator beacon) as used by sailors and wilderness travellers in North America.

Though more reliable and designed to communicate with a regional Search & Rescue network, setting off your PRB or pressing '911' on your Spot is unlikely to result in anything much in the depths of the Karakum desert or anywhere in the interior of Africa, despite what it may do in Alaska or the Caribbean, for example.

The good thing with a Spot or similar device compared to a PRB is that it **contacts specified individuals** who know what you're up to, rather than an anonymous S&R base. These individuals can hopefully act on your plight, although who they call and who can actually mobilise a rescue in Turkmenistan without dropping a huge bill in your lap is the big question. In a real fix a **satellite phone** is so much better.

Such a situation befell AMH contributor Andy Pag in northern India in early 2010. Being very popular with jihadis and smugglers throughout North Africa and west Asia, Thurayas were **banned in India** following the Mumbai attacks of 2008. Unfortunately, Andy – along with the other billion people in India – was the first to find this out, which led to a short spell in prison followed by a few months of legal procrastination before he was let off with a 1000-rupee fine. Like GSM phones, sat phones can be easily tracked, so unless you know better, hide them well at borders and in dodgy countries save their use for emergencies.

Satellite trackers

The simplest device to let others know where you are is an easy-to-use **personal tracker** like the palm-sized Spot 2 GPS Messenger. No doubt more sophisticated units will appear and it's quite possible that a GPS-enabled smart phone will do the same. Once turned on and locked onto the satellties, a Spot can send your position with either an 'All OK', a 'Help' (or another predetermined message set by you on your Spot account webpage), to anyone's email or mobile on your list from almost anywhere in the world. You have to subscribe to the service, which costs at least $100 a year, as well as navigate the convoluted Spot website to set up your unit, but it still works out cheaper than daily text messages and best of all, gives peace of mind to those back home.

A Spot 2 can also be configured to pinpoint your position every ten minutes on an embedded Google map page. Doing so, the AAA batteries may last up to two weeks and it's worth knowing that Spots require **lithium batteries** which aren't so easy to get hold of; other types may not work even though the lights will blink convincingly. That's one problem with Spots; you're never really sure if the information has been received so it's best to advise people back home not to rely on it completely; for that texts are still best.

Summary: basic comms for overlanding
- One mobile phone per person and the means to charge them.
- Local SIM cards bought as you go.
- A tablet or a laptop with an ethernet cable for internet cafés without wi-fi.
- Satellite phone for emergencies or where no GSM coverage.
- Spot Messenger or similar to record your position on a website.

Maps and route finding

Although more than one rider has boasted of setting out with just an inflatable globe or no map at all, there's more than enough adventure waiting for you out there so you'll want a map of some kind to estimate distances, find towns with fuel, contemplate interesting-looking diversions, and to help you navigate through or around a congested city.

Mapping these days comes in four forms: traditional inexpensive **paper** maps; the same map in **digital** form on CD or a download to display on a screen or print off – a raster map; scrollable and zoomable **vector maps** for satnavs like Garmin Zumos which can be expensive, or free from OMS (see p131), as well as **online** maps like Google Maps which of course require internet.

PAPER MAPS

The digital revolution may be mapping the world for us using online satellite imagery and routeable street-level satnavs, but until internet access becomes an atmospheric phenomenon and we can project a usefully sized holographic screen from our smartphone, some sort of **paper mapping** is still desirable. Light, portable, robust and battery-free, as with books there's still no better way of easily displaying

and accessing a large amount of information over a large area in a simple and inexpensive medium.

In the 1970s the Cold War saw costly global mapping programmes that are never likely to be repeated. As a result the entire planet is covered by detailed **large-scale maps** from that era down to 1:200,000 scale. These maps may be old, but as change in many wild places is often geological rather than historical they can still be useful. These maps include the **American TPC** and **ONC** aeronautical maps (slowly being withdrawn) and the **Soviet series** in three scales (more details about both on 🖳 www.sahara-overland.com/maps) available as official or bootleg digital downloads for little more than the cost of the paper version. Touratech QV mapping uses these maps with annotations.

Map scales

A paper map's scale is given as a ratio of how much smaller that map is than the actual land surface: a 1:1,000,000 (1m) scale map is a million times smaller than the area it represents. This can cause some confusion as what are called small-scale maps have a bigger ratio number like 1:4m and cover a larger area in less detail. Small scale = small [amount of] detail but big number and area; large scale = large [amount of] detail.

METRIC AND IMPERIAL MAP SCALES

Map scales are given in metric or imperial ratios. Most of the world uses metric, even the UK; the US and a few other places hang on to imperial. With the metric format millimetres are easily translated into kilometres. With US mapping, imperial measurements like inches and miles prevail and so it's common for map scales produced there to have some abstruse ratio like 1:633,600. This might not mean much to anyone apart from the map being 633,600 times smaller than real life, but it happens to equal an intuitive 10 miles to 1 inch. The 1:4m Michelin, for example, represents 40km to 1cm, or 63.1 miles to 1 inch.

Maps using either scales are fine, but out in the overland zone imperialists will want to try and get used to **thinking metrically**. As 1km is 0.621 of a mile, a quick formula is to **halve kilometres and add a quarter to get miles**: 100km / 2 + 25% = 62.5 miles. Near enough. You may even want to get your bike's analogue speedometer changed to a metric instrument. Some modern digital speedos like Yamaha's XT660Z can be configured to display mph or kph. Very handy.

Small-scale maps with scales from 1:2m to 1:5m give you a big overall picture of an area, which makes them great for planning a trip, if not necessarily for following a route. A good example is the Michelin 700 series of maps covering Africa at 1:4 million. Riding in an unfamiliar country, anything beyond 1:5m scale becomes progressively less detailed and so less useful.

Medium-scale maps between 1:500,000 and 1:2m are the optimum for riding. On a 1:1m map, one millimetre represents one kilometre on the ground (1cm = 10km, 1 inch = 15.8 miles). If the cartographic design is good, the map will be easily interpreted and the millimetre/kilometre relationship makes distances on the map easy to visualise. A typical 1:1m map might cover between six and eight degrees of longitude and from four to six degrees of latitude, which at the median latitude of the two tropics (currently 23° 26' 16" north or south of the equator) is around 600–800km (370–500 miles) from east to west and 440–660km (270–410 miles) from north to south.

Anything **large scale** below 1:500,000 (1cm = 5km, 1 inch = 7.9 miles) is where terrain and landforms as much as any tracks govern where you can ride. In other words, when things get gnarly you'll need knobblies and a large-scale map to work out a way through.

As you can see though, you can potentially cross a 1m-scale map is a couple of easy days and so for a long ride that can add up to a lot of maps which is why a small scale map or driving atlas is preferred, backed up with maps in a GPS or satnav.

Latitude and longitude

If you expect to be using GPS to calculate your position on a paper map rather than just relying on a spot on your satnav, you'll need maps with a **lat–long grid** (otherwise you can skip this bit). This is a printed grid that criss-crosses the face of the map, and not just a lat–long scale shown around the edges; not all maps have this.

Latitude and longitude is a grid system used to pinpoint a location on the spherical Earth using horizontal (latitude) and vertical (longitude) measurements. (If ever you forget which is which I find the expression "in southern latitudes" helps). The equator is the zero line of reference for latitude, dividing the globe into northern and southern hemispheres. The Greenwich or Prime Meridian is the zero line for longitude, dividing the world into western and eastern hemispheres.

Lines of latitude are parallel, horizontal rings stacked up like cake layers. They divide the globe into surface bands at equal distance from each other so that anywhere on the globe each degree of latitude is about 110km or 68 miles (or 60 nautical miles) apart. One minute of latitude (a 60th of a degree) equals one nautical mile or, more usefully on land, 1.85km or 1.15 miles. One second of latitude (a 60th of a minute) equals 30.8m or just over 101 feet.

Lines of longitude all converge at the poles, slicing the earth into vertical segments like a Terry's Chocolate Orange. The width of these segments varies, being widest at the equator where, like lines of latitude, they're around 110km apart. Moving away from the equator lines of longitude converge towards the poles, where they meet.

The lat–long grid divides the globe into **360 degrees** (abbreviated as °). Each degree is divided into 60 minutes (abbreviated as ') and each minute has 60 seconds (or "); this is easily remembered as °, ', ", or zero, one, two. Positions are shown with latitude (N or S) followed by longitude (E or W).

With this system of co-ordinates it's possible to give a **grid reference** for anywhere on the planet to an accuracy of 15m using just six digits of latitude and seven digits of longitude. A grid reference in the traditional format looks like this: N35° 02' 45.44" W90° 01' 22.56" (Graceland in Memphis). However, these days seconds have been superseded by decimal fractions of minutes, so that the grid reference for the home of the undisputed King of Rock 'n' Roll would now be written as: N35° 02.757' W90° 01.376', although for navigation purposes rounding it up to N35° 02.8' W90° 01.4' is sufficient.

The default on Google Maps uses decimal degrees so Graceland is 35.045956, -90.022933. The first figure is called a northing and if it's preceded by a minus it's south of the equator. The second figure is an easting, but being preceded by a minus in the case of Graceland means it's west of the Greenwich meridian. With this system the ° symbol is not used and the + symbol is considered redundant. You can set a high-end GPS and most satnav units to show a position in any of the above formats, and probably a few more besides.

Locating your position on a map

Locating your position on a map can only feasibly be done with a scale of 1:2m or less; beyond that, accuracy becomes hit and miss. If you expect to be doing this, a clear plastic ruler can help.

Putting a straight edge along a line of latitude will reveal that the seemingly horizontal line actually curves upwards in the northern hemisphere and downwards in the south. Meanwhile, measuring the distance between vertical lines of longitude will show them a little closer together at the top in the northern hemisphere and vice versa in the south. Only the equator can ever be depicted as a truly horizontal line. Depending on the map's projection, lines of latitude curve along a radius from the nearest pole, while longitudes diverge from the nearest pole. This means that **trying to draw your own grid** on a map with any degree of accuracy is not as easy as it sounds.

LIFE ON THE ROAD

Know your maps

There's a lot to be said for taking an interest in your maps. Inspect your route or area closely before you go there, study the key and see what everything means and how **relief and road hierarchies** are depicted. Although it might be the information you most need, not all maps are dependable in giving you an idea of what a road or the terrain may be like, so you'll soon learn if a map can be relied on.

You might occasionally expect to find that what's shown as a track on a map has now become a two-lane highway on the ground, but most frustrating is when what's depicted on a map as a good road turns out to be a track, especially if you're in a low-slung cruiser. Assuming a perfectly good road was not dug up in some barmy prisoner rehabilitation scheme, this is incompetent map-making and, like a travel guidebook making up information, you rightly begin to lose confidence in the product.

Along with accuracy, the best cartography offers a balanced combination of **clarity and detail** that enables you to read the terrain like a book. If you're lucky enough to live near somewhere like Stanfords Map Centre in London, you can inspect over half a dozen maps of the same country. Compare scales, prices and clarity and see which suits you best; not everyone likes the same look. On both my Sahara and Morocco websites (linked from the AMH website) I give detailed descriptions of the mapping choices covering those territories. The paper selection reviewed for Morocco gives a good analysis of the best European map publishers, which can probably be translated to their maps covering the rest of the world. Some recommendations are also given in the Route Outline sections.

In my experience it's a mistake to assume that, prior to producing a **new edition**, paper map publishers get someone to drive all the roads on a given map – even if you might think that's the whole point of a road map. On occasions I've found a redesigned cover is all you get with a new edition. For the retail price and volume of sales, it's just too expensive to get maps updated on the ground, especially with online mapping racing ahead. The reward for all this effort and expense will just be copied by other mapmakers.

In countries where the Latin alphabet is rarely used on road signs – including China, some Arab-speaking countries and Russia (see p223) – having a map using the **local alphabet** can be useful. Even if you don't understand it, a local will, and you can also compare the illegible (to you) squiggle on a road sign with the matching squiggle on the map, to work out where you're going.

SATNAV AND MAPPING

After centuries of paper mapping we're now becoming accustomed to using routeable satnavs to get around. We key in a destination and an on-screen map guides us all the way there, while if you can hear it, a soothing but authoritative voice tells us which turns and junctions to take along the way. It's a graphic, map-based version of what you might get in the 'Destination' menu on Google Maps.

In a foreign country that has satnav mapping coverage it also saves struggling with paper maps and illegible road signs when you want to be concentrating on navigating the mayhem around you. The problem is that this won-

LIFE ON THE ROAD

THE DIFFERENCE BETWEEN SATNAVS AND GPS

Satellite navigators such as the TomTom or the Garmin Nuci/Zumo have come to be known as **satnavs** (below centre). They feature a small touch screen and built-in street-level vector mapping that moves continuously, showing your position. Among many other features, satnavs are **routeable**, which means you can key in a destination and they'll work out what they think is the best way to get there by following the road network, with optional voice prompts.

A traditional GPS unit (below left) from Garmin or Magellan among others is more suited to non-motorised navigation in wilderness areas where there are few roads or landmarks, or at sea. The built-in map that comes with a new GPS unit is usually pretty basic and will get worse once you leave the territory where you bought it, to the point where it might only show borders and a few cities and towns. However, as on satnavs, better maps are around.

The common 12-volt cigarette lighter power plugs supplied

with your satnav or available for your GPS unit won't always keep a good contact on rough tracks so it's worth either hard-wiring them or converting the ends to more secure **DIN plugs** as used on BMWs and Triumphs, among others. If contact is lost for a split second your unit reverts to batteries (if fitted) and is usually set to turn off in 30 seconds. With a GPS unit you'll also lose a track log, if you were recording one. A satnav losing contact is less of a drama as most rarely depend on the track log feature, if included.

Many **smart phones** like the Nokia pictured right have a GPS and vector mapping facility just like a satnav, though operating full time in GPS mode eats battery power, so find a way of plugging it into the bike on the road. Assuming you won't have world mapping in your smart phone, it can at least be used as a way of acquiring a waypoint. With a waypoint and a paper map with a lat–long grid and no one around to ask, you can at least figure out if you're in Kazakhstan or Kyrgyzstan.

der of technology has yet to cover the world adequately and it'll be many years before it reaches the levels of street-by-street mapping we're used to in Europe and North America.

But some countries are already giving it a go. Right now you can buy downloadable maps for a Garmin or TomTom satnav for South Africa and East Africa, Turkey, Chile, Brazil and Argentina, western Russia, India, Malaysia and Thailand – the total cost: several hundred pounds. Very often not all corners of the country are covered in the detail you may be expecting, and many interesting places – some Andean countries of South America, Central America, much of Africa and Asia – are not yet mapped.

As with computer software, certain advocates of **open sourcing** like www.openstreetmap.org have taken it on themselves to try and map the world and then offer their versions for free, or for a minimal price; in places these have better detail than what Garmin and the others sell. Other sources of downloadable satnav mapping include 🖳 www.gpsunderground.com or 🖳 www.gotrekkers.com, though there are often arcane importing hurdles.

Just remember, it can be a mistake to rely solely on satnavs as you may do back home. Above all they lack the **big picture** around you, currently something that can only be achieved with a paper map.

LIFE ON THE ROAD

A slim but unweatherproof Garmin Nuvi costs from £70 used and will survive downpours tucked behind a screen. Their bulkier, bike-based Zumo unit is much more costly.

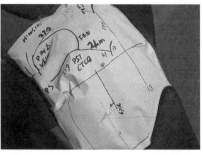

Old school nav still works as well as ever.

Maps for your satnav

For a GPS or satnav unit to be useful in a navigation sense, they're best combined with imported mapping onto a GPS unit with a **usefully sized screen**. Aim for a 5-inch diagonal screen as found on some TomToms and Garmins.

Cars can use a laptop running GPS software plugged into a regular GPS receiver to display their position; on a bike this is not practical although now with Garmin CustomMaps it's at possible to eliminate the laptop and scan, calibrate then import a digital image of a decent paper map (a raster map) into a Garmin GPS unit, providing it has enough chip power to display it. You could even scan in a satellite image which you'd imagine will be the next level in satnav display options; photographic 'streetview' type imagery is already available. Whether you can be bothered to do any of this is another matter, though it would work well in remote areas where proprietary satnav maps have not caught up and probably never will. Even then you can just whip out a paper map down to 200,000 scale and transpose your lat and long off the GPS.

Digital maps

Raster maps can be bought (see above), but now any map in digital form, even a scanned paper map, can be used as long as it's been **calibrated**, something that's easily done with software like OziExplorer, Fugawi, TTQV, or MacGPS Pro, or as an image layer imported onto Google Earth and manipulated. The accuracy of your position on such a map will depend on how accurate the map was in the first place (a matter of distortion or 'projection' – the perennial cartographic quandary of displaying a spherical object like a planet in a two-dimensional plane like a sheet of paper or screen) and how well it was scanned. Scanning a map is a time-consuming task and can be an infringement of copyright. Of course it's only the former that puts people off, so have a dig around to see what's online.

Among others, the German mapping house Reise Know-How covers the whole world except far eastern Russia with over 160 maps, all of which are available as **digital pre-calibrated raster maps** for the above-listed software except MacGPS Pro; they cost around €15 – ironically about twice the price of the identical plastic paper map. Other far-sighted mapmakers may be following suit, but hopefully with the price the right way round.

Also from Germany, Touratech (🖳 www.ttqv.com) sells all sorts of digital mapping for GPS units (as opposed to satnavs). In places the detail matches or exceeds mapping sold by TomTom and Garmin, but then so do the prices. Although I've not used their maps, knowing Touratech's background I suspect their mapping catalogue is bound to be more practical in the AMZ than the more urban or domestic offerings available for satnavs, but be warned, you need to get right into digital mapping to get the best out of TTQV. Unless you're a computer techie you may find yourself pulling your hair out trying to get an expensive new map to display on your satnav.

Recording or following a track log
One thing a GPS can do that most low-end satnavs can't is record your track. A **track log** can be set up to record your position – or 'drop a breadcrumb' – every 10 seconds, 10 metres, or as frequently as you like. All your unit needs is the **memory** to store all this data, either built in or on a removable mini-SD card. Your position, distance, speed, altitude and other parameters are also recorded on a track log, which can be fun to review once it's downloaded and viewed with the software listed below.

You can also do this 'remotely' with the Spot II as mentioned earlier and have your position pop up on an online map viewable by anyone you like, with just a ten minute delay. You can then save your route as a track log (such as the Kolyma Highway recorded by Kym Bolton: see my OLH Website), as a Google Earth file for all to view, or even **import** it into another GPS unit.

Tracking down the right river crossing on the steadily disintegrating Kolyma is an example where such information can be useful, but then you have to remember that like others, Kym managed to drive the Road of Bones in the first place *without any GPS data*, just his common sense. On off-road routes it certainly helps, but in my experience some travellers can get a bit obsessed with accumulating masses of waypoints, POIs and track logs for anything and everything.

Online maps
As long as you have internet you have access to the vast range of global mapping available online from Google or Microsoft's Bing, to name just two. Both offer **WYSIWYG aerial imagery** supplied either by NavTeq or Tele Atlas, with a quick random check showing Google being far superior in resolution.

As mentioned already, aerial images are very useful, especially in cities, but the plain map graphic screens can be a less cluttered way of getting a good city-centre map. Using a screen-grab feature or software like Google Map Buddy to make a bigger-than-screen-sized map, you can then calibrate it by layering it over Google Earth (as explained earlier), download it to view as an image or print it off. Doing this you then have **a paper or GPS raster map** of just about anywhere in the world, with Google Map back-up to help identify actual buildings from a waypoint so you know what you're looking for when you get there. With a wi-fi or GSM signal it's possible to cut out the paper element and view such a map on a smart phone or iPad, except that with a phone you'll be paying heavily for the privilege anywhere abroad, unless you use a local SIM card. Some can be bought for internet-only use costing just a euro a day.

Don't forget that in most cases, unless you're engaged in some black op, entirely adequate paper maps exist individually or can be found in guidebooks. Also be aware that out in the world, paper, digital and online maps will never

... successful navigation anywhere requires keeping track of two things: where you are now and which way you want to go.

be able to keep up with what you might actually encounter in any given place or season. At this point you'll be no better off than Lewis and Clark, Marco Polo or Bilbo Baggins and will have to pull up and **ask a local**.

FINDING YOUR WAY AROUND

Stepping back a bit from the mind-boggling possibilities of digital mapping, successful navigation anywhere basically requires keeping track of two things: where you are now and which way you want to go. To do this you can deploy any number of the navigation aids listed here.

Compass and trip meter

When travelling in unfamiliar territories it's always useful to know **which way is north**, not least when trying to ascertain whether you're heading in the right direction out of a city. As long as you can see it, the position of **the sun** will help you with this. Using an analogue watch, point the hour hand at the sun; halfway between that point and 12 on your watch is south in the northern hemisphere (or north when south of the equator). After some practice you can be accurate with just a quick glance at the sun and the time.

A **magnetic compass** is easier to read and doesn't need an external power source, but when used on or close to a bike can become unreliable due to interference from steel components and the electrical field. I keep one in a sleeve pocket where it's vibration free, easy to read and is usually with you when you get lost on foot in the souk before they lock you in for the night.

Get into the habit of resetting the **trip odometer** on your speedo/trip computer or your GPS each time you fill up with fuel. The odometer can vaguely help establish your position and is the most reliable way of gauging how far you can ride on a tank or if your bike is using more fuel than normal.

Not getting lost

Blindly following roads or tracks without giving a thought to landmarks, orientation or maps is the most common way to get lost. If in doubt, stop and think or settle on ending up somewhere unexpected – it's all part of the adventure. Otherwise look around you, consult your map or ask a local. If none of this is possible and you haven't a clue, **turning back** is the most sensible action. At some point along the way you just came you were not lost.

Lost near towns

Between towns there's usually only one main road heading in one direction, but getting confused near settlements is a universal experience, especially settlements that are inland or lacking in some other helpful geographical landmark to narrow your options, be it Bogotá or a Turkish village.

The bigger the settlement the more roads converge, offering a baffling choice of routes as well as more distractions than you can handle while trying not to run over a street vendor. Especially in the countryside, routes might connect a village to all sorts of places: the river, another village, a rubbish tip; or it might start off in your intended direction only to turn away or peter out.

To-ing and fro-ing across town is more frustrating than unnerving, though it's something that, where available, good satnav mapping can minimise.

Ask the audience

Asking someone can be a hit-or-miss affair which is why we cling so dearly to our nav gadgets. A lot depends on who and how you ask. Don't make Tony Christie's elementary error of **pre-suggestion** by asking 'Is this the way to Amarillo?'. Instead, take a tip from Dionne Warwick and enquire 'Hello. Do you know the way to San José?'. It won't guarantee a correct answer but hopefully won't elicit the **automatic affirmative** nod just to please or get rid of a stranger. Although you may be steaming from the ears by this stage, remember to be polite and, as with all exchanges, start with greetings and handshakes.

> Don't make Tony Christie's error of pre-suggestion by asking 'Is this the way to Amarillo?'. Instead, take a tip from Dionne Warwick and enquire 'Hello. Do you know the way to San José?' There's a big difference.

Unless you're in a place where people might be literate, avoid asking locals to look at your map; in the remote corners of the AMZ it's generally only tourists who use and understand maps. However, drawing a mud map in the dirt, or in the dust on your tank top can be useful.

It also helps to **ask the right person**. I've found policemen, soldiers and older men to be the most reliable, knowledgeable and straight. Women and young girls might rarely travel out of the village and could be unaware of anything beyond a limited radius; they will seldom be drivers, and are less likely to speak English than their menfolk. In some remote places they also may be embarrassed by your attention; elsewhere they'll enjoy teasing you. Groups of kids or young boys may mislead you for a laugh, to get a tip or cadge a free ride to impress their friends.

Sometimes it's less hassle to just try and work it out for yourself, which eventually you always do. As one traveller reported in an earlier edition of AMH: *'I learned quickly that you never believe what anyone says without getting a few second opinions. Usually you get a variety of contradictory responses and either have to go for the most popular answer or choose the guy who seems most intelligent and trustworthy.'*

Lost in the wilderness

Getting completely lost is very rare, but even when you're just temporarily disorientated you can soon become anxious, especially if there are other worries pressing on your mind or it's getting dark. At times like this you must use your logic and common sense to work out where you went wrong.

It's almost always your navigational mistake and not the commonly blamed map, 'magnetic rocks' affecting the compass (though this can occur), or the Pentagon messing about with the GPS signal in your locality. Even if reading and trusting the veracity of maps can take some time, good navigators never forget their own fallibility.

The most common reason for getting lost is not paying attention to your orientation, then jumping to conclusions and **making the situation fit the** facts. Suddenly you become aware that your direction doesn't quite match the bearing suggested on the map and after a while a road curves off in the wrong direction. The thought of turning back is frustrating, but sooner or later common sense tells you that things are not right. It takes some experience, but in the city or the bush, after a while you soon gain a feel for whether a road or track is the one you want to be on.

Stop and have a good look around. If you're out in the wilds, **get on to high ground** and scan around. Assess the 'quality' or feel of the track you're on; does it appear less travelled? Are there telephone or other power wires that'll lead to a village for sure? Is a track corrugated or showing other signs of frequent vehicular use, or just littered with the bones of your predecessors? Check your position and bearing from the GPS if you have it. Look at all the facts objectively, not just the ones that agree with your preferences. Above all, rest assured there was a point, not too long ago, when you weren't lost. If you can't correct your mistake, **go back** there, waiting till daylight if need be.

With a set of knobblies you may think you can go anywhere, but where it's even possible, taking **cross-country shortcuts** as a way of getting back to where you were can often get you in more trouble. Unless you can clearly see where you're trying to get to, keep it simple and retrace your tracks. Apart from the fact that it may be very slow going, short cuts are also a good way of falling off and getting trapped under your bike, and off track like this you're on your own. Always play it safe and go back the easy way, however galling it seems, or be prepared to face the consequences.

Riding together

Getting completely lost is rare, but on or off the highway or in a busy city, losing sight of your riding companions is not so hard to do as you battle with the traffic. This will happen for sure so before you set out, establish some clear rules and signals. The simplest **signal** should be flashing headlights: 'I am slowing down or stopping' – on seeing this the leader should stop and wait or turn back if necessary. For this reason it's worth having a **rear view mirror**.

On the dirt or in town, a common way to lose each other is when the leader stops to wait for the follower to catch up. After a while of waiting and wondering, the leader retraces his route to look for the other rider who in the meantime has raced ahead to catch up the leader who is nowhere in sight. It is the responsibility of all riders to look out for each other – this should stop any arguments about whose fault it was. The leader should slow down or stop if he gets too far ahead of the group, who in turn should keep together.

If you do lose sight of each other in town, get the mobiles out or continue to the previously agreed location. Out in the desert ride to some high ground, turn off your engines, look around and listen for the others. In this position you're also more likely to be seen by the others too. Failing this, an **agreed procedure** should be adhered to. For example, after a certain time out of contact, you should all return to the point where you last stopped or spoke together. If fuel is critical you should stop ahead at a clear landmark, such as a village or junction. If phones work, use them. The whole point of riding together is to give each other much-needed support so resist any individualistic tendencies while traversing remote tracks.

SURVIVAL

Besides breakdowns (see p172) or an accident (p166), a more serious situation might occur when you find yourself trapped under or alongside an irretrievable bike. Once you're sure you're in trouble follow the '3 Ps' below:

Protection (shelter)

Arranging shelter from the elements will greatly extend your ability to survive. In the case of an injured partner, shelter will be essential while you go for help. Depending on where you are, this means erecting shade or a windbreak if you're not carrying a tent. Get in the habit of wearing some kind of head covering to minimise heat loss or sunstroke; a crash helmet or a scarf will do if you've no hat. With protection secured you can now turn your attention to either recovering your bike, rescuing your partner, or preparing to walk out.

Position

If you've been keeping track, your position should not be hard to pinpoint. It may be just a short walk back to the last village, where someone can help you drag your bike out of a ravine, or it may be miles to a minor road. If you're sure no one will come this way you must be prepared to walk back to the last sign of human presence.

Look on the map to see if there's some place to get help which you'd overlooked. Consider torching your bike, or just a smoky component like a tyre or a seat, but *don't waste smoke and signals on the off chance that they may be spotted.*

Provisions

Establish how much food and water you have and how many days it will last. **Water** is by far the most critical aid to survival. Wherever you are you can survive a lot longer without food which you should consume frugally anyway, as digestion uses up water. Staying where you are obviously uses less energy but might not be an option offering much hope. If there's a river, stick close to it, settlements or human activity usually accompany them.

SURVIVAL DOS AND DON'TS

- **Don't go alone** into remote areas in bad weather.
- **Know your limits.** There's no rescue service.
- **Avoid known danger areas** where there are bandits, terrorists, wars or landmines.
- **Don't travel in desert regions in summer or high mountains in winter.** Summer is when most desert travellers die because, survival margins shrink drastically.
- **Know where you're going.** Keep on the track and avoid cross-country short-cuts. Carry adequate route information, navigational tools and communications devices.
- **Never carry on when lost.** Stop before you go too far, accept that you've made a mistake, and if necessary retrace your steps.
- **Carry enough fuel and water** for your entire planned stage, including a reserve. Difficult terrain and physical activity will greatly increase consumption of fuel and water.
- Even before things go wrong, **avoid wasting water**. Get into the habit of being frugal with your washing and cleaning needs.
- **Carry essential spares and tools and know how to use them.** You should at least be familiar with tyre removal and repair, and fault diagnosis (see p170).
- If travelling in a group **keep your companions close** or tell them what you're doing and where you're going, both when riding and when going for something like an evening stroll.
- **Avoid riding at night.** Even on the tarmac roads there's a danger of unlit vehicles and stray animals.

Wild camping

On the road it's surprising how rarely you actually need to camp. Werner Bausenhart (*Africa: Against the Clock on a Motorcycle*), managed to ride a Funduro up and down the continent over several weeks without ever spending a night in a tent. In Asia and South America overnight accommodation is even easier to come by, although the moto-vagrants who call themselves *Terra Circa* spent almost every night out during their ride across Europe and Russia. Not taking camping gear should mean you need carry less stuff, though it rarely works out like that.

The truth is, disregarding the savings in paying for accommodation, **camping wild is part of the big adventure**. There will come a day when you either have to, or want to park up in a nice spot and enjoy a night out. Sure it means a whole lot of extra gear, but that should really add up to no more than 5–10kg extra. In return you get the autonomy not only to ride where you like but also stay where you like.

Sleeping, cooking, eating and **drinking** are the basic elements of camping (washing too, I suppose). The greater the comfort and efficiency of these elements, the better will be the quality of your camping experience and on a long ride it needs to be. As with all biking gear, it depends how committed you are to saving space and weight.

Even before you get to settle down for the night, for lunch stops and the like, do yourself a favour by **parking well off the road or track**. Besides the safety factor of not getting run over or choked by dust from passing lorries, this avoids giving too much of an open invitation to chancers or the inquisitive – particularly relevant when you're too close to a settlement.

Once you get used to wild camping it'll be the nights spent out in the mountains or deserts, or the occasions when you get invited in by the rural locals that'll make up some of the best memories of your moto adventure.

DEALING WITH ONLOOKERS

It's amazing how in certain countries, even if you think you're miles from anyone, an **audience** will emerge, seemingly from thin air. Initially you may think this is all part of the travel experience, but being stared at by 22 kids as you eat your lunch is not a normal situation.

In many poorer countries where the concepts of privacy and personal space are not so sought after, the idea of sleeping alone and away from others out in the bush is regarded as suspect or deviant. Don't be surprised if, just when you've pitched the tent and donned your slippers, a local or even an army patrol rocks up to see what you're about. Out of concern they may even advise you this is not such a good place to spend the night on account of bandits or wild animals, and that there's a perfectly fine hotel half an hour down the road. It can work both ways of course; as often as not you'll be invited for a meal, when it'll be your turn to see exotic people enacting mundane tasks.

CHOOSING A SPOT FOR THE NIGHT

All this underlines why it's a good idea to try and not be seen heading for your night's camp and once there, **not to be visible to passing traffic**, or at a point where you're far enough to discourage casual visitors. This can be easier said than done but will make for a more relaxing night. The first night or two wild camping alone can be frightening, and over the months you're bound to have a couple of unnerving encounters.

A grassy knoll in the Karakoram.
© Margus Sootla

As the sun sinks lower it's common to keep riding on, 'just over that rise', to find somewhere that feels right, until it's too dark to see anything and you end up sleeping in a roadside ditch alongside a dead dog. Try and pin down a place **before it gets too dark**, especially if you may have trouble getting far enough off road.

If you're confident you won't disturb someone or cause a commotion – the usual problem with wild camping, rather than issues of security – the answer can be to go right up to some isolated dwelling and **ask** if you can camp nearby even if that won't be so wild.

If the road or track you're following is surrounded by fields and you decide to camp among them, you can be pretty sure that in a developing country you won't get the hostile 'gerrof moi land' reception from a farmer that you might back home. Nevertheless, on arable land make the effort not to ride over or trample crops, or upset carefully dug irrigation ditches.

Be careful about how far and how hard you roam in your search for some nocturnal seclusion too; you don't want to make any manoeuvres or river crossings that may be difficult to reverse the following morning. It can also a good idea to **switch off the lights** if possible, to avoid attracting attention.

Once you find a good spot, give yourself a few minutes to adjust and absorb your new locale. You may have been so intent on finding a place that you haven't noticed someone's nearby shack, an awful reek of undefined roadkill, clouds of mosquitoes stirring from a stagnant pool, or a slavering pack of rabid dogs zeroing in on your camp from all directions. And almost perfectly **level ground** is also more important than you think.

Trees of course make the ideal cover, and it's also worth noting that areas of loose sand will lose the day's heat quicker and so get colder than rocky places. Altitude above 1000m (3280ft) will also have a noticeable effect on overnight temperatures, though it may be something you want in the tropics.

It can be quite unnerving when someone looms up out of the dark to 'say hello' and you have your camp spread out all over the ground. Depending on their behaviour, you never know if they're just being friendly while emboldened by drink, are on the scrounge, or have other ideas. In this situation you may prefer to **move on** to avoid the nagging fear of theft. As said earlier, it's the main reason why camping far from a road and at least initially being discreet with your lighting are good ideas.

LIFE ON THE ROAD

Moto camping gear

Many motorcyclists are into activity sports like rock climbing, mountain bikes or kayaking and may have their own ideas on what follows; for the rest here are some very basic guidelines on acquiring gear. Carrying camping gear on a bike rather than on foot, I'd suggest that a **lack of bulk** is more important than light-weight. An extra 5kg is a lot when you're hauling a backpack over the moors, on a bike it's a gallon of fuel, so don't get too hung up on the scales.

If you don't own and use good gear already, the £700+ you might spend on a quality set up may be a bit galling for the nights you actually use it. In much of the AMZ you don't need to camp and in Asia accommodation can be cheap, but would you rather spend the night in a €3 roach hotel or out in the wilds? Like I said, wild camping is part of the adventure.

Top: a £10 single skin cheapie keeps the wind off but can be too small for regular use.

Tents

On my early Sahara trips I never carried a tent or even a mat; I just unrolled my sleeping bag on my jacket, dozed through the night, woke up aching and will doubtless have arthritis in a few years. These days I usually carry either just the inner tent against insects or the outer against rain. In still conditions a tent adds about 5°C or 9°F to the ambient temperature inside, though as importantly it can be a psychologically comforting shelter, or an annoyingly claustrophobic cocoon. I err towards the latter and for this reason I think a tent should be on the large side so you can get in, spread out and have room for your luggage. If you're planning on spending several days in one place you'll also appreciate a **bigger tent** and on a warm, windless night you always have the option of simply lying on it like a groundsheet.

There's no need to splash out on an expensive ultralight design built to withstand a Himalayan blizzard and there's no real need to faff about with guy lines unless it's a gale (guying a tent in wind can stop flapping which can otherwise keep you up all night). For most situations a simple two-pole crossover design will stand up without pegs or guy ropes and cost as little as £10/$15 for a single skin cheapie. In a basic tropical hotel it can also act as a mossie net but outside you'll need to quickly weigh it down with either your baggage or pegs, because in windy situations they can take off like kites.

For me the best sort of tent is one where you can erect the inner alone as an insect dome or just the outer for the space; not all tents can do this. An ultra-basic alternative is just a tarp some 12 feet/3m square. Attach one corner to the bike's bars and peg and weigh the other three down. In town it can act as a bike cover, too.

Sleeping mats and bags

Closed cell foam sleeping mats are bulky for the comfort they offer. Nowadays, though expensive for a piece of open-cell foam in a bag with a plug, the self-inflating Therma-Rest-type sleeping mats work amazingly well. I managed for a few years with a three-quarter-length Ultralight model which rolls up to around two litres in volume; now I use an Exped Synmat Ultralight of half the volume with basic, sand-proof plugs rather than valves. One tip that really helps in the sands is digging a shallow, mat-wide **trench**; it vaguely replicates sinking into a soft mattress and so greatly increases comfort.

As for **sleeping bags**, compactness and efficiency within your budget is what it's about as long as you recognise that a good mat makes all the difference. Get the best bag you can afford which can mean spending over £150/$250. Aim for a three-season bag rated as comfortable at freezing point. A boxed foot and a 'mummy' head cowling alone are worth an extra 'season's' rating.

Goose down still can't be beaten as a filler and should not be confused with inferior *feathers* which are sometimes in the mix. Not only does down fluff out to fill a large volume (the key to insulation), it still *compresses* better than any man-made fabric and will do so for many years so it takes up less room – the weight saving is negligible. The drawback is that down clumps up when **wet** and takes a long time to dry.

In my experience **synthetic bags** loose their loft after what might effectively be only a few weeks use; and warmth for warmth they're always bulkier than down too. A hiker might use and so uncompress their synthetic bag every night; on a bike it may be left compressed for weeks – bad for synthetic recovery but no problem for down which feels nicer too.

Whatever you use, **air** your bag out every morning by turning it inside out and letting it hang in the breeze, and decompress it every chance you get. Especially with down you want to stretch the washing cycles out as long as possible as it reduces loft in the long run; use a liner or wear something.

Lighting

On long winter nights you'll need some lighting; a good spread of light around your camp makes life much easier, although I find most nights you don't need a torch except for specific tasks. The bike's parking light is too weak and the main beam risks flattening the battery so an LED **head torch** is the way to go. Lately Petzl have gone over the top with the Nao at over £100; something simple like a Petzl Zipka

(right) is incredibly compact, even if they don't exactly set the night ablaze.

Cooking

Running a motorcycle it makes sense to use small **petrol (gasoline) stove**. You have a tank full of the stuff so if you ever run out, not being able to cook up a brew is the least of your problems. Getting into camping takes some adjustment and clumsy accidents are common when you're tired or still getting used to the whole business. A reliable, uncomplicated and stable stove goes a long way to minimising this.

Top: Primus RBJ on the Shandur Pass. Note the ally windshield.
Below: Coleman Featherlite drinks like an old V8 but keeps on going.

The problem with petrol stoves is modern ones are designed to run on '**white fuel**', a cleaner fuel than that which comes out of most outback bowsers. Lead-free gasoline is better as prolonged use of low octane leaded fuel may eventually clog your stove's generator (pre-heater pipe; not all have them) or jets with soot. I'd guess this process takes a couple of months of daily use, so either take a spare generator or take a gamble and hope the stove won't block before you get back. Top your stove up with unleaded when you can and before you get deep into the bush where ordinary leaded fuel may be all you'll find.

Using local leaded fuel your stove may spurt and smoke a bit before it fully warms up, but once hot, petrol stoves put out much more heat than propane and, being under pressure, are more resistant to wind. Jetboil apart, the windshields which come with most stoves are pretty ineffective, so work out a proper wind break to increase efficiency and save fuel.

Anything that claims to run on **multi-** or **dual-fuel** is either a play on words (ie: it runs on leaded *and* unleaded – big deal), a compromise in the jet size, or requires fiddly changing of jets. On the road you need a simple petrol stove, not something that claims to run on diesel, kerosene, white fuel and Orangina.

The Coleman 533 I used for years (renamed a 'Sportster' in some markets) claimed to run on white fuel and unleaded, but I've always run it on African fuel with an occasional burn-through on unleaded when I get home. It was still on the original generator when it finally fell apart and I've heard that if it blocks up you can take out the wire inside, try and clean it or eliminate it altogether to get a rougher flame. To start it you simply pump it up, turn on the fuel and light it. This sort of ease of use is the key for all sorts of overlanding equipment and I now use a more compact Coleman Featherlite.

Which brings us to what I call 'red bottle' stoves or 'RBJs' with the fuel bottle (usually red) attached by a hose or pipe to a compact burner. I've tried an early Optimus Nova which squirted fuel from the clip-on connection, watched new Primus and MSR stoves spluttering and then permanently blocking after a couple of hours' use, despite cleaning and replacing parts. Others have reported reliable results from RBJs whose variable reliability could be down to lean running so it doesn't run out halfway up the Eiger, but they cost twice as much as a gas-guzzling Coleman, require fiddly assembly which can lead to leaks or blockages, and regular cleaning maintenance, the last thing you want

MY KINGDOM FOR A CHAIR

Not all may agree but I think a light camp chair is no extravagance, especially for those at an age when joints don't bend like they used to. Let others scoff, then wait for them to ask: 'ooh, can I have a sit?'.

Some sleeping mats come with accessory frames to run the mat as a plush, lean back chair. Or on the right, a $70 Monarch from Alite in the US pivots on its back legs (like you were told not to in school) but weighs just 600g (21oz) and assembles in a minute. Best of all it's tougher than it looks.

to do when you're hungry. Another drawback many also mention is the **noise** of some RBJs and the poor heat control: all or nothing.

Whatever you get, consider a stove's **stability**, both on the ground and for holding pots; there's nothing more frustrating than watching your half-cooked carbonara alfredo tip into the dirt. Unlike say a Jetboil, in my experience Coleman models are ideal in this respect: the squat compact shape of the one-piece unit sits securely on the ground, and the wide burner gives off plenty of heat and support for a pot.

One-pan cooking

It may sound extreme but a half-litre **mug** and a one-litre **pan** with a lid will do. A plate is unnecessary and a spoon and a penknife are all the cutlery you'll ever use. You can cook your rice/pasta, put it in the mug with a lid on top to keep it warm, and then, if you're not simply throwing it in with the pasta, cook whatever else you have, chuck the pasta back in and eat with just a pan and a cup to wash. Avoid pouring hot water away: use it for soup or washing up.

Don't get drawn in by trick titanium cookware from camping shops. A sturdier stainless saucepan with a spot-welded rather than riveted handle will take rough use and sand cleaning without getting grubby or bent.

Water containers

In hot lands the best way to carry water while riding is a **hydrator** in your backpack or a sleeve fitted in the jacket so you can drink while riding. Camelbak set the ball rolling years ago; Platypus is another brand but I've found their less pliable bladders can acquire pinprick leaks. With either you don't have to buy the full pack, just buy a bladder and hose which fits in any daypack, melting a hose hole on the top of the bag for the hose. I prefer a pouch (right) for a 1.5L plastic water bottle attached somewhere to the bike.

Your main water container should ideally be around **10 litres**; a sturdy **water bag** works best and optimises space. MSRs are pricey but tough though caps leak; take a spare.

LIFE ON THE ROAD

Off-highway riding

It's possible to traverse South America, Asia and finally even Africa without leaving the tarmac. But wherever you go in the world, mastering the techniques of riding your heavy motorcycle off sealed highways will be one of the major elements of your adventure. When there's a trail of dust billowing off your back wheel you can't help thinking you really are far away from home and heading deep into the unknown. It's out here that adventures are ripe for the taking, from uninterrupted vistas across the wilderness, to unexpected encounters with the people you'll only meet in the back of beyond.

On the dirt, traction is unpredictable and constant reading of the terrain ahead is vital. It's this involvement that makes off-roading so rewarding. Ever since Kenny Roberts rewrote the book on GP racing, it's common knowledge that today's top racers developed their rear-wheel steering and sharp reactions from sliding around on dirt bikes. And besides the improvements to your road-riding skills, off-roading provides the exhilaration of road racing at a fraction of the speed. By the end of the day you'll be parked up in some scenic and remote location, shagged-out, filthy, but satisfied. Unless I'm very much mistaken, it's largely what adventure motorcycling is all about.

Gently does it

Riding off-road is fun, but until you get the hang of handling your loaded bike on various surfaces take it easy. As a general rule you'll find **50mph/80kph** is a maximum cruising speed on any dirt surface. At speeds greater than this it's not possible to react quickly enough to the ever-changing surface – riding on dirt is never predictable which is part of the fun but also a danger.

Adventure motorcycling is not about smouldering kneepads; it's about surviving the long ride so never take risks, resist the impulse to show off and always ride within the limitations of:

- Your vision
- The terrain
- Your experience
- Your bike's handling abilities

Ready for a beating

Be in no doubt about the hammering your bike is going to get on dirt roads, or the just-as-frequent broken tarmac roads that you'll encounter. Much of the advice on bike preparation given in earlier chapters is concerned with limiting damage when riding over rough terrain. Lightly-framed dual sports bikes with heavy loads or cast-wheeled road tourers were not built for a beating on corrugated tracks, and frame, rack or tank fractures are common mechanical problems. Besides offering agility in the dirt, a lightly-loaded bike will put less stress on the already hard-working wheels, suspension and transmission and luggage rack. Make sure they're all up to it.

DIRT ROADS

Most of your off-highway riding will be on rural dirt roads rather than cross country. At their best these tracks are straight and flat, with a smooth and consistent surface requiring only slightly reduced speeds. But dirt being what it is, this won't last for long and most tracks will have been rutted by heavy traffic, washed-out by rains, blown over with sand, littered with rocks and, likely as not, corrugated.

Corrugations

Corrugations are another name for the washboard surface which an unconsolidated track develops as a result of regular, heavy traffic. The accepted explanations for these infuriatingly regular ripples of dirt are braking and acceleration forces of passing traffic or the 'tramping' shock absorbers of heavy trucks.

In a car you grit your teeth and pray that the shock absorbers won't explode; the best solution is to accelerate up to about 50mph/80kph and skim across the top of each ripple, so reducing vibration dramatically. On a bike, the same practice gives a smoother ride too, but at this speed your wheels are barely touching the ground and your traction is negligible. In a straight line this is not too dangerous, but on a bend it's possible to skim right off the track.

Wealthier countries grade their corrugated dirt roads once in a while but the honeymoon only lasts a few weeks. In the developing world, the passing of a grader is most likely an annual event just after a rainy season.

The good thing is that on a bike you only need a tyre's width to get by and you'll often find corrugations shallowest or non-existent on either edge of the track, though rarely for more than a few metres at a time. You'll find yourself forever weaving around trying to find the smoothest path. On a plain it might be easier to avoid a corrugated track altogether and ride in far greater comfort and freedom alongside the track, but realistically this option is rare.

Corrugations do have one small saving grace. If ever you're lost or wondering which way to go, the most corrugated track is the one most frequently used and probably the one you want to follow. But overall, corrugations are just a miserable fact of dirt-roading and a good place to have knobbly tyres with slightly reduced pressures, a well-supported subframe and a comfy seat.

When the going gets rough, stand up

Standing on the footrests over rough ground is probably the most important technique beginners should master because when you're standing up:

- Suspension shocks are taken through your legs not your back.
- Your bike is much easier to control.
- Being higher up, your forward vision is improved.

Contrary to the impression that standing up makes your bike less stable, in fact it has the opposite effect. It transfers your weight low, through the footrests, rather than through the saddle when you're seated. This is why trials riders and

LIFE ON THE ROAD

Weight forward, knees and elbows bent to absorb the impacts.

motocrossers always tackle tricky sections standing up on the pegs.

When standing up, **grip the tank** lightly between your knees to give your body added support and to prevent the bike from bouncing around between your legs. As you get the hang of things, standing will become instinctive. You'll find it's not always necessary to stand right up; sometimes just leaning forward, pulling on the bars while taking the weight off your backside will be enough to lessen the jolt. In a nutshell: **sit down when you can, stand up when you must**.

RIDING SAND

Sand can be great to ride over if it's consistently firm, but in somewhere like the Sahara riding on sand requires a high degree of concentration and it's at its most demanding when riding through very soft fine sand alongside dune areas or when forced along a track rutted by passing cars. Riding *along* rather than just across a sandy creek presents the most difficult condition that a desert biker regularly encounters. Here, fine waterborne sand is washed down by flash floods, and you can find yourself riding standing up in one- or two-foot-wide ruts for miles at a time. Extremely tiring! Realistically this is not a scenario that trans-continental motorcyclists will gravitate towards, but for those that do more detailed guidelines are in my *Sahara Overland* book.

Low tyre pressures

By dropping the air pressure to as little as 5psi (0.3 bar), a tyre flattens out and its 'footprint' on the sand lengthens significantly (rather than widens, although it does that a little, too). Doing this changes your normally round tyre into more of a caterpillar track, increasing your contact patch and improving your traction dramatically, even with a trail or a road tyre. It can mean the difference between riding confidently across a sandy section or slithering around barely in control, footing constantly, losing momentum and finally getting stuck or falling over – every few minutes.

The trouble is that in this severely under-inflated state a tyre gets much **hotter**, due to the internal friction created by the flexing carcass (just as you get hot doing exercise). Softened by the heat, a tyre becomes much more prone to punctures. Keep your speed down on very soft tyres and be sure your security bolts or similar devices are done up tight as it's in just these low-pressure/high-traction situations that the dreaded tyre creep (see p84) occurs.

Knobblies at reduced pressures make all the difference.

LIFE ON THE ROAD

Momentum and acceleration

These are often the only two things that will get you through a particularly soft stretch of sand, so don't be afraid to stand up and accelerate hard at the right time. A quick snap of the throttle in a middle gear gives you the drive and stability to blast assuredly across a short, sandy creek as you try and lighten the front wheel to stop it getting buried. No matter how much your back wheel weaves and bucks around, keep the power on and your backside off the seat for as long as it takes. So long as the front wheel remains on course you're largely in control. Keep off the brakes, especially the front. If you need to slow down use the engine to decelerate and be ready for the bike to become unstable. The reason is that loose sand builds up in front of the front wheel and so messes up the 'self-straightening' caster effect of the fork-axle relationship. With caster lost, the front wheel wants to flip to the side. Keeping the power on helps cut through loose sand and minimise sand build up.

Riding like this is very tiring, but in most cases even trying to slow down and stop will mean falling over or getting bogged. Sand riding can be hair-raising stuff and you'll often come close to falling off, but the above techniques are the only way to get through soft sand short of paddling along at 1mph.

Sandy ruts

About 20mph/30kph in second is the best speed/gear combination to maintain when riding along sandy ruts, the low gear and high revs giving quick throttle response to further difficulties you may encounter. Slow down through the gears not the brakes and don't be reluctant to rev your engine hard if necessary. It's in this situation where unreliable or ill-tuned engines begin to play up or overheat.

If you're in a deep rut, stay in it and don't try to cross ruts or ride out

Sometimes the ruts just win and it can be a long ride on a K100. © Edde Mendes

unless absolutely necessary. If you must change ruts, hurl your bike and your weight in the preferred direction of travel while standing up and gassing it... but don't expect to get away with these kind of moves on a tanked-up 1200.

RIDING MUD

Even on a 120kg competition bike with fresh knobblies, mud and especially bogs or swamps can present the dual challenge of negligible traction and treacherous suction. No two ways about it, riding this sort of terrain on a portly overlander is plain exhausting. While sand riding responds to certain acquired techniques, the occluded consistency of water-logged terrain has no cut and dried rules, but if you can:

- avoid big mires as much as possible.
- ride in one rut and stick to it, either attacking it standing up or, if you don't feel confident, paddling or walking or being helped across.
- ride through slowly to avoid drowning the engine or being knocked off by submerged obstacles.

LIFE ON THE ROAD

Slimy going requires a steady hand;
standing up helps to control and balance the
machine.
© C. Siewald

Some tracks crossing the Congo and Amazon basins and in far eastern Russia are notorious riding challenges. Hundred-metre-long puddles stretch before you with vehicles sometimes backed up behind a bogged-down truck.

On a bike, tyres are critical: aggressive treads at low pressures make all the difference, but blasting into a huge puddle on an African track is a recipe for a muddy face plant. If you can't find a way around the side, recognise that it's going to be a slow and tiring paddle, and be ready to stop if the trough deepens. You're usually forced to ride through the trenches dug by the last truck's spinning wheels, but depending on the period since the rains ended, these pits can drown an entire car. If you're not sure, **wade through first**.

Bogs and swamps

The large expanses of water-logged wilderness found in temperate zones can be harder still to deal with, and any tracks through this sort of terrain tend to be few and expensive to maintain. Perhaps the best known examples are found in far eastern Russia such as the original Old Summer Route of the Kolyma Highway between Yakutsk and Magadan (see p233), only rideable in summer by which time the tundra melts into a quagmire.

This is a tough place to ride alone: in a desert you can extricate a bike from sand with a little digging, and along the flooded channels of central Africa there are usually enough other travellers or villagers around to help out. A bike ridden up to its bars into a Siberian bog could take days to extract.

Learn to recognise what sort of vegetation inhabits water-logged ground, be it reeds or moss; keeping to high ground is not always the answer. Even with help, in terrain like this your mileages may drop to single figures while your ability to deal with this exhausting pace can be numbered in hours.

RIVER CROSSINGS

Who can resist the thrill of cutting a big V-shaped shower of spray as you blast across a shallow river? The other end of this photogenic scenario is a bent crankshaft in an engine ruined by hydraulic lock: the consequences of a piston sucking in and trying to compress uncompressible water.

The first thing to do when you come to a substantial and unfamiliar water crossing is to stop and have a good look. Just because tracks lead down one bank and up the other doesn't mean the crossing is rideable. Distant storms can raise an unfordable creek miles from the actual downpour in a matter of hours. And in a few more hours that river might be just a series of trickling pools again. Furthermore, in recreational or farming areas 4WDs can churn up the river bed, creating mud or ruts which can easily tip a bike over.

Walk first

If in doubt about the river crossing **walk across first**: a pair of wet trousers is less inconvenient than a drowned engine. Walking across establishes the strength of the current, the nature of the river bed and, of course, the maximum depth.

If you feel the combination of current, river bed and depth make riding possible ride the bike through slowly, following the exact route of your foot recce. Generally, if you can walk it unaided, you can ride it, otherwise walk the bike across on a running engine (right, middle). Still waters are usually deepest, so pick a spot just above some rapids; the water may be moving fast, but it's shallow. Keep the revs high in first or second gear. This helps run through any electrical spluttering, avoids stalling and keeps a good pressure of exhaust blowing out of the silencer.

Generally the 'plimsoll line' on most conventional engines is halfway up the barrel and below the air filter intake, but wet electrics can snuff out an engine blasting through a two-inch puddle.

Waterproofing the electrics on your bike should have been part of your pre-departure preparation, but before you take the dive, spray in and around the plug cap and other vital ignition components with a water dispersing agent like WD40 or GT85. Remember that the consequences of

Top: Recce-ing to ride through a river while balancing on a pipe – that's extreme!
Middle: it may look shallow but when you're worn out it's best to take the easiest way; one stone could flip you. © Walter Colebatch.
Bottom: except for photos, keep splashes to a minimum. © C. Siewald

LIFE ON THE ROAD

falling over are almost as bad as riding in too deep; keep your finger over the kill switch and use it the moment you lose control. Once on the far side expect your brakes not to work and a bit of spluttering as the engine steams itself dry.

Walking the bike

If riding is too risky, walk your bike across with yourself on the **upstream** side of a current so there's no chance of getting trapped under the bike should you fall. If your baggage looks like getting soaked, unpack it and bring it over on your shoulders. Whether you walk the bike across with the engine running or not depends on the risk of water reaching the air intake. If you go for a running engine keep your thumb on the kill switch in case you fall or it gets deep.

Truly, madly, deeply

Very rarely you might come to a river crossing which is way too deep to ride through but which, for whatever reason, you simply must cross. With careful preparation it's possible to totally submerge a bike providing the fuel, induction and exhaust systems are completely sealed off.

Doing this is no small job and you risk ruining your bike, so make sure there's no alternative. Naturally the maximum depth you can walk through is limited by your height, but realistically don't attempt anything deeper than the height of the seat and don't try this radical procedure alone.

Before you go ahead, establish the answers to these questions first:

- Is there a bridge or a ferry in the vicinity or a shallower place to cross?
- Can you get the bike in a boat or the back of an AWD truck, as in Siberia?
- Do you have the means to waterproof the bike and get across without putting yourself in danger?
- Are you sure there are not more such rivers ahead?

If the answer is 'no' this is what to do:

- Remove as much weight from the bike as possible, including the tank.
- Turn over the engine so that it's on compression with both sets of valves closed (this only works with singles).
- Plug the exhaust securely and disconnect the battery.
- Take out the air filter, wrap it in a plastic bag and reinstall it.
- Fold over all oil tank, battery, engine and carb breather hoses so they're sealed and tape them up.
- If you have some rope, set up a line from bank to bank, or to the bike so someone can help pull it through from the far bank.

Once the bike's virtually submerged there is no rush, take it easy; don't be distracted by bubbles rising from the bike; whatever's leaking it's too late to do anything about it now. On the far bank let the bike drip dry – do not attempt to start it until you're sure it's fully drained. Pull out the exhaust bung and stand the bike on its back wheel draining any water which may have leaked in. Release the breather hoses and drain the carb. Take out the air filter, drain the airbox and reinstall the filter. Remove the spark plug and turn over the engine, hoping that no water spurts out of the plug hole; if it does check your engine oil over the next few miles of riding. If it's turned milky it's become contaminated with water and you should change it or continue slowly until you can. Once all these procedures have been completed check for a spark and if all's well, fire the bike up and hope there's not another deep river a few miles further down the road.

DROWNED ENGINE: WHAT TO DO

The worst has happened and your bike has taken a lung-full while running, or has fallen over and filled up. It's not the end of the world; this is what to do:

- Stand the bike up and drain the exhaust.
- Drain the petrol tank.
- Take out the spark plug and kick or tip out water.

- Drain the carb and dry the filter.
- Remove the stator cover (on the left side of most singles), drain and dry it.
- If the engine oil has a milky colour, it's contaminated with water and needs changing.
- Once everything has dried out, test for a spark first and, if the bike runs, give it a full re-lube at the earliest opportunity.

Health and medical emergencies*

DR PAUL ROWE

The key principle to avoiding illness and injury on your trip is that prevention is far better than cure. However, with some prior planning and a small first-aid kit you will be able to deal with most ailments which arise, to keep you and your group riding.

First-aid kit

A small plastic box is ideal and should include the following:
- Paracetamol
- Strong painkillers (analgesics)
- Anti-malarials
- Antacids
- Anti-diarrhoea tablets (Loperamide 2mg)
- Laxatives
- Antihistamines
- Rehydration powders
- Broad spectrum antibiotics (eg amoxicillin 500mg)
- Multi-vitamins

Equipment
- Latex gloves (good for oily repairs too)
- Tweezers (for tick removal)
- Sterile syringe set with two hypodermic needles per person
- Sterile dressings, plasters, bandage
- Alcohol wipes ('Sterets'); can also be used to start fires
- Superglue
- Antiseptic cream
- Durapore tape
- Safety pins
- Thermometer
- Savlon antiseptic concentrate
- Steristrips

Good **painkillers** could make the difference in being able to carry on riding in an emergency, so see your doctor prior to departure and request a supply of Codeine Phosphate 30mg or Tramadol 50mg tablets. Also ask for some amoxicillin or similar antibiotic (beware of any group member with penicillin allergy) as wound infections, dental abscesses, ear and urinary infections are all more common during remote travel.

Although contrary to the manufacturers' advice, a lot of space can be saved by removing tablets from their blister packaging and putting them into small zip lock plastic bags. Just remember to label them clearly.

* This page also appears on the website under Resources

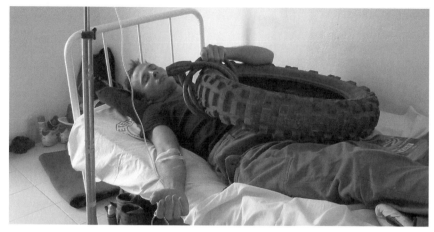

Illness, including malaria, is much more likely if travelling in the hot season. © Jeff Condon

Obtaining supplies

Between a friendly doctor and your local pharmacy you should be able to obtain most of the kit for your trip. For anything else, try these sites:

UK	BCB Ltd 🖥 www.bcbin.com
	Lifesystems 🖥 www.lifesystems.co.uk
	SP Services 🖥 www.spservices.com
	St John Ambulance Supplies 🖥 www.stjohnsupplies.co.uk
US	Safety Central 🖥 safetycentral.com
Canada	Mountain Equipment Co-op 🖥 www.mec.ca
Australia	First Aid Kits Australia 🖥 www.firstaidkitsaustralia.com.au

Minor injuries

Minor cuts and grazes are common ailments. Apply the following general principles:

- Stop the bleeding.
- Clean thoroughly to reduce risk of infection.
- Keep it dressed to maintain cleanliness.

Bleeding is stopped by simply applying **direct pressure**, elevating the limb and bandaging firmly to hold the dressing in place. Dilute some Savlon concentrate in clean water and clean wounds thoroughly, picking out any gravel or other foreign material. If the wound is gaping you can close it with either Steristrips or ordinary household superglue (Loctite). Hold the wound edges together and smear the glue along the surface, maintaining that position for one minute. It will flake off after a few days once it has done its job. Steristrips are sticky paper strips which are very good at holding wound edges together but are less effective in humid environments.

Foreign bodies should be removed whenever possible but otherwise can be left in place for removal by a surgeon once you return home. The exceptions are any organic material (wood, splinters, thorns, fangs) which are likely to become infected or anything embedded in your palm or sole which will become too painful for you to function normally. For these you will have to venture to a local medical centre for removal. Any spills which leave gravel in your face need to be cleaned meticulously or may leave permanent scarring.

Planning for serious injury, illness and evacuation

Most riders give little forethought about what would happen if they were to become incapacitated during their trip. Thankfully these events are rare, but some pre-trip planning will help things run a lot smoother if things go wrong.

A worst-case scenario can be broken down into the following stages:

Casualty event → First aid → Stabilisation → Summon/move to help → Casualty evacuation → Repatriation.

Consider what you would do at each stage after initial stabilisation, which is dealt with later in this chapter. Go through some scenarios in your mind asking yourself questions about how you would cope with an emergency at different parts along your proposed route.

How will you raise help? Will there be a mobile phone signal or do you need to carry a satellite phone? Are there any dwellings or bases with VHF radio? **Who will you call?** Is there an ambulance service and if so will you have to pay cash? Can you leave your travel plans with someone who will come looking for you? How can you signal an aircraft? How long might it take to get rescued? A list of worldwide contact numbers for local police, fire and ambulance can be found at 🖳 www.sccfd.org/travel.html.

If you're spending a significant amount of time in an area it may be worth identifying where the local hospitals are, roughly the level of care they provide and whether there are likely to be any English-speaking staff there.

In the event of a **serious accident** the involvement of an established international recovery agency can be a godsend. These 24/7 organisations are dedicated to the evacuation and, if necessary, repatriation of those injured or taken ill overseas. However, aeromedical transfer can get extremely expensive so you need to be sure that your travel insurance includes cover for this eventuality. Your insurance company will want to be involved from the earliest stages and can be a useful ally at this stressful time so should be contacted at the first opportunity.

First-aid training

Ideally, all members of a group should have some first-aid training. If you travel alone you take an accepted risk, but prior first-aid training could still save your own life. In the UK conventional first aid is taught by St John's Ambulance Service (🖳 www.sja.org.uk), the British Red Cross (🖳 www.redcross.org.uk) or look for 'first aid training' in your region.

However, practising first aid in a remote environment with poor communications, adverse conditions and sub-optimal transport can all get challenging. Add to this that the responsibility may fall on you to straighten broken limbs, stem haemorrhaging and all the rest, it would be wise for at least one in a group to undertake one of the more advanced first-aid courses aimed specifically at expedition first aid.

Aeromedical emergency transfer agencies

First Assist	🖥 www.firstassist.co.uk
Aeromed 365 (UK)	🖥 www.aeromed365.com
Air Ambulance Network (USA)	🖥 www.airambulancenetwork.com
Swiss Air Ambulance	🖥 www.swiss-air-ambulance.ch

It is a good idea to keep all your **important information** and phone numbers together for use in an emergency. Write all of the following onto a piece of card, laminate it and keep it with your passport:

- Information about any medical conditions you have, prescribed medications and known allergies.
- Blood group if known.
- Next of kin with contact details.
- Contact numbers of insurance company, travel agency and some international medical evacuation agencies.
- One fallback number at home who can be contacted in any emergency to help you summon assistance.

First aid and basic trauma management

Significant injuries are rare amongst motorcycle travellers, despite the perception that it is a 'dangerous' form of transport. The key factor to improving survival in the event of a serious accident is prompt access to definitive care, i.e: a hospital with surgery and intensive care facilities. As soon as you have made the scene safe and performed a brief Airway, Breathing and Circulation assessment ('ABC', see below) your priority is to get help to the scene or, depending on experience, location and vehicles available, perform a rapid stabilisation and transport to hospital.

ABC

Although there follows a brief description of the ABC approach to trauma, it must be emphasised that a book is no place to learn such skills. Any group embarking on a serious motorcycle journey needs at least one person who is trained in first aid, for whom this should be an *aide memoire*.

A   Airway and Cervical Spine

The airway extends from the mouth down to the larynx and ends where the trachea (windpipe) divides into the left and right lungs. After trauma the airway may be obstructed by dislodged teeth, blood, facial bone fractures or, most commonly, the tongue falling back into the pharynx (back of the mouth) because the patient has been knocked unconscious. The signs of an obstructed airway include noisy breathing, gurgling and distress. A patient who can talk has a clear airway.

If you suspect airway obstruction you must carefully remove any obvious blockage from the mouth and then perform a **jaw thrust** which will lift the tongue clear of the back of the mouth thus opening the airway. To do this, approach the casualty from their head end, place your thumbs on their cheekbones either side with your middle fingers tucked in behind their jawbone (mandible) in the groove just below the earlobe. Now push the jawbone vertically up towards the sky and hold it there, checking again to see if air is now moving in and out of the patient's lungs. This manoeuvre is safe even in the presence of a possible spinal injury because the head is not tilted – only the jawbone is moved. Basic airway management of this type is the most important skill for any casualty carer. Without a clear airway the casualty will die in minutes.

Cervical spine protection is included with Airway in ABC because of its fundamental importance. What is meant by this is that the force of impact may have fractured neck bones (cervical vertebrae) or disrupted the ligaments which hold the vertebrae together. Any further movement such as turning the head or moving the casualty without proper stabilisation could push the broken bone fragment into the spinal cord thus permanently paralysing the patient from the neck down. However, a patient who is confused, has the distracting pain of a broken limb, or is buzzing from an adrenaline surge may not perceive the pain of a fractured vertebrae, so it is prudent to **assume that every trauma victim has a spinal injury**. Keep the patient still and their head supported in line with their body until professional help arrives.

B   Breathing

Management of specific chest injuries is beyond the scope of this book. However, you can help inbound medical personnel to guide you by exposing the casualty's chest and relaying to them the following information:
- Respiratory rate, i.e: number of breaths per minute.
- Whether there are any open or gurgling chest wounds.
- Whether one side of the chest is moving more than the other.
- Respiratory distress: is the patient talking normally or short of breath?
Repeat your observations every few minutes.

C   Circulation

Bleeding from open wounds may be easy to identify and stop but not from broken bones or internal organs. As an adult begins to lose some of their five litres of circulating blood, the body compensates by going into shock. This medical application of the word shock refers to significant blood loss not psychological fright.

Signs of shock
- Fast heart rate.
- Fast breathing rate.
- Paleness.
Signs of severe shock include:
- Reduced consciousness level.
- Weak pulse; may be too weak to feel.

At an **accident scene** there are several things you can do to reduce bleeding:
- Always remember scene safety; airway and spinal injury first, no matter how spectacular a wound initially appears.
- Apply firm pressure to wounds. If blood soaks through, apply more padding, always keeping the original directly pressed on the wound.
- Elevate injured limbs.
- Lay the casualty down and raise legs.

- Realign and splint broken bones.
- Internal bleeding into the chest, abdomen or pelvis can only be fixed by surgery. The best way to help here is to summon medical help as quickly as possible.

Fractures and splints

Broken bones are extremely painful, with most of the pain coming from the broken bones grating against each other and the jagged ends sticking into the surrounding muscles and skin at unnatural angles.

It follows that the pain can be greatly reduced by repositioning the broken limb into its normal realignment and holding it in that position. A comfortably splinted arm could make it tolerable to ride pillion on a bumpy track.

In addition to pain relief, the other major benefit of splinting fractured limbs is to reduce blood loss from the ends of the broken bones. To improvise a splint you will need something soft around the limb to provide padding, such as clothing or a sleeping mat, followed by something stiff to fasten to the outside to provide rigidity eg sticks or tent poles. Straighten whilst providing traction (pulling along the length of the limb) and have the splint ready to apply by testing it on the good side beforehand. For the patient this will be extremely painful but you will rarely do any more damage and the end result will be worth it.

Once a limb is immobilised it must be elevated, either in a sling for an arm or onto a padded pannier for a leg.

Other points regarding bone and joint injuries

Dislocations occur when a joint comes out of its socket, typically the shoulder, elbow, fingers or kneecap. The joint will be very painful, immobile and appear deformed compared to the other side. It needs to be located back into the socket by a medically-trained person as soon as possible.

Fractures where the overlying skin is broken are called open fractures. These are serious injuries and need urgent medical attention. Spinal, pelvis, and leg fractures require a stretcher and proper immobilisation so are impossible to transport by motorcycle.

A fractured **collar bone** (clavicle) is relatively common following a fall from a motorcycle. The treatment here is to hang the affected arm in a sling for four weeks. Although intensely painful, there are reports of people continuing to ride with this injury.

Helmet removal

It cannot be emphasised enough that **at the scene of a motorcycle accident, leave the casualty's helmet on until professional help arrives**. Attempts to remove a helmet by untrained persons can worsen a fractured neck and cause permanent total paralysis or even death. Even if you have had a little training or read the description that follows, the attending paramedics will have performed this manoeuvre many times, so leave it to them. This is the case in all developed countries but where trained help is in short supply you will be glad you practised amongst your group beforehand.

However, a description of the correct technique for helmet removal is included here on the premise that in a remote motorcycling emergency where the casualty's airway is compromised, some knowledge is better than none at all. If you're heading on a long, remote trip, go on a first-aid course which covers helmet removal and practise at home until you can get the helmet off without moving the neck at all.

Two rescuers are required. Some of the latest helmets feature removable padding to make this task easier.

● **Step 1** Rescuer 1 kneels above the patient's head. Grasp the helmet as shown left with fingertips curled around its lower margin touching the mandible (jawbone). Hold firmly to immobilise the head in line with the body.

● **Step 2** Rescuer 2 kneels alongside the patient's torso, opens the visor and checks the airway and breathing, then undoes or cuts the chin strap.

Rescuer 2 then places one hand so that the mandible is grasped between the thumb on one side and the index and middle fingers on the other side. The other hand is placed at the back of the neck with the finger tips reaching up under the back of the helmet.

The rescuer now clamps the patient between their forearm (front) and (wrist) (back) bracing the head, taking over in-line immobilisation.

● **Step 3** Rescuer 1 now pulls the sides of the helmet apart and rotates the helmet up and backwards by pulling the mouth-guard over the patient's nose.

● **Step 4** Next the helmet is rotated the opposite way so that the back of the helmet slides up around the curve of the back of the head.

● **Step 5** Now Rescuer 1 can gently pull the helmet off. After helmet removal, in-line immobilisation must be maintained at all times.

LIFE ON THE ROAD

MALARIA

Malaria is endemic throughout the tropical world as far north as southern Turkey, down to the northern part of South Africa. It kills 1–2 million people every year, with travellers being more susceptible than those indigenous to malarial areas.

Since the disease can only be transmitted to humans by the mosquito, the simplest measure is to **avoid being bitten**.

Mosquito avoidance
- Wear long sleeves and long trousers between dusk and dawn when mosquitoes are active.
- Use insect repellent containing DEET (50% is enough) applied to all exposed skin.
- Use individual lightweight mosquito nets. Soak in Permethrin every six months to increase insect repellence.
- Use vaporising insecticides or slow-burning mosquito coils in sleeping areas.

Antimalarial medication
There are two vitally important points here which cannot be stressed enough.
- Taking these medicines alone **will not prevent you from catching malaria**; they must be combined with the anti-mosquito measures listed above.

- The course of tablets must be **completed as directed** (ie. four weeks after returning) even if you are symptom-free, as the organism can lie dormant in your liver.

The choice of anti-malarial drugs which your doctor will prescribe depends on geographical area, time of year and emergence of resistant strains in that area. The tablets will be either daily or weekly. Most of the drugs available will have some side effects, the only one worthy of mention here being Mefloquine (**Lariam**). The side effects of this have been well publicised and include stomach ache, diarrhoea, insomnia, loss of co-ordination and psychological changes, albeit in a minority of people.

However, it is effective against the most dangerous form of malaria (multi-resistant Plasmodium Falciparum strains) and currently recommended for high-risk areas in Africa, the Amazon and South East Asia. Due to the possibility of intolerable side effects occurring, it's advisable to start taking Mefloquine up to a month prior to departure to allow time to change drugs if necessary.

Useful malaria info websites
- www.malaria.lshtm.ac.uk
- www.malaria-reference.co.uk

Immunisations

Vaccinations need to be sorted out at least **six weeks** prior to departure as some may require several doses and also to allow time for your sore arm and mild flu-like symptoms to subside.

They're available from your doctor or travel clinic. Depending on where you're going and your prior immunisation status, your doctor will select vaccinations based on current state Health Department and WHO guidelines. Owing to these variables your vaccination list might not exactly match that of your travelling companions – a source of anxiety for some but nothing to worry about.

Online you will find a useful vaccine recommendations generator at 💻 **www.fleetstreetclinic.com**.

Apart from Yellow Fever, which remains the only disease for which you must hold a WHO-approved certificate for entry into some two-dozen countries, mostly in **Latin America** and **Central Africa**, there is no legal obligation to have any of these jabs prior to travel.

Vaccination course notes

Hepatitis A	Single dose.
Hepatitis B	Three doses at 0, 1 and 6 months. Transmitted by sexual intercourse and blood. Advisable for a prolonged trip.

Japanese B Encephalitis	Three doses at 0, 7 and 28 days. Recommended for Southeast Asia. Rare but fatal in 30% cases.
Meningitis	Single dose. Africa's 'Meningitis Belt' runs from Senegal to Ethiopia.
Rabies	Three doses at 0, 7 and 28 days. Rare but 100% fatal. Prior vaccination only buys time and medical attention must be sought in the event of contact with source.
Tetanus	Single dose. Get up to date before any trip.
Typhoid	Oral or injection. Common in all developing countries.
Yellow Fever	Single dose.
Diphtheria, Polio & Tuberculosis	(BCG) Vaccinations are routinely given in childhood in developed countries. If you think you may not have had them, ask your doctor about a booster dose.

With all these conditions it is worth remembering that having a vaccination does not make you immune and it is always best to avoid coming into contact with the source of the disease in the first place. Having said that it is important to keep in perspective that all these conditions are incredibly rare and it would be a shame to let paranoia about contracting some exotic condition dissuade you.

There are many sources of information about travel vaccinations and other health issues on the internet:

Medical Advisory Service for Travellers Abroad 💻 www.masta-travel-health.com

World Health Organisation 💻 www.who.int

Travel Health Online 💻 www.tripprep.com

Travel Doctor 💻 www.traveldoctor.co.uk

Diarrhoea

Loose bowel movements occurs in up to 80% of travellers, usually simply from an altered diet or the stresses of an upset body clock, while infective diarrhoea is caused by contaminated food or water. It follows that the latter may be avoided by taking food handling and preparation precautions:

- Prepare your own food.
- Wash hands frequently.
- Protect food from insects and rodents.
- Keep food preparation surfaces spotless.
- Cook food thoroughly and eat immediately.

In addition be particularly cautious with:
- **Shellfish and crustaceans** As filter feeders they tend to concentrate whatever organisms may be in the local sewage outfall which may also contain poisonous biotoxins.
- **Raw fruit and vegetables** Although 'healthy', the locals may well use human faeces as fertiliser. Clean thoroughly or peel.
- **Dairy products** Boil milk before consumption.

Infective diarrhoea may be caused by viruses (which will not be helped by antibiotics), bacteria (E. Coli) or other parasitic micro-organisms (eg Giardia,

Campylobacter, Shigella). Whatever the cause, the symptoms will be loose stools, abdominal cramps and loss of appetite with or without vomiting and high temperature. There may be bloody diarrhoea. These illnesses are usually self-limiting and will settle in a few days without treatment. One exception is amoebic dysentery (caused by an organism called Entamoeba) which is distinguished by a slower onset and bloody diarrhoea without fever. Medical attention with a full course of medicines for around two weeks is always needed.

Treatment

The most important aspect when treating diarrhoea of any cause is **adequate rehydration**. Powder sachets (eg Dioralyte) should be made up with clean water or you can make your own by adding **four teaspoons of sugar plus one teaspoon of salt and a little lemon juice to a litre of water**. Water which has been used to boil rice makes a good alternative.

Antidiarrhoea tablets (Imodium, Arret, etc) temporarily mask the symptoms but prevent the body from flushing the harmful bacteria from the intestines. As such they are best avoided unless you absolutely have to keep riding. The antibiotic Ciprofloxacin (500mg taken twice a day) is effective against most infective causes of diarrhoea but it is only worth considering obtaining a supply from your doctor if you're heading somewhere very remote or tropical.

Medical assistance needs to be sought if you have:
- Diarrhoea for more than four days.
- Diarrhoea with blood.
- Fever (temperature greater than 39°C/102°F) for over 24 hours.
- If confusion develops.

Spiders, snakes, and scorpions

Films like *Arachnophobia*, *Anaconda* and *The Mummy* have much to answer for. Apart from some non-venomous blood-sucking/flesh-eating spider species, none of the above has much to gain by running up and biting you; you're just too big to eat. They will only resort to doing so as a self-defence measure if they feel threatened.

Of the many **spider species** throughout the world that will give a painful bite, only **four** are actually dangerous to humans. The Sydney Funnel Web is the most poisonous, although no fatalities have occurred since the introduction of antivenom in 1980. First aid for a bite by this spider is similar to that for a snake bite (see below). The other notorious species include Latrodectus (Black Widow, Redback), Loxosceles (Recluse spider of North and South America) and Phoneutria (Brazilian Wandering spider), all of which caused fatalities in the days before the introduction of antivenom. Treatment of these bites consists of cleaning the site, applying a cold pack, giving a pain killer and getting the victim to a hospital.

Snake bites

Irrational fear of snakebites is common among travellers despite the fact that they are exceedingly rare and, with correct management, **hardly ever fatal**. The most sensible precaution with snakes is simply to avoid the places where they are likely to be. This means wearing covered footwear in long grass or deep sand, stepping well clear of fallen trees and avoiding hollows. Never approach or provoke a snake.

When camping, keep your tent zipped up at all times, shake out your boots, helmet and jacket each morning if left outside, and be extra careful when collecting firewood. Snakes are attracted to your campsite for warmth (your cooling engine or warm body) and food, such as rodents feeding on your scraps. If any of your group is unlucky enough to get bitten by a snake, you will need to take the following action:

- Reassure the victim. They will be terrified and as such their heart will be pumping harder, accelerating the venom through the system.
- Calmly explain that a tiny minority of snakes are lethal to humans and of these, only 10% of bites inject enough venom to be harmful to an adult. You can also add that death from snakebite occurs after hours or days, not immediately as depicted by Hollywood.
- Cover the bite with a clean dressing. Never suck or wash a wound as it does not help and the hospital will need to swab the site to identify the venom.
- Bandage the limb tightly, starting nearest the heart.
- Immobilise the limb by splinting it, eg by strapping a stick to it as any movement speeds up the spread of venom.
- Give paracetamol or codeine painkillers, **not aspirin**.
- Transport to hospital immediately, keeping the patient as still as possible.

If you're alone follow the same protocol but leave out the splint – you will still be able to ride. Move quickly but do not run. Never attempt to kill or capture the snake. Ignore local snake-bite remedies – it's the **antivenom** available from a hospital which will save your life should envenomation have occurred.

Scorpion stings
Although dangerous scorpions do exist in Africa, North and South America and the Middle East, the chances of a sting being life threatening are almost zero. The most common effects are severe localised pain, swelling and numbness which begin to subside after one hour, similar to an intense wasp sting. Signs of a more severe sting include sweating, shortness of breath, abdominal pain, high temperatures, progressing very rarely to death. Antivenom exists for these cases. Debate exists as to whether it is necessary to visit hospital after a scorpion sting at all. I would say almost certainly not unless the symptoms are progressive. First aid is as for spider bites (see opposite).

Back pain
Long days spent hunched over the 'bars (as opposed to *at* bars) makes back pain common amongst motorcycle travellers, even in young people and those who have never had any previous problems. Poor posture and relative inactivity cause the muscles of the lower back to go into painful spasm and can irritate the nerves where they run through the muscle causing pain down the back of the leg. This is **sciatica** and symptoms can be very debilitating.

LIFE ON THE ROAD

The muscles in question do not work in isolation but rather in an important balance with other muscle groups, namely the deep abdominal muscles (Transversus Abdominis), deep back muscle (Multifidus), pelvic floor muscles and the diaphragm. The key to alleviating low back pain is to redress the balance by exercising these other muscles – something which can be done with a few simple exercises as you ride:

- Regularly tense your pelvic floor muscles gently and hold for 10 seconds whilst breathing normally. These are the same muscles you use to stop yourself passing urine. If you feel your abdominal wall muscles tighten you are clenching too hard.
- Tilt your pelvis by pushing your hips forward so that your back is straight from top to bottom. Hold for 15 seconds.

These principles and exercises are the fundamental basis of **Pilates**, a system of exercise which can be of great benefit to back pain sufferers. If you are prone to back pain when you ride you would be well advised to go to some Pilates classes prior to embarking on a long trip. The numerous subtleties are best taught by an instructor and you will learn a number of exercises which you can do while riding.

Exercise
Although motorcycling undoubtedly uses up more calories than driving a car or sitting at home channel surfing, it's important for your general wellbeing to do some **regular aerobic exercise** at the end of a day's riding. Anything which gets your limbs moving and heart pumping will make you feel healthier, sleep better and have more energy to cope with whatever the trip throws at you. Playing keepie up with a hacky sack or running after a frisbee are good sociable activities using items which take up little room in your panniers. Skipping with your tie-down rope is another good one.

Dentistry
The phrase 'prevention is better than cure' has never been more applicable when it comes to teeth problems on the road. A visit to the dentist several months in advance is an essential part of your pre-trip preparation for the following reasons:

- Almost all dental problems are predictable.
- Any small, previously unnoticed dental cavity can turn into a painful infection under the conditions of poor oral hygiene associated with overland travel.
- As Dustin Hoffman found out in *The Marathon Man*, toothache can become one of the worst types of pain and can be incapacitating.
- Dentists are few and far between in the developing world.
- Hygiene standards are not assured in such places. Transmission of HIV, Hepatitis B and C are possibilities.

Should a gum infection occur the symptoms can be subdued with painkillers, frequent teeth cleaning, hot saltwater mouthwashes and the antibiotics from your first-aid kit. **Oil of cloves** is a well-known remedy to numb toothache.

Altitude sickness

Humans can start to feel the effects of lack of oxygen over about 2600m/8500 feet, a height at which your bike engine will still be functioning without a problem.

Most people will feel unwell if they ascend above 3000m (9850ft), with much variation in individual symptoms and their speed of onset. Headache, fatigue, shortness of breath, dizziness and difficulty sleeping are the common complaints which develop within 36 hours and settle within a few days as acclimatisation occurs. They occur simply due to lack of oxygen and are nothing to do with your level of physical fitness or smoking. Acclimatisation is the process by which the body adjusts to the lack of oxygen with increased heart rate, faster breathing rate and more frequent urination. Vivid dreams are normal during this time.

Acute mountain sickness is the most severe form of altitude sickness experienced by mountaineers who climb too rapidly. It can be fatal and must be treated by immediate descent, although ordinarily would not occur at altitudes normally attainable by a motorcycle.

Heat-related illness

Heat-related illness describes a range of symptoms which occur as the body temperature rises; from heat cramps through to heat stroke which can be fatal. Humans need to maintain their internal (core) body temperature within a relatively narrow range of their normal temperature of 36.5°C/97.7°F in order to function properly. Heat acclimatisation is a process that occurs mainly during the first ten days after moving to a hot climate and is aided by exercising at cool times of day for an hour. The body adapts by gradually lowering its core temperature and making the sweat less salty, meaning that you actually have to **drink more** to stay healthy once acclimatised.

The important factors leading to the development of overheating are:
- High ambient temperature.
- Humidity: cooling by sweating is less efficient in high humidity.
- Heat production: exercise, feverish illness.
- Reduced heat dispersal: heavy protective clothing.
- Dehydration.
- Bodily factors: obesity, lack of acclimatisation.
- Alcohol: exacerbates dehydration, reduces perception and appropriate response to overheating.

Symptoms of heat illness include headaches, muscle cramps, nausea and fainting. Swelling hands and feet are common after travel to a hot climate but settle in a few weeks. Any reduced consciousness or confusion in a person with body temperature over 40°C means that **heat stroke** is setting in, requiring urgent cooling treatment and transfer to hospital.

Treatment of heat illness in all cases consists of **cooling and rehydration**. Stop all activity, find shade and lie in a place which allows air to circulate. Evaporation is an efficient cooling technique: undressing the patient, keep the skin moist while fanning. Bathing in water, application of ice packs or transfer to an air-conditioned environment/vehicle also help.

LIFE ON THE ROAD

WATER PURIFICATION

Water is lost through sweating, urination and vomiting and in hot climates must be drunk constantly. Even then, it's common to be squeamish about water when on the road. A life lived off tap water makes you forget that this is a natural resource which falls from the sky. Along with **wells**, rivers in wilderness areas as well as shady rockpools in desert areas are most likely all safe sources of natural, clean water.

Polluted water is most commonly found around places of human activity, caused by poor sanitation and unhygenic practices. Luckily, **bottled water** is now commonly available throughout the world. Use it but check the cap seals as refilling empties is a well-known scam in poorer countries. Eliminating bugs from water can be done in three ways:

- Boiling for four minutes (but see below).
- Sterilising with chemicals like chlorine, iodine or silver.
- Filtration.

Filtering in the Hindu Kush; slow work but better than the trots.

Boiling uses up fuel and, along with tablets, does not remove impurities in dirty water. Furthermore, water boils below 100°C as altitude increases, so add a minute to your boil for every 1000 feet/300m above sea level.

Sterilising tablets (or liquids) are a less fiddly way of getting pure drinking water. Cheap and effective, their drawbacks include giving water an unpleasant taste (especially chlorine-based tablets), the need to wait from ten minutes to two hours to take effect, and the fact that they can't remove impurities. Iodine can be poisonous if overdosed and silver compounds are slow. For visibly dirty water pouring through a rag helps as it may remove cysts in which bugs like giardia or amoebic dysentery lie dormant.

Manually-operated **filter pumps**, like the well-known Katadyns or MSRs, are fast but expensive and if a ceramic core cracks as it gets thinner, it's had it. These types of pumps are slow and may require cleaning every litre in silty conditions so do your best to pre-filter water.

TRAVEL HEALTH TIPS

- **Get immunised** against commonly-known diseases.
- **Avoid getting bitten** by insects, snakes, rodents and, of course, larger predators.
- **Take malaria pills** – better still use a mosquito net and repellent.
- **Take a first-aid kit** containing at least the items listed on p151.
- **Drink frequently**, particularly at altitude, and if necessary rehydrate (see p160).

- Be sure that your **water source** is clean.
- **Eat nutritious** freshly-cooked food and avoid re-heated meals.
- **Travel insurance** is useful but in the end medical cover is more important than property insurance.
- **Back home**, if you don't feel well (readjustment often produces some ailments), consult your doctor and tell them where you've been.

When things go wrong

Not every day on the road will go as you'd wish and if you're very unlucky you might find yourself in a nightmare-like situation, made all the more stressful because you're abroad. The most common misfortunes on the overland trail are serious illness or injury, road accidents, trouble with the law, and theft. Much less common dangers include rape and assault, armed robbery, kidnapping, the total loss of your bike and being imprisoned.

Travelling in foreign cultures has its perils, and if you find yourself in one of the above scenarios it's as well to remember that the rules, laws and customs of your home country won't apply. Getting out of a legal tangle could be as simple as paying off the right person. With any other show-stopping catastrophe, your best option may be to get back home with the help of travel insurance and your government's representative abroad.

Before you leave it's worth apprising yourself of exactly **what your government can do for you** when things go wrong abroad; this should be set out on their foreign office or travel advice website. It may not be as much as you'd hope, because they're bound by the laws of the nation that hosts their diplomatic mission. One further caveat: if an insurance provider can find a reason for not paying out on a claim, expect them to try their utmost to do so. See p21 for more on buying the most **appropriate travel insurance**.

SERIOUS ILLNESS OR INJURY

When you or one of your party is afflicted by a serious illness or major injury, or has been in a road accident (for more on which, see below), it's time to make use of your travel insurance. This is what you're paying for and the person on the end of the all-important helpline will be practiced in dealing with your predicament even, in my experience, up to the point of offering basic medical advice to keep a person alive. It's worth locating this **helpline number** on the policy document and recording it in a few other places, including on your mobile phone. There's advice on **trauma first aid** in the preceding section

However, don't expect travel insurance costing a pound or two a day to get you the sort of emergency support that expensive sporting events or rallies can muster. Once you make the call they won't mobilise International Rescue and despatch a Chinook full of nurses to pluck you from your predicament by nightfall. Instead, in most cases the patient must be brought to a town or city with a hospital, a journey which, depending on the condition of the patient and access to painkillers, can become very uncomfortable.

> ... don't expect travel insurance costing a pound or two a day to ... mobilise International Rescue and despatch a Chinook full of nurses to pluck you from your predicament by nightfall

LIFE ON THE ROAD

Getting to a hospital will be the priority, and better still, to a hospital in a city with an international airport. You may want to contact your embassy at this time, especially if you've been injured in a criminal attack. If nothing else, embassy staff should be able to recommend local medical facilities as well as legal help, money transfers and so on. If you find yourself needing medical help then consider the following issues:

- How far do you need to travel to reach a decent medical facility? If your condition is serious think about initiating some standby treatment if you have some.
- Public hospitals in many developing countries can be poorly maintained. Mission hospitals or private facilities can be a better bet.
- Healthcare workers in some places are demoralised and underpaid. Be polite and don't make criticisms openly. Clarify issues about payment up front.
- Check the expiry date on any medicines prescribed and what the ingredients are.
- If you're seriously ill and in need of hospitalisation, contact your insurance company straight away. Remember this is exactly what it's for and failure to do so may invalidate any future compensation. If necessary they may organise evacuation by air.

Once a seriously ill patient is stable, the travel insurance provider will almost certainly organise **repatriation**, but this is unlikely to be a Lear jet loaned out by *Médecins Sans Frontières*. If the patient is able to go on a scheduled flight, even in a wheelchair with a drip, that's what they'll use, although transportation to and from the airport and at any stopovers should be covered. If any payments for medical services have to be made, make sure you get receipts or guidance from the insurers on how to proceed.

If you don't have travel insurance you'll be on your own of course, though this need not mean financial ruin. Getting out of a fix can cost no more than the price of a visit to a hospital and then, if necessary, the next flight home.

ROAD ACCIDENTS

A 2010 report by the FIA (💻 www.fiafoundation.org) estimated that annually 25,000 tourists die abroad as a result of road accidents and when others are involved, be they drivers, pedestrians or even livestock the situation can become extremely intimidating. The familiar procedure of the speedy arrival of police, ambulances and the exchanging of insurance details could be muddied by the formation of a curious and possibly hostile crowd.

Small inter-vehicle shunts with minimal damage usually don't need to result in the police being called, and can either be shrugged off or **settled on the spot**; if all are in agreement, it's the best way to resolve the situation. A local in the wrong might well offer to get your bike repaired; you may want to do the same if you feel you were at fault.

If you've seriously **hurt or even killed someone**, most likely a pedestrian, then you're just going to have to ride out the events and hope for the best. This must be understood though: in the poor countries through which you'll be riding it's a mistake to think a **pedestrian** should not be wandering along the road in the first place. Even on a motorway of some kind, in most countries the road is also the **pedestrian's right of way**; in countries like India, it's the right of way of a good few animals too, many of them extremely valuable or even sacred.

Following an accident, it's best not to admit any liability, even though you may get locked up for a short while until things are sorted out. This is the time to get in touch with **your government's representative**, if there is one. If the details are not to hand (check the city listings in a guidebook), it may be simpler to call someone at home and ask them to track down the contact details for you online.

Motor insurance bought locally ought to cover you for such events, but it's not uncommon to regard it as having little actual value save being something to present at checkpoints. While having it may not magically solve the situation, not having it will certainly make the situation worse.

If you're thought to be in the wrong, local mobs can gang up on you and, in some places, victims who are probably desperately poor can see the chance to make a buck. I read recently of some overlanders in Ethiopia being charged several hundred dollars for running down a cow. On a bike that would take some doing, but in similar situations travellers have been advised by well-meaning policemen to **swiftly leave the scene** and not come back. At other times the policeman or other authority figure may insist or suggest some sort of **on-the-spot compensation**. It's up to you to judge whether it's required, fair, or extortionate, but as a foreigner on a flashy bike, you won't have too many cards in your hand. Many travellers are so freaked out and indeed outnumbered that they'll happily pay anything to get out of there fast.

THEFT AND ROBBERY
As long as travellers have travelled, brigands and swindlers have preyed on them. The perils of travel are much reduced in comparison to 500 or 2000 years ago, although the need for vigilance both on the road and in foreign settlements has always been the same.

Accept that on the road it's possible that you may lose something or even everything, through carelessness, bad luck, **theft** or outright robbery. Much has been said about the need to keep your valuables safe, but in the end it's all just stuff that can be replaced, albeit at a price and great inconvenience. This is just a simple fact, the not-so-glamorous side of travel.

Theft is just a pain, from your person or your bike; the perpetrator is long gone before you noticed anything is missing. **Robbery or mugging** is another matter. During the months preceding your departure, it's likely at least one person – an individual who watches a lot of tabloid television and doesn't travel much – will have expressed alarm at your adventurous itinerary. 'Africa/ Iran/Colombia, are you crazy?' You might knock back some bluff reply, but underneath you can't help thinking they might have a point.

More city strategies
Cities anywhere are the lairs of thieves who prey on conspicuous and gullible tourists. Markets and crowded travel termini are favourite haunts for pickpockets. If you find yourself wandering into these places check that everything is zipped up and be alert. Try to keep the evidence of your wealth or your confusion under wraps. **Wallets** should always be zipped into inside jacket pockets or kept in money belts, not bulging in a trouser pocket, and

cameras should not dangle temptingly around your neck. If you're walking around with a day pack on your back, don't put valuables in there; I find a **shoulder bag** that swings round to the front where you can see it is better.

Avoid gazing cross-eyed at town plans on street corners with your mouth half open. In dodgy cities like some African and Latin American capitals, **plan your route** before you walk out of your accommodation and when you do walk, imitate the advice given to women walking alone at night: march with a single-minded purpose that emits the signal loud and clear: 'Don't even think about it, punk!'. Beware of pats on the shoulder, newspapers, flowers or babies being shoved in your face, people claiming to be wiping bird droppings off your coat, and any other number of distractions which are **set-ups** for snatches or pickpockets. If you expect to be coming back drunk from a bar in the early hours, carry only things you can afford to lose.

Guidebooks advise leaving your valuables in the hotel's safe or at reception, but not all **hotels** you'll stay in will inspire such a feeling of security, so some travellers prefer to keep valuables on their person at all times. It's best never to leave valuables in your hotel room.

Getting robbed

While theft is usually an urban problem, robbery, or what's quaintly know as banditry, usually occurs in rural or remote regions, and is as likely in the US or the Ukraine as anywhere else. Again, be wary of set-ups like a **feigned breakdown**. Generally, a family group sat at the roadside by a steaming car will be what it seems, but a couple of shifty-looking sleazebags may have other plans. If you're unsure of the situation, **keep moving**; someone else will help them soon enough if they really need it.

If the game is up the important thing to remember is that assuming they're not severely intoxicated they've little to gain by harming you as that could result in a whole lot more trouble. Acting as a submissive tourist is the best strategy. Valuables are what the robbers are usually after, not your bike. Galling though it may be, **let them have it all**.

Carrying weapons for self defence

Many bikers wonder whether they should carry a weapon as a means of self defence and, if so, what kind. You might imagine situations where it could be reassuring to have some mace, thinking that pepper-spraying an assailant would be an effective deterrent but less risky than a knife or a gun.

The fact is, you'll almost certainly never need to act like this, and possibly won't even have the aggressive instinct to do so when you should. Your best weapon is the common sense to **avoid or flee** such situations, although you never know what you might manage on the day. One mild-mannered overlander I know managed to relieve a drunk, threatening soldier of his AK-47 and later bent the AK's barrel sideways in a tree in his bid for world peace.

Most of us have never seen a **handgun** and would consider the idea of carrying one abroad absurd, but for overlanders from societies where gun ownership is widespread, the prospect of travelling without a gun may unnerving, even if they know it's bound to be illegal. Using a handgun or even a knife to protect yourself might be advisable if you're prepared to face the consequences, including getting it wrong. When you're feeling a bit insecure it can be fun to fantasise about wasting the dirtbag who tried to rob you, but most people appreciate that real-life armed struggles and fights aren't the beautifully choreographed balletics from *The Matrix*, but clumsy affairs.

Mace or **pepper spray** sounds like a more innocuous and compact alternative to a Glock and is recommended in some ursine habitats and sold elsewhere as an urban self-protection agent. But again, ask yourself how

You got me! © Walter Colebatch

often are you likely to come up against a witless sole assailant who can be taken out with a quick squirt? The reality is if you're indeed under attack and unable to flee, you'll be either petrified or just very frustrated that it's happening.

POLICE TROUBLE

It pays to be on your best behaviour abroad, if for no other reason than you can land yourself in trouble for any number of unknown and unexpected transgressions. These can include immigration or visa infractions, a road-traffic offence or accident, entering or 'spying' in a restricted area (including some border areas), possessing illegal drugs or bootleg DVDs, smuggling (including prehistoric artefacts or fossils), not fully declaring something (including certain foods and gadgets), talking with the wrong people or just being in the wrong place at the wrong time, political or religious insensitivity including insulting behaviour, or being disrespectful about the head of state. This list goes on.

Once they have you they'll be in no rush to admit a possible mistake and release you. You don't have to be in a North Korean-style police state to recognise that **human rights** in many of the countries you plan to visit are woeful; falling foul of the system and having to undergo even a short spell in prison could be traumatising. Whatever you think of the quality of policing back home, it'll be heavenly compared to the pitiless contempt for citizens' rights you're likely to encounter abroad. You can also be **set up** for any of the above offences by corrupt police or vengeful locals who you may have annoyed.

If you're **arrested**, the first step is to get in touch with a friend or family member and then your local embassy, high commission or consulate, or an embassy or honorary consul that might represent your country. This is vital if you're not to disappear because you'll be helpless and need people on the outside to fight your case.

Drugs

Drugs offences probably get more young overseas travellers in trouble with the law than anything else. Not a few of them have been set up by dealers or guest-house owners working with the police. The best advice must be to just say no while you're on the road, unless you're clearly in a comfortable situation. Otherwise, along with any number of other traps you can fall into, there's too much at stake.

LIFE ON THE ROAD

Bike maintenance and troubleshooting

Even today a motorcycle is a fairly simple machine and one on which it's easy to see or feel if something is wrong and to track it down quickly. As a result of that you can pretty much coincide a service and check over with your oil changing intervals of every few thousand miles. Due to superior oil filtration technology modern machines like Triumph's Explorer have service intervals of 10,000 miles, but out in the dusty, demanding AMZ doubling your oil change intervals is one of the best things you can do to ensure engine longevity, especially if you're running on ordinary local oils. This is where older machines which run cooler and are in a lower state of tune have their benefits, being less sensitive to sub-optimal fuel and oil.

Unless you've run your bike for a while, or took a thorough test trip, there are sure to be tweaks you make in the early days of your big trip as you settle into the machine: suspension, tyre pressures, ergonomics, adjusting loads. Otherwise, do a checkover at the end of rough stages of several days, be it dirt tracks or bad roads. **Home-made fittings** are especially prone to failure on the first corrugated track.

Brushing from a jar of your top-up oil helps clean the chain and works once a handy aerosol runs out. A stick under the rack props the wheel up on the side stand.

Lubing the chain

Where present, it's worthwhile lubing the drive chain frequently as chain and sprockets can be a pain to replace out in the world and are heavy spares to carry. Keeping an eye on the tension as well as a little daily lubing can double the service life. **A little lube applied regularly** is the way to go and stops your back wheel getting covered in muck. For most of us, a tin of aerosol spray from home won't last and may be hard to buy on the road, so instead apply a little engine oil from a squeeze bottle or off a toothbrush on the **inside** of the lower chain just before it engages the rear sprocket while the wheel spins in first gear on the centre stand or while propped and lean over on the side stand. Heavier non-synthetic gear oil will cling better, a garage will top you up a half-pint's worth. All this messing about can be automated by fitting a Scott Oiler system, the cheaper Loobman or making such a device yourself.

IMPROVISED REPAIRS

Making your own repairs is something that worries inexperienced riders, and there's often justified nervousness about getting what might be a bad job done by a local metal basher. Often all you need is to bodge something to keep moving. It's actually very rare for a bike to be completely stranded and unrepairable and it's worth recognising that, even though you may not think so now, the more irresolvable the problem, the greater will be the ingenuity of you or the people around you in fixing it.

Even if it's not your nature, try and develop a systematic, logical approach to **fault diagnosis** and, if necessary, a lateral approach to problem solving.

GETTING PARTS

Messrs Honda, Suzuki and Yamaha may sell motorbikes in every corner of the world but that doesn't mean that parts for your Euro/US model, not to mention Aprilia, BMW or Cagiva will be available or even obtainable in far flung places.

Having witnessed a Thai parts supplier stuff my piston in his pocket, hop on his scooter and disappear off into the Bangkok traffic in a trial-and-error search for some piston rings that 'might' fit convinced me to forget the expense and have parts couriered out from home. The resulting series of catastrophes, by people who really should know better, remains the most frustrating part of my trip. How can it take *two months* to get a gudgeon pin for Honda's ubiquitous XR400?

Should you need parts from home, to minimise the risk of waiting weeks or even months for them to arrive try the following:

● Before you leave, try to find one, or preferably two, parts suppliers who specialise in your bike; make and model. Big multi-franchise dealerships often carry plenty of parts for the latest pocket rockets but very little for trusty old overlanders.
● Phone them up and tell them what you're doing and where you're going. Ask them: will they ship parts abroad and if they have done so before.
● Check how much stock they actually carry. Some companies who claim to have every part available often don't.
● If they don't have a part in stock, ask where would they get it from. Some UK dealers, for instance, get their parts from mainland Europe which takes longer and the savings aren't always passed on to the customer.
● Get contact details, especially email address, phone and a contact name.
● Do a little research on your bike. Are there any parts notorious for failing and/or being difficult to obtain? Dependent on cost, you might want to pre-order a part or maybe leave it with a reliable friend.

● If you do order parts from abroad, use a courier like DHL or FedEx. Regular postal services may offer a 48-hour international parcel service, and indeed your package might reach the destination country in that time, but when it hits customs it will probably just stop dead.
● Couriers usually offer a customs clearance service, and although more expensive, if you consider the cost in time, money and sheer frustration of hanging around for weeks, they represent good value.
● Expect the worst. Sadly, it is possible someone along the line will mess it up. Think about what could go wrong and plan accordingly. Always give detailed instructions and information and keep track of all involved.
● Make sure the shipper provides you with the courier's tracking number. Most couriers offer a web-based tracking system – use it! As soon as your package has landed get in touch with the nearest courier office, preferably in person and with all your documentation. Keep the pressure on. The slogan 'every second counts' doesn't always apply in some parts of the world.
● If second-hand parts are being sent, make sure they are completely free of oil, uranium, anthrax or any other substance that could be deemed 'hazardous'. Airlines can get funny about what's in a package. If in doubt, check with the courier or airline first.
● Ask your supplier to reduce the value of each item on the invoice and therefore the amount of duty you will have to pay. But don't get too carried away; customs aren't stupid.

If it all goes wrong, don't get stressed. Ranting and raving may make you feel better, but will make your situation worse.

The above may seem excessive, but it's all based on real life incidences which have left people tearing their hair out. A few hours' pre-departure preparation could save a lot of time on your trip. RICHARD VIRR

LIFE ON THE ROAD

Fault	Possible cause	Possible cure
Engine won't turn over; dim or no lights.	Flat battery, faulty alternator (see p177).	Find another battery or jump start; in freezing conditions pre-warm the engine and battery.
Lights are fine, but starter won't engage.	Some sort of starter safety cut-out in operation.	Is the stand up, box in neutral and clutch in? If not, a switch may think it is.
Starter motor spins but won't engage.	Can still be a weak battery or a worn starter. More likely a dodgy solenoid switch or a jammed Bendix gear.	Sharply tap the starter housing with rock or hammer to release jammed Bendix. Or remove to check and clean the solenoid.
Engine turns over but won't start.	No spark at the plug. No fuel.	Check for spark by removing a plug and turning engine over while holding the plug against the cylinder head. Check fuel level or find blockage or air lock.
Engine running badly or misfiring.	Inadequate battery charge. Poor fuel mixture. Blocked fuel filters. Faulty EFI; dirty plugs. Very high altitude (see p174).	Charge or replace battery. Check for air leaks in the fuel system. Check plugs. Check fuel pump. Check/replace fuel filters.
Oil pressure light won't go out, even above 2000rpm.	Faulty oil-pressure switch (unlikely). Engine-oil level low or oil very old (thin). Badly worn engine, (usually associated with tapping or knocking noises).	Check oil level. Check oil switch. Change oil. Rebuild engine following a cylinder-compression check (easily done with gauge).
Overheating.	Engine speed too high or ground speed too slow for ambient conditions. Broken fan Loose or worn radiator cap or leaking hoses. Insufficient coolant or oil level. Radiator fins blocked or mashed. The bike is overloaded. Old, worn engine.	Check oil and coolant levels, radiator and cap (squeeze hoses); leaks can evaporate almost instantly. Check fan switch or wire to horn button. **Slow down** if it's 45°C in the shade and roadside reptiles are fainting! You're expecting too much and need a new or bigger engine.
Flat battery.	Discharged overnight; faulty alternator. Low fluid level in unsealed battery.	Jump start; recharge battery. Top up with distilled water, though any water will do in an emergency.

LIFE ON THE ROAD

Fault	Possible cause	Possible cure
Ruptured brake line.	Damage, rust or perishing.	Slow down and replace when possible.
Leaking radiator.	Rust, damage.	If you don't have a radiator sealant, use curry powder, egg white, or ground cork – anything that will swell or harden as it's forced through the leak. Alternatively, remove the radiator and repair with solder using a flame-heated tyre lever.
Split radiator hoses.	Old age, wear or poor fitting.	Bind tightly with duct tape, though replacement is better. Carry spare hose clips.
Broken or leaking exhaust.	Vibration, old age, rust.	A fracture mid-pipe can be splinted with a cut-open tin can and a pair of hose clips or lockwire. Leaky joins can be filled with a soft metal. Up to a point bikes can run OK without much of a silencer.
Cracked metal fuel tank or engine/gearbox casing.	Rock or accident damage, weak mounts, vibration.	A bar of soap rubbed into a cracked tank is an old bodge though 'chemical metal' epoxy pastes made for the job are better. Plastic tanks can be repaired with epoxy glue.
Engine cuts out in hot and slow conditions.	Vapour lock – occurs when petrol vapour blocks the passage of liquid fuel through the fuel pump (carb engines only). (See also p60)	Let everything cool down or drape the fuel pump with a wet rag to cool it and condense the fuel vapour. Only a short-term solution.
ECU error code appears.	ECU registers a fault (there may not be one).	Establish fault or clear error code with OBD reader (see next page).
Exhaust pops and bangs on hard deceleration.	Unburned fuel is leaking into the exhaust system and exploding there.	Exhaust valve may need adjusting (not closing fully) or is burned out and needs regrinding against the cylinder head. This is not a serious problem.
Brakes are mushy and lack power.	Air in the brake fluid.	Bleed the system (see next page).

LIFE ON THE ROAD

ENGINES AT HIGH-ALTITUDE

Carbs work best mixing consistent levels of fuel and air. At anything above 3000m there is increasingly less air and your bike (especially smaller engines) will run 'rich', which actually means 'run very poorly indeed'.

Fitting smaller jets inside the carb can be a fiddly roadside job; lowering the carb needle is a bit easier. Both tricks reduce fuel flow so lean out the mixture to balance it with the reduced levels of oxygen in the air. More air is easier still: temporarily removing the air box lid or even the air filter (if not dusty) will go some way to rebalancing the mixture.

All these steps will have to be reversed once you lose height. Bikes with EFI have far fewer problems at altitude.

Lacking a dust-controlled diagnostic suite, **improvisation** is at the heart of many roadside remedies and is how many of the developing world's vehicles keep running. It's beyond the scope of *AMH* to offer detailed guidelines so this advice is generalised, but with just about all the remedies listed here it pays to ride slowly initially and to check a repair frequently. Very often a first repair is not initially effective, especially if sensitive to vibration, and you may have to try something else. These ideas cover only vital items that must be addressed to maintain mobility. Usually, as long as you get the engine running, however badly, you can keep moving.

Now wash your hands

This can become messy work. If you're not using disposable latex **gloves** (available in bulk from car shops or chemists), carry re-usuable heavy-duty washing-up or gardening gloves. Alternatively, wet your hands with soap, allow them to dry and go to work. Once the job's done you'll find that with a little added soap and water, grease and oil will rinse off much more easily. If you forget to do this then washing your hands afterwards in a mixture of washing-up liquid or soap and **sand or sugar** is also an effective way of cutting through oily grime.

FAULT DIAGNOSIS AND FIXES

If you don't know exactly how engines work look at it this way: will it start; will it run; will it go, steer and stop? Engines **won't start** for two main reasons: a lack of electrical power or fuel. More rarely some mechanical issue like a broken starter motor may be the problem, or, more commonly these days, a relatively insignificant electronic malfunction like a blown fuse may disable your CANbus controlled engine by default, though this stuff is happening less and less as these systems evolve.

Should an **error or fault code** appear somewhere on the dash, getting on the internet to find out what it means may help track down the problem. It's not uncommon for non-terminal error codes – to do with emissions, for example – to flash up even if the bike seems to be running fine. Ignore these.

Once running, if **engines** perform badly or intermittently, it's usually due to a poor air/fuel mixture, though again on modern, electronically-managed fuel injected engines, a loose connection, faulty battery or some electronic sensor may be the cause. Despite the fact it needs very clean fuel at high pressure, electronic fuel injection hasn't proved to be a weak spot on modern bikes. If anything EFI bikes run better in a wider range of conditions.

Assuming the engine started and is running sweetly, only some element of the **transmission** can still be a problem – brakes and steering usually leave you something to get by with. Steering head and wheel **bearings** usually give a lot of warning before they collapse completely, but they are consumable parts whose life will be shortened in dusty or wet conditions. Certainly on a old bike, new bearings all round are a good idea before departure.

A **clutch** should not go without warning either, unless it's been ragged in which case you have yourself to blame, such as riding a loaded bike hard uphill in soft conditions on a hot day. Just like you, a clutch can only take so much. On a bike it's usually the friction plate(s) that goes – a single 'dry' plate on big GS boxers (like a car), or wet plates in oil as on most other bikes. Some hyper-slippery synthetic oils don't marry so well with wet clutches. Again, on an old machine it's worth fitting a new one. Gaskets can be made from cardboard, providing the single piece is big enough, or just use gasket sealant.

With **brakes** the usual problem with bikes is a sticking piston in the caliper, down to old age, rust or gunge – or the sensation that the brakes have gone mushy which means air has got into the brake fluid, again usually due to old brake lines which may themselves bulge and lose braking power as they age (the reason steel braided brake lines are better). To bleed a brake have some fresh brake fluid – you may need 100-200ml. Locate and fit a spanner

(usually 8 or 10mm ring) to the bleed nipple down on the caliper (pictured right), fit a clear hose to the nipple and dip the other end into a jar with a bit of brake fluid in it. Then with the master cylinder reservoir open, operate the brake – as you feel resistance open and close the bleed nipple quickly to eject hopefully aerated fluid. Then close the nipple, release the brake lever and repeat, not forgetting to top up the reservoir as you go. When what comes

out at the caliper has no air in it, you have succeeded in purging the system with new fluid.

Gearboxes give lots of warning, often thousands of miles, before they pack up entirely, but it is going to be a major repair when you get round to it.

What follows are some other leads on solving common problems. Your vehicle repair manual may have more ideas.

Common battery problems

When you run into electrical problems – the vehicle is dead or won't start – before testing the alternator as described on p177, check the fuses and then the battery terminals. It's possible to have low-wattage items such as small lights working but not have enough electrical power running from the battery to

RECHARGING ELECTRONICS

Never mind the bike, these days you need a full array of cables, adapters and chargers to keep your show on the road.

Above all, make sure it all works *before* you leave, make use of the bike's 12-volt charging capacity (the USB 12-volt cig charger centre right is very useful, for example) and if possible, have back-up methods of charging gadgets (wall, bike, solar, storage battery) as well as importing data from SD cards.

turn the starter motor. A quick wiggle or twist of the cable clamps may be all that's needed. Even if they're not loose on the **battery terminals** from shaking, oxidisation can make a poor contact (which is why terminals are covered in a grease like Vaseline). If poor contact looks like the cause, try filing the inside of the battery clamps and the lead battery terminals, and make sure the clamp is tight on each terminal. Because terminals are made of soft lead, they can erode over the years so that the vehicle's original clamp cannot tighten properly around it. Don't forget to check where the battery's **negative lead** is earthed, usually at the bike's chassis. Rust can develop here too, degrading the contact. After unbolting, this is easily remedied with a file, or by rubbing the removed lead on a rock until it's shiny bare metal again.

Next, if the battery is not a maintenance-free sealed item, check the **electrolyte fluid**. With the battery level (in the horizontal sense), electrolyte acid should cover the plates of all six chambers. If it doesn't (it's common for levels to be uneven), top them up with **distilled water**; the battery may well recover, but you ought to wonder why the levels have suddenly dropped unless you've not checked them for months. At worst, the battery is being overcharged by a faulty voltage regulator on the back of the alternator.

To top up, any water will do if you're desperate, but don't confuse boiled water (sterilised) with distilled water. Boiled water may well be *more* mineral-rich (less distilled) than normal water; it's the evaporated steam that, once condensed can be called mineral-free or distilled. You can make your own by making a still but as Ray Mears has proved, this can take some time.

Of course this is all a comforting old-school scenario of roadside diagnostics, at which many of us have become master practitioners. These days an **error code** on the instrument panel might also highlight an electrical fault. You can now get error code readers or emergency diagnostic code readers like the GS911 gadget for just about all GS BMW models. They work with your PC or smartphone – this is the way electronic roadside repairs are going – and most importantly can read and then **clear** an errant fault code. Quite possibly it's something you'd never have known about in the old days until that component or system failed. **Loose or worn connections** will still probably be the physical cause of such a malfunction, but to that must be added the array of **sensors** and other electronic components that monitor or manage a modern bike's functions, all of which can complicate matters.

Charging system – the alternator

When due to age, wear or possibly overuse (too much drain on the electrical system), an **alternator** starts malfunctioning (it can become only partially efficient), your bike may continue running as normal, but the battery won't be getting adequately charged. After a few hours, or if you suddenly increase electrical consumption by turning on headlights for example, the **red charge warning light** (usually a 'battery' icon) and maybe a fault code will light up on the dash. Lights will soon dim and the engine may misfire or stop.

On seeing this warning light **don't stop the engine**: chances are the battery won't have enough power to restart it. Instead turn off what electrical ancillaries you can. Modern engines rely very much on correct levels of electrical power, if not sensitive electronic management, and engines will shut down very quickly if the system voltage drops minimally.

Ascertaining the voltage

Before you stop the engine make one more test. Get a **voltmeter** or multimeter (a device for testing electrical circuits and levels), set it to DC and check the voltage across the battery terminals with all lights and so on turned off. With the engine running at about 2000rpm it should read between 13.5 and 14.5 volts – normal for a 12-volt battery. If the voltmeter reads much less than 12 volts with the engine running, the alternator is not functioning fully. You can make further checks by turning on lights and revving the engine. The reading across the battery terminals should still show around 14 volts as the alternator adapts to the added load on the battery. If it reads less than 12 volts, or worse still is dropping before your eyes, it's more proof that the alternator is kaput.

If it rises way over 14 volts as you rev the engine the **regulator** isn't regulating and may have already damaged your battery.

With alternator problems usually one of the three sets of copper windings inside the body has broken or shorted out. They can only be repaired by a specialist so replacement is the simplest route. It's not always possible to see the break in the windings, but if on removal and disassembly they appear black rather than coppery, it could be a bad sign.

Rear shock

Exacerbated by force-multiplying leverages, the modern single rear shock on a loaded overlanding bike running over rough terrain can have a hard time. Bathed in waste engine heat, it creates heat itself as the friction of internal valving tries to dampen the coil spring's in-built tendency to

What looks like a carved up tyre returns some damping to this cooked GS11 shock.
© Margus Sootla

rebound. Coil springs themselves rarely break, and if they do the way they're wrapped around the damper's body means they just drop by one coil. More commonly seals on the pressurised inside wear out or burst, something which usually requires a professional rebuild. BMW GSs running two-up, especially the 1150s, are not immune to this problem which can be temporarily fixed as shown on p177.

Worrying noises

Diagnosing errant sounds from your engine takes experience and is another good reason to take the bike on a test run for a few days as the added weight could reconfigure the harmonics. Obviously noises you need to react to swiftly include something scraping along the road or an ever-louder tapping or knocking from the engine. Low-octane petrol or high temperatures can also make an engine sound noisier. After riding off road it's not uncommon for a stone to get caught in the brake disc cowling or under a bash plate and rattle annoyingly. Don't beat yourself up about over-reacting to or being paranoid about noises. It's quite easy to isolate and so diagnose a noise while riding along by following these actions:

Noise	Possible cause
Only at a certain speed or increases with speed?	It could be something loose on the bodywork/exterior or speed-related resonating.
Only in a certain gear?	It's probably a faulty gearbox. While riding along, pull in the clutch and let the revs drop. If the noise is still present it's not associated with the engine and is coming from the gearbox, wheels or bodywork.
Noise drops off as the revs drop, with the clutch in.	It's the engine or clutch. Stop soon and investigate.
Engage neutral and rev the engine.	If the noise increases with revs it's coming from the engine.
Engage neutral and coast.	Does noise match the vehicle's speed as it slows down? It could be the shaft drive/chain or wheel bearings.
Sirens.	Pull over.

Jump leads and push starts

It's said that CANbus bikes are not suited to jump starting and some leads come with built-in 'surge protection' devices to stop the ECU from getting a jolt, but be that as it may, a pair of home-made jump leads at least a metre long and with croc clips each end are well worth carrying with you. If you don't have them, any bit of thick wire will do, the clips just save you having to use hands to press the wire against the terminals

Push starting an XRL for a bet – I lost. Carry a small set of jump leads.

Push starts are best achieved in a high gear but will be hard work without a downhill, especially on big singles. If the engine is cold and you have a kick start, pull the clutch in and take a few swings to clear the plates. Then, put the bike in second gear and pull it backwards onto compression. This way, when propelled forward, the piston(s) will get a good speed before it hits compression and the spark. Start off in neutral and, once moving at a good speed of 10mph or more, pull in the clutch, click up into second and dump the clutch as you jump down onto the saddle. The mass of your weight will help load the back tyre and make it grip rather than spin. The key is to synchronise dumping the clutch with dropping onto the seat – easier if you are astride the bike and whizzing downhill rather than gasping as you run alongside. **Towing** is another way of doing it, but obviously has perils of being pulled over. There is also footage online of bikes being started when parked **back to back** with wheels touching, like a rolling road. It's worth a try.

Air filters

Along with clean fuel and motor oil, your engine's longevity, like your own, will be extended by breathing clean air. In an urban setting it's not so vital, but riding on dusty tracks or in arid and windy conditions for weeks at a time will clog up the filter. Black exhaust smoke can mean the engine's **running rich** (not enough air in the air/fuel mixture), which can be due to a blocked filter.

Loose or split induction hoses, as well as a damaged or incorrectly fitted filter, are worse for engine wear than a blocked filter, which merely reduces performance, and so the filter, airbox and attachment hoses should be inspected occasionally and will need to be **cleaned**. Some bikes may have a light that comes on when the air filter is clogged, but it takes a lot of dust and neglect to get this bad. Far better to clean the filter before that happens.

It pays to work out where your bike actually **draws its air**. Some trail bikes have poor designs which throw dirt from the back tyre straight in. It's also good to know your 'plimsoll line' when you're riding through rivers.

I find greasing the inside surfaces of the airbox catches dust and sand and so keeps the element cleaner for longer, but eventually it'll need cleaning.

Foam filter maintenance

Most bikes run **open-cell foam filters**. Again these must be cleaned and re-oiled with a special air-filter, but with this sort of maintenance will last much longer than a standard paper filter.

If you're heading into dusty desert conditions it can save time to carry a spare, pre-oiled filter which you can quickly and easily replace to clean the dirty one later on. The correct tacky **foam-filter oil** (available in aerosols and from dirt-bike shops) doesn't seep down and dry out as engine oil can do, but if you take it and it runs out, clean engine oil is better than nothing. Clean the filter in fuel, let it dry, oil it and squeeze out the excess – a messy job made less so with rubber gloves or by squeezing the foam inside a plastic bag.

LIFE ON THE ROAD

Washing a foam filter in fuel. Use gardening gloves for messy tasks like this.

Adventure motorcycling – the bird's eye view

Lois Pryce advises on the pleasures and pitfalls of women riding solo.

I'm pleased to say that the last few years have seen an increase in the number of women entering the wonderful world of adventure motorcycling, either solo or as part of a couple. But outside the Western world, a woman on a motorcycle remains an unusual sight and you'll still be regarded as something of a novelty once you venture into the AMZ: Africa, Asia or Latin America.

A mud-splattered woman astride a loaded up bike, rumbling into a remote village, is not something those villagers will forget in a hurry. Although your status as a travelling circus act can sometimes feel over-whelming, all well-travelled women riders report countless incidents of immense kindness, generosity and encouragement from men and women alike (if you exclude officers of the law, of course). There is definitely a hearty dose of goodwill out there for female adventure *motards*.

It's a man's world
The feminist revolution didn't make much of a dent outside the West so in the developing world as a general rule men do the drinking, smoking and driving (sometimes all at the same time) and women look after the home and have babies. This is of course normal life for the majority of the world's population, but it can be a bit of a culture shock to the independent Western woman arriving on a motorcycle fresh out of emancipated Europe or North America. Bear in mind though that in their world you yourself are a one-woman, two-wheeled, travelling culture shock. You'll be a novelty item everywhere you go, so expect to be stared at, pointed at, quizzed and (hey, if you're lucky) even poked and mauled. There's nothing quite like being surrounded by a crowd of shouting, sleeve-tugging men yelling 'where is husband?' to make you want to roar off into the distance. While this can be intimidating at times, it's gen-erally borne out of genuine curiosity, so if you can grin and bear it with a friendly smile, and brush off unwanted overtures without bruising anyone's ego, you should manage to ease your way out of most situations leaving everyone's pride intact.

DIFFERENT STROKES FOR DIFFERENT FOLKS
Although there are some generalisations that can be made about the experi-ence of being a woman on the road, situations differ depending on where you are. Culture and religious beliefs will determine a large part of your experi-ence and how you're viewed as a female, especially if travelling solo.

Latin America is a popular destination for women riders, as it's certainly one of the safest and most comfortable places in which to travel, once you get your head round the idea that the Latin male ego is as fragile as his country's economy and must be indulged. When you enter Mexico from the US there's no official sign saying 'Welcome to Machoworld – you are now entering the land of the Latin Lover' but it's obvious that from here on, you're playing by a different set of rules. Masculinity reigns supreme and the division of the sexes is abundantly clear. Machismo is as much a part of the Latin American culture as dictatorships and civil war, and this is simply a fact that one has to accept. On the whole this macho approach manifests itself as chivalry rather than lechery but nonetheless, travelling solo in this part of the world can require some re-adjustment of your behaviour and at times, severe gritting of the teeth. But there's no use in allowing it to wind you up as this only provides extra entertainment for your 'admirers' while spoiling your day. It's hard, but any feminist principles are best left at the Mexican border in the receptacle provided.

Him indoors, her on the road.
© Lois Pryce

Africa is a tougher proposition. The Muslim countries can be an isolating experience for women who often find themselves facing what can appear to be hostility from the male population. It takes a reformatting of one's cultural hard-drive to understand that when someone refuses to speak to or look at you, they're in fact being respectful rather than rude! Often you'll encounter complete incredulity that a woman is capable of riding a motorcycle 'like a man'. In the Algerian Sahara I was once detained at a highway checkpoint, just because I was a woman and even though I was with a tour agency escort in a car (the rule for all tourists in Algeria). Even then, the rewards to be gained from travelling by motorcycle through this beautiful and fascinating part of the world far outweigh any negatives, and for a less intense version, Morocco and Tunisia provide a more tourist-friendly, Westernised experience.

South of the Sahara being ignored will be the least of your problems. The attention you will garner as a girl on a motorcycle is usually completely harmless but it can be intimidating when each time you stop you're surrounded by a clamouring group who think nothing of touching you and your belongings. You do eventually get used to it and realise that your sense of 'personal space' should have been sent home with your feminist principles. Like most places on this earth, the further away you get from heavily populated areas, the more pleasant your African experience will be. But as opposed to Latin America where women are revered, albeit in a sexist fashion, life is tougher in Africa for women. This is apparent everywhere and is mirrored in the way they're treated in a society which operates on a 'survival of the fittest' basis.

Many women riders report favourable experiences in Asia, especially in what are thought to be challenging countries like Iran and Pakistan, where they tell tales of lavish hospitality and genuine friendliness. Any lascivious behaviour you may encounter is usually the result of a guy conflating his internet porn with re-runs of Friends, and can be handled with a firm brush-off, or just a firm brush, if you have one handy. As a woman you're rarely viewed as a threat and if you're travelling solo you'll often find that the locals will feel

LIFE ON THE ROAD

Ladies on the Loose DVD
Inspiring – even for blokes.

sorry for you. In these more family-centred cultures it's inconceivable that a woman would want to put herself in such a supposedly dangerous situation! So rather than the predictable horrors that the folks back home will warn you about, you may find it's the excessive hospitality that gets you in the end! It's a good idea to carry photos of your family, invent a 'respectable' profession like a teacher, and talk about your father a lot.

Travelling in Muslim countries does of course bring its own set of rules for women travellers; simple things like shaking hands or walking alone with a man can be misread and in places the dress code required is not exactly conducive to motorcycling. It can be a frustrating business to have to constantly cover up, especially in hot weather, but the best approach is to think of the photo opportunities – you can't beat that bike 'n' burka shot!

Ahead of the pack

As a motorcyclist you already have a huge advantage over the average gap-year student trudging her sorry way along the backpacker trail. This is alarmingly apparent as soon as you get off the bike and change into your flip-flops for a wander around town, only to find yourself accompanied by the hissing and catcalling of over-attentive local men. Although you're not totally exempt from harassment while riding – filtering through grid-locked, sweltering Lima while being barraged with lewd suggestions from the stationary cars was one particularly memorable day for me – the bike will almost always help in gaining you respect. Arriving in a town on a motorcycle invariably raises you to near-male status from some men's viewpoint, while promoting you to a Wonder Woman figure in the eyes of the women who, never having even contemplated leaving their village, let alone on a motorcycle, will proclaim you to be very brave. Just don't tell 'em how easy it is or the world will fall apart!

Him indoors

Out in the AMZ family and married life feature more prominently than in Western society and you'll frequently find yourself being quizzed about your personal situation. As well as discussing your family and carrying photos of them, it's also a good idea to invent a husband who has just nipped off to buy some bike parts (or another suitably manly pursuit).

Throughout Latin America I wore a fake wedding ring, giving me instant respectability and helping me out of all sorts of tricky situations, including negotiating my way through a Mexican roadblock with a hastily concocted tale of my devoted spouse urgently awaiting my arrival in the next town. But where my imaginary husband really came into his own was at police and military checkpoints where I was regularly met with the two standard questions: 'Are you married?' 'YES!' and 'Do you have any drugs?' 'NO!' Get these answers the wrong way round and you could find yourself on the receiving end of a marriage proposal from a prison warder.

WOMAN, KNOW YOUR PLACE
While the Benny Hill-style pestering is undoubtedly annoying, it's usually harmless and often tempered with a gentlemanly regard for old-fashioned chivalry. God forbid that a woman should adjust her chain tension or even check her oil unaided! Maybe some of you female readers are expert motorcycle mechanics, but my skills in that area are rudimentary, and let's face it, men do seem to know more about this stuff. So when Jose (who was pinching your arse in the supermarket a few hours previously) spies you by the roadside miserably watching oil pouring out of your crankcase, any unsavoury thoughts are banished by the gleaming opportunity that has presented itself: to be a knight-mechanic in shining armour! Tools, pick-up trucks, friends, brothers are all rounded up and an unholy cacophony of banging and clanking ensues until you're up and running again, with not a pinched bottom in sight. There is only one rule in this situation which must be heeded: Do not offer any advice. Even if you absolutely know they're doing something wrong, or they've picked up the wrong size socket, or haven't replaced the washer or whatever. Don't try telling them. As far as they're concerned, you wouldn't know an 12-mil ring from a loaf of bread. And more importantly, they don't want you to know anything – it'll only spoil their fun and offend their sensibilities. So just sit there, let them over-tighten the bolts and make precise adjustments by hitting things with tyre levers, because y'know what? They'll fix it a whole lot quicker than you will. Once again, a feminist stance has about as much currency here as the Argentinean peso in Alaska.

Trust your instincts
Of course you don't want to go around shunning contact with every swaggering moustachioed man you see (er, actually maybe you do). But there's that fine line to be trod between using your common sense and turning into a paranoid wreck. The communicating and mingling with the locals is all part of the experience, and travelling by motorcycle makes this a much more viable prospect than it is for the backpackers who are bussing it from one tourist attraction to the next. Your common sense will naturally find that correct level of wariness while still satisfying your urge for adventure. Just remember to be patient and genial while retaining an air of confidence, even if you don't feel it at the time. Some of the people you meet may not see things the way you do, but for the short time that your paths cross, it doesn't really matter.

And finally...
In the run up to your departure you'll be inundated with horror stories from well-meaning friends, colleagues and family members. 'You'll get raped!' I remember one panic-stricken acquaintance of mine declaring hysterically as I set off into Mexico. These people must be ignored. Of course, one can't deny that bad things can happen and that there are nasty people out there. But this is as applicable to Tunbridge Wells as it is to the Congo. It may be worth pointing out to the doom merchants that good things can also happen and there are nice people out there too. Alternatively, you can save your breath and start packing. Sure, you'll have some tough days, miserable days, and days when you wish you hadn't got up; it's the same for all independent travellers. But you'll never wish you hadn't set off.

Filming your trip

We have the technology to self-shoot adventure films from places that most TV production companies wouldn't go to for less than £100,000 plus expenses. Today, compact **still cameras** and even phones can shoot HD film while tiny **bullet cameras** can mount in places you'd not risk with proper cameras.

So the fabulous technology may be there, but what hasn't changed is the **planning, commitment and techniques** required to produce something that will captivate someone other than yourself. Filming your trip can easily dominate and even disrupt your journey, but when properly edited, the results will be a lifelong souvenir of something you'll probably only do once. If you want to do more than merely assemble a bunch of never-to-be-edited footage (that unfortunately ends up on youtube anyway), here are some tips.

CHOOSING A CAMERA

You can get great results, save space and learn what works by experimenting with the ever-improving video capabilities of a **digital still camera** recording onto **SD cards**, even if a well-featured **camcorder** is a more intuitive tool for filming. I shot what I thought was a great little film in the Sahara on a Lumix TZ6 worth £100. Dust sucked in through the zoom lens ruined it within a month, but for what it cost the results were worth it. Video and audio quality will be rough, but for internet or home-viewing it's fine if used right (see next page). Still cams (get two) have the advantage of being handy, light and low-profile, all at a minimal expense.

With a camcorder, **SD cards** are the way to go on a bike – compact, easy to buy and no moving parts like an HDD or tape. Note that Sony use their own more expensive memory stick. Choose a camcorder with **manual options** and

EATS, SHOOTS AND LEAVES

I messed around with Super 8 in the 80s making rubbish, but in 2000 got a Sony TRV900 three-chip camcorder to shoot a desert tour and later, *Call of the Wild* in northwest Canada and *Gorge Riders* in Australia.

They sold as VHSs then DVDs, and versions appeared on a National Geographic Channel show about home-shot adventures. I wrung that TRV dry and learned a whole lot more from reading *The Complete Idiot's Guide to Making Home Videos* which you can still buy on Amazon for a cent. All the key points are in there loud and clear: keep still, watch the audio and compose a clear story.

DVDs like *Desert Riders* (narrative) and *Desert Driving* (instructional) honed my skills and also got on TV, but with Vimeo and youtube, selling DVDs is not worth the bother now when you think of the huge production effort and expense required. I've done well enough and got shooting out of my system so am now happy to put my more interesting travel adventures straight to internet, using compact still cameras and a GoPro, and so spending days rather than weeks editing.

On a solo bike trip I'm not sure I'd bother filming; doing a good job gets in the way of your ride. If it was a few of us doing something epic like *Desert Riders*, I'd make sure we all had the same cam and used them.

whatever you get, switch off the inter-polated '**digital zoom**' forever, the quality is dire. Rely on optical zoom up to 10x – beyond that you need a tri-pod anyway as the shake will be terri-ble. Much more useful is a **wide-angle adapter** on a camcorder lens – put one on and you'll never take it off except for long zoom shots. One reason why I like Lumix compacts (right) is that they've always erred towards a wide angle – so much better for film or stills.

My basic still kit: an oversized Gorillapod will last longer; GoPro HD needs light for decent exposure and is fiddly to use, but is light as a feather; below an LX5 Lumix with manual options; bottom, a Panasonic FT2 waterproof still camera; slim enough for quick shoots. All these cameras shoot in HD. Right: read that book or something like it.

High definition (HD) is all the rage and looks great but note that it takes three or four times the space of standard def (SD) and later on, editing in HD will require a powerful comput-er. Some camcorders can export HD as SD for quicker editing. That way should National Geographic Channel ever want to buy your footage you'll have it in far more valuable HD. **Widescreen** (16:9) is now the norm. Certainly for travel the widescreen format works best.

Essential accessories

Before you even think about it, get a **spare battery** or two, and if they're non-OE clones, make sure they work. As mentioned, camcorders err towards ridiculous zoom ranges at the cost of wide. Screwing a wide-angle lens reduces the chance of things being out of the picture when you're not viewfinding and close-up handheld shoots inside tents and the like ensures two talking heads can easily fit in the frame with the all-important mic close.

Overlooking the importance of **audio** is the biggest mistake beginners make; it's easier to watch poor film with good audio than the other way round. Still cameras will have crumby mics so make sure you always speak to it no further than arm's reach. Even prosumer camcorders have duff mics because audio is a whole parallel science. Budget on an auxiliary mic that'll require assembling onto the camera body each time. It's a pain, but in situations like a piece-to-camera (P2C), the results will be worth it. Be aware of **wind noise** obliterating worthwhile audio on the move. A furry windsock on a shotgun mic will be needed, or experiment with the camera position, speeds and shout-ing. For static P2Cs get an inexpensive **tie-clip mic** on a 3-4m lead so you can shoot good audio without the camera being right under the subject's nose. With a fur head it may work on the move too if clipped close to your mouth.

A full-height **tripod** sounds excessive on a bike but all the 'image-stabilising' gubbins inside cameras can't hide a handheld shot and too much handheld (like *Blair Witch Project*) can make viewers nauseous. For a light cam-corder an inexpensive tripod will do, but get one with a 'fluid-head' to enable smooth pans. Otherwise, with a still camera, use a **stick** or trekking pole or a chunky Gorillapod.

You need a few good-sized **memory cards**, but be sure your camera's chip doesn't bog down running a 32gb card and know that a smaller card will lose less. Back up frequently and always have a spare battery on the go. Get **RAM mounts** and something like a monopod, trekking pole or a Manfrotto Magic Arm so you can shoot back on yourself, or clamp a bullet cam around your bike for interesting cutaway angles.

Extra **lighting** is more of a studio issue. Outdoors, where you'll be most of the time, natural light is by far the best. In the evening rely on the ambient tones of firelight or well placed head torches for detail. Modern cameras can manage very well in low light and any grain merely adds to the atmosphere. Avoid the horrible green-toned night-vision setting unless you're remaking *Dawn of the Dead* with Nicholas Cage; use a lighter flame for a warmer hue.

Pack a soft **shaving brush** or microfibre cloth and use them regularly. As with all your **rechargeable** electric components, get a lead to charge off the bike's 12V power take-off or a storage battery like a Power Monkey as well as a wall plug. The only **filters** you need are a clear UV or polarising item on the lens, more for protection than effect.

Two riders, two cameras

With a **pair of cameras** it's easy for two of you to produce a creditable movie; you'll get more than twice the value from having a 'second unit'. We did just that with a pair of Lumix FT2s on a paddling trip in northwestern Australia one time. As we travelled we shot the approach by van, small plane and 4x4 and then on the river shot each other, P2Cs and whatever else we saw. At the end we combined the footage and had more than enough good material to make nearly an hour's film for youtube.

Cameras don't have to be identical, just make sure the **movie settings** are to maintain a consistent quality when edited together (on Lumixes I use HD Quality and Motion jpeg mode, not AVCHD). There's nothing much you can do about the audio and wind noise with still cams; it'll all be part of the guerrilla film-making style.

Very light, fixed-focus, wide-angle **helmet cams** like the GoPro HD have really come on. You can put this camera in its waterproof case in places you'd not risk a proper camera. There's no viewfinder and the controls are hit and miss on earlier versions – you'll get a lot of footage of you staring at the lens to check the red record light is blinking. The other problem is the muted audio inside the waterproof case; if you're going to talk to it, take it out of the case, but even like this don't expect audible results on the move.

SHOOTING

As TV viewers we know instinctively what works and what looks good, but hand us a camera and we act differently. Trying to match the quality of pros takes commitment and skill. Get into the habit of watching TV documentaries with a film-maker's eye or watch other adventure motorcycling DVDs like *Mondo Enduro* (shot in the 90s) or *Terra Circa, GlobeRiders Iceland Adventure* or *Long Way Round* – the polar extreme of *Mondo's* budget but a good way to scrutinise professional shooting and editing. You'll see they all keep the camera still, are creative in the shots and let the picture tell the story, not the other way round. Out of the box many home shooters blow it with excessive **zooming** and **panning**; one guy I knew used his camcorder like a garden hose or a torch, as if he was hunting for rats in the undergrowth. Resist 'wow-look-at-this' 180-

degree pans – and if possible use a tripod, or rest your elbows on the tank or a stick, or brace yourself against a tree. Resist zooming across the full range too, and unless the action demands it, pan and zoom *slowly*. Avoiding these two pitfalls, developing a steady handheld style and watching the audio will get your travel movie off to a great start.

If you're shooting yourself doing a P2C walking along handheld, or sitting by a tripod, use a camcorder's LCD screen flipped round if you must, but remember to look and talk *to the lens*, not your image on the LCD; another newbie pitfall and another reason why a wide-angle lens is a great idea; you don't need that distracting LCD to make sure you're in shot. As it is, use the LCD sparingly to extend battery life and, while you're at it, avoid any in-camera editing gimmicks like sepia tone or fades; that's better left to the editing stage and anyway should be kept to a minimum.

Shot list

A journey is really the same repetitive sequence of sleeping, eating and riding, but with the thrill of an ever-changing location and your reactions to it. It may help to have a list of basic, everyday 'must-get' shots covering every element of your journey, starting perhaps with your preparations long before your departure, such as poring over maps, setting the bike up and of course setting off. Once on the road, shots can be predictably divided into: camping/domestic; on the move; and locations (more on p188). Tick them off or keep tally as you get them so you know you have a full range of 'fillers'. You'll find you shoot too much early on; don't worry about it, digital memory is free and erasable.

Camping/domestic

Eating, drinking, cooking, and checking the bike – these daily activities give a flavour of life on the road and a pause between the action on which you can add a voice-over later. Shoot them in a photogenic spot as locations change. These are the quiet and still times when you make **diary P2Cs** in a nice setting to give a feeling of progress. A P2C is best preceded with a distant '**wide-establisher**' (WE) shot to give a sense of place, then cut in to show your mate doing the chain tension while saying what a fantastic day you just had. If you forget you can do the WE after of course, just watch the **continuity** if props or positions have changed.

Until you get used to it, I find it's easier to sound less stilted in a P2C if you're engaged in a menial task or even just walking along, rather than sat in front of a camera with someone shouting 'action!'. When you're done, zoom and pan out slowly to an owl flying across the face of the rising moon. And unless you were very lucky, make a note to download some owl-hoot audio off the web when you get home.

Riding shots

You're starring in your own road movie, about as dynamic as it gets. These shots will provide the **drama** you need between the more contemplative pauses. Who can fail to be impressed by a bike hammering past in a trail of dust with the snow-clad Andes as a backdrop, you battling through a muddy Congolese trench or giving a running commentary on rush hour in Lima? This is where a bike is an unbeatable filming platform or subject.

LIFE ON THE ROAD

On the bike get short shots of you riding, a close shot of the starter button, the speedo or GPS, side views out, back shots at you, under shots, you name it. Experiment! All these laboriously set-up multiple viewpoints might only work for a few seconds and be suited to a fiddly GoPro, but really help set your film apart from lazy 'hosing'.

Distant **passing shots** of the bikes take a lot of effort, especially when alone, but they're worth it. More than one bike helps of course, as do mobiles to co-ordinate things. The effort made in scrambling up a hill to get a distant shot of the bike crawling across the wide-open plain adds drama and perspective to your adventure. (Tip: after a stiff climb hold your breath, or bring the tripod to avoid having your off-screen panting ruin the audio).

Be creative: get low, locked-off kerbside shots of the bike rushing by. Let the bike enter the frame, pan with it for a bit and then let it leave the frame while fixing on something in the background, and all possible variations on this shot. Get moving shots of another bike but remember shots of the bike moving across the frame must match. If the sequence has the bike shot moving left to right across the frame, all other shots and cutaways must be from the same **PoV** (point of view), or at least not moving in the opposite direction.

Locations

You'll notice how often TV documentaries use **still shots** to slow down the pace or set a scene. Have the confidence to do the same, allowing the ambience – be it birdsong, music, crackling fire or city hubbub – to tell the story.

Filming **locals** is tricky without making them act self-consciously. In reality, unless you establish their trust (which can take a good few hours if not days) or find a clandestine way of shooting, the results won't be subtle but will be better than nothing. Consider how you'd react if some tribesmen came to your place of work and started filming your exotic activity. Discretion and distraction might work, as does having one of you engaging with the subject.

Don't worry about having to voice the entire story to the camera on location. Especially in the early days you'll almost certainly babble and that can't be got rid of. Don't state the obvious; there's no need to say 'Well, here we are changing a tyre, *yet again!*' – we can see that and anyway, it's boring. Let a well written post-production **voice-over** (VO) fill in the gaps in the narrative more succinctly. And back home, if it's recorded in a local sound studio with professional mics and not behind the sofa, so much the better. Type up your VO script, practise at home for what sounds good, then hire a studio for an hour.

For any sort of multi-bike adventure it's well worth designating a **principal shooter** and establishing an understanding with all involved not to goof off or play up to the camera; it looks amateurish. Inevitably some individuals will seek attention and play up while others avoid it. A thoughtful shooter will sense people's needs and limits, and after a while everyone will get accustomed to the filming and ignore the camera which will be the goal. If as a director you get frustrated with your subjects not being telepathic, remember this is their adventure first, and a film set second.

Use your camera as often as not as a **sound recorder**, grabbing any atmospheric audio like a muezzin's chants, birds, music, animals and local chatter (although many generic sounds are easily found on the web). These can be used in conjunction with a series of stills – handy if you missed some footage.

Review and storage

It's important to **review your footage** in the early days, either in the camera if you have battery power to spare, or on a laptop/tablet. This way you can be sure you haven't been shooting on some wrong setting or with the mic off. There's so much to think about it's bound to happen, so better to learn from your mistakes early as you'll only get one chance.

Do you lug around a laptop or do you find a way to slot your material directly onto a storage device? Whichever you choose, a vibration-proof **solid drive**, not a spinny HDD, will be more immune to vibration, be smaller and use less power. Have a capacity of at least 500gb and use it or the laptop regularly to download or review material and edit and delete poor sequences to save space or having to wade through masses of it later.

EDITING

Shooting well is a sweat and takes commitment; I find the real creative satisfaction in film-making lies in the editing, especially if you're confident you managed to shoot enough good material. As a rule a polished hour of watchable film requires **ten times** the raw footage from a beginner and up to 100 hours of work to edit. Editing can be made so much easier if you planned the shoot well with a shot list so you know that a certain scene has all the necessary elements: a wide establisher, close-ups, some cutaways and of course good audio. If some key narration got lost during a noisy scene you can always add subtitles; used judiciously this can add to the drama.

Importing and reviewing takes hours and hours but it needs to be done to get a full picture of what you have. It's probably best not to leave it till the end of an 18-month RTW trip. For reviewing I find it helps to **log** and time each clip in a big notebook as you import or review partway through the journey, with a brief description and quality rating such as 'x' for 'crap' to '√√√' for 'pure gold'. For example:

Folder G East Turkey:	Zoltan to Schmoltan (dates)		
Clip #025	13.40 to 14.12 sec	Leaving Z	√√

Remember, 90% will be in the 'x' category so unless you've been lucky enough to capture a full-scale alien invasion in HD across a brilliant sunset, religiously **dump** anything that's out of focus, shaky, badly composed, badly exposed, badly lit, boring, or inaudible.

You'll be amazed how a good **soundtrack** can transform an ordinary film. Copyright-free music can be cheesy and getting decent music written is hit and miss unless you have talented contacts. Buy local CDs to get a feel, but at least make the effort to credit the musicians.

Avoid post production **gimmickry** like bouncy titles or swoopy transitions. Watch TV and learn: you'll realise they keep it simple because a good, well-shot story stands on its own merits without a blobby/spinning transition.

When it comes to **self-producing** your finished film, you can burn DVDs slowly off a computer one at a time and use your printer to create labels and cover inserts. **Mass production** has a unit price of around £2 for 1000 boxed and labelled copies. Unless you have contacts, are very lucky, have done something really exceptional, or happen to be a celebrity, my advice is forget about selling to mainstream TV. Get out there and shoot a film for your own creative satisfaction, then slap it on the internet for all to admire.

LIFE ON THE ROAD

Shipping overseas

Horizons' **Grant Johnson** *on crossing the parts you cannot ride.*

If you're going to ride the world eventually you'll encounter either a large body of water or a no go area. Either will require transporting the bike. There are two main options and a number of creative alternatives.

Sea shipping should be less expensive than by air, but port charges at both ends can actually add considerable amounts to the cost. I know of cases where shipping relatively short distances was more expensive than flying. Then there is the question of risk – ports are much more prone to theft or damage than airports. Finally, how much will you spend during the 3 to 10 weeks before your bike arrives; many people overlook the time and cost in **waiting for your bike** to arrive or be released, although it can work at either end of a big trip when you're back home while your bike's at sea.

Creative alternatives to shipping include leaving your bike overseas. Peter and Kay Forwood left in 1997 for an RTW trip on a Harley Davidson, but periodically left the bike behind and returned to Australia to replenish funds. One thing to consider is that some countries (such as Malaysia) accept the Carnet de Passage, and others (such as Thailand) stamp the vehicle information into your passport on entry, so you cannot leave without the bike. One rider had to ride from Thailand into Malaysia in order to fly back to England temporarily without his bike.

Sea freight

The decision whether to use air or sea is often made when you do the first check on price – an airfreight company will quote say US$1500, and by sea freight it's only US$800. Sounds like an easy choice. However, where it all goes wrong is when the bike arrives at the destination and you find out that there are port charges. To unload the container from the ship is US$50, to move the container to the other end of the dock is US$75, to unload the container and get your crate out is US$100, to move your crate to the shipping company is US$50, and paperwork costs for customs and fumigation add up to several hundred more. All of a sudden it's not such a good deal anymore.

It's worth appreciating that sea freight is best suited to low-value bulky commodities like crude oil, ore or livestock. Even new Chinese cars can be considered low-value and bulky. But a motorcycle is a small, high-value item of little volume, yet is a single consignment liable to the same series of charges as a quarter million tons of coal. Moreover, the money, in our experience, is the minor aggravation – what's worse is when the bike doesn't arrive as promised. One traveller shipped out of the UK to Ecuador, planning on three months travelling around South America. As a former RTW traveller she was experienced so left lots of time but on arrival no moto. A quick call to the shipper in the UK revealed that the bike was still there, waiting for a ship.

The sea freight for another couple ended up taking over six weeks from the UK to Mombasa. This story illustrates the risk of dealing with small companies and agents versus larger shipping companies who have their own staff at both ends. I've heard of loads more horror stories like this, but the lesson here is that sea shippers do not give you the full costs. No matter what they promise, it's not a guarantee.

If the bike isn't there when you are, you can spend a lot of time on foot or in taxis, and a lot of frustration dealing with shippers, forwarders and customs. As mentioned above, it's safest to ship the bike home after a trip, when it doesn't matter so much how long it takes. Ports in Europe and North America aren't usually as expensive as most of the rest of the world, but whatever port you choose, you're much better off choosing a **busy, high-volume port**, even if it's not the nearest to your destination. For more on single-vehicle shipping check out the detailed, 20-page article by Doug Hackney in Chris Scott's *Overlanders' Handbook*.

Air freight

Transporting your bike by air is **much more reliable** even if some countries' airlines are increasingly reluctant to put these 'dangerous goods' inside their passenger planes. You might have to look for an air cargo company. It has become especially difficult to ship a bike into and out of the **USA**. Many travellers find it's much easier to ship via **Canada** when travelling to North America, and in fact one of the major shippers to and from the USA, *Motorcycle Express*, is based in the USA but primarily ships via Canada. You'll

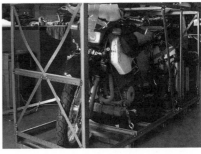

A metal frame crate with a DR650 heads for Far Eastern Russia. © Sean Flanagan

find a directory of air freighting agents at 🖳 www.azfreight.com. In the UK James Cargo has made a good name for itself as a specialist on airfreighting bikes out of the UK.

Most other countries aren't a big problem, but you'll often find that the airline doesn't want to deal directly with you; they prefer you to use an agent, and very often the agent's fee is money well spent.

Crated versus uncrated

Whether you ship crated or uncrated, you'll usually only be required to drain the fuel from the tank, and possibly disconnect the battery or leave it behind. Some, however, will require the bike to be crated, which will involve either building a crate or preferably, finding a friendly motorcycle dealer who has crates to throw out. These days most have metal frames (see above) which are harder to customise – wood is easier to DIY.

Air freighting uncrated is a lot less hassle of course and common on some routes like Panama to Colombia or Ecuador with Girag, though they suggest you film-wrap your gear for security. Lufthansa may well still ship uncrated to anywhere they fly; Frankfurt is their European hub.

LIFE ON THE ROAD

Air freighting tips

They may insist you remove the battery, even if it's a sealed item. This means you'll have to buy a new battery at your destination. Some travellers have carefully packed the battery in a box and attached the box to the crate floor, with other gear (that won't get damaged by any acid fumes) covering it. Or you could just stash a sealed battery in your baggage, after thoroughly insulating the terminals with melted wax or tape – at least it looks like you tried to be safe if it gets discovered.

We usually leave the front wheel on when shipping – it can be an advantage to be able to just wheel the bike out of the crate and ride away. All I usually do is take off the mirrors and windshield, but it does cost a little more. Sometimes the warehouse where you pick up the bike will insist you take the crate away. We've always been able to get around this, but it's taken some persuading in the USA where unions and safety regulations are strong.

Weight versus volume

If the weight is over a certain level you pay by weight, if under you pay based on volume. Bikes are bulky, and you have to work hard to get the volume down in order to pay the weight price. But you can also sometimes find that there's a big **price break** over 300kg, enough to make sure you save money by getting the weight over 300kg, not under. Ask many questions about price breaks, and what happens if the weight is more or less, as well as the breaks on volume if any.

Other packing tips

Don't fully compress the forks; use a block, if possible. The bike should be tied down on its blocked suspension, about halfway down. It should not be resting on the stands, only on its wheels, and vertical. Use up to six good tie downs and don't skimp on the crate.

To really squeeze the volume down, take the front wheel off, rest the bike on the sump and tie it down securely. You can also take the rear wheel off, front fender, panniers, and the handlebars. Just unbolt the handlebar clamp(s), leave the cables and wiring attached, and turn the bars sideways, wrap up and secure. Always remember that the goal is to make the crate smaller.

There's more on HU database at 🖥 www.horizonsunlimited.com/tripplan/transport/shipping

Colour section (following pages)
● **C1** Mudbrick mosque in Bobo Dioulasso, Burkina Faso. (© Margus Sootla).
● **C2 Left, top**: Shortcut from Angola to Cabinda across the Congo estuary. (© Margus Sootla). **Bottom**: Namibian dunes. (© quadsquad.org). **Right**: Negotiating a heavy swell on the road to Mamfe, Cameroon. (© Henri Conradie).
● **C3** Twilight near Maun, Botswana. (© Daan Stehouwer).
● **C4 Top**: High road between Ollague and Calama, Chile. (© Duncan Hughes). **Bottom**: Dodging the spray aboard the *Stahlratte* en route to Colombia. (© John Martin).
● **C5 Left, top**: Quiet night in Damascus. **Bottom**: Open-heart surgery in the Tian Shan, Kyrgyzstan. (© Dave King). **Right, top**: High pass in Ladakh, northern India. (© Jörn Buchleitner). **Bottom**: A rude shelter on the eastern BAM track, Russia. (© Walter Colebatch).
● **C6 Left**: Hajar mountain lookout, Oman. (© Margus Sootla). **Right, top**: Taking a breather near Song Kul lake, Kyrgyzstan. (© Dave King). **Bottom**: On the road to Zanskar, northern India. (© Jörn Buchleitner).
● **C7 Top**: Shady spot on the Lake Turkana route, northwest Kenya. (© Jay Kannaiyan). **Bottom**: South Angola shore (search: 'Angola, it's not like they said'). (© Erik van der Meulen).

C7

ASIA
ROUTE OUTLINES

4

From Istanbul or the Urals to a stone's throw from Alaska – and from above the Arctic Circle to below the equator close to Australia, **Asia**, the world's biggest landmass, just about has it all. And for an overland motorcyclist matching the right season with the right bike and gear, it's all rather easier than you might think. Asia offers sealed highways of varying quality from the Bosphorus to the Indian subcontinent and now right across Russia to Vladivostok.

Part of the appeal of riding in Asia is its rich historical and architectural heritage, a range of fabulous cuisines as well as the **low cost of living** in the south of the continent (potentially much less than Africa or Latin America). In places fuel prices can be among the lowest in the world too, though they're finding methods of making you pay in other ways.

WHERE TO GO
Apart from North Korea and Burma which are closed to overlanders, hot spots include **Syria**, parts of the **Russian Caucasus**, as well as all but the Kurdish north of **Iraq**, **Yemen** and **Afghanistan** away from the Wakhan Corridor. **China**, **Saudi** and **Vietnam** severely restrict, control or complicate independent travel with motor vehicles, and importing a bike into **Japan** gets difficult and expensive.

VISAS FOR ASIA
Visas will have a major impact on your route because getting them for Russia, Iran, India and some of the Central Asian 'stans' can't always be done in an adjacent country in a day or two, let alone at a border. Some, like Iran, will take weeks to acquire, something that's best done before you leave. In Turkmenistan you might find yourself racing across, simply because a short transit visa means you don't have to pay out for the escort that's required with the longer tourist visa. Russia offers an easy solution – one long duration visa.

Knowing this and all the rest, long before you settle on your country-hopping itinerary, get yourself clued up online with the latest requirements, costs and availability of Asian visas.

CARNET COUNTRIES IN ASIA

Bahrain, Bangladesh, Cambodia, India, Indonesia, Iran, Japan, Kuwait, Malaysia* Nepal, Pakistan, Qatar, Singapore, Sri Lanka.

* If arriving by ship as opposed to visiting from Thailand overland.

THE ASIAN CLIMATE

For trouble-free bike travel across Asia there are two things you want to avoid: the tropical **monsoon** on western coasts from June to October, and, more importantly, **winter** anywhere north of the Himalayas.

For Asia-bound riders starting from either Europe or the east, if you're heading towards India, leave in summer and ride into the autumn. If Central Asia or even just eastern Turkey is your destination, plan to arrive in the spring or early autumn – winters in the Asian interior are extreme. Further north, eastern Siberia will only be rideable in the late summer (see p229).

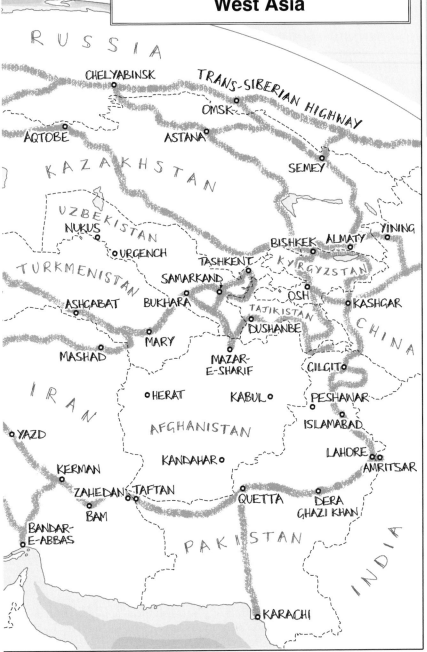

Main overland routes across West Asia

PRINCIPAL ROUTES: TAÏGA, HIGH ASIA OR TROPICS

Unless you're a family of Yakuts heading for a snorkelling holiday in Sri Lanka, Asia overland can be considered a **lateral transit** and broadly speaking there are three principal routes:

- The Trans-Siberian route and its adventuresome offshoots runs across Russia to Vladivostok from where ferries reach to South Korea.
- The 'Silk Route' links the Caucasus with the mountains of Central Asia, to join eastern Russia with Mongolia, or western China for India.
- Finally, the 'Road to Kathmandu' runs from Turkey and Iran to India. From here you need to freight onward or take on China.

Coming from Europe, around Turkey and Iran the high and low routes interweave with the middle route but as you move east the mass of China divides your options. On this eastern side the mainland termini of all routes are more specific: possibly Magadan but more likely the conurbation of freighting sea terminals around Vladivostok in Far Eastern Russia (FER) and with ferry links to South Korea and on to the port of **Busan**, or **Singapore/Kuala Lumpur** (Port Klang) on the equatorial mainland of Southeast Asia. These are the **key ports** you'll want to ship to if you're approaching Asia from the east.

Mile for mile, culturally, historically and scenically **Central Asia** offers the diversity that Russia lacks, but is similarly **carnet-free**. It was through this region that the fabled 'Silk Roads' developed two millennia ago; a network of trade routes along which not only silk, but paper and gunpowder and, of course, ideas shuttled west to Europe via places like Samarkand before trade passed into the hands of western Europe's 17th-century seafaring empires.

For the time being **China** sticks to its historic isolationism, at least for motorcycling – on a bicycle you can go pretty much where you like. Otherwise you'll need to organise the expensive escort and permits months in advance. Borders in the far west and east of **Mongolia** means this distinctive and undeveloped country can be transited in full via Ulaanbaatar any way you dare, or you can use the route to the north from Ulan Ude in Russia. The only entry point into China is south of UB on a track that becomes a road to Beijing.

The adventure begins. © Nathan Coy

Turkey

Traditionally, coming from the Balkans, **Asia** begins once you cross the Bosphorus from Istanbul into Asia Minor. As a taste of what lies ahead, rather like Morocco, **Turkey** offers just enough challenges to stop you falling back off the learning curve. Although a long way from western Europe to be treated as a test run for the big trip, it's a destination in its own right, full of fascinating sites that you wouldn't want to rush, even if you could. The east and north-east regularly feature as highlights in trip reports, although in the ethnically Kurdish areas along the Iranian and Iraqi borders, watchtowers and checkpoints are a common sight and tensions occasionally escalate.

Most travellers will get a **visa** issued at the border for around €15. Here you can also buy **motor insurance** for another €30 for up to three months. And that's just about it, no other obscure taxes or requirements or letters of introduction. Enjoy it, this could be the last easy, European-style border for a while.

The downside is that Turkey boasts **fuel prices** as high as just about anything you'll pay in Europe. This may well dictate how many miles you cover here, but whichever way you go, it's hard to choose a bad route.

At the far end of Turkey the party could be about to end so brace yourself. Excluding going back home, you have three or four choices:

- Ferry from Trabzon to Poti (Georgia) and either on to Ukraine or Russia.
- Into the Caucasus and up into Russia or across the Caspian Sea to Turkmenistan.
- Southeast into Iran, either direct or via Kurdish northern Iraq.
- A ferry to Cyprus and then Israel or direct to Egypt for Africa.

NEGOTIATING THE MIDDLE EAST

At the time of writing (you'll get used to hearing that phrase...) what has become a civil war in **Syria** looks as if it'll get worse before it gets better. Despite its hitherto discreet profile on the geo-political stage, Syria is said to be a key in keeping the Middle East from unravelling any more than it has, something which many observers fear will happen if the Assad government falls.

Riders were still managing to swiftly transit Syria between Turkey and Jordan in a day or two in early 2012, following protracted border searches and escorts. Up to that time visas were issued at the border only if there was no Syrian consulate in your home country. Otherwise you needed a visa in advance issued in your home country which, depending on where you're from, is very unlikely as things stand.

With non-Kurdish Iraq still far from stable, the Syrian conflict has greatly added to the disruption of overland traffic from Turkey to Africa and Arabia. Currently the options are **ferries** running between Mersin in Turkey and Egypt, or from Turkey via Cyprus to Israel's border with Egypt. Don't even think about slipping along western Iraq between Turkey and Jordan, or for example crossing Yemen, even if there are boats from Djibouti and a ferry from Dubai to Bandar Abbas in Iran. A French biker came very close to being kidnapped while trying that in 2011, despite travelling with an armed escort.

As a result of this Jordan has become a bit of a dead end, even with a daily ferry between Aqaba down the eastern arm of the Red Sea to Nuweiba in the Egyptian Sinai (⌨ www.abmaritime.com.jo). Instead travellers are either arriving in Israeli ports from Cyprus or other European ports with Grimaldi, or taking a hit-and-miss RoRo ferry service launched in 2012 between Port Said and Mersin in southeast Turkey.

Be aware that even though **Israel** can stamp you in and out on a piece of loose paper rather than in your passport, countries like North Sudan, Iran and possibly Libya have been known to closely check the dates and places on passport entry and exit stamps for Jordan and Egypt. If they find they're not on the same day or recognise the point of entry was at an Israeli border, they may well turn you away, especially if they're having a bad day or don't like the look of you. In fact, you rarely hear of it.

THROUGH THE CAUCASUS AND ACROSS THE CASPIAN

WITH CHARLIE WEATHERILL

For many the Caucasus represents the jumping off point – the sudden transition from the home comforts of Europe to the rigours of Asia – although over the past few years **Azerbaijan, Georgia** and **Armenia** have become significantly more tourist-friendly and overlanders may feel that they're still in eastern Europe.

If you're shooting through, be sure to visit **Tbilisi** and **Kakheti**, Georgia's wine region (and home to a number of beautifully situated monasteries) as well as Azerbaijan's unspoilt and mountainous northern regions – **Kifl** and **Lahıc** being two of the area's highlights. We found the *Lonely Planet* guide for Georgia, Armenia and Azerbaijan a decent travel companion. As these are former Soviet republics, **Russian** is the most useful **language** here, though English will be understood too.

Despite the brutal secessionist wars in nearby Chechnya, it's become possible to enter the Russian republic of **North Ossetia** at Kazbegi on the road from Tbilisi to **Vladikavkaz** (200km). Be wary in the unlit tunnels on the Georgian side and buy Russian insurance (*strahavanie*) in the village of Chmi or Vladikavkaz, 38km from the border (MCK, first floor; N43° 01.45' E44° 40.83') and close to the town of Beslan, site of the notorious 2004 school siege.

Fuel, money and internet

Petrol is around two thirds cheaper, than Europe. **ATMs** are widely found in all major cities and many regional towns. Some fuel stations in Georgia and Azerbaijan take credit cards, as do many hotels in major towns.

You'll find plenty of high speed internet cafés in all major cities as well as **free wi-fi** in hotels, smarter cafés and restaurants, especially in the capitals. Internet access is becoming cheaper as connections become faster and more widespread; expect to pay no more than around $1 an hour.

Riding in the Caucasus

As for local driving standards, the exuberant Georgians are the most aggressive and impatient, although outside the major cities there's very little traffic. Road manners in Armenia are good whilst Azeri truck drivers should be passed with caution. Driving standards in Baku are far more chaotic than the rest of Azerbaijan, so be prepared.

These days **traffic police corruption** has virtually been eradicated, so if you're stopped for speeding and have been riding recently in either Russia or Central Asia, offering to pay your way out may be the wrong thing to do.

Motor insurance is only compulsory in Azerbaijan where it should be issued to you at the border for around $15. You'll be unlikely to obtain motor insurance at any Georgian or Armenian borders, although it's possible to buy it in the major cities, if you can be bothered.

In Georgia, **Imedi** (🖳 www.imedi-l.com) provide local and Green Card insurance (useful if you're transiting Georgia on the way home) and have offices in Tbilisi (20 Chavchavadze Avenue) and Batumi. Note, if you are entering Turkey from Georgia it'll cost you far less to obtain your Green Card in Georgia than it will from a European company or at the Turkish border.

T R I P   R E P O R T
TRANS ASIA ~ F650 GS DAKAR

Name	Bjorn
Year of birth	1975
Occupation	Photographer
Nationality	German
Previous travels	Europe, South America, SE Asia
Bike travels	Europe

This trip	UK, Central Asia, China, Australia
Trip duration	13 months
Departure date	May 2008
Number in group	1
Distance covered	48,000km

Best day	Too many
Worst day	Tajik washboard with broken subframe
Favourite places	Iran, Tajik, Nepal people. Malay food.
Biggest headache	Kyr-China border closed; traffic in India
Biggest mistake	Not enough time in some countries
Pleasant surprise	Things always work out alright
Any illness	Trots in Bukhara
Cost of trip	~$1000 a month
Other trips planned	I kept going for another two years

Bike model	F650 GS Dakar
Age, mileage	2005, 22,500 miles on departure
Modifications	Forks, brakes, iridium spark plugs
Wish you'd ...	Fitted a new shock
Tyres used	Tourance and ContiTKC 80
Punctures	1 nail in Pakistan
Type of baggage	Alu boxes

Bike's weak point	Soft suspension with heavy panniers
Strong point	Solid engine, good fuel economy
Bike problems	Leaking shock
Accidents	A couple of light falls
Same bike again	Possibly, but BMW service was poor
Any advice	Not right now

Entry points

Apart from North Ossetia, the only **overland entry points** to the Caucasus from Europe are between Turkey and Georgia, at **Batumi** and **Vale**. Turkey and Armenia's borders remain firmly **closed** whilst crossing from Turkey to the Azeri enclave of Naxçivan limits you to exiting either into Iran via Culfa-Jolfa or returning to Turkey.

EU and US nationals don't require visas for Georgia (Australians and New Zealanders do at a cost of around 60GEL or $30 at the border) and there are no entry taxes or other hidden costs. Customs officials these days are very efficient and corruption is virtually non-existent.

Once you've explored Georgia's mountains, monasteries and wine regions you have three options: north to Russia, south to Armenia or east to Azerbaijan. Note that if you cross into Armenia and then subsequently attempt to enter Azerbaijan, you may be **refused entry** into the country if the Azeri officials notice your Armenian visa in your passport (at best, it'll certainly slow down the immigration process). Conversely, there's no problem entering Armenia with an Azeri visa stamp in your passport.

Whichever way you do it, crossing into **Armenia** is relatively expensive: visas are available at the border for $10 per person but you'll have to pay around $65 in road and 'ecological' taxes to bring your bike in for up to 15 days. A 30-day vehicle permit is available, but will set you back around $100 in taxes. Have plenty of photocopies of everything or they'll charge you their rates to do it. It's only possible to exit Armenia via Georgia or Iran – you can't get back into Turkey from here. If crossing to Iran be sure you have your visa and note that you'll have to pay another spurious $25 departure tax.

Azerbaijan and the road to Baku

Crossing to **Azerbaijan** from Georgia is straightforward though you'll need to obtain your Azeri visa prior to arriving at the border. The border crossing at **Lagodekhi** is more straightforward and foreigner-friendly than the crossing at Krasny Most. Visas can be arranged in Tbilisi; a 30-day **tourist visa** takes three days to process and costs $101, whilst a 5-day **transit visa** can be issued on the same day for around $40. Note that Azerbaijan insists on the payment of a hefty **temporary importation deposit** (up to the full documented value of the bike) if you're entering on anything other than a transit visa. Although the deposit is refundable upon re-export of your bike, this is why most shoot through on a **transit visa** to catch the rail freighter across the **Caspian Sea** to either Turkmenistan or Kazakhstan – see below.

Exiting from Azerbaijan to **Iran** at Astara is straightforward, providing you have your Iranian visa (technically these can be issued in Baku, but may take up to three weeks). Most travellers expect to need a carnet for Iran, although it's unofficially possible to get the border officials to issue an Alternative Transit Document on the spot for around $200.

Across the Caspian Sea to Turkmenistan

The idea of crossing the Caspian Sea between **Baku** and **Turkmenbashi** in Turkmenistan or **Altau** in Kazakhstan (from 12 hours) has a romantic ring, but the reality is a hassle-prone requirement, usually to get round Iran. The hassle adds up to grumpy and corrupt officials, the uncertainty in securing a place as

ASIA – ROUTE OUTLINES

well as getting off swiftly, and more bribes at either end. The vessels are actually rail freighters with a few spare cabins, not a P&O pleasure cruise with a karaoke happy hour. And because there's only one berth at Turkmenbashi, you can be stuck on board for a day or more waiting to disembark, or even longer should storms hit the Caspian.

© Nathan Coy

If leaving from Baku enquire at the ticket office at the port (N40° 22.47' E49° 51.94'; the Lonely Planet Baku map marks the ticket office, customs and the loading point) about the next departure and again, get on a list. Tickets are not sold until the departure is imminent and once that's decided, loading can happen very quickly so don't stray too far. In 2012 passenger tickets cost $110 per person for a basic en-suite cabin with a window, and the same again for your bike plus another $20. There's a café on board but that can run out of food so bring enough food and water for up to two days. The less used ferry to Aktau is about the same price.

Heading west, aim for the customs office at Turkmenbashi port (N40° 00.37' E53° 00.89') and put yourself on a list for the next sailing. There will be a $20 departure tax and other small fees, but you pay the passenger cost to the crew and for the bike once you disembark at Baku.

If entering Turkmenistan on a transit visa, it's advisable to just obtain a letter of invitation rather than a full visa, and then get your transit visa on arrival. This way your visa will start the moment you arrive rather than having a fixed start date, so you won't encounter any problems if the ferry is delayed.

As mentioned, if you're transiting **Turkmenistan** and leaving via the Caspian, you won't be allowed to enter the country except on a tourist visa, meaning an expensive daily escort which is part of the deal. Guide-free transit visas are only valid for five days and are only extendable in the capital Ashgabat, a day's ride from Turkmenbashi. The authorities are fully aware of the ferry delays and so won't issue transit visas if leaving that way.

If you're entering Turkmenistan on a pre-arranged transit visa (as opposed to the Letter of Introduction option), your visa dates are fixed. Should you be delayed for four days getting into the country, you'll only have one day to leave Turkmenistan. As it's over 1200 kilometres along the only M37 main road to the Uzbekistan border post, this is not a realistic prospect. Kazakhstan visas are valid for one month so won't present problems with ship delays.

Disembarking at Turkmenbashi, there is a raft of entry fees, taxes and fuel waivers to pay before you can clear customs. A fixer will help you understand a little more clearly what you're paying for, but the costs will be the same. You should receive a **receipt** (*polichenie*) for everything – ask for one before you hand over any money. Unless you're on a transit visa your most important document will be a green A4 sized 'map' certificate, detailing your approved route through Turkmenistan. Without a guide, the customs process can take up to eight hours so note the parking charges in the port.

Iran

WITH ANDY PAG

Don't be nervous about visiting Iran, even if every once in a while we seem to be on the verge of some sort of airstrike by the west, with all the consequences that entails. For many overlanders Iran is an unexpected highlight of their journey across southern Asia, with some of the most cultured and welcoming people you'll meet. Iran is more developed than many expect, except they've taken their own route. Absent here are all the familiar icons of Western consumer culture – Pepsi, iPod, Burger King – that pervade the rest of the planet, although many are present under local names.

The roads are in great shape and the range of **landscapes** from mountain, lakesides, coasts and desert is especially striking. Human rights for Iranians may not be so rosy, but regionally the country is far from unique in this aspect. Providing you **behave respectfully** – which off the bike includes **women** wearing a head covering and unrevealing clothing – you'll not be harassed by officials for your nationality, despite the high profile posturing of politicians on the international stage. Foreigners' movements within the country are not tracked too closely, though Iranian friends might be checked up on, so as in many countries like this, beware of putting locals in compromising situations and avoid **political discussions** unless you know better.

VISAS

This is the main stumbling block. Getting a visa depends on your nationality and the diplomatic ambience at the time. For Brits and especially Americans, the process can still be slow and if **American** overlanders manage to get a visa at all, they may have to pay for an escort, as do most Americans who fly in as part of an organised tour. You'll find using an approved **visa agency** speeds up visa acquisition greatly; indeed as with Russian visas, it can be the only way to get one at all. With fees, this adds up to £100 for Brits applying in the UK and takes at least a month (in the UK 🖳 magic-carpet-travel.com have a good reputation, or try 🖳 iranianvisa.com).

What you actually get is an approval number sent out from Tehran. With that you go to your nominated consulate to pick up the actual visa. In Turkey they are found in Istanbul, Ankara, Trabzon and Erzurum. The good thing is Iranian visas are usually valid for **three months** before they expire. Once in the country, you get the usual 30 days which can be renewed if you have a good excuse.

LANGUAGE, MONEY AND INTERNET

Farsi is the national language, not Arabic as some assume, but many young people will speak English. The currency is the **rial**, currently about 16,000 to the euro, though Iranians commonly quote prices in toman: one toman equals ten rials so that's 1600 toman to a euro. You can get by comfortably on about 40,000 toman (€25) a day. Bring cash – foreign credit cards won't work in Iran.

Don't be too irked if you discover you're paying ten times what locals do to get into museums and the like. It's official policy, the same in many neighbouring countries and anyway, it's still pennies. Less officially sanctioned overcharging goes on in some hotels so be prepared to bargain (although hotels do pay higher taxes for foreign guests).

Internet and **mobile phone** access gets restricted by the state at times, but **cyber cafés** with slow connections are everywhere. Reception for foreign mobile phone service providers is patchy; local SIM cards are easily bought and much cheaper, but even they can be hit and miss.

MAIN BORDER CROSSINGS

Iran has borders with seven countries, but most overlanders are transiting between Turkey and Pakistan, or possibly to or from those two countries via Turkmenistan or Iraqi Kurdistan (see box below). A **carnet** is required, though it's said that a local version – an Alternative Transit Document – is available at the border for about $200. As you'll need a carnet for Pakistan and India, you may as well include Iran.

There are two border crossings with Turkey. **Dogubajazit – Bazargan** is used by most, a busy commercial border that's open all year but can be slow and a little corrupt. Southeast of Van in the midst of a similarly militarised zone of Turkish Kurdistan, is the **Esendere – Sero** crossing. Less used by travellers, foreigners can be treated like VIPs on both sides of the border though in midwinter this crossing may be closed.

There's a guarded car park on the Turkish side where you can camp although the toilets are right out of Elm Street. Show your passport to any official that makes eye contact and they'll either wave you in the right direction or stamp it and fling it back at you. To get your carnet stamped, add yours to the stack belonging to the Turkish traders crossing the border in minivans.

TRANSIT OF IRAQI KURDISTAN

Hard though it may be to believe, for the last few years it's been quite feasible, and indeed straightforward and safe by regional standards, to cross the northernmost edge of Iraq administered by the Kurdistan Regional Government. The band of Kurdish-controlled territory reaches no more than 150km in from the Turkish and Iranian borders.

Fifteen kilometres south of the Turkish town of **Silopi** is the Turkish frontier post which leads to **Zakho** in Iraqi Kurdistan. Here a regional **visa** is issued for some ten or fifteen days either free, or about a dollar a day. No carnet is required and there are no other costs.

Bring **dollars**; nothing else will work to change into Iraqi dinars, although you can even pay in dollars for most things. **Petrol** is low octane but works out about 20% of the price in Turkey (among the most expensive

in the world). Other commodities and services are also said to be cheap.

Once in Iraq, most will be heading for Iran, southeast via Dohuk to the capital Erbil, Mosul and, skirting Kirkuk, on to Al Sulemanyah for the Iranian border near Marivan, a distance of some 450km. Or there's another crossing riders have used to the north at Rawandiz for Piranshar in Iran. The roads leading into Iran from either of these obscure frontiers are not the finest.

Many riders report a warm welcome in Iraqi Kurdistan (and in the Kurdish areas of neighbouring countries too), although entering Turkey from Dohuk can lead to an interrogation and search. It's good to know that Turkey is particularly hostile to Kurds and 'Northern Iraq' and bombed Iraqi Kurdistan in 2011, while the PKK rebels have waged a guerrilla war against Turkey since 1984.

On the Iranian side expect a cup of tea and officials speaking good English. They'll guide you through the entrance process which involves a thorough search and triple check of your documents and chassis (VIN) number. There is no fuel tax in Iran (despite what some might try on) and the fuel card system – Iran's way of trying to curb smuggling – may be a thing of the past or not affect you.

ON THE ROAD IN IRAN

It's at least 2400km from Turkey to Taftan just inside Pakistan, but as always and visa duration notwithstanding, if you can get off the direct trans-national highways so much the better. Along with the wide open desert and distant ranges, the **architecture and bazaars** in cities like **Esfahan**, **Yazd** and **Shiraz** as well as the ruins of **Persepolis** and what's left of Bam are what you've come here to see. As a guest in Iran, you'll be waved through toll booths and attempts to pay will be met with a confusing look to the sky and tut, the Iranian equivalent of shaking your head.

Fuel

With **fuel prices** about the cheapest in the world, both locals and tourists could only officially buy subsidised petrol with a pre-paid **fuel card** which tourists bought and loaded with credit at the border. The cards could supposedly be topped up on the road, but there are no refunds on your unused quota. Now it seems the cards have been abandoned and you just pay around 700 toman for unsubsidised fuel (about 45 eurocents) at the pump – the attendant may use his own card. As it's still so cheap, most aren't bothered with chasing down a card, even if they can.

Highway madness

Iranian drivers are fast and frightening and so riding through cities can become a contact sport until you get a feel for the rules. Let me save you some time: there aren't any. A motorway may have three marked lanes following the Western convention; actual lane capacity depends on how many vehicles can fit abreast without the outside ones falling off the edge or having a head-on. In Teheran it's often less stressful to arrive or leave in the dead of night.

Steady, predictable riding is the key to avoid being shunted. Keep an eye out for cars reversing fast or driving in the wrong direction on the motorways. Usually they're thoughtful enough to confine themselves to the hard shoulder, but it's not uncommon to find traffic coming straight at you in the fast lane.

Roadside recoveries

When you need a break the better roadside fuel stations will often have restaurants and resthouses, as well as mechanics. As for **food**, the only complaint might be that the ubiquitous **kebab and rice** gets pretty repetitive in Iran, but try *dizzy* as an alternative. It involves lamb stew and pitta, but you'll need to ask the waiter to show you how to eat it and so provide some all-round entertainment. Eating out isn't cheap in Iran, so to save funds be prepared to cook. At the same time the generous Iranians make it hard to pay for anything out of your own pocket, part of a social custom called *tarof*, so put up a fight to pay if your host is clearly being generous beyond their means.

To Pakistan

On the east side of the country, the Iranian police will escort you the 400km from the city of Bam via Zahedan to the **Pakistani border** at Taftan. As with so many of these escorts, it's a largely futile exercise intended to protect you from the bandit hordes and means progress will be slow as you'll have to stop at check points along the way for escort changeovers. As things stand, there's little chance of making it from Bam to Taftan in a day.

... until you get a feel for the rules. Let me save you some time: there aren't any. A motorway may have three marked lanes following the Western convention; actual lane capacity depends on how many vehicles can fit abreast without the outside ones falling off the edge ...

ASIA – ROUTE OUTLINES

Fill your tank with cheap Iranian fuel well before the border as Pakistani truck drivers and Baluchi smugglers can run the final filling stations dry. As a last resort you can get cheap smuggled fuel in Pakistan.

Entering Pakistan you'll be competing with local lorry drivers for the attentions of those little rubber stamps and their uniformed keepers. The Iranian side involves visiting an unfathomably high number of counters with hand-written ledgers, something that must be tackled in a specific order which you'll eventually divine. Once you've patiently endured watching Iranian officials valiantly trying to make sense of your unfamiliar documents, there's a tough initiative test to find the actual exit to Pakistan.

Pakistan

Perhaps because **English** is widely spoken, many overlanders have traditionally found Pakistan, its people and landscapes, to be another unexpected highlight on the ride to India. Visas are still issued without difficulty, but since late 2008 the security situation has worsened so convoys of siren-wailing **police escorts** herd overlanders swiftly from the Iranian border at Taftan the 1500km via Multan or Lahore, close to the Indian border at Amritsar. Unless you manage to evade these escorts, before you know it you've crossed the width of the country and it's all over which, as those who've visited in happier times will know, is a great shame.

The good news is that from Lahore you're allowed to travel unescorted, which means you can slip off and head north to Islamabad from where you can continue up the fabled Karakoram Highway right through to China.

VISAS

Costs vary greatly according to nationality; it's best to get them before leaving as they're valid for up to six months. Otherwise Letters of Introduction (LOI, get used to the idea) from your embassy can help. Visa extensions are obtainable in Islamabad, but take up to a week to sort out, so go for the longest duration tourist visa to avoid the hassle of extending. If coming from China, it's certainly possible to get a temporary visa for around $30-90 at Sost (more on p210).

BORDERS, FUEL AND RISKY AREAS

If you clear the formalities at Taftan after around 2pm, expect to be told you have to stay the night at the border, before being allocated a free and compulsory armed escort for the ride across Baluchistan to Quetta and right across Pakistan to Lahore on the Indian border. The customs compound is a safe haven for overnight camping, and the head of customs may have his cook rustle you up a curry in exchange for a few of your tales from the road.

Pakistani frontier officials are friendly, straightforward and fast by Asian standards. A **carnet** is necessary, though bikes have been allowed through without them in the past (an apocryphal story you'll hear from many carnet lands). There's one official border crossing to Iran, at Taftan, one to India at Lahore and a seasonal one with China at the 4700-metre Khunjerab Pass, the highest border crossing in the world. As for the Khyber Pass crossing into Afghanistan, it's unlikely you'll want to go there just yet. Elsewhere you can rely on sealed roads between Iran and India. Away from the Iranian border, fuel is up to five times more expensive; **petrol** goes for about Rs107 a litre.

The 630km between the border and the first big town of **Quetta** can all seem a bit close to Afghanistan's Helmand province for some people's liking. In 2012 a British aid worker based here was abducted for ransom and subsequently killed, so there is something to having an escort in this area. Expect a rough, hot, dusty ride as the road is in bad shape east of Dalbandin, with sand tongues and even steel ropes or chains hung across the road near checkpoints which can be difficult to spot at low sun angles.

Depending on checkpoints and escorts, you can ride between Quetta and the border in about ten hours, but two days is considered normal and gives you a chance to enjoy the great Baluchi hospitality. There's a rest house at Dalbandin halfway along; camping elsewhere (should it be possible) may be either inadvisable or memorable.

Travellers have long been warned of bandits in **Baluchistan** and in Sind Province (Karachi and Hyderabad), as well as to avoid travelling at night or in remote areas, a precaution that's become more widespread in recent years. Certainly the south-west corner of Baluchistan, south of the Quetta road down to the coast, is an area few overlanders visit, and is best left that way.

What's known as **Waziristan**, the region bordering Afghanistan, more or less between Quetta and Peshawar and part of the former North West Frontier Province (NWFP) was never under state control and is now the main front line with the Taliban. This was a region overlanders often had difficulty in visiting even in the good times, and these days it's unlikely you'll get anywhere near it, nor would you want to.

Since 2008 even Peshawar has become too dangerous to be visited for too long by conspicuous foreigners, and the route down the west side of the Indus from Peshawar via Dera Ishmail Khan to Quetta is said to be closed to overlanders.

NORTHERN PAKISTAN AND THE KARAKORAM HIGHWAY

The way things are at the moment, Pakistan can be a hard nut to crack, but one highlight that many riders agree is worth the effort is following the **Karakoram Highway** (KKH) and its offshoots up towards the Chinese, Indian and Afghan Wakhan borders.

All of northern Pakistan is designated tribal territory that never really came under state control, although that can be said for much of the country. However, it's the significant **cultural difference** between what used to be called the Northern Areas, now Gilgit-Baltistan through which the upper KKH passes – and the legendarily notorious region once known as North West Frontier Province alongside Afghanistan, which will impact on your experience. It could be summed up on the one hand by the proud, xenophobic and ethnically Afghani Pashtun who occupy the former NWFP (and who probably make up the core of the Taliban) – and the more tolerant and approachable Balti followers of the Ismaili Muslim sect living in the north of Gilgit-Baltistan. Here women and girls are more conspicuous and unveiled, social attitudes are more progressive and even Ramadan is not so strictly observed. 'For us, every month is holy' a guy told me in Karimabad with a smile.

With mountaineers still drawn to several of the world's highest peaks and the less driven attracted to the 'Shangri-La' reputation of the Hunza valley, tourism in the area collapsed following 9/11 and with all that's followed it has barely recovered. And yet the few who make the effort to get up here, even if it means going back down to the baking plains again, admit it's one of the best stages on the road to Kathmandu.

To get a feel for this area, download the excellent free **map** of the KKH at 🖳 www.johnthemap.co.uk. On paper I found the two-sided Nelles 1.5m map of Pakistan was the best, as was the better-than-average Lonely Planet **guidebook**. I also used Trailblazer's *Himalaya by Bike* which gives a very detailed and well-mapped account of the KKH including spot heights, along with 10,000 kilometres (6200 miles) of other high mountain routes in this part of the world, including the Indian Himalaya (see p218).

The Karakoram Highway

The Karakoram Highway runs for 1300km (800 miles) from Islamabad over the 4693m (15,397') Khunjerab Pass on the Chinese border and on to Kashgar in Xinjiang. Built in the 1970s and regarded as one of the engineering wonders of the world, it's become one of the world's great rides, tracing a former arm of the Silk Route along the Indus valley which in places is lined with thousands of petroglyphs dating back 5000 years. It also passes through the densest concentration of 7000 metre peaks in the world and it is this dramatic contrast with the surrounding peaks towering over the Indus and later Hunza valleys far below which makes the KKH so special, especially compared to the higher roads of Ladakh and Spiti in India (see p218).

Part of the reason for all this mountain drama is that the Karakoram is one of the most **seismically active** areas in the world, where the Indian continental plate pushes under the Asian plate, raising the Himalaya and the adjacent ranges as it does so. Because of these steep, loose slopes, at any point along the mountainous stages of the KKH landslides frequently block the road after a downpour or one of the frequent tremors. Diggers are used to moving in fast to clear the blockage, but as you'll read below, bigger landslides can disrupt travel on the KKH for months.

Altitude and lodgings

The effects of high altitude can easily be overlooked when sat on a bike. Until that is, you need to do something like stand up. The quick way to acclimatise is to **drink lots of water** and once above 3500 metres or so, aim not to sleep more than a couple of hundred metres higher each night. If you feel bad the answer is to **descend immediately**. Even a few hundred metres does the trick.

Lodgings along the way are plentiful and a **fuel range** of 250–300km will cover you. Most towns will have some sort of hotel, though they can get pretty grotty in the villages. If you want a change from camping, look out for the PTDC motels (🖳 www.tourism.gov.pk) dotted around the north. They cost around $20 half board, but are often set in great locations.

The lower KKH

Leaving Islamabad, an **alternative summer route** to the KKH towards Chilas runs up into the hills at Murree, on towards Muzaffarabad and over the 4170m (13,681′) Babusar Pass. In doing so it avoids the lower reaches of the KKH in Indus Kohistan where the welcome is not always so warm from the Pashtun villagers, to whom a stranger is an enemy they have not glared at yet. Even before the Taliban came on the scene, when blood feuds were running in Kohistan, police would often escort travellers through to beyond Chilas, and they still do so today. After Chilas, you pass the bulk of Nanga Parbat mountain whose 8126m (26,660′) summit is just 40km away, but towers nearly four and a half miles above you.

From Chilas towards the Chinese border and even before the 2010 floods, there's a lot of **road-widening** construction going on, with frequent detours and long sections of gravel. Pakistan is trying to make sure the port of Karachi gets its share of goods exported from western China via the KKH.

Excursion to Skardu

Even if you're not planning to cross to China then, access permitting, northern Pakistan still has a lot to offer, with two or three good excursions off the KKH. Late spring and early autumn are the best times to travel, but the KKH itself is open all year as far as **Gilgit**, situated at only 1500m and some 600km (370 miles) from Islamabad.

A few miles before Gilgit, the Indus river heads off eastwards towards Skardu, at times a precipitous and narrow road you'd not want to attempt with your Vario panniers on full extension. Over the churning Indus far below the occasional, quake-proof suspension bridge straddles the tectonic front line, leading to isolated villages and their surrounding terraced plots.

Skardu (2500m, 8203′) is set in a vast desert-like basin with roads leading to the area's famous peaks and the disputed Line of Control with Indian Kashmir. The route to Askole and K2 is constantly being rebuilt with some very rough sections and quite daunting hairpins high above the river. East from Skardu to Khapalu is sealed, beyond to Hushe is rough or blocked, but offers astonishing scenery below the 7800m peak of Masherbrum.

T R I P R E P O R T
TOUR OF INDIA ~ ENFIELD BULLET

Name	Dan M
Year of birth	1974
Occupation	Teacher
Nationality	British
Previous travels	Yes; live and work abroad
Bike travels	NZ, US, France, Thailand on all sorts

This trip	Tour of India
Trip duration	25 days
Departure date	December 2008
Number in group	1
Distance covered	3600km

Best day	Kerala backwaters with elephants
Worst day	Mumbai to Kochin in 3 days
Favourite places	Sentinels of the Himalaya
Biggest headache	Roads – average speed can be 30kph
Biggest mistake	Riding at night. Unnecessary pressure
Pleasant surprise	Delhi based rental agency 10/10
Any illness	No
Cost of trip	£1800
Other trips planned	London to Almaty

Bike model	2007 Enfield Bullet 500 rental
Age, mileage	2000km
Modifications	Alu luggage, crash bars
Wish you'd ...	nothing. All fine.
Tyres used	Local brand
Punctures	0
Type of baggage	Alu boxes

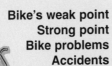

Bike's weak point	In the context of India – none!
Strong point	Fuel economy, 76–108 mpg!
Bike problems	Minor short circuit. Fixed for a dollar
Accidents	A front end slide on diesel
Same bike again	Yes. It's the fastest thing on their roads
Any advice	Armour under light clothes = less hot

Gilgit and the high road to Chitral

Gilgit is no picture postcard settlement, but a sprawling administrative centre set in a basin and hosting occasionally violent altercations between the Shia and Sunni. In the bazaar you'll wonder just how many mobile phone boutiques a town needs. From here there's an easy route that lacks the exposure of the Skardu road, around 360km (220 miles) west to **Chitral** over the 3720m (12,205') **Shandur Pass**, of polo field fame and with a couple of fuel stops on the way. It's a spectacular ride up to the broad, yak-dotted plateau where the Pass is situated; a great place to camp or even spend a day or two.

Continuing east, you now pass into the Hindu Kush and the NWFP, or Khyber Pakhtunkhwa as the province is now known. The road deteriorates as you drop down past Mastuj and Buni, leading to Chitral, just 30km from the Afghan border. Over the domes of the town's mogul mosque the distant peak of Tirich Mir is visible to the north. Chitral is a congested, one-street town lined with bazaars. Since 2008 the ride over the 3118m (10,230') Lowari Pass towards Peshawar is thought to be too risky, so the only way out is to return to Gilgit, but it's still worth it as an excursion if you've taken a liking to the area.

Hunza and the road to Kashgar

Continuing on up the KKH beyond Gilgit, the ascent begins in earnest and soon you arrive at the fabled **Hunza Valley** where people were thought to live to over a hundred on a diet of apricots and sunshine. With the mass of Rakaposhi (7788m, 13,453') to the southwest, most hotels are based in the town of **Karimabad** (Hunza), although Altit is friendly and cheap.

In January 2010 a huge landslide blocked the entire Hunza valley at the village of Attabad 14km up the road. Very soon a **lake** backed up drowning four villages and over 30km of the highway. There's talk of lowering the lake level, re-aligning the KKH as well as occasional blasting to widen the spillway, but for the moment regular boats can transport a bike for the two-hour trip. The 🖳 www.pamirtimes.net website is the place to catch up on the current lake situation. Locals were said to be digging their own bypass track.

Passu is a small village near which the Batura glacier nearly reaches the highway and where a famous cluster of spire-like peaks rise above the valley. Some 84km short of the Khunjerab Pass, **Sost** (2790m, 9150') is a rough and

ready trading post where the Pakistani border formalities are done. Without a **Chinese visa** and all the escort arrangements (which take months to organise), Sost is where you'll need to deposit your passports if you wish to make the two-hour excursion up to the Pass as the valley tightens in around the frost-mangled KKH. Jammed in an ever-narrowing cleft, one-in-one scree slopes teeter just a tremor or a downpour away from the next landslide.

The KKH closes in. © Iris Heiremans

Into Xinjiang, western China

As you emerge at **Khunjerab**, the land opens right out into broad valleys dotted with grazing camels. Just below the pass is the Chinese immigration post at **Pirali** from where smooth asphalt rolls down 125km (78 miles) to the ethnically Tajik town of **Tashkurgan** (3115m, 10,220′) where more formalities will be required.

Pirali; welcome to China (got any oxygen?).

From here it's another 275km (170 miles) to **Kashgar**, over the 3995m (13,107′) **Ulugrabat Pass** where Karakul Lake spreads out beneath the 7546m (24,757′) snowy mass of Mustagh Ata peak. From the lake you drop down through the Ghez river canyon, pass a checkpoint and head on through Tajik farming villages and past the hazy Pamirs to **Kashgar** from where the cost of the daily escort in China might see you regrettably rushing on to Kyrgyzstan border posts at the Torugurt or Irkeshtam passes.

That money will not necessarily have been wasted because, as a way of getting between Central Asia and the Indian sub-continent, this passage through the farthest corner of Chinese Xinjiang over some of the world's greatest mountain ranges is well worth the months and few hundred dollars it may cost to organise the chaperoned transit of China over, say, five days. Coming from Europe and Russia via Central Asia, picking up the KKH to Pakistan, visiting India and then heading back via Iran and Turkey is one of the greatest overland journeys you can do.

India

I have to say that after nearly ten years on the road and well over 70 countries, India was the most difficult place to ride a motorcycle. You're left totally drained at the end of each day to the point that I was unable to enjoy the riding. Your concentration and awareness has to be full-on and 360° every second you're on the road. It's exhausting.

Lisa Thomas ⌨ www.2ridetheworld.com

You'd think if you've ridden all the way overland across Iran and Pakistan, India would be just another crazy south Asian country, but within a short distance of the border you'll see that yes, there is an eleven on the scale after all. This land of over a billion, the world's biggest democracy (for what that's worth) can still take your breath away: the pollution and filth alongside beauty and ancient splendour, the anarchic road manners and scoffing at safety or even common sense despite a suffocating bureaucracy, and of course the wealthy but growing elite amid a mass of the world's poorest people. Over 3000km from tip to toe and almost as wide, you can't expect to see it all, but if you give it a try you'll come back with some tales to tell.

It's not for everyone and sounds daunting, but once you catch on and recognise that the Highway Code is just something to feed to a goat, riding a bike in India becomes 'adventure motorcycling' alright.

Riding here could be likened to a computer game with a time travel element. You'll be fighting for your place on the road with every mode of land transport since they invented the wheel or slung a noose around an ox. Horn-steered Tata trucks and buses trail a wake of carcinogenic soot past Victorian three-wheeled contraptions, slick Bajaj scooters and blacked-out Mercedes, while among them all a meagre pedestrian leads a cow to market with a tree trunk on its back.

It's not for everyone and sounds daunting, but once you catch on and recognise that the Highway Code is just something to feed to a goat, riding a bike in India becomes 'adventure motorcycling' alright. By turn terrifying, exhausting and frustrating, above all it's an unforgettable sensory feast to which it's hard to feign indifference. All you have to do is learn fast and then keep up. Many riders get on their knees in thanks on crossing into Pakistan, knowing that India is behind them. And Pakistan is thought to be so dangerous the police escort you across at high speed.

VISAS AND BORDERS

Visas are available in Islamabad in three days with a Letter of Introduction (LOI). Try to get the longer, **six-month** visa, even though it starts on the date of issue. An LOI is not required for a visa issued in your home country. Costs start from around £30 or $45 for a standard single entry 90-day tourist visa.

The only land border to **Pakistan** is at **Wagah–Atari**, 20km from Lahore and 40km from Amritsar, open daily 10am-4pm. Arrive early and bring lunch as the immigration process on the Indian side can take hours (the Pakistani side, by contrast, is relatively efficient). Vehicles are often searched for drugs. You must have a **carnet** and you should try to buy **third party motor insurance** at the border, although you might have to wait until Amritsar for this.

There are several crossings into **Nepal** (see p221) which include Sunauli in Uttar Pradesh to Bhairawa (south of Pokhara) and Raxaul in Bihar to Birganj (south of Kathmandu). It's possible to cross from India to **Bangladesh** at various points, but the most straightforward is at **Benapole**, 75km north-east of Calcutta. The Indian side is shabby, but the Bangladeshi side is highly efficient, especially for foreigners. Your carnet will be required in Bangladesh, but bear in mind that even after India you might still find the Dhaka–Chittagong Highway a recurring finale of *Scrapheap Challenge* on crack. The only overland route into **China** is via Nepal.

PRACTICALITIES

Part of the fun is that **English** is widely spoken, even to a limited extent in the smallest villages. Amex travellers' cheques are accepted in most banks and **ATMs** can be found in major cities and tourist areas.

The black market or licensed **money changers** might offer a slightly better exchange rate and will definitely be much less tedious than major banks.

Main overland routes across India and western China

ASIA – ROUTE OUTLINES

INDIA – YOU'RE STANDING IN IT

Bovids

General Purpose House Cow (GPHC). Varying in colour from brown to black and white, they wander aimlessly through traffic. Dangerously limited ability to reason.

Buffalo. Black with laid back horns. Used for working the fields, pulling carts and obstructing traffic. Walks slowly and once moving keeps going in that direction no matter what. Make sure you're not coming the other way.

Brahmans or 'Sacred Mobile Roundabouts' (SMR). Grey to white, smaller in the south, up to 1.8m tall in the north. Cocky, will not budge under any pressure. Creates its own roundabout with other Brahmans. Has eyes with 180-degree vision. Objectionable 'Holier than a GPHC' attitude. Immune to all intimidation; scoffs at warp-factor air horns.

Goats

Commonplace and also contemptuous of traffic. Whole families cohabit in permanent squalor on median strips. The young ones are dangerous as they make sudden moves and lack respect.

Pigs

Have the tendency to cross the road in gangs and change course midway. Often seen stranded across median strips where they are able to disrupt both directions of travel. Nevertheless, said to be highly intelligent, verging on conspiratorial.

Dogs

Less intelligent than a GPHC with learning difficulties. Minor hazard.

Monkeys

Very dangerous and unpredictable – jump out of the bush screaming and race along the road baring their teeth. Avoid braking hard on any Fresh Flat Monkey Formations (FFMFs), which otherwise have passed their most dangerous phase and are on the path to reincarnation.

Old men on pushbikes

There are two varieties. First is the 'I can't afford a hearing aid. Pardon?' type. Prone to making sudden right turns with perfectly bad timing. The second variety usually wears glasses fashioned from sawn-down coke bottles polished with coarse sandpaper and held on by copper wire. These guys steer straight towards you with an 'I can't believe my eyes' attitude and change course just prior to impact.

Truck/bus drivers

The biggest threat to road users on a daily basis. Drip-fed on amphetamines and have adapted the Nietzschean axiom 'That which does not kill me and is not an SMR can be run at/run over/run off the road.'

Government vehicles and army jeeps

Attitude: 'We own the road so we drive in the middle – what are you going to do about it/ I am too important/have a big gun'. Yield or face the consequences, including several forms requiring stamping and countersigning by India's speciality: a Permanently Unobtainable Person (PUP).

Grain crops in need of thrashing

Can appear on the road in all arable areas up to a foot deep. Apply the same caution as with FFMFs. Dry stalks can block your radiator or wedge against your exhaust and set you ablaze.

Everything else I forgot to mention

Whatever it is, it's out there on the road and heading for you!

RICHARD WOLTERS

Bureaucracy for anything from buying a train ticket to extending a visa is truly mind-boggling. It's often easier for a travel agent to organise tickets for you. If you're heading away from big towns, have a stash of pounds, dollars or euros and keep hold of small denomination rupees. Petrol pump attendants always have lots of change but small shops don't.

There's something to be said for not using the ubiquitous Lonely Planet **guidebook** if you want to avoid the tourist tramlines and ghettos; break out and try the *Footprint India Handbook* in conjunction with Nelles or LP maps. The *Rough Guide to India* is also very comprehensive, and now covers Kashmir again. A great Indian **road trip website** with a lot of knowledgeable local content, as well as routes you've never heard of, is 🖳 www.indiamike.com. Local SIM or **phone cards** or even phones are easily bought and much cheaper than your own and **internet cafés** are widespread.

Accommodation in India is cheap, plentiful and usually good quality. A budget of around £10-15 or $15-25 per night will usually find you in a decent mid-range hotel, outside of Delhi and Mumbai (where that price range can more than double). Excepting the mountainous north, **wild camping** in a country of over a billion people is not so easy. Expect visitors.

As for the **best seasons** for riding, the hyper-humid build-up (late March and April) as well as the subsequent **monsoon** (May–late September) are well worth avoiding. Riding into the cool post-monsoon season makes more sense, unless you're heading up to Kashmir and Ladakh where the cool Himalayan season runs from the clearing of the snowed-up passes in June until September. After mid-September it's said the road crews of the Border Roads Organisation (BRO) stop clearing the bigger landslides or early snowfall until the following summer, although it's possible to keep riding up there well into October; there's more on p218.

ON THE ROAD IN INDIA

Driving in India is about as chaotic and unpredictable as it gets and the driving rule 'Might is Right' is the only law both here and in Bangladesh. Bus drivers are particularly deranged and seem to be chasing impossible schedules. Exploit your bike's agility and ABS if you have it, but don't get carried away; **keeping pace with the local flow** works out best so a small bike is fine here. Even on a 120-horsepower adventure moto with titanium lasers you're still at lower-foodchain levels on the road. Some riders have suggested viewing other road users as having only blinkered forward vision; nothing else exists which is why a **loud horn** is vital. Rear view mirrors are merely for hanging tassles or judging squeeze-through width.

'Be careful, I hear India is the worst driving in the world.'

Locals have no faith in the traffic police (who are virtually non-existent anyway) or the judicial system, so if you're involved in an accident the usual advice is to disappear as quickly as possible, irrespective of whose fault it is. With the countless hazards that Indian roads throw at you (see the opposite page for a partial list), **avoid riding at night** if you can help it. Potholes, cows and the homeless all roam the roads at this time, so if you must do so, ride with full beam on (everyone else does), cover the brakes and take it easy.

Aside from the ceaseless widescreen chaos and carnage, there are few other tricks to master in India. *(continued on p220)*

'Be careful, thanks for that! Russia was bad at the time, Iran was controlled mayhem, Pakistan was all they could do, India is ... beyond all belief. No brakes – no problem ... no horn = accident, no end of smashed trucks/buses. Now I drive more aggressively and Danielle does not shout in my ear – perhaps she is speechless or her eyes are tight shut. I will miss this one day but for now it is sometimes over the top. You should try it!
Bob Goggs

INDIA ON AN ENFIELD

Once built in Chennai (Madras) using the original casts from the parent company in Redditch, Royal Enfield India is currently experiencing a renaissance. The beloved vintage-style cast-iron models are no more; the new lineup now features Unit Construction Engine (UCE) models, a move necessitated by emission regulations. Royal Enfield India has been dragged into the 20th century, still clutching its pushrod single engines.

The company seems to have made all the right moves though, with unprecedented popularity in India and around the world. The designs have been freshened and technology upgraded but amazingly they've managed to retain the original's inimitable character. But it's not all sunshine and roses.

Today, there are three types of Enfields, each available as a 350 or 500cc: the old cast-iron (CI) models based on the original British dies; the aluminium-engined models developed with AVL in Austria; and the current (UCE) models with the gearbox in the crankcase like all modern bikes.

Though each of these models has a different heart they retain the look and character of the original classic and the 'Export model' Enfields sold abroad continue to be superior to the ones you buy in India.

Bullets have been described as 'always sick but never terminal': if you're expecting modern Japanese reliability, a Bullet isn't for you. But a tune-up (plug, points, tappets) every 500km will go a long way to keeping the show on the road.

The challenging nature of Indian roads make things interesting and will mean your top speed is around 50mph/80kph on any machine. If you're planning on a lot of highway riding, it's safe to assume a daily average speed of 25mph/40kph. In this sort of environment the Enfield is perfectly suitable and will give you a journey to remember along with plenty of roadside encounters. The bike's poor reputation is somewhat exaggerated: treat it right and it'll last.

For a Himalayan adventure a 500cc bike is best; this motor will chug steadily over the world's highest roads. Down on the plains and in the south the 350 is fine.

Model differences

All AVL and UCE models and some of the later CI models have the gear lever on the left, a five-speed gearbox and more reliable electronic ignition. Older Bullets have the shifter on the right as in the British Royal Enfield era. A popular crash scenario for nascent Bulleteers involves stamping on the gearlever thinking it's the brake.

New Enfields

Modern India is in the midst of a love affair with the Royal Enfield. As a result there's a six-month waiting list for some models. If you're unwilling to wait, many dealers will sell you a brand-new bike at a premium.

    Classic 500 Rs 150,000
    Classic 350 Rs 121,000
    Thunderbird Twinspark (350) Rs 125,000
    Bullet Electra Twinspark (350) Rs 125,000
    Bullet 350 Twinspark Rs 121,000
    Desert Storm (500) Rs 159,000

Reliability

Though the new UCE models have made great strides in reliability compared to the older CI models, it's the AVLs that are most reliable. They enjoy the advantage of being built on a decades old platform, with better mechanicals where it matters most. The present UCE models, being first-generation, still need some kinks to be ironed out.

Spares

The diversity of models and the new-found popularity has resulted in a spares shortage, especially for the newer models. Spares for the 350cc CI are most readily available, even in small towns. The rarer 500cc models have a perennial spares availability issue. Karol Bagh district in Delhi remains the best place to get spares at the cheapest rates in India, though check the origin.

Buying used from travellers

Departing foreigners advertise in travellers' hotels in areas like Paharganj or the New Delhi Tourist Camp. Standard price for a CI 350, regardless of age, is around Rs 40,000; you'll rarely pay more than Rs60,000. Right now Rs100 equals £1.16, US$1.80 or €1.48.

Used dealers and rentals

The main Delhi bike market in **Karol Bagh** has several dealers, the best known being Lalli Singh (🖳 www.lallisingh.com). Many people have positive things to say. I had a good experience with SoniMotors (🖳 www.sonimotors.com) who rented me a 500cc Bullet with toolkit and sale-or-return spares (very few needed) for just Rs300/day,

INDIA ON AN ENFIELD

but current prices are around Rs1000/day. Tony Bullet Center (🖳 www.tonybullet centre.com) also has rentals. Rentals in Manali or Leh cost much more and the bikes are substandard.

All the above offer no time limit repurchase at 30% less than you paid. Depending on your bargaining skills used prices are around a third higher than buying privately. If you're planning on using a bike for more than about six weeks, it works out cheaper to buy and sell than to rent. The owner of Nanna Motors, near New Delhi Tourist Camp, is a good mechanic (recommended by owners of foreign machines) and can sometimes help with bike purchase (including new bikes). In the summer season his son also runs a garage in Manali.

Modifications
After crash guards, the most popular modification is an after-market exhaust. A short pea-shooter silencer gives the best looks and sound, but you'll find many others in Karol Bagh, with varying levels of loudness.

A common issue when touring is fouling the air filter due to oil overflowing from the catch can. This happens if the catch can is not drained or when the bike falls to the right. A simple fix is to remove the air filter and fit an old style one that sits outside the right-side tool box instead.

Useful minor extras for Indian touring include: petrol filter, fueltap lock, battery isolation switch, different handlebars and a reshaped seat to improve handling and comfort as well as crash bars, racks and super-loud horns. None of these add up to more than a few thousand rupees.

Running an Enfield
Get used to the fact that you'll spend a lot of time nurturing your machine. Apart from regular carb cleaning, check nuts and bolts frequently – Enfields shake themselves to pieces on pot-holed Indian roads. As said before, a plug, points and tappets check every 500km will be time well spent.

Passing about one per hour, getting to know your nearest Enfield-wallah isn't difficult. These roadside 'mechanics' who over many decades became intimate with the CI models, haven't spent similar time with the AVL and UCE models so if you have one it would be better to visit an authorised company workshop. Spares are available in all but the smallest towns. Besides the usual items, carry cables, spare tubes, a chain link, rectifier and a coil. Always try to buy original Enfield spares, cheaper imitations have an even shorter service life. If you're heading up to Ladakh and Zanskar, it's best to carry all necessary spares with you.

Be prepared for roadside repairs everywhere and anytime, although most towns have a dedicated Enfield 'metalbasher'. Note that it's worth supervising all work to check it's actually being done and that no old parts are being substituted. You have been warned.

Prices for common repairs are: puncture Rs50; carb' clean Rs50; oil change Rs600; rebore and new piston from Rs3000 to Rs13000 depending on the model; fitting new clutch plates Rs450. In India **petrol** costs around Rs70 a litre and a 350 Enfield will return around 80mpg or 25-35kpl.

Documents/regulations
It's not strictly necessary to get **ownership papers** in your name as long as the owner on the documents has signed the transfer. That said, a sale letter from the seller stating you to be the buyer will do too. If planning to sell the bike in a state other than the one it's registered in, you must obtain a 'no objections' certificate. Most dealers will organise a name transfer for a fee although being India, this can take a few weeks.

Third-party **insurance** is mandatory, if worthless. It costs around Rs850 (£10) a year, and is obtainable at any insurance office. Any driver's licence will do. In practice almost every foreign rider can get by in India with his own driving licence as the average policeman doesn't even know what an IDP looks like. However, if entering overland it would be sensible to be armed with an IDP. **Helmets** are required in India.

Taking a Bullet out of the country
Since about 2000, it's only possible to ride your Indian-registered Bullet to Nepal. Under new regulations, riding one back to Europe or wherever is virtually impossible. The only realistic way to do it now is to buy a Nepal-registered 'export model' in Nepal, have your Carnet de Passage issued in your home country and ride it through India to Pakistan and back to Europe.

GAURAV JANI

EXPLORING THE INDIAN HIMALAYA

I haven't ridden all of this route or been to 'mainland' India for any longer than necessary, but a great fortnight's riding is to be had up in Indian Kashmir. All the things that can get to you down on the plains: traffic, congestion, heat, filth, are less oppressive up here where a laid back Buddhist culture and its ancient monasteries (gompas) have survived for centuries. The fact that you'll be riding over some of the world's highest roads is almost a side issue. Providing you have a head for heights and good weather, in the 2-3000 kilometres between Amritsar and Shimla you can't fail to have a fabulous ride.

For a fuller picture check out the lively Indian forum: www.bcmtouring.com/forum/ladakh-zanskar-f24. You may also want to read the box on riding at altitude on p174 as well as the information on p163; a breakdown at over 4500m (14,800') while unacclimatised could get nasty.

> ## CAUTION!
> ## YOU ARE AT 17586 FT (5360 M)
> ✓Do not exert
> ✓Try not to spend more than 20 minutes here
> ✓Refrain from smoking
> ✓In case of breathlessness and/ or chest pain, seek medical attention immediately
> ✓Protect your eyes from sunlight by wearing goggles

Srinagar to Shimla

If coming from Pakistan, swing north at Amritsar for the city of Jammu and on to **Srinagar** at just 1600m (5250'). This conservative Muslim corner of India is not without its sectarian troubles and has a heavy army presence. Renting a houseboat out on Nagin Lake is the done thing here; the guidebooks can tell you all about that. With that ticked off, you're ready to ride east some 440km to Ladakh's capital, Leh. Following the alpine Sindh valley, 110km from Srinagar is your first pass, Zoji La at 3545m (11,630') after which you coast down to Drass which one day in 1995 awarded itself the accolade of 'second coldest village in the world' at minus 60°C (for the coldest see p234).

You might try and shoot through militarised **Kargil** (fuel) just a couple of miles from the disputed Line of Control with Pakistan and just 90 kilometres from Skardu, just off the KKH. All along this section of the road you'll encounter army convoys who expect you to get out of the way, pronto.

On the way up to Namika La at the village of Mulbekh (fuel), you'll pass your first **Buddhist stupa** (shrine) and the pass itself (3700m, 12,140') is decorated with colourful prayer flags, something you'll be seeing a lot of in the coming days. After a brief dip, you reach Fotu La (4105m, 13,469') the **high point** on this ride to Leh and where you actually crossing to the north side of the Great Himalaya Range. Some 15km down the road is **Lamayuru** with its clifftop gompa. If you develop a taste for them, another hour down the road are a couple more at the peaceful villages of Alchi and Likkir.

You're now riding along the valley of the **Indus river** which flows some 3000km from Mt Kailash in Tibet to Karachi in Pakistan. About 30km from Leh is a viewpoint where the clear turquoise green Indus mixes with the sediment-heavy Zanskar river coming up from the south (or so it was for us).

If you arrive mid-season **Leh** can be a throng of backpackers and other tourists in search of Shangri-La (that's not another pass), but unlike most of them you have your own wheels and if your head's up to it, set off the 40km up to **Khardung La** – at 5359m (17,582') one of the world's highest drivable passes, but there's a higher one on this ride.

If you just want to tick off the pass you can probably get by without the Inner Line permit and leave your passports at a checkpoint on the way up. If however, you want to head over and down to the remote **Shyok and Nubra** valleys, get the permit and a extra fuel (Deskit might have fuel). You'll get as far as they let you up here, as the Nubra Valley leads north to the Saichen glacier where even the Line of Control gets blurred. One night in 2012 the 'two bald men fighting over a comb' stand-off between the Indian and Pakistani armies was again questioned when 138 soldiers stationed at one of the highest and coldest outposts on Earth were buried by an avalanche.

EXPLORING THE INDIAN HIMALAYA

If you're ready for more it's possible to continued south-east from Khalsar junction along the Shyok valley to Aghyam and turn south here over the 5200m (17,060') Wari La to **Taktok**, close to a junction with the road that leads to the **Pangong Tso lake**, a popular day trip from Leh via Karu. That involves crossing the **Chang la** pass (picture left) while over the lake there are views east to Tibet. It's said foreigners can't ride beyond Pangong towards Chushul, but Guarav Jani's film *Riding Solo To The Top Of The World* describes the ride along the very border of China to the isolated gompa at Hanle.

Leaving Leh to take the popular ride to Manali you'll need a range of 350km assuming you top up at **Karu** (the turn off for Wari La and the Nubra loop, or Pangong Tso lake). Locally, 2-litre Coke bottles are used as fuel containers, the reasoning being that if they can survive transportation from the bottling plants down on the plains to Ladakh without exploding, they'll manage a couple of days with petrol in them.

At **Upshi** you turn south for Rumtse and the **Tanglang La** (5300m, 17,388') with an optional diversion to Tso Kar lake on the far side. Alternatively, with a bit of off-roading ability, carry on another 100km up the Indus valley to Mahe Bridge and turn east for Puga and Polo Kongka La (4970m, 14,587') which leads down to the other side of Tso Kar (Tso Moriri lake may not be worth the effort) and so the Manali road near the road camp at Dibring, some 25km south of Tangling La. This will add some 100km to the range you need between Leh and Thandi. Whichever way you got here, you're now on the Morei plains, an arid 4500m basin between more high passes. At the southern end the road drops into a canyon and **Pang**, a string of seasonal tents and cafés, followed by an impressive climb up to Lachulung La (5077m, 16,656') and another pass before dropping down the heaped hairpins known as the **Gata Loops** from the base of which it's a short ride to **Sarchu**, offering more rudimentary lodgings and food.

Beyond here you cross back to the south side of the Great Himalaya Range at **Baralacha La** (4918m, 16,135') where the long descent brings you out of the barren heights down into more vegetated, inhabited and finally forested lands for fuel at **Thandi**, some 385km from Leh.

Most now will scoot up the Chandra river valley to the hamlet of Gramphoo and turn off for the 3988m (13,061ft) **Rohtang La**, the most treacherous of all of the Manali–Leh passes. Set against the south-facing flank of the Himalaya, it catches all the north-bound monsoonal rains and is usually the first to get either drenched or snowed up, while the northern passes you've just crossed remain cold but dry as a bone. At any time the road can become a mud fight past a line of mired trucks heading up to re-supply the military camps. The **Leh–Manali Highway** is officially open from around June until September 15th, but this is the cut-off date the BRO (Border Roads Association) are obliged to clear passes in the event of early snow. Roads can be open beyond that date.

Manali is covered by the guidebooks, but if you're not ready for Babylon just yet, at Gramphoo take the rough track along the Chandra valley up to Kunzum La (4501m, 14,767') and cross the watershed into the fabulous **Spiti valley**.

Soon after Kato village the road bridges the Spiti river. Although it's a dead end for anything other than a moped, riding up towards Chicham reveals some spectacular Bryce-Canyon-like *hoodoos* (rock spires) along the Spiti's eroded banks. Chicham, along with more touristy Kibber on the far side of a deep gorge covered by a span (cradle on a cable), are among the world's highest villages.

Back in the Spiti valley you pass the gompas at Kei (and the track back to Kibber) to arrive at the town of Kaza (fuel, restos, guest houses) where you'll need an **Inner Line permit** to ease below the Chinese frontier at the bridge checkpoint at Sumdo. Beyond here the famously unstable slope at Malling used to cause headaches and require a span as at Kibber. Now they've built a road around the top to Nako village, though it still won't take much of a tremor or downpour to set off the tethering rubble slopes.

Mile by mile you now lose height until you've passed the new dam works and at **Rampur** are barely over 1000 metres and experiencing an oxygen high.

Now back down among distinctive **Lahaul**'s pine forests, it's a day's bend-swinging up again through the trees to the busy hill resort of **Shimla**. where you can pull up and look back at your photos of what has been a mind-blowing ride.

(continued from p215)   The **police**, whilst certainly corrupt, are generally insipid and if you're ever stopped and asked for 'baksheesh' then hold your ground, be firm and rude if necessary, and don't give in. Hard and fast traffic laws are unheard of in India.

Petrol is around Rs70 per litre (about €1) and easy to come by, but if you're exploring the more remote back roads of central India don't miss a chance to fill up when you can. **Motor insurance** is required but being India, getting some takes a bit of effort. Try to get it at the Pakistani border or the first big town.

Where to go

India is a vast country, packed with geographical, cultural and ethnic diversity. From the snowbound Himalayan expanses of Ladakh to the deserts of Rajasthan; the lush alpine valleys of Kashmir and Himachal Pradesh to the steamy tropics of Kerala; the cosmopolitan frenzy of Mumbai to the mist-clad plantations of Assam. There is **too much to take in**, even with a few months and your own wheels.

Your entry point and ultimate destination beyond India might dictate your itinerary. If **shipping** onwards from India chances are you'll finish up in Mumbai, Chennai or Calcutta but as a rule, clued-up riders try to avoid getting involved with shipping out of or into India. Life is just too short for that. Flying your bike out of Nepal is the preferred method, with plenty of agencies in Kathmandu specialising in that service.

Head for the hills

Aside from some of the classic high mountain **road trips** (see box on p218), there are a handful of must-sees down on the plains, if you can put up with the fellow tourists. A ride encompassing **Delhi, Agra, Varanasi** and not least **Rajasthan** would leave few people disappointed and would include many of India's cultural highlights, although you'd struggle to find yourself much off the beaten track.

Possibilities for exploring India's vast centre will give you a memorable taste of more remote, local life. Consider setting out across the **Deccan Plateau** and visiting the beautiful hill station of **Pachmarhi**, the caves at **Ellora** and **Ajanta**, the erotic 10th-century temples at **Khajuraho**, and then ending up in either **Mumbai**, **Goa** or if time permits, beautiful, tropical **Kerala** in the deep south.

Riding east of **Calcutta** can be difficult but will be rewarding – the remote and intriguing states of **Sikkim**, **Nagaland** and **Arunachal Pradesh** all require special permits from the police but this area is far removed from the rest of India, both culturally and geographically. Far-east India isn't without its problems and ongoing insurgencies in **Manipur** mean this part of the world may remain off-limits for a while to come. But does it really matter where you go or what you see? Much of the fun of India is simply the day-to-day riding, observing and surviving life on the roads – hair-raising and exhausting yes, but once you're used to it, a colourful and unforgettable experience that you actually might miss one day.

NEPAL AND TIBET

WITH ANDY PAG

For once getting a **visa** for Nepal couldn't be easier, and after being in India a while some travellers experience a kind of reversed form of post-traumatic stress disorder which can lead to dizziness and euphoria. Simply rock up at the border and pay for 30 or 90 days. At $40 a month it's no give-away, but after the bureaucracy of India or restrictions in Tibet, you'll be glad to pay the premium for the easy service. You can stay for up to five months per calendar year on a tourist visa, and it takes just 20 minutes to renew it once inside the country, at £2 a day. If you've made it this far then you'll know what to do at the border. Seek out the customs and immigration huts and smile as you watch them adorn your prized documents with a selection of fine inks.

Coming from India you'll be pleasantly surprised that **lodging** and **meals** can be as cheap, although at 115 rupees (Nrs) a litre, **petrol** is a bit more expensive. At least the air isn't perpetually filled with the sound of truck horns, and not every oncoming vehicle is trying to rush you on the path to reincarnation. None the less, be prepared to be sent diving for the grassy verge every now and again, though rest assured that if you're on the verge of a precipitous mountain drop, they'll usually allow you to stand your ground. Trucks and buses will speedily use the full width of the hairpin switchbacks no matter how blind the corner is.

As an **overlanders' hangout** Kathmandu with a vehicle doesn't have a lot going for it. I found **Pokhara** to be nicer and there's a free campsite with a toilet block in the tourist Lakeside part of town, as well as a more secluded spot at Palme, five kilometres up the lake track.

The Tibetan capital of **Lhasa** is just 1000km from Kathmandu along the **Friendship Highway** – one of many such named roads in east Asia. With a Chinese visa and Tibetan travel permit, a bus tour via Everest Base Camp (Tibetan side) is fairly easy to arrange at the cost of around $100 per day. Riding up there on your own bike is not something you can organise on the hoof in Kathmandu. Special group visas as well as permits must be applied for months in advance – there's more on p246. A quote in 2011 for a 4x4 and three motos to cross from Nepal to Kyrgyzstan via Lhasa over three weeks came to £7300, excluding fuel, food and lodging, and with the guide sat in the 4x4. The cost for a similarly long transit eastwards to Laos might be a little less.

Note that the G219 road across the **Tibetan plateau** to Kashgar stays well above 4000m (13,100') and frequently crosses 5000-metre-plus (16,400') passes between Lhasa and the G315 Khotan road southeast of Kashgar. Whichever direction you do this, it may be better to grab a week's acclimatisation at around 4000m in a neighbouring country rather than suffering in China at over $100 a day. Once on the plateau there's no quick way down if altitude sickness strikes, bar an emergency flight out of Shiquanhe (aka: Ngari or Gar) airport, near the Indian Kashmiri border.

© Bob Goggs

Russia

WITH CHARLIE & NINA WEATHERILL

Easier access to the Russian Federation opened up following the fall of the USSR, proving that overland travel isn't always becoming ever more restricted. The bad old system has gone, to be little changed by a not-so-great new one, only now the withdrawal of state support has left much of the countryside and particularly the Far East high and dry. Infrastructure crumbles away from economically unviable areas as in fits and starts the huge country judders along under its own weight. As the Russians might put it phlegmatically '*mi dyshajem*' (we're breathing) and as in so many places in the overlanding firmament, it's the resolve and hospitality of the poor struggling against all odds which leave the main impression – along with the entrenched bureaucratic pedantry and small scale corruption of the authorities.

Scenically, mile for mile Russia is not so grand but the further you range from the Russian homeland in the west, the more the aforementioned spirit will strike you, for these are essentially Europeans estranged in a frontier land where by and large, their forebears were exiled to work the gulags.

At 17 million square kilometres (6.6m square miles) the half of this land mass above 60°N probably has the lowest population density in the world and geographically, 'Europe' ends rather too neatly at the **Ural mountains**, running from the Arctic Ocean down through the Kazakh border to the Caspian.

Away from the southerly network of the **Trans-Siberian** railway and highway, land-based travel can be arduous. In winter major rivers such as the Ob, Yenisey, Lena and Kolyma become navigable ice roads or *zimniks*. In the short northern summer melted snow saturates the top soil and any attempt at building and maintaining a highway becomes literally undermined as an annual temperature ranging 40°C either side of freezing point sees roads expand, crumble or get washed away by floods.

Rail links to navigable rivers are most effective because, as you'll read below, for all but the most specialised off-road vehicle, land travel away from these routes is extremely slow.

The former gulag prison camps which mushroomed across this region during the 1930s in an effort to accelerate the Soviet Union's industrialisation, are today in ruins or have evolved into isolated frontier settlements, populated by descendants of the inmates and guards. They endure because, as a geologist from Magadan put it 'we have all the elements of the periodic table, and we have them in industrial quantities'.

Do yourself a favour and learn the **Cyrillic alphabet** (see opposite) so you don't end up in Xandyga when you wanted to get to Huevos Rancheros; it's not totally alien to the Roman alphabet and numbers are the same. English or German may get you by in the West, but not east of Irkutsk. Learning a few phrases greatly enhances your trip so carry a phrasebook or visit 🖥 www.rt.com/learn-russian.

BORDERS

Borders are the place to demonstrate your fine mastery of Russian, if you have it. They'll appreciate it and the arduous processes should take less time and be more fun. Forms are normally in Russian, so try and find a female officer – they are ever more frequent at border posts these days – as they'll always be the first to help you and may even write out your forms for you.

Assuming all your paperwork is in order there's no need to pay out any bribes to anyone during the process. You'll get there just as others have done before you. Without help, expect to be there for several hours. Consider yourself lucky that you're not a truck driver coming from Latvia, at the wrong end of a 50km queue and a three-day wait. Unfortunately, the need to **re-register** and renew permits continues once you're in Russia.

VISAS AND REGISTRATION

Although there's periodic talk of easing regulations with the EU and allowing a reciprocal 30-day visa to be issued at a border, the process to get into Russia is at least simpler than it used to be. Now it's merely expensive and, as with Iran and the 'stans, a cosy alliance with certain **visa agencies** has become established. They do all the work for you, including obtaining the so-called **letters of introduction** ('LOIs').

The most basic is a **single-entry tourist visa** which lasts for 30 days and costs around £116 through an agency in the UK, less for other EU nationals and from $180 in the US. A **double-entry** visa allowing a second 30-day visit within a year costs about 25% more and both take at least a week to issue. You must have confirmed accommodation or transit information for every night of your stay in the country, but the small fee for a visa support letter can get round this requirement.

CYRILLIC ALPHABET

Cyrillic letter	Roman equivalent	Pronunciation*	Cyrillic letter	Roman equiv	Pronunciation*
А а	a	father	П п	p	Peter
Б б	b	bet	Р р	r	Russia
В в	v	vodka	С с	s	Samarkand
Г г	g	get	Т т	t	time
Д д	d	dog	У у	u, oo	fool
Е е	ye	yet (unstressed: year)	Ф ф	f, ph	fast
			Х х	kh	loch
Ё ё	yo	yoghurt	Ц ц	ts	lots
Ж ж	zh	treasure	Ч ч	ch	chilly
З з	z	zebra	Ш ш	sh	show
И и	i, ee	seek, year	Щ щ	shch	fresh chips
Й й	y	boy	Ы ы	y, i	did
К к	k	kit	ь		(softens preceding letter)
Л л	l	last	Э э	e	let
М м	m	Moscow	Ю ю	yu	union
Н н	n	never	Я я	ya	yard (unstressed: yearn)
О о	o	tore (unstressed: top)			

* pronunciation shown by underlined letter/s

Anything of longer duration or with multiple entries is classified as a **business visa**, although you don't have to be involved in any sort of commerce. Costs for a double-entry 90-day business visa start at nearly £200 for Brits (30% less for most EU citizens) and take at least two weeks to issue; to get it within a week the price is nearly double. Prices and delivery times **for multiple-entry business** visas lasting six months start at around £400 and take two weeks. Visas need to be used within a year, which is longer than most.

With a visa like this you could just about fill up the riding season to-ing and fro-ing between the Baltic and the Pacific, while visiting Central Asia, Ukraine, Mongolia and, if you're quick, the North Pole. However, technically the consulate can refuse to issue a multiple-entry visa if you don't have a previous Russian visa in your passport, although as with all things Russian, this law is rarely enforced consistently. Unless you're sure you'll be in Russia for only a couple of weeks, get the longer lasting business visa; Russia is a big country.

This is the former USSR and so getting a visa is just the start. Within 72 hours of entering the country (excluding weekends and holidays) you must **register** your visa with the Office of Visas and Registration (OVIR, aka UFMS, Federal Migration Service Organisation). Your passport or the immigration card you filled out at the border is stamped, and you obtain a **registration slip** showing the period you're registered to stay in any one place. In addition to the dates, it'll also include details of where you're staying. Very often the **hotel** you're staying in immediately after crossing the border will do this for you for a minimal charge. However, this applies more to the popular tourist cities of Moscow and St Petersburg in the west. In many provincial cities some hotels will register your visa for a fee, even if you're not lodging there.

If you're not passing through the west or are camping, a **Registration Support Letter** will help you register yourself at the nearest OVIR. You'll be asked to complete a **Notification of Arrival form**; it's in Russian so you may need some help; see the image on 🖥 www.realrussia.co.uk. Give the top part back and possibly get another stamp on your migration card or passport.

It's not over yet. In theory once on the road you need to register in any sizable town within three working days but, if you're not staying there for three working days or more, then technically there's no need to register. However, on the road it's worth doing so once in a while and getting another **registration slip** to avoid any potential problems with 'gaps' in your registration. And don't forget to de-register your visa back with the OVIR every time you leave Russia if you're on a multiple-entry visa.

There are obviously plenty around, but Brits have recommended the 🖥 www.realrussia.co.uk agency. Its website is clearly designed, up to date and shows graphics (including translations) of immigration documents. It also has a useful list of **restricted provincial cities** with details of where and how to register should you not be staying in a hotel. They include Barnaul or Novosibirsk if coming out of north-eastern Kazakhstan, Gorno-Altaysk if coming out of north-western Mongolia, Irkutsk north of Ulaanbaatar, plus Vladivostok and Khabarovsk. They even run a forum to discuss Russian topics. Things will have almost certainly changed since this was written; pay them (or somewhere like it) an online visit to see what's new.

ASIA – ROUTE OUTLINES

TRIP REPORT
RUSSIA ~ HONDA AFRICA TWIN

Name	Ergman B
Year of birth	1977
Occupation	Civil engineer
Nationality	Turkish
Previous travels	Turkey, Iran, Kyrgyzstan
Bike travels	Turkey

This trip	Russia
Trip duration	5 weeks
Departure date	July 2010
Number in group	1
Distance covered	16,000km

Best day	Every day
Worst day	Riding into Irkutsk
Favourite places	Novosibirsk
Biggest headache	Everyday bike reload again and again
Biggest mistake	Too many miles a day.
Pleasant surprise	Friendly people
Any illness	None
Cost of trip	€2000
Other trips planned	Mongolia, Kazakhstan, North Africa

Bike model	Honda Africa Twin
Age, mileage	14 years, 90,000 km
Modifications	Hand guards, higher screen, K&N
Wish you'd ...	had heated grips
Tyres used	Mitas E07
Punctures	None
Type of baggage	Hand made alu boxes

Bike's weak point	Basic rear shock
Strong point	Bulletproof and troublefree
Bike problems	Leaking radiator
Accidents	I slide on melted tar near Samara
Same bike again	Yes
Any advice	Learn some basic mechanics

ASIA – ROUTE OUTLINES

Vehicle documents

A translation of your vehicle ownership document will be useful if stopped, although the temporary importation permit (see below) issued at the border ought to suffice. Get an IDP too. **Motor insurance** (*strahavanie*) you buy at the border and pay in roubles at around $10 a month.

No carnet is required; instead you get a 14-day **temporary importation permit**. This can be extended at a main customs office at their discretion, but reasons for the extension and all other details have to be stated in Russian on the application form. As Chris W from 🖳 www.realrussia.co.uk writes '*If you don't speak and write good Russian, it's virtually impossible to apply for an extension, as you need to see a senior customs officer and explain your reasons verbally, to get a permit valid for the whole of Russia. We used an interpreter, who cost us about 5000 roubles for the whole day spent at the customs building.*'

Obviously any extension can only be to the end of your visa registration period (maximum six months; not possible everywhere but no problem in St. Petersburg for example). If you leave Russia for the 'stans or wherever, the permit expires and if you come back you have to start again. Get a **customs declaration form** (sometimes available in several European languages) and indicate on it that you're temporarily importing a bike. Insist on a stamped copy that includes a description, otherwise there'll be problems getting out of Russia. As you ride away from a border after what may have been several frustrating hours bouncing around chasing documents and stamps, resist the urge to wind it open; just down the road radar speed traps or more document checks are likely.

ON THE ROAD

Petrol prices in Russia start at around 30 roubles a litre for 80–95 octane (about $1 or €0.77). Generally fuel costs more in the far east and in western cities. If you're visiting Kazakhstan, petrol costs about the same as Russia; in Mongolia it's about 20% more and in Ukraine about 40% more than Russia. The police in **Ukraine** are no different than anywhere else by the way; you'll find nifty tips on driving there at 🖳 www.go2kiev.com/view/driving.html. To stop run-aways, at most fuel stations you pay first, then they turn it on. As some have found, if the nozzle has no trigger you can get splashed in the eye when your tank's full. On the trans-Sib east of Chita there are **roadhouses** every 150km or so, but in the sticks you know the drill: fill up or run out.

Driving standards in Russia are poor; a combination of uncarworthy roads, unroadworthy cars, **drunkenness** and a healthy dose of machismo, evoking Putin in one of his raunchy vids. Once you factor in dealing with the *militzia*, in big cities it may be easier to park up and get around by taxi or even on foot. **Radar traps** and checkpoints are found on the edge of every town as well as places in between, and you'll almost certainly be stopped for speeding or crossing solid white lines whether you were or not. **Speed limits** are 60kph in town, 110kmh on motorways or as signposted. Maximum fines for moderate speeding are only around 300 roubles; but just 5kph over the limit will get you a ticket unless you settle on the spot and negotiate the fine.

They'll want your passport, immigration documents, registration slip, IDP, TIP and anything else you've got ending with P, to copy into their ledgers.

If they don't ask for these immediately it's probably a prompt for a bribe (*straf*) of 300 roubles or less, or maybe just a friendly chat about your cool bike. Carry photocopies of everything as losing one item can mean having to cough up a bribe or a spell in the salt mines.

There are a couple of Russian road-atlases or, as they call them, auto-atlases, such as the 2008 edition pictured right from  www.allmaps.ru (420 roubles or £9/$14). They cover just about all of the ridable parts of the country at scales from 1:200,000 in the west to 1:3 million in the east, and are occasionally available from specialist map shops in Europe or North America, but at three times the price. Once in Russia these atlases may take some tracking down outside the big cities. However, unless you're roaming off the beaten track, a regular folding road map, either European or Russian produced, will do you. You'll find Russian editions for sale in fuel stations. Of the proprietary digital maps to import into your GPS from the likes of Garmin, their current Russia download costs £85 and is hopeless in the east, just where things begin to get interesting. The best available will be on OSM 🖳 www.openstreetmap.org. And although it's all in Russian, web browsers can translate 🖳 www.roads.ru/forum to get up-to-date news of the state of roads.

DODGING THE POLICE – THE OTHER 'GREAT GAME'

Thanks to a combination of increased poverty and unforgotten Soviet policing styles, **bribery and corruption** are a way of life in Russia and the 'stans' of Central Asia. It can be a daily occurrence, so the quicker you accept it and learn to play the game, the less stressful and more enjoyable your trip will be.

Ultimately, if you don't give the police a reason to stop you, you should be in the clear. The first handy thing to know is it's easier for them not to stop you if you don't make eye contact, so remember: sunvisors down and tunnel vision whenever you see the cops. Learn the rules of the road, though admittedly this is trial and error. Here are some pointers to get you started:

- Speed limits are generally 90kph (56mph) on highways and 60kph (37mph) in towns. As in Europe, town limits start at a sign and end at the same sign with a red line through it. Except that in Russia these signs can be miles after the last house to give the radar cops a chance.
- Never cross a solid white central line. Cross on dashed lines only, or use designated U-turn areas. After speeding, this is a common trap.
- Signs often tend to tell you what you can do, rather than what you can't. In most major cities such as St Petersburg, Moscow, Almaty, Bishkek, Tashkent and Ashgabat, if there's no turn left sign then you can't.
- Slow down if you see a police car, even if you're under the speed limit.
- If an oncoming car flashes you, it's probably because there's a police radar check up ahead. Alternatively, you're in the way and he's coming on through regardless.

Checkpoints, speeding and bribes

At **checkpoints** make sure you closely observe the painfully slow speed limits. If there's a 'Stop' sign, wait there until you're waved on, even if it's just 10m to another one. This 'double stop' combination is a nice little earner for the militzia; don't give them the satisfaction!

When you're **stopped**, first find out why. They may just be interested in where you're from, especially on a bike. If they request your documents, again, politely ask why – '*prabliem?*' ('Is there a problem?') and add that you're a simple tourist. Be reluctant to hand over essential documents if you suspect the policeman may be difficult and will need inducement to give them back, but definitely don't refuse to hand them over.

If you're stopped for **speeding**, ask to check their radar read-out (they should show it to you anyway). If the speed limit is 60kmph, it's often set to go off only marginally higher, say 65kph. For a minor offence that's 10–30kph over the limit, a smile, chat and the offer of cigarettes may be enough; if not then generally pay no more than the equivalent of a $5–8 'fine' or *straf*. That's about 150–240 roubles.

For that amount don't push your luck and expect or ask for a receipt, and bear in mind that they'll often initially ask you for something exorbitant like $50. Negotiate the figure down by showing them the contents of your wallet, which at all times contains no more than 150–240 roubles. It's even worth having a special 'Russian' wallet set aside for such occasions.

If, however, they're claiming you were doing 140kph when you were actually doing 59 (it's not unknown!), then ask to see the radar, the speed sign and argue for as long as it takes. When they ask to see your passport, show them a copy of the photo page. Similarly, have copies of your visa and ownership documents and present these instead of the real thing.

It's illegal to pay traffic fines in dollars in any CIS country, and if they ask for dollars then smile and deny that you have any (*U menya niet*; 'I have none'). It's a form of bargaining though don't treat it as such. Usually they'll then ask for a hefty sum in local currency which will be more than is in your Russian wallet. You should end up paying no more than $8 unless you were more than 40kph over the limit, or have jumped a red light, both of which are much bigger fines. You may find yourself in their sweaty, nicotine-tinged Lada whilst negotiating the *straf*. Don't let this put you off, it's all part of the experience and who knows, you may have never seen the inside of a Lada up close before.

If you speak Russian, above all don't waste this fine talent on the police. Make their job as tedious as possible by smiling a lot, repeating 'tourist' and lowering your IQ while looking confused and babbling. If you're lucky, they might give up on you as a bad job; their next victim will be along shortly.

WESTERN RUSSIA

Western Russia feels like Eastern Europe, and if you're from Europe and are no stranger to centuries-old buildings, aggressive driving or a bored cop with a radar gun, you may not be so impressed with heartland Russia compared to what lies ahead – or indeed to the south via Turkey and the Caucasus. Many people find a warmer welcome along with a more adventurous frontier ambi-

VODKA

One of the most common phrases you'll hear in Russia is 'Davai! Malinka vodka!' which literally means 'come share a little vodka with me and we will end up drinking for two days and departing the best of friends'. Initially this can be a very enjoyable aspect of Russian hospitality, but after weeks of people rushing up thrusting bottles of vodka in your face it gets a bit much. Just saying *niet, spasiba* will not always be enough. Although no one's ever tried it, claiming you have half a liver or no kidneys *(nie imiyiu nikakiye pochki)* might stop further pleadings.

SHAUN MUNRO

ence in the distant outposts and even the huge cities of Far Eastern Russia. If you're Pacific-bound, you're almost certainly going to have to go into west Russia; just remember it's another country out east.

Founded in the late-17th century, the city of **Yekaterinburg** on the eastern flank of the Urals will mark your entry into Asia. There are some beautiful buildings from that era mingling with grittier Soviet-era structures and it was here in 1918 that the Bolsheviks murdered the ruling Romanov family.

Heading east of the Urals the adventure approaches, but not until you've traversed the thousand-mile wide basin of the Siberian Plain and reached Novosibirsk. The principal overlanding route now closely parallels the Trans-Siberian Railway, indeed it's the only route that traverses the entire country. Even then, it only goes as far as Vladivostok; nearly 10,000km from Moscow but still 2500km short of the easternmost continental extreme at Cape Deshneva on the Bering Strait.

To the south-east of Novosibirsk lie the **Altai mountains** and a sealed road right up to the western entry into Mongolia at Tsagannuur (see p241). Even if you're not heading for Mongolia, the wild Altai region (and Tuva to the east) are well worth exploring. You now leave the waterlogged Siberian plain and ascend imperceptibly onto the like-named plateau towards Krasnoyarsk on the Yenisey River, the natural boundary which separates western Siberia from the more interesting eastern side.

NORTH OF THE TRANS SIBERIAN

Looking at a map you'd think there's only one major highway to Far Eastern Russia, and you'd be right. That road parallels the Trans-Siberian Railway and is now sealed right through to Vladivostok. While the surface lasts it's easy riding in most weathers. But there's another, less well-known railway reaching to Far Eastern Russian's Pacific ports; the 4400km (2700-mile) 'Baikal-Amur Mainline' or **BAM** which runs around the north side of Lake Baikal to meet the Pacific at the port of **Vanino**, opposite Sakhalin Island. Where there is a railway there's a service road. Or so you'd hope.

Now becoming as well known as the Kolyma Highway, the BAM was a failed Stalin-era project built over the bones of tens of thousands of Russians or WWII prisoners of war. Work was suspended on Stalin's death, but in the mid-1970s in the face of cooling Soviet-Sino relations, the BAM project was revived by Brezhnev. A strategic back-up to the established Trans-Sib was thought to be needed, as even with Mongolia as a buffer state, in places the Trans-Sib ran rather too close to the Chinese border.

GUIDEBOOK FOR THE BAM

In the mid 1990s Trailblazer published *BAM Railway Guide* by Athol Yates. No one had ever heard of the BAM and it briefly achieved cult status among train enthusiasts as the new thing to do. The book expands on the riches, attractions and history of the area and helps underline the fact that eastern Siberia is not just a wasteland of former gulag camps turned into mining outposts.

Whether you'll have the spare energy to appreciate these finer points while battling your way across the BAMsky Trakt is another matter. By the time you read this, the last handful of copies of the 2001 edition o *Siberian BAM Guide – Rail, Rivers & Road* (expanded by Nicholas Zvegintzov to include the **Kolyma Highway**) may still be available on 🖳 www.trailblazer-guides.com.

Completed at huge cost, the line has recovered from being a Cold War white elephant and instead of supplying secret bases and gulags, today trains run along it day and night, transporting goods from the Pacific ports, serving private mines and sustaining the depressed communities strung alongside it.

The BAM track traverses just a fraction of Russia's vast eastern wilderness, buried in turn by winter snows then flushed by the thaw before a brief, hot, insect-ridden summer – the only time to consider riding the BAM. If you're finding the Trans-Siberian Highway a bit of a yawn and think the Kolyma (see p234) is too obvious, take off along the BAM and see how far you get. This is one biking adventure that will require a steely determination to deal with the relentless obstacles.

In 2009 Walter Colebatch set about logging new routes up here (🖳 www.sibirskyextreme.com; 'SEP') and he and his chums managed most of the BAM in a westerly direction. Walking rivers and small lakes will be necessary and at any time of year violent **windstorms** can rush out of the northern plains, and downpours can raise river levels, turning tracks into quagmires.

Nearly ten per cent of the line is made up of rail bridges, well over 4000 span hundreds of rivers and seasonal swamps. You may think that as long as the locos keep running, these rail bridges could be ridden over. Sadly *niet*. Armed guards control major rail bridges and even just walking across a bridge to ask permission to ride across can earn a hostile reproach: *zapresheni!* (forbidden) so where guards are present, tread gently.

Along the BAM

At the western end the BAM Railway branches off the Trans-Siberian Railway corridor at Taishet, 300km east of Krasnoyarsk. Another 260km further on towards Irkutsk at **Tulun**, a road leads north towards Bratsk to meet the railway. From here it continues to Ust-Kut and an alternative northern route to Yakutsk (via a ferry-barge to Lensk). After Ust-Kut you reach Severobaikalsk on the northern tip of Lake Baikal, about 1000km from Taishet and where during high summer passenger hydrofoils run down the 650km to Irkutsk.

At **Novy Uoyan**, 150km east of Severobaikalsk the western end of the maintained road **ends**. Things now begin to get complicated as the BAM and its adjacent track run into the Severomuisk Ranges. The road gets steadily worse with the first of many broken bridges, as the neglected track returns to the bush. Near **Severomuisk** a ten-mile rail tunnel runs into the mountainside. The service road follows the old, pre-tunnel railway route over the pass and last

TRIP REPORT
POLAND-MAGADAN ~ KTM ADVENTURE

Name	Maciek S
Year of birth	1978
Occupation	Computer programmer
Nationality	Polish
Previous travels	Europe, Siberia, Ivory Coast
Bike travels	Large amounts

This trip	Poland to Magadan
Trip duration	3 months
Departure date	June 2007
Number in group	3
Distance covered	23,000km

Best day	Every single day
Worst day	Few hours after arriving in Magadan
Favourite places	Georgia, Armenia, Pamir, Mong, RoB
Biggest headache	Crap fuel in Tajikistan for a while
Biggest mistake	One more person needed.
Pleasant surprise	KTM very nice to ride *and* bulletproof
Any illness	Vomit both ends from mutton meat
Cost of trip	$3000 + $1000 plane from Magadan
Other trips planned	Maybe Africa again

Bike model	KTM Adventure 2007
Age, mileage	Nearly new, 2000km
Modifications	Yes, including air mixture carb screw
Wish you'd ...	All was perfect
Tyres used	MT21
Punctures	None for me, other two had a couple
Type of baggage	PVC kayak bags

Bike's weak point	Too sexy
Strong point	Sexy! suspension, tank, power, weight
Bike problems	Dirt in carb, frame cracked for others
Accidents	Road zero, dirt plenty
Same bike again	Yes
Any advice	Enjoy it 777.7%, it will last for ever

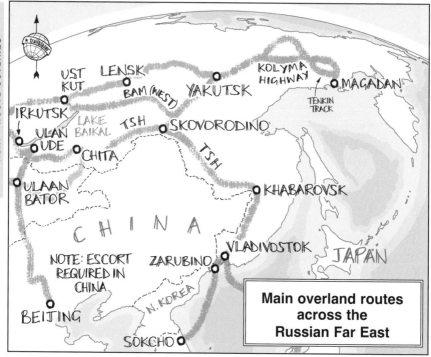

Main overland routes
across the
Russian Far East

told, was said to be in good shape. Seven hundred increasingly gruelling kilo-metres from Baikal you arrive at the town of **Nova Chara**, its unexpected dune field at N56° 50' E118° 8', and the remains of the sinister Marble Canyon gulag nearby. On the way you pass the gold mines around Takshimo, the fittingly named hamlet of Shivery and not least, the bowel-slackening exposure of the **Vitim River bridge** (see p354), a slender 400-metre-long raised causeway clad in loose or rotting sleepers. It leads to the town of Kuanda, lavished with a few kilometres of tarmac to prematurely celebrate the BAM's 'golden spike' event in 1984, when construction crews from either end met and joined up the line.

Soon after Kuanda the road bridge over a small river 50km east of the Vitim is no more. In 2009 the SEP bikers got permission to use the rail bridge; a few days later the Polish 4x4s weren't so lucky and were towed across the metre-deep river by the tracked 'ferry-tug-truck' stationed there.

By Taluma, nearly halfway to the Pacific, you emerge from the hills where some maps show a track cutting directly east to Neryungri and Chulman on the Amur-Yakutsk road. Alternatively, stick with what's known and follow the BAM for another 400km to **Tynda** and quite probably an overdue rest and repairs. You're now a couple of hundred kilometres north of Skovodorino on the Trans-Siberian Amur Highway, and as far east as most get on the BAM.

It's nearly 2000km to the next city of **Komsomolsk** on the Amur River. What the SEP and an earlier Polish motorcycle expedition confirmed is that between **Verkhnezeisk** (about 250km east of Tynda on the north side of the huge Zeya reservoir) and **Fevralsk**, you can only get through during winter on the *zimnik* 'ice road'. In summer the track is impassable even in the big 6WD Ural trucks and the rail bridges are categorically *zapresheni*. So, from the Trans-Sib corridor in the south, a good track leads 200km back up to **Fevralsk**, but even from here to Novy Urgal it will be hard riding.

After **Novy Urgal** the next 500km to Komsomolsk-na-Amure ease up, or at least are used more frequently by locals, and from there the final 400km to the coast are drivable in good weather on most bikes, even if no road is shown on some Russian maps, including the atlas on p227.

EAST OF IRKUTSK

A thousand kilometres from Krasnoyarsk, **Irkutsk** is a city with a distinctive European feel. Founded in the mid-17th century a few years after Yakutsk, unlike the former it retains a largely Russian rather than native Yakutian population. A beautiful road leads around the edge of Lake Baikal to Ulan Ude and the start of the Wild East.

Ulan Ude is the capital of the Buryat Siberians and where you can turn south for the main route into **Mongolia** (more on p241). From **Chita**, another former 17th-century Russian outpost, the **Amur Highway** runs all the way to Vladivostok. Arching around the Chinese border (which hereabouts is the course of the Amur River) a short distance after Skovorodino the **Amur-Yakutsk Highway** leads up to the city of that name and so the Kolyma Highway to Magadan, the easternmost point on the Russian mainland accessible in summer.

North to Yakutsk

Soon after Skovorodino, depending on recent weather the promisingly named **Amur-Yakutsk Highway** can be 1150km of either recently graded fast dirt, or all-out mud wrestling carnage. It crosses the BAM route at **Tynda** and is interspersed with sections of asphalt, crossing two mountain ranges before dropping into the Lena basin. With a northbound railway ending about halfway at Aldan, there's more traffic than you'd expect and along the way there are plenty of roadhouses and towns. Getting into Yakutsk itself requires ferrying across the Lena River, now 4km wide, from Khachykat to Bestyakh on the west bank, about 80km upstream from Yakutsk. Run by a local journalist ⌨ www.askyakutia.com is an English-language resource for this whole region, listing many recent travellers' reports. Another good local resource in four languages is ⌨ www.yakutiatravel.com.

Yakutsk and the Kolyma Highway to Magadan

On a slightly lower parallel than Fairbanks in Alaska, **Yakutsk** is just 400km south of the Arctic Circle (which is accessible along the river or by plane to Zhigansk). If the road is in good shape Yakutsk could be worth the return 2300km trip up from Skovo', even if you're not planning to continue to Madagan. As various private interests tear their way into the region's mineral deposits, the city is one of the few in Siberia that seems to be prospering and as mentioned earlier, possesses a notable proportion of native Yakut (also known as Sakha) as well as Evenk inhabitants. Most likely though, you'll only find yourself in sunny Yakutsk if you're heading to, or have come from, Magadan. And for you, Magadan really is the end of the road in Russia.

Kolyma Highway – 'The Road of Bones'

As it's become well known, traversing the Kolyma Highway has evolved as a kind of adventure bikers' rite of passage, rather like crossing the Sahara once was. There are even organised tours now. Built in the 1930s at great human cost to help extract the region's mineral resources, in the decades following the collapse of the USSR, the 'Road of Bones' had already fallen into disuse. Like the BAM railway service track mentioned earlier, countless bridges have collapsed, the track has subsided and maintenance of a rideable way falls to the last party to pass by, these days mostly 4x4 and moto adventure tourists.

From Yakutsk via Khandyga to Kyubueme is about 700km of good gravel road involving **ferries** across the Lena and then the Aldan rivers. Most significantly in recent years an 'all season' route has been completed arcing 650km north from **Kyubueme** via the mining outposts around **Ust Nera**, before turning down to meet the original route at spooky, deserted **Kadykchan**. The direct 400km central section of the original 'old summer road' (OSR) between Kyubueme and Kadykchan via Tomtor-Oymyakon (the only settlement) has been officially abandoned. No local who simply wants to get to the other end of the Kolyma Highway would bother taking the OSR these days because between Tomtor and Kadykchan you're on your own and may well get stuck.

Fast, cold rivers, frail bridges, mires and flooded sections of track and no support – it's all part of the challenge of the Kolyma's OSR. Depending on the weather and time of year, the normal way via Ust Nera may not be any less of an adventure but at least it's regularly used. If you just want to enjoy some remote scenery there's something to be said for going this way but as the whole thing is a dead end ride, most come here to get stuck into the OSR, an endeavour that typically takes at least a **week** between Yakutsk and Magadan, but with as little as two days of it along the abandoned central section.

Coming from the west or north, some 52km south of Kadykchan is the settlement of Bolshevik just before the main road continues northeast for Susuman. At the junction here you can follow the more scenic and less truck-riddled alternative – the so-called **Tenkin Track** – via Ust Omchug (food, fuel) to rejoin the main road at Palatka, just 80km from Magadan where you either turn back or ship your bike out – usually to Vladivostok or thereabouts.

THE AMUR HIGHWAY TO VLADIVOSTOK

Beyond Skovo' fresh tarmac unrolls before you: the Amur Highway to Khabarovsk. How the new highway will survive the road-wrecking 80°C temperature variations of the Siberian seasons remains to be seen. Like a similarly long section of the Trans-Sahara Highway in Algeria completed in the early 1980s, there may well be one mythical year, sometime around 2012, when the length of the highway remains intact, before frost heave, pounding trucks and floods begin to break it up and money runs out to do anything about it.

Roadhouses with **food and fuel** are plentiful, although secluded wild camping is not so easy as the road is built up over the swamps and Armco may stop you getting off the road to good spots. Day and night you're bound to encounter the near-constant convoy of used Japanese cars which head west daily from Vladivostok to cities like Yakutsk, Ulan Ude and Irkutsk just as fast as the roads will let them. With bodywork covered in cardboard to protect it from stone chips, if you have bike trouble they'll offer you the sort of solidarity you'll not find in the west.

Khabarovsk is a relative late developer, but with Vladivostok is now among the biggest cities in Far Eastern Russia, with up to three quarters of a million inhabitants. You'll see many Japanese and South Koreans establishing businesses here, and with a **Chinese consulate** at the Lenin Stadium (N48° 28.8' W135° 02.8') on the west side of town just north of the city beach, there's a chance to nip over the Amur for a day trip to China (without the bike, of course).

Vladivostok and the end of this particular road are just 850km away, through the wooded hills where once the Amur Tiger – at up to 400kg, the largest member of the cat family – harried the railroad builders of the late 19th century until its private parts got ground down for aphrodisiacs. Perennially miserable weather doesn't make Vladi the most inspiring place to end your trans-continental trek, but as you'll read, it needn't be quite over yet.

GETTING OUT OF VLADIVOSTOK

You'll find the Vladivostok ferry terminal (N43° 06.8' W131 53.1') right opposite the grand station at the very end of the Trans-Siberian Railway. Twice a week in summer a ship runs to Fushiki (40hrs, booking info ⌨ www.bisintour.com). Japan may be a rewarding destination, but prefers exporting bikes, new or used. Getting a bike in requires a document verifying your carnet. Although one or two have managed it, don't expect to get far out of Fushiki or any other Japanese port without a carnet that's been verified. This document can be obtained from the Japanese Automobile Federation (JAF; ⌨ www.jaf.or.jp/e) who have an office in Toyama, near Fushiki (see website below). The paperwork will be waiting there as long as you've contacted JAF in Tokyo in advance and faxed them your carnet. Chris Lockwood's Japan website has plenty of details on the bike import scene: ⌨ www2.gol.com/users/chrisl/japan.

Probably put off by the expense of Japan, most choose **South Korea**. The **Dong Chun ferry service** runs one to three times a week to **Sokcho**, South Korea, just south of the DMZ and some 200km east of Seoul. Ferries leave once a week from Vladivostok or twice weekly from **Zarubino**, 220km south of Vladivostok towards the North Korean border. The big advantage of Zarubino is that it's much quieter than Vlad, making it a more efficient way to leave or indeed enter Russia. Prices in 2012 for the 12-hour crossing from

Zarubino added up to a hefty $700 plus $300 per person. Hotels are also said to be expensive in Vladivostok, so if you already have the schedule from Zarubino, head directly there off the M-60 at Ussuriysk, 90km north of Vlad.

Because there's no carnet agreement with South Korea, on arrival you have to lodge a fully **refundable deposit** which is officially supposed to be 40% of your vehicle's value. Even without an advanced knowledge of Korean, recent reports suggest negotiation down to a more tolerable 20% or more is not too difficult. You have to pay in Korean WAN (there's a bank at the port) and if you're counting the pennies, **fuel up in Russia**; in Korea it's around double the price.

Once in Korea you won't be going that far anyway, most probably **Inchon airport**, on an island 70km west of Seoul (via a bridge that's closed to bikes...), or the port at **Busan** in the south. Wallenius Wilhelmsen (⌨ www.2wglobal.com) has cargo services running eastbound while www.eukor.com can ship a bike to Europe for around $1000.

Going in the other direction towards Russia, as already advised head for Zarubino rather than Vladivostok before they read this and catch on. There are customs declaration and immigration forms on the boat and once in Zarubino a freight guy will organise your temporary Russian registration document in the customs office. It's valid for up to six months and costs $100 or so.

Central Asia

CHARLIE WEATHERILL

Assuming you're wanting to get round the north side of Afghanistan, the four smaller 'stans' of Central Asia offer a challenging alternative to hauling along the Trans-Siberian Highway in Russia. Kazakhstan adds up to the fifth 'stan, an interminable steppe the size of Western Europe, but most riders enjoy the actual riding across the yurt-clad pastures of Kyrgyzstan or the high Pamirs of Tajikistan. The Silk Route cities and fiery deserts in Turkmenistan and Uzbekistan add up to more cultural experiences or put bluntly, unavoidable transits to get to the epic riding in the eastern 'stans.

The distances that need to be covered on **poor roads** or tracks in Kazakhstan can be mind-numbing and innumerable Soviet-era legacies survive in the form of corrupt traffic police aggravating bureaucracy, registration issues and complex visa acquisition.

But fear not. On the ground, central Asian people – be they Kazakh or Kyrgyz, Turkmen or Tajik – are amongst the most hospitable you'll meet, and the irritations will always be worth the effort.

Language, maps and money

Although **Uzbekistan** and **Turkmenistan** are slowly moving to modified Roman alphabets, learn the **Cyrillic alphabet** (see p223) so you can understand the road signs. **Russian** is still the lingua franca throughout the 'stans although the universal 'Salaam aleikum' of Islamic lands will always be appreciated.

Gizi Central Asia and Kazakhstan **maps** (1:3,000,000) cover the entire region effectively and the German *Reise Know-How* (1:1.7m) provides better detail and information on smaller routes. As for **guidebooks**, Lonely Planet is the major player for Central Asia.

ATMs are found in all cities but very rarely anywhere in between. Fuel stations will generally only accept **cash** – although in an emergency you'll probably be able to pay for your fuel in US dollars at a terrible rate. After US dollars, euros will be the most useful **hard currency**. Uzbekistan is the only 'stan where a currency black market of up to 40% more prevails. Changing dollars is not difficult here. **Credit cards** are really accepted only in expensive hotels in large cities, and the occasional Western supermarket aimed at ex-pats in places like Almaty and Bishkek.

BORDERS

All Central Asian borders are generally open daily from 8am to 5pm. Chinese road borders with Kyrgyzstan are at the 3672-metre (12,100') **Torugurt Pass** 180km north of Kashgar and the 3005-metre (9859') **Irkeshtam Pass** which is 240km east of Osh, 80km from Sary Tash and about 250km west of Kashgar. It has a slightly better reputation for formalities but a long rough track up from Sary Tash. Expect both to be closed at weekends and on public holidays on

ASIA – ROUTE OUTLINES

WEST ASIA ~ HONDA XR250S

Name	Ilias V
Year of birth	1984
Occupation	Waiter
Nationality	Greek
Previous travels	Backpacking in Italy
Bike travels	None out of my country

This trip	Turkey, Iran, Pak', India, Nepal, C. Asia
Trip duration	Over two years
Departure date	April 2007
Number in group	One
Distance covered	73,000km

Best day	Amazing off-roading in Spiti valley
Worst day	Wheel bearing went in remote Pamirs
Favourite places	Indian Hims, Tajikistan Iran
Biggest headache	Corruption in ex-Soviet countries
Biggest mistake	No kick-starter
Pleasant surprise	Amazingly hospitable Muslims
Any illness	Small infections here and there
Cost of trip	€10,000
Other trips planned	RoW!

Bike model	Honda XR250S
Age, mileage	10 years old, unknown mileage
Modifications	Just about everything
Wish you'd ...	added a kick-starter
Tyres used	TW302,-1, TKC80 + Asian crap
Punctures	12
Type of baggage	Zega + soft bags

Bike's weak point	No kick!
Strong point	Light, simple and reliable
Bike problems	Diaphragm, reg-rec, wheel bearing
Accidents	Three minor ones
Same bike again	Similar, but with a you-know-what
Any advice	Keep it simple

either side. The 🖥 www.advantour.com website has additional information on these passes.

Turkmenistan's borders require mind-boggling paperwork; up to three-dozen stamps before you can enter! Here, a pre-arranged **guide** is mandatory to ride through the country on anything other than a five-day transit visa and despite the exorbitant expense – about $100 a day or about half of what you'll pay for the whole crossing – a guide certainly helps at the border. Stantours (🖥 www.stantours.com) and DN Tours (🖥 www.dntours.com) are experts in arranging self-drive logistics and guides. **Getting into Kyrgyzstan, Uzbekistan** and **Tajikistan** is less complicated. The general rule with border paperwork is, if you need it, someone will ensure you have it before you're allowed to leave the border area. A **carnet** is not recognised here; keep it stashed.

Customs declaration form

As in Russia, a **customs declaration form** must be completed in duplicate, sometimes triplicate. The form is normally in Russian (sometimes you might get an English one) and it's **essential** it's filled in correctly, so if in doubt get an official to help you. Both copies are signed and stamped and one is retained by you until you leave the country.

Due to its currency black market, Uzbekistan is the only country where you must accurately declare the amount of dollars you're officially importing. What you don't declare can be used on the black market, just make sure the stash is not found on departure.

Vehicle importation or transit certificate

This varies from country to country and some charge a fee, for example $20 in **Tajikistan**. The form varies in colour and is usually hand-written. Most countries will give you 15 days on your certificate, or as long as you ask them for, though **Uzbekistan** can be difficult and may insist you can have only three days to transit the country; ask for more if you get a chance.

Vehicle tax or transit fee and motor insurance

A transit fee is seemingly is only necessary for Tajikistan and Turkmenistan, and costs $20 in the former, with another dose on the way out. A dollar amount is calculated on your pre-approved route mileage in Turkmenistan. Turkmen fees are complex and expensive: expect to pay around $150–250 in transit fees, comprising the mileage-based fuel price differential, mandatory third party liability and numerous documentation fees.

Insurance is required in Kyrgyzstan, and theoretically a legal requirement elsewhere, but only Tajikistan and Turkmenistan demand you get it at the border. As for the others, it's sometimes available at the borders and buying it is up to you.

Vehicle documents

Throughout the 'stans a multi-lingual translation of your vehicle ownership documents (in the UK known as an International Certificate for Motor Vehicles) may be useful if stopped, if nothing more than to add to the 'document surge' with which you can bore and confuse your tormentor.

Obviously, you'll need your domestic driving licence; an International Driving Permit (IDP) to back it up helps. Theoretically, none of the CIS countries now require your bike to be declared in LOIs, visas or passports so you're not 'attached' to your machine and may be able to nip out of, say, Kazakhstan.

VISAS AND REGISTRATION

Unfortunately the entire visa system throughout the stans is in a constant state of flux and the degree of time, paperwork, difficulty and cost involved varies considerably. Use what follows as a guide only.

Kyrgyzstan is the easiest place to obtain a visa – if you happen to fly in you get one for free. A one-month single-entry visa is usually obtainable the same day from Kyrgyz consulates in all Central Asian capitals, with no LOI required. They're similarly easily obtainable in 24 hours at the Kyrgyz embassy in London. There is no requirement to register once in the country.

For **Kazakhstan** no LOI is required for most nationalities when obtaining a standard one- or two-month single- or double-entry visa. Visas are obtainable in Kazakh embassies in Bishkek, Tashkent and Dushanbe and take 1–3 days to process. All overland arrivals must register with the OVIR (and get another stamp on your entry card) within five working days of entering, or face a hefty fine when you leave the country. Officially it's $130.

An LOI is no longer required in **Tajikistan** either. Their embassy in London issues two-week or one-month single-entry visas for £60. Visas issued in Bishkek and Tashkent take between one and three days and cost between $80 and $120. You'll also need a GBAO (Gorno-Badakhshan Autonomous Oblast) permit to ride the **Pamir Highway**, obtainable from numerous travel agencies (including Stantours) from $25–50, or from consulates or embassies (including London) when you apply for your visa. Generally costs are around £50 in London or $10-25 from other consulates.

Registration with a stamped receipt is no longer required assuming you're on a single-entry, 30-day tourist visa, although you'll be 'registered' in a book at every military checkpoint along the way.

An LOI may not be required for **Uzbekistan** if obtaining a visa from embassies in Europe, although one is still required if getting a visa from a consulate in a neighbouring country. LOIs are obtainable from numerous travel agencies including Stantours and Arostr (🖳 www.arostr.uz). Processing time is 7–10 working days and cost is around $40–60. The visa cost varies from $70–110 depending on where you're from and where you obtain it. The Uzbek consulate in Bishkek, Kyrgyzstan is one of the more straightforward and in most cases issues visas on the same day.

Turkmenistan remains the most difficult 'stan for visas, but it's easier than it used to be. An LOI is required for all foreign nationals entering on a tourist visa. With a LOI, your visa can be obtained at the border (if you have a guide, inform them beforehand that you intend to do this). Visas generally cost $70 for 10 days – longer stays are possible if you book and pay for a longer 'tour'.

As a rule visa extensions are not possible in Turkmenistan although (as in all other Central Asian countries) in emergencies this can be done in the capital. No LOI is required for a **transit visa**, although these can take 10–14 days to process and approval is often not guaranteed.

ON THE ROAD IN CENTRAL ASIA

In Kazakhstan, Kyrgyzstan and Tajikistan, away from the principal cities there's a lack of traffic though like Russia, beware of **drunk drivers** and old Ladas with no brakes. As in most Asian countries, drivers will pull out of side roads without paying too much attention and in rural areas **goats, sheep and cattle** are a common sight on the roads. Big cities tend to be more aggressive – you'll get used to the 'Central Asian traffic light creep' and drivers in Almaty can be pushy towards bikers.

By far and away your biggest headache whilst riding in the 'stans will be the *militzia*, universally corrupt and dedicated to self-enrichment. You can't blame them, really – they're paid a pittance. **Checkpoints** entering and leaving major towns are a favourite cash-cow, as are cunningly hidden radar speed traps. Always play the 'dumb foreign tourist' as explained on p228.

Speed limits tend not to be clearly demarcated. Work on 90–100kph on rural highways (though in many places the road condition will make these speeds unachievable) and 50–60kph in towns. Many towns have signposted 40kph and even 20kph zones around schools and police tend to congregate round these areas.

Both routes between Khorog and Dushanbe in Tajikistan are prone to landslides which can shut them for weeks on end, especially in the spring. Access and road improvements in the Pamirs are constantly hampered by mudslides, floods, political unrest and earthquakes. It's all part of the adventure.

Fuel

Fuel prices range from 60% to 70% less than Western Europe for 90–92 octane petrol. Old style, 80-octane leaded petrol is widely available and cheaper, still feeding a generation of near-fossilised Ladas.

Parts of southern Kyrgyzstan and the Pamir region of Tajikistan experience regular **fuel shortages** which lead to dramatic price spikes. In these areas the only way to get fuel is to seek local advice, but beware of water and other contaminants. Having the smallest Mr Funnel or similar **fuel filter** might not be a bad idea out here.

In **Uzbekistan** petrol shortages are not uncommon, so fill up whenever you can. Petrol in **Turkmenistan** is among the cheapest in the world but as a foreigner they get you with a **fuel tax** at the border, calculated on the mileage for your pre-approved route through the country making the 'real' cost around $0.45 per litre. The vast distances between towns in **western Kazakhstan** means fill up from KazGaz and Gazprom fuel stations whenever you can at around $0.40 per litre.

VEHICLE MAINTENANCE

Even though the roads may take their toll on your bike, at least in Central Asia there are plenty of **decent mechanics** around to help fix the variety of problems you're likely to encounter. Virtually every small town in Central Asia has an old boy in a shed with a spanner, an oxyacetylene torch and an incredible level of resourcefulness. As long as you don't have serious engine problems, you should be able to get most things sorted quickly and cheaply.

MONGOLIA: YOU ARE THE ROAD

Don't miss a chance to visit Mongolia, one of the world's great AM destinations; your 'golf course' riding fantasy made real and on an epic scale too. Accommodation can be grotty or overpriced in the few tourist areas so a **tent** is a must – it's how most countryfolk live. **ATMs** work in fully westernised Ulaan-baatar (UB), elsewhere they're rare so carry US dollars or the local tugriks.

English and Russian are useful **foreign languages** and the ring-bound 1:1m *Monsudar Mongolian Road Atlas* has the best **map** detail, though don't assume a bold red line adds up to any sort of a road. Otherwise US TPCs work well with GPS. **Petrol** works out around $1.40 a litre, but quality drops out in the sticks. The same goes for **drinking water** so fill up regularly or plan to filter.

Visas and borders

Four land borders are open to foreigners at present: **Altanbulag–Kyakhta** south of Ulan Ude; **Tsaagannuur–Tashanta** in the far west, 600km south-east of Barnaul in Russia, and **Ereentsav-Solovyesk** 1000km east of UB and some 250km south of the Trans Sib – handy if going to Vladivostok (or coming from there with a visa in hand). Turning up at the **Zamyn Uud–Eren Hot** for China requires months of preparation. Considering where you are, formalities are straightforward; allow a couple of hours and a couple of dollars to maybe get your tyres disinfected plus $30 for **motor vehicle insurance**. Carnets out here are nothing more than a type of Cornish ice cream. Americans get a three-month visa at any border, most others get it in advance and it's valid for 90 days.

Mongolian consulates in Siberia
Irkutsk
11 Lapina ul.
N52° 16.8' E104° 17.1'
30-day tourist visa for $100 same day, $55 next day (pay in roubles).
Ulan Ude
Near corner of Prostsoyuzaya and Lenina ul; look for a large domed roof.
N51° 49.9' E107° 35.0'
Planned stays longer than a month require registering within a week of arrival at the Aliens and Naturalisation Office at the Ministry of Transport off Genghis Khan Ave, in UB (N47° 54.6' E106° 54.8'). Get thoroughly deregistered there before departure.

If not riding there consider putting your bike on the **Trans-Siberian railway** in Moscow. Direct trains to UB leave weekly, take five days but cost from $800.

Riding and running a bike

'Extreme continental' is how they classify the Mongolian **climate**, which means two out of three days are sunny and rain is rare. UB's average annual temperature is actually a couple of degrees *below* freezing so don't expect to break out in a sweat, even in mid-summer in the Gobi, while elsewhere or at other times, be ready for snowy sub-zero episodes even if the aridity makes deep snowfall rare. Up in the Altai it can be freezing at any time.

There are three paved roads in Mongolia emanating from UB: up to Altanbulag; west to the touristy Kubla Khan capital at Arvaiheer and east 300km to Ondorkhan, with another 600km to the Russian border at a braided track down to China. Elsewhere is common land with no fences, few signs and indistinct tracks. Once you get your head around the fact that you are the road, it's an easy country to get around compared to the bug-ridden waterlogged taïga to the north. Pick a spot on the map and as long as the steppes are dry and mountains, deep rivers and lakes permit, you can ride straight there. Therefore, unless you have the migratory instincts of an Alaskan salmon, a GPS and a good map like the TPCs mentioned is useful and as in Russia, watch out for drunk drivers at all times of day, and avoid riding at night. Checkpoints are rarely troublesome.

Mongolians are honest and friendly but it's not unknown for things to disappear overnight so sleep with everything inside.

Cheeky Mongolian. © Tom Bierma

ACCOMMODATION

Standards of accommodation are improving throughout Central Asia, though it's not always cheap. Expect to pay between $50 and $70 for **guesthouses** in the capitals and other major cities where you want to get your bike off the road. Outside the cities, roadside *gostinitzias* or *chai-khanas* (teahouses) are good, inexpensive alternatives. It should be possible to avoid the decaying and overpriced Soviet bunker-hotels, although for the experience you should consider staying in at least one. If **wild camping** try to attach yourself to a local roadside café, yurt or farmhouse to legitimise your presence and provide some extra security for the night. If this isn't possible, make sure you're **out of sight** of the road, thought you're only ever likely to get hassle from a passing drunk or the *militzia*. Additionally, camping with a local family will doubtless provide memorable hospitality for which many of the Central Asian peoples are famed.

Elsewhere, Kyrgyzstan and the Pamir region of Tajikistan have extensive **homestay** networks which are cheap, convenient and delightful experiences. They cost around $10–15 per person half board.The flat deserts of Uzbekistan and Turkmenistan don't lend themselves so well to wild camping. There are many **B&Bs** in the touristy cities of Bukhara, Khiva and Samarkand.

Southeast Asia

CHARLIE WEATHERILL

Cheap living, good roads in places, a great climate in season, **food** and scenery and amazing beaches and islands all combine to make Southeast Asia one of the world's **most popular tourist destinations**. It's all here from the isolated Angkorean temples deep in Cambodia's jungle; the western ranges of Thailand; the Ho Chi Minh Trail in Laos and Vietnam or Malaysia's rugged and relatively unspoilt east coast.

This region has been well and truly discovered, and on a bike the thought of slugging it out with hordes of frizzy-haired backpackers and package tourists might not sound too appealing. But having your own wheels opens up numerous adventures off the beaten track in Southeast Asia. You'll have no difficulty avoiding Thailand's heaving beaches and the tourist tramlines of Chiang Mai, or skirting the tourist trails of Cambodia as well as picking and choosing your remote jungle destinations in Laos.

Southeast Asia comprises seven mainland countries and three island nations. On the mainland, all except **Vietnam** and **Burma** are accessible, though **Singapore** can get complicated and expensive. For the time being Burma's land borders with everywhere except China remain firmly shut and this situation is unlikely to change soon, even with the recent rapprochement Meanwhile Vietnam still doesn't officially permit entry to foreign vehicles, unless they're from neighbouring Cambodia, Laos or China. Of the island nations, **Indonesia** is the easiest to reach, although the numerous ferry rides can become tiresome.

Consequently this section focuses primarily on the four easy overlanding countries: **Thailand**, **Cambodia**, **Malaysia** and **Laos**. Like Japan out of South

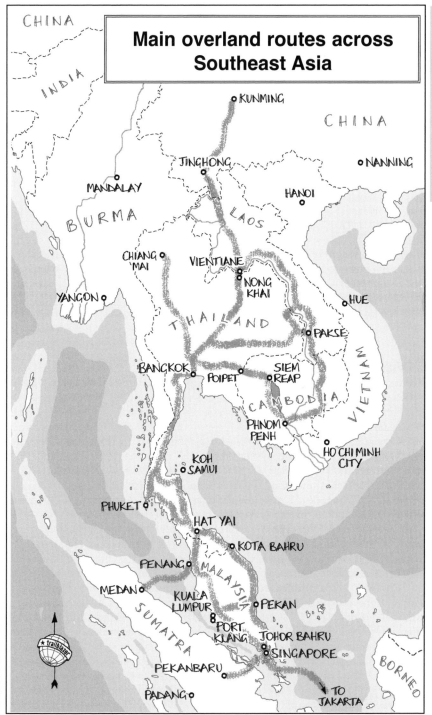

Main overland routes across Southeast Asia

Korea, you may find Singapore and the other five countries including Burma more easily visited as a regular tourist without your bike.

PRACTICALITIES

Visiting the selected region can be regarded as a bit of a **holiday** if you've come from India or China. **English** is widely spoken, as is French in much of Indochina. **ATMs** are widely available throughout Singapore, Malaysia and Thailand, and **credit cards** are widely accepted at major fuel stations. Conversely, ATMs can only be found in major cities and tourist destinations in Laos and Cambodia and fuel stations want cash. In these two countries it's usually possible to pay for all your fuel in **US dollars** which will save endless trips to ATMs which often don't dish out more than the equivalent of $70 per transaction. There are no currency **black markets** in any of these countries, save for a slight discrepancy in Cambodia.

Maps and internet

Besides **OSM** options for your sat-nav, *GeoCenter* have several **maps** covering the entirety of Southeast Asia (1:2m) showing enough big picture detail without becoming cluttered. *Gizi* and *Insight* also have good overview maps. In Laos and Cambodia, *Gecko Maps* (1:750,000) have excellent local detail including identifying roads that are impassable during the monsoon. The *GT Rider Touring Map of Laos* (1:1m) is waterproof, and GT also has smaller maps covering parts of Chiang Mai in northern Thailand. The associated website, 🖳 www.gt-rider.com, is a good resource for anyone riding in northern Thailand and Laos.

BORDERS

Throughout Southeast Asia you'll need your original **vehicle ownership documents**, your domestic driving licence and an IDP. Your bike is not stamped into your passport in any Southeast Asian country. Crossing from **Singapore** to **Malaysia** and vice versa is relatively straightforward. For many nationalities visas are not required for either country, although both will want to see a **carnet**. With a bike, **Singapore** is often considered more **hassle** than it's worth; for more information on riding in Singapore, check 🖳 www.lta.gov.sg. You'll require an **International Circulation Permit** (ICP, S$10 in Singapore) in both Malaysia and Singapore – essentially a blue disc that's affixed to a windscreen; you won't be able to purchase third party insurance without an ICP.

Crossing into **Thailand** from any neighbouring country is straightforward, if a little slow sometimes. A carnet is not required, instead you'll be issued with a temporary importation document (in Thai) that you hand back when you leave. Buy motor insurance at, or very near, the border.

Crossing to **Cambodia** from any of its neighbours is refreshingly swift, efficient and corruption free (Thai customs officials aren't averse to conning tourists out of a few dollars for 'form fees'). A **carnet** is required but motor insurance is not, and is difficult to obtain at any border point. You may have to hunt around to wake up the boy in charge of the Lao-Viet Insurance Company kiosk. Don't worry if you can't get insurance at the border, get it when you can – no one seems to be too strict on this regulation.

Shipping from Singapore to **Indonesia** can be relatively swift and straightforward; companies such as Samudera (🖳 www.samudera.com) regularly ship containers from Singapore to Batam, Palembang and Jakarta in addition to numerous other smaller Indonesian destinations. You'll need an IDP and motor insurance to ride in Indonesia. Driving standards here are amongst the worst in Southeast Asia. **Ro-Ro** ferries operate between Bandar Lampung and Jakarta (crossing about one hour) and between almost all of Indonesia's islands. Bear in mind that safety standards are abysmal and

Three little piggies go to market © James Rix

dozens of sinkings every year result in the annual loss of thousands of lives.

VISAS

With the region being so open to tourists, many countries don't require visas, or issue them at land borders. Visas are generally be paid for in US dollars. For **Malaysia** no visa is required for British, US, Australian or EU nationals for stays of 1-3 months; same with **Singapore** which issues 'Social visit passes'. For **Thailand** a free 15-day visa waiver is issued on arrival. This can be extended by 30 days at the Thai Immigration Department in Bangkok, or by exiting and re-entering the country at any land border for another 15 days. **Cambodia** issues E-visas online, otherwise get a 30-day tourist visa issued on arrival from $20-35, dependent on nationality. **Laos** also does a 30-day tourist visa at land borders from $20-35.

All foreign visitors require visas for **Indonesia**. Sixty-day single-entry visas are issued on arrival at principal airports (including Jakarta) and some sea ports for around $55. Visas in advance are obtainable from consulates in most neighbouring countries including Singapore, in 2-6 days.

POLICE AND FUEL

Outside of Singapore and Malaysia, police in all Southeast Asian countries are not averse to a bit of petty bribery. If you're stopped by the police, don't attempt to speak the language, be polite and be firm. Spurious accusations of petty offences should be strongly denied; if it's speeding then ask to see the radar reading (Thai police are especially fond of estimating your speed 'by eye' rather than using a radar gun). Continual harassment is very unlikely and with a little patience the police will usually let you carry on without relieving you of any cash because it's far easier for them to pick on the poor locals.

Police at **checkpoints** may occasionally want to see your documents – showing your vehicle ownership documents, driving licence and IDP will usually suffice. Unless you're in a restricted area (in Long Chen in Laos, for example, or near some sensitive parts of the northeastern Thai–Cambodia border) checkpoints are unlikely to give you any hassle.

Petrol prices in Southeast Asia average out at around $1.70 a litre, or a dollar in Indonesia. Fill up in larger towns and on highways to avoid the risks in buying out of bottles from roadside sellers. Fuel is subsidised in Malaysia but all foreign vehicles are supposed to buy 97-grade which is up to 50% more than 95-grade and halfway between the above two estimates.

China

CHARLIE WEATHERILL

Riding in China gets expensive and on discovering the costs involved, most choose to give it a miss or make short transits such as between Pakistan and Kyrgyzstan via Kashgar in the far west. To ride in China you will need:

- Customs, national and regional permits for every province you plan to visit
- Chinese driving licence
- Temporary Chinese registration plates for your bike
- Motor insurance
- Government approved escort in a car at all times to ensure you don't stray. You cover their food and accommodation.

All documents are in Chinese and incredibly complex to obtain without the services of an **agency** to sort out all the paperwork and provide an escort to meet you at the border. This all-in service costs the equivalent of an eye-watering **$100–200** per day. Considering the average wage in China, this might appear like extortion, but there's no way round it. If you want to ride from Central Asia to the subcontinent, via **Kashgar** is still the easiest and shortest route and should cost around $600–800. The bureaucracy is reduced on this transit as you're only visiting **one province**. Although fast disappearing under monolithic Chinese skyscrapers, the ancient, Silk Road city of Kashgar and the distant Pamirs mean it's well worth it, especially with the reward of Pakistan or Kyrgyzstan at the other end.

Otherwise, consider how much you really want to see China and whether it might not be less hassle without your bike or as part of a big Asian tour where costs get diluted. China is big, expensive and tiring, and the principal points of interest are very far apart. Aside from Tibet, Yunnan, Szechuan and parts of Xinjiang, much of the scenery leaves a lot to be desired and the entire east coast has been concreted over, so plan your route carefully!

AGENCIES

With China and the Chinese, you get what you pay for. The more reputable and reliable the agency, the more they'll cost, but the less chance there is of something going wrong. Try to avoid outfits who make it all sound far too cheap and easy – if seems too good to be true, it is. Rest assured, if you've only paid $100 for all your paperwork, it will prove insufficient and you won't be able to bring your bike across the border, no matter how much you plead.

On longer transits **your guide** will make a huge impact on your experience. Many travellers report that, as in so many countries, their guides have been at best incompetent and at worst dishonest, so be vigilant and make sure you have all the information on the places you want to visit; don't depend on your guide alone.

Recommended agencies

NAVO (🖥 www.navo-tour.com) are the market leaders in arranging self-drive trips in China and are used by many tour operators. They're also the most expensive, but bargain hard and present alternative quotes as this can lead to a good discount. Their guides vary in quality and experience, but your all-important paperwork should be faultless.

On the Road in China (🖥 www.ontheroadinchina.com) is a Western-run outfit that specialises in self-drive tours and might accommodate overlanders with their own bikes. China Highlights (🖥 www.chinahighlights.com) and Drive in China (🖥 www.driveinchina.com) offer self-drive tours with their own vehicles, but might arrange an itinerary with your bike.

AT THE BORDER

China has land borders with 14 countries, more than any other. Some are open to all, some are closed to foreigners and others are closed, vacuum-sealed and razor-wired. The following borders are open to foreigners with their own transport, albeit with varying degrees of difficulty:

Bordering country	Chinese province	Border town/post	Comments
Nepal	Tibet	Zhangmu	
Pakistan	Xinjiang	Khunjerab	
Kyrgyzstan	Xinjiang	Irkshstan	The easier Kyrgyz crossing
Kyrgyzstan	Xinjiang	Torugat	
Kazakhstan	Xinjiang	Horgos	
Mongolia	Inner Mongolia	Erenhot	The only Mongolian border open to foreigners
Russia	Inner Mongolia	Manzhouli	
Vietnam	Guangxi	Youyiguan/ Pingxiang	Can close suddenly. Vietnam difficult to enter anyway
Vietnam	Yunnan	Hekou	
Laos	Yunnan	Mohan	
Burma	Yunnan	Ruili	Not realistic at present
Hong Kong	Guangdong	Shenzhen	

NAVO will be able to provide up-to-date advice on the current border situations – check with them and other sources as all these border situations can change suddenly. The China–India border has been closed since the war of 1962 and is unlikely to reopen, although if any, the Sikkim border point would be the most likely to do so.

T R I P   R E P O R T
BURKINA FASO TO FRANCE ~ MOPED

Name	Vincent C
Year of birth	1979
Occupation	Not decided yet
Nationality	French
Previous travels	India, Nepal, Bangladesh, SE Asia
Bike travels	None

This trip	Burkina Faso to France
Trip duration	Six months
Departure date	January 2005
Number in group	1
Distance covered	11,873km

Best day	Riding off-road in Mali
Worst day	Not being able to ride Western Sahara
Favourite places	Villages between Mopti and Bamako
Biggest headache	Convincing Guinea army I wasn't a spy
Biggest mistake	Seat, got a sheepskin in Morocco
Pleasant surprise	Few problems with moped paperwork
Any illness	Just the usual
Cost of trip	€3000
Other trips planned	Bien sur!

Bike model	Peugeot 103, 50cc
Age, mileage	New
Modifications	None, just luggage
Wish you'd ...	Used a different bike!
Tyres used	OE, then €3 cheapies
Punctures	7
Type of baggage	Soft bag in front, hard case on back

Bike's weak point	Lack of speed, comfort and power
Strong point	Strong, lot of fun, people really liked it
Bike problems	Weak transmission eaten by sand
Accidents	Nil
Same bike again	Hmmm, why not
Any advice	Get fake papers for some borders

AFRICA
ROUTE OUTLINES

5

Africa presents the biggest challenge of the three continents covered in this book, or at least that's how some perceive it. Many accomplished riders have travelled the world and the seven seas, but have never set foot in Africa. As always, it's not as bad as you hear and the hotspots are established, well known and easily avoided. Moreover, Chinese road builders are having a bitumen BBQ down there and the former gaps on the main routes in the Congo, north Sudan and northern Kenya are shortening year by year, or have closed up altogether, so a road-oriented bike becomes less of a handful. Of course it remains to be seen how these rapidly-built roads will handle a few monsoons or Saharan summers under the wheels of the typically overloaded local transportation.

The **headaches** of riding across Africa include regional conflicts, road conditions, the climate (in the wrong season) and petty corruption, but in a handful of key places **visas** will be the dominant issue. Lately, a few countries midway en route now claim only to allow entry if the visa was issued in your home country, or present other mind-numbing hurdles. As always this varies with your nationality, where you attempt the application, where you cross a border, and not least, the cut of your jib or their mood. What works for one rider one week becomes a brick wall for you, and so as much as anywhere in the AMZ, all your advance planning may have many ends. It's part of the adventure of course, but when it can't be unravelled can also lead to unplanned expenses in flying your bike around. Having a **second passport** can definitely help here when making visa applications, as well as having enough **paperwork** on hand (relevant or otherwise) to choke a hippo.

In North Africa this situation turned dramatically in 2011 when what became known as the '**Arab Spring**' led to long-overdue popular revolutions right across the southern Mediterranean. The consequences of this upheaval aren't over yet and have had a major effect on trans-African routes.

And yet behind all this aggravation is the appeal of the fabulous imagery and landscapes we're all so familiar with and, less expected by overlanders, the generosity and warmth of the ordinary people you'll encounter, people who struggle to survive under some of the most blatantly mismanaged kleptocracies on earth.

REGIONAL EXPLORATIONS

As much as any other continent, overlanders feel the need to take on a **trans-African crossing** from Casablanca or Cairo down to Cape Town, not least because it's one of the great overland routes, and as a biker any rain you'll encounter won't be the miserable, warmth-sapping experience of temperate climates (though on an equatorial track it may have other energy-sapping consequences). Furthermore, when starting from Europe, once you're south of the Sahara you may as well keep going. Getting to Sudan from Egypt or Senegal from Morocco is no effortless 'there-and-back' jaunt, and once in these countries your regional roaming options are still limited by topography, climate and politics. So, unless you're an old hand, initially at least, most see Africa as somewhere to just get through, rather than a place to explore.

One exception is **Morocco** (see p255). With just enough of an edge to keep you on your toes, it offers the perfect introduction to Africa and makes a great place for a shake down for longer travels in Africa or elsewhere.

The other exception is **southern Africa**. Relatively stable, sharing the time zone with Europe, and with winter (the northern summer holiday season) being the best riding season, many tour operators offer **fly-in tours** here. From South Africa itself, visits to half a dozen nearby countries can be ticked off as far north as Kenya and on tour you can have the ride of your life, even if – or perhaps because – it's all organised for you.

In between lie the feral republics of **central Africa**; principally the Democratic Republic of Congo (DRC). No one heads here for kicks as they do in the places mentioned above, not least because issues with Angolan visas can mean an onerous 2400km run through southern DRC from Zambia (see p269). Probably more than anywhere else in Africa this is a place to grit your teeth and battle through and as such, along with a central Saharan crossing (where possible, see p253), it'll be the bit you'll dread most but remember best.

TRACKS4AFRICA AND OTHER RESOURCES

A GPS is invaluable in many ways, from saving you fuel by ensuring you take the correct turning, to offering a beacon to aim for in a large chaotic African city, or for tracking down those unsigned immigration huts. A couple of good things to load up on your GPS before setting off are **Tracks4Africa** (🖳 www.tracks4africa.co.za) and **Camping Weld** (Google: 'Camping-Welt.zip').

T4A collects and configures user-generated data sent in by overland travellers supporting the project. Tracks are mostly collected in southern Africa, but the less detailed, but still routable, West Coast Africa map for around €12 and Angola for the same price are a bargain. You usually get waypoints for border immigration posts as well as main roads in each large city, along with overlanders' haunts and various other points that might be useful (tyre repairs, mechanics, restaurants, embassies and so on). I found it invaluable and it works with Windows, Mac or an SD card. If you find an error, let them know; that's how things like this improve.

Camping Weld is free to download and contains hundreds of campsites and embassies divided into country folders. Some are a couple of years old now but you're bound to find something useful there. Finally, pay a visit to 🖳 www.africa-overland.net, an overlanders' hub. It takes a bit of digging around but can be a great resource for potential bushcamps.

Darrin Johansen

MAPS AND GUIDEBOOKS

The three 1:4m scale **Michelin maps** (Nos 741, 745 and 746) are traditionally regarded as the best navigational companions for crossing Africa, but in central Africa they aren't really keeping up with the road-building – no paper map is. A road may be where it says on a map, but whether it's a still-steaming blacktop with a crisp white line down the middle, or a motocross course, you'll just have to ask locally or find out for yourself.

Lonely Planet, Rough Guide and Bradt produce regional guidebooks in paper or ebook form with useful titles for parts of North, southern and East Africa, but keeping up with the less visited countries in print is not viable either. The internet fills the gaps: **LP Thorn Tree** (⌨ www.lonelyplanet.com/ thorntree) or of course the **HUBB** ⌨ www.horizonsunlimited.com/hubb.

WEATHER IN AFRICA

When considering crossing Africa two climatic factors ought to govern your departure date and your route: summer in the Sahara and the equatorial monsoon. **Summer in the Sahara** need not be perilous down the all-sealed Atlantic Route to Senegal, or from Egypt to Khartoum, until something goes wrong. When it does, unless you're able to act decisively, your margin for survival shortens very quickly when it's 45°C (113°F) in the shade. More commonly though, the Saharan summer is a time of sandstorms and hazy skies when the night time temperature may stay above 30°C for weeks. This round-the-clock heat puts greater stress on your body and engine so travel becomes a matter of endurance rather than enjoyment.

© africansupertramp.blogspot.com

In central Africa the **rains** fall for up to ten months a year, certainly from June to September alongside the equator, and to a lesser extent from February to April when the rut pictured above right will be one long pool. South of the equator the **sealed road network** makes the rains in eastern and southern Africa from November to April much less of an issue, although your ability to explore off the beaten track will be greatly reduced.

If heading across the continent from Europe and wanting an easy time of it, **set off around October or November**, riding into the Saharan winter and the central African dry season.

FUEL PRICES AND MOTOR INSURANCE

Check the latest, but broadly speaking **fuel prices** in Africa range from heavily subsidised in oil-producing nations where it's cheaper than bottled water, to some of the highest around. In the Maghrebi nations of Algeria, Libya and Egypt fuel costs from **12 eurocents** a litre. Sudan, Nigeria, Angola and possibly Congo are midway at around four to six times that price, with South Africa and Namibia also much cheaper than their neighbours. Zambia, Malawi and Mozambique are especially expensive.

In between you find fuel prices either equivalent to European levels which are around €1.40 ($1.76) a litre, or at about two-thirds of that figure. There's more on world fuel prices on p15 and prices can shoot up to well above normal levels in outback areas.

For EU nationals your domestic **motor insurance** can be extended with a **Green Card** to cover only Morocco and Tunisia. Elsewhere you buy as you go, but countries in a given region often band together in economic zones or common markets (sometimes sharing a currency too) so that one policy covers all participating countries. In West Africa the ECOWAS agreement (🖥 www.ecowas.int) covers just about all of the region, while on the east side COMESA does the same from Sudan to Zimbabwe, and ECCAS covers Central African states from Chad down to Angola. Certainly in the ECOWAS zone motor insurance bought there – known as a *carte brune* (🖥 www.brown-card.ecowas.int or 🖥 www.cima-afrique.org) will be valid in all the countries as far as Chad, so it's safe to buy motor insurance for the several weeks you may expect to spend in that region.

Trans-African routes

Locals in Angola check out the pannier map.
© africansupertramp.blogspot.com

More than ever these days, riding across Africa (typically a ride of at least **7500 miles/11,000km** and two months) is like a game of snakes and ladders and it's not uncommon to have to change your itinerary on the eve of departure because something new has come up. As a rule, political instability is quick to develop and slow to subside, while lawlessness in the remote corners of an ostensibly stable country is also a hazard to overlanders who blunder in there.

Once in a while some brave or unhinged individual manages to get across a country or region long thought to be deadly. The word spreads, others follow and the ladders shift; the Lubumbashi–Kinshasa route in DRC (see p269) is a recent example of this. Often this is a result of the already-mentioned logistical and bureaucratic contortions in **getting visas**, and not least the **expense** of merely getting from one end to the other. At least these days the news of new visa regulations spreads quickly via the internet. All you have to divine is whether they're there to stay, the result of some diplomatic spat or an upcoming election, and whether they'll even be implemented. As said elsewhere, very often obscure border crossings may not have got the message yet, and the key things with visas and immigration stamps is that once you're in a country, you're in and ought to be able to stay there for the duration of your visa.

ASKING DIRECTIONS IN AFRICA

On stopping to buy water, a snack or confirm directions at times young men were 'in my face' and the attention could be intimidating. One time a local farmer among the group seemed especially aggressive. I didn't take it personally and it was interesting to note that when I addressed him directly, answering his questions genuinely and asking some myself, he seemed to come around – indeed warning off a couple of other young smart asses who were suggesting exacting a 'toll' from me.

I had a similar experience in Cameroon. Stopping for directions at a fork, I chose someone whose appearance suggested some 'worldliness'. He was a teacher who instantly took responsibility for the situation but as the inevitable crowd gathered the usual argument broke out and things became quite heated. I was to experience this further into central Africa and knew it was a cultural trait that didn't necessarily mean what it would back home in Ireland.

Remaining unperturbed was the best strategy. My defender had a stand off with one chap, accusing him of saying 'silly things' about me. The other guy backed off, things calmed down and the teacher would not let me go before I knew exactly where I was, the name of every village and even the hills all the way to Bamenda, my destination.

HUGH BERGIN
🖥 www.kilkennytocapetown.com

EAST OR WEST SIDE?

Short version: the **Nile Route** down the east side (from Khartoum east into Ethiopia and then down into Kenya, Tanzania and southwards via Zambia, Malawi or Mozambique to South Africa) is easier, better developed and offers more classic African sites, from the Pyramids to Kilimanjaro, Victoria Falls and Table Mountain. The **western route** (from Cameroon through Gabon, Congo-Brazzaville, DRC then Angola or Zambia) needs stronger nerves, greater patience, more visas and an appetite for adventure. Coming from Ethiopia, on the east side the riding eases once you're past Nairobi.

And as things have been in recent years, once you start down one side it's fairly arduous or dangerous to ride across to the other until you get down to Zambia. The enduringly ungoverned east of DRC as well as the Central Africa Republic (CAR) see to that. Crossing the width of Chad to or from Sudan is not currently possible either. If you're thinking of riding **there and back**, visas and other challenges fall into place a bit easier if you go down the west side and up the east.

North Africa and across the Sahara

North Africa can provide a taste of the continent which is distinctly different from sub-Saharan Africa and it was desert biking which begat the popularity of adventure motorcycling. The problem is that the best countries for deep desert travel; Libya, Algeria and parts of Niger and Egypt, all now require an expensive **escort**, and following a 4WD is not exactly adventure biking.

The **Sahara** has for centuries been a barrier separating Black Africa from the Arab-influenced Mediterranean. In the 1980s the classic routes ran from Morocco through Algeria and the central Sahara down to Mali or Niger. Then

in the 1990s political troubles beset northern Algeria and an unconnected desert-wide Tuareg rebellion in the south cut off northern Mali and Niger. The region closed and the **Atlantic Route** developed as the pressure on overland access sought another way.

Independent travellers returned to Algeria in 2000 and made hay while the sun shone because the party would not last. Around the same time Libya started opening up to tourism. Then Western tourists became targeted for kidnappings by Islamist groups starting in Algeria in 2003, followed by Mali, Tunisia, Mauritania and Niger. Now, post-Arab Spring, the great routes through the central Sahara look less accessible than ever.

But even in the good years there were no more than three or four trans-Sahara routes for tourists: the Atlantic Route from Morocco to Mauritania (now all sealed), Algeria to Mali (all piste, long closed), Algeria to Niger (250km piste but insecure or closed) and the all-sealed Nile route via Lake Nasser to Sudan. Only the first and the last of these routes are currently viable so unless you make the effort to deviate, the Sahara can be over before you know it. The HUBB Sahara forum or my 💻 sahara-overland.com website will have the latest.

TUNISIA AND LIBYA

Accessible on **ferries** from Genoa or Marseille to Tunis, it was events in Tunisia which kicked off the Arab Spring, but following the demise of Gaddafi in 2011, an RPG-equipped genie was let out of the bottle. After a brief lull – a common situation following a violent upheaval which can sometimes work to your advantage if you're quick – even the **coastal transit** between Tunisia (the border at Dehibat–Wazin near Nalut may be best) and Egypt has become dicey. Clan-based militias have been settling scores or vying for influence so Libya's not really ready for tourists, and as it is overlanders require a €300 'business' visa. And while a **guide** may not be mandatory with this visa, depending on the situation he may be a good idea to get you into Libya and through the many checkpoints along the coastal route run by local factions.

Things may not escalate in Libya, but along with Syria (see p197), this has meant that simply riding overland to Egypt from anywhere other than Sudan has become difficult. Currently **east Mediterranean ferries** are the least complicated way to get to Egypt.

ARABIC NUMERALS										
0	1	2	3	4	5	6	7	8	9	10
٠	١	٢	٣	٤	٥	٦	٧	٨	٩	١٠

MOROCCO AND MAURITANIA

Coming from Europe, **Morocco** (right) is the best destination for an eye-opening experience of North Africa. Here you'll find ancient Moorish cities on a par with their counterparts in western Asia, as well as a range of tracks (*pistes*) rising over the High Atlas to the fringes of the Sahara.

Ferries leave the southern Spanish ports for northern Morocco round the clock and cross in as little as 20 minutes. There's no need for a carnet or, in most cases, a **visa** for Morocco, making entry and paperwork relatively undemanding. Even then, if it's your first time out of Europe, Morocco can be intimidating and at the border a local helper may be worth the small tip, if not sticking with someone who knows the ropes.

Imperial cities excepted, northern Morocco is not so interesting. The fun begins in the **Atlas** which, along with the desert in southern Morocco, is best in

ALGERIA

For the adventurous rider in search of the Sahara, Algeria has it all. You can explore a fantastic range of landscapes between the Hoggar mountains near Tamanrasset and the Tassili plateau along the Libyan border (pictured below), or the more open country to the west of the trans-Sahara Highway. It's all here: long, easy and spectacular routes over dunes, mountains and plateaux.

Algeria also has a reputation as a dangerous place, partly due to the gruesome civil war of the 1990s (few tourists went there then), but more significantly from the serial abductions of 32 tourists on bikes and in 4x4s in the Tassili region in 2003. It was actually an exceptional event for Algeria which has not been repeated on that scale. The Algerian security services appear to be on top of it and so the kidnappings have continued in some adjacent countries.

Since that event **escorts/guides** are now mandatory for travel in the Algerian desert; you won't get a **30-day visa** (best applied for in your home country) without an invite from an agency that'll meet you at the border and stay with you for the duration. The idea and the cost (typically €**100–150/day**) of tagging along puts many off Algeria, but once you've seen the desert there you'll only regret not having gone there sooner. Use the car to carry your gear and even a cook.

For the trans-African rider Algeria has open borders to the south only with Niger on the trans-Sahara route from Tamanrasset to Agadez. There are Mali and Niger consulates in Tamanrasset, but visas for Niger have become hit and miss so better to get a Niger visa in Europe and a double-entry visa for Algeria in case you don't like what you find at the Niger post of Assamaka and want to turn back.

Although there was talk of it in 2011, **borders** with Morocco have been closed for years, the track to Mauritania is well beyond the range of a bike and far from safe, the same goes for access to Mali, Libya and, at the moment, Niger – though of all those Niger may improve. Which leaves only Tunisia and a ferry back to Marseille or Genoa.

MAURITANIAN AND MALIAN VISAS IN RABAT AND NOUAKCHOTT

Mauritanian embassy, Rabat
6 Rue Thami Lamdawar
Rabat-Souissi
N33° 58.8′ W06° 51.6′
Single entry 150DH or €15. Mali embassy's
in the same street, 100m away at #7. For photos and copies there's a supermarket at the
crossroads about 100 metres away.

In Nouakchott
Ave de Palais des Congres
N18° 06.5′ W15° 58.7′
Fee, about 6500UM.

See 🖥 www.sahara-overland.com/country
for the latest details.

---

the **intermediate seasons** when it's neither baking at over 40°C (104°F) or freezing on the High Atlas, where snow can block the few road passes. At any time
of year in the mountains you can expect sudden downpours which run down
the Atlas's steep slopes to cut through roads or tracks.

Petrol costs about 60% less than in Europe, while food and lodging can be
less than half, especially away from the tourist traps and resorts. All these
qualities make Morocco an ideal place for a test run, but also add up to a great
short-range overland destination in its own right. For the long version, along
with 10,000km of GPS routes and all the rest, see my *Morocco Overland* book
(latest edition, 2013) with updates at 🖥 **www.morocco-overland.com**.

To Mauritania

Even before they sealed the Mauritanian portion a few years ago, the **Atlantic
Route to Mauritania** was a rather dull way of crossing the Sahara. Inland
access to Moroccan-controlled parts of Western Sahara is limited and even
then, not so interesting so most bomb down the coastal highway to the
Mauritanian border where a few kilometres of sandy piste lead across No
Man's Land. Stick to the used tracks here as there are landmines around and
people have been blown up while needlessly following their own routes.

As long as you have your visa, entry into Mauritania near Nouadhibou is
fairly straightforward. Small bribes or presents are sometimes asked for; a
taste of things to come.

Mauritania

Many travellers initially don't take to Mauritanians; as yet unacclimatised to
culture shock, they're tempted to speed south to the grubby capital of
Nouakchott for Senegal or Mali. The country's reputation was damaged in
2008 when the Dakar Rally was cancelled, and by a handful of attacks and kidnappings of western tourists soon after. But security wise Mauritania has got
on the case while as yet not insisting on border-to-border escorts which means
you can roam the southwestern corner of the country; anywhere to the north
or east is largely trackless and less safe.

With the right bike and some company, for a **taste of the Sahara** take the
sandy, 520km two-day run east along the railway towards Atar. Spend some
time exploring the Adrar Highlands region as far as Chinguetti or Ouadane
(the giant 'crater' of Richat nearby is only impressive on Google Earth). Then
take the more demanding 400km crossing south to Tidjikja, possibly hiring a
guide. From Tidjikja it's best to head for Kiffa and ride into Mali sooner than
later. All up this'll add a fortnight you won't forget and an African highlight.

West Africa

West Africa covers the sub-Saharan region from Senegal as far east as Cameroon and Chad. Much of it was once under French colonial rule and today **French**, and to a lesser extent English (in the Gambia, Sierra Leone, Liberia, Ghana and Nigeria) will be the **languages** you'll use the most. A romantic idea many have is riding all the way along the **Atlantic coast**; the problem is that between Dakar and the Ivory Coast border, there is no road and some countries in this corner of West Africa can be hard work for a

'Everybody keep still!' Piroguing in Togo.
© africansupertramp.blogspot.com

beginner. Coming from the north and still wet behind the sidepanels, most riders choose to make it easy on themselves by reducing the borders and so visas to save their energy for central Africa where there'll be less choice. As it is, since the Arab Spring, right across West Africa anti-government protests and coups (or coup plots) have become more numerous, and with key countries like Mali and Nigeria suffering, overland travel has lately taken a dive.

In 2012 **Mali** north of the Niger river was over-run by Tuareg rebels armed with Libyan army surplus. They've since lost control to AQIM (Al Qaeda of the Islamic Maghreb), declaring Sharia and an independent homeland called Azawad. As a result western governments are now getting edgy, but AQIM have operated up there with impunity for years and the barely populated desert north of **Timbuktu** has long been off limits.

The situation in Mali is currently unresolved, with talk of ECOWAS troops helping reclaim Azawad, but although no one's sure who's actually running the country, southern Mali and Burkina are calm enough to cross. In the event of that changing for the worse, it'll be a lot of visas at around €60 a go to border hop from Senegal via Guinea to the Ivory Coast (via Sierra Leone and Liberia if you wish). From there you can continue along the Gulf of Guinea states to Nigeria and so Cameroon, gateway to equatorial Africa.

Local currencies in West and Central Africa

Travel in this region is eased by the CFA currency which is shared by Senegal, Guinea Bissau, Mali, Ivory Coast, Burkina Faso, Benin and Niger. It's abbreviated on currency websites as CFA XOF. The other **CFA currency** zone (CFA XAF) covers six Central African countries: Chad, CAR, Cameroon, Congo, Gabon and Equatorial Guinea.

You can't use one in the other zone, except possibly near borders between the zones. The international rate of exchange is the same for both and pretty stable at about 655 to a euro.

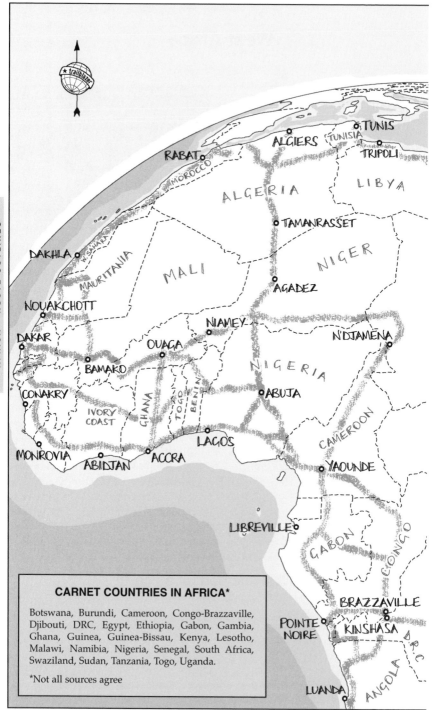

CARNET COUNTRIES IN AFRICA*

Botswana, Burundi, Cameroon, Congo-Brazzaville,
Djibouti, DRC, Egypt, Ethiopia, Gabon, Gambia,
Ghana, Guinea, Guinea-Bissau, Kenya, Lesotho,
Malawi, Namibia, Nigeria, Senegal, South Africa,
Swaziland, Sudan, Tanzania, Togo, Uganda.

*Not all sources agree

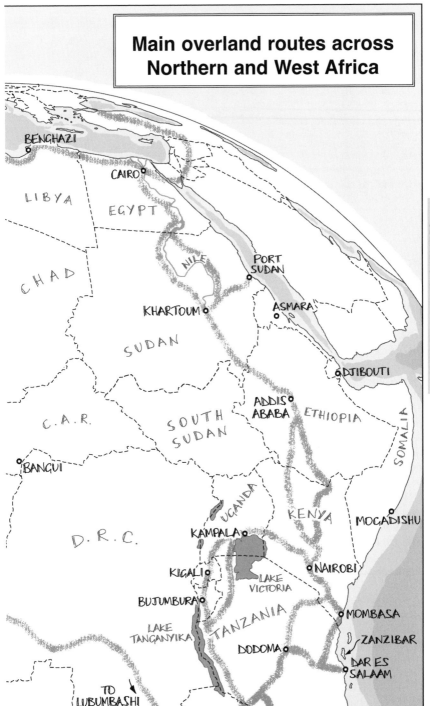

Main overland routes across Northern and West Africa

AFRICA – ROUTE OUTLINES

WEST AFRICAN VISAS

Burkina Faso consulate, Bamako
Off rue de Guinee, just east of the US
embassy. N12° 37.9' W08° 00.9'
Three photos and around 24,000CFA for a 30-
day, single-entry visa issued same day, but
now you pay the same at the border.

Nigerian consulate, Bamako
South of the bridge, close to the *Sleeping
Camel* on the RN7 to the airport. N12 37.0'
W07 58.6'.
Displays a visa price list for each country.

**Ghana consulate in Ouagadougou,
Burkina Faso**
Ave d'Oubritenga.
N12° 22.7' W01° 30.6'

Four photos and around 15,000CFA. Issued
in 1–3 days.

Nigerian visa in Accra, Ghana
Akasombo Road, Airport Residential Area.
N05° 36.7' W00° 10.8'
Two photos, two copies of passport, application form, Ghana visa plus itinerary, insurance, vehicle ownership papers, carnet and
at least $100. At the border you may need to
show a Yellow fever certificate.

Benin visa in Accra, Ghana
Switchback Lane, Cantonments
N05° 35.2' W00° 10.8'
Two forms, two photos, 10,000CFA.
Issued same day.

SENEGAL, MALI & BURKINA FASO

Leaving Mauritania, the border on the Senegal River at **Rosso** has long had a
reputation for petty intimidation and corruption on both sides of the frontier.
Because of this, most choose to avoid the ferry here and ahead 50km downstream to the **Diama** dam bridge, but during the rains this route gets closed, at
which time Rosso have you where they want you. It may not be a great introduction but welcome to **sub-Saharan Africa**.

At Rosso without a carnet you must pay up to €200, and even then they
lately make you ride down to the docks in Dakar within 48 hours (extensions
available in St Louis) to get the carnet stamped, rather than at the border like
anywhere else. Once on the way, several **checkpoints** on the road to St Louis
might also be angling to dish out fines for minor or invented transgressions.
Regional **Carte Brune insurance** is sold at the border for up to six months.

Like many African capitals, **Dakar** may be a grind but Senegal is a wonderful country. The old colonial capital of **St Louis** just down from the border
is well worth a stop; the ever helpful Zebrabar, some 18km south of St Louis
(N15° 51.9' W16° 30.7') is a popular hangout for overlanders. However, unless
you're heading for Gambia and maybe ending your trip there, you may choose
to avoid the needless hassle at Rosso altogether and head directly from
Mauritania into Mali.

The road is sealed from Kiffa to Nioro in Mali and carries on down to
Bamako, and there's a sealed route coming in from Tambacounda in Senegal via
Kayes too. Unless things take a huge turn for the better, don't carry on to Nema
in Mauritania; it's too close to AQIM/Azawad areas on both sides of the border.

If entering Mali without a visa, it's said to be possible to obtain a two-day
pass at these borders and continue to Bamako, though it may cost you. Again,
Bamako can be a little crazy and even risky after dark, but it's a useful place to
obtain visas. Just south of the main bridge, *The Sleeping Camel* (N12° 37.53' W07°
59.28') is the traveller's haven and a good place to get information.

Located a thousand kilometres northeast of Bamako, since 2012 **Timbuktu**
has become an outpost of Tuareg-controlled Azawad territory and is current-

TRIP REPORT
TRANS AFRICA ~ YAMAHA 660 TÉNÉRÉ

Name	Luke Steele
Year of birth	1978
Occupation	Diesel mechanic
Nationality	New Zealand
Previous travels	Many places but not Africa
Bike travels	Europe

This trip	London to Cape Town via west coast
Trip duration	Three months
Departure date	June 2009
Number in group	Three
Distance covered	24,000km

Best day	Into Namibia after Angolan visa dash
Worst day	Ekok to Mamfe (Nigeria–Cameroon)
Favourite places	Windhoek, Namibia
Biggest headache	Decent food and accommodation
Biggest mistake	Taking a MasterCard...
Pleasant surprise	... Visa-friendly ATMs everywhere
Any illness	Crook stomach
Cost of trip	20,000AUD
Other trips planned	Not at the moment

Bike model	Yamaha XT660Z Ténéré
Age, mileage	2008 model, 15,000km
Modifications	Yamaha bash plate, bars and guards
Wish you'd ...	not fitted those crash bars
Tyres used	Metz Tourance, Conti TKC80, Mich T63
Punctures	Three
Type of baggage	Yamaha Panniers, Tatonka Barrel Bag

Bike's weak point	Rear end sags when fully loaded
Strong point	Fuel range
Bike problems	Broken frame, skid plate & crash bars
Accidents	No
Same bike again	Maybe KTM690E or Adventure version
Any advice	Go with friends you can trust

ly subject to Sharia law. The last European tourists to get there in 2011 ended up kidnapped or shot, and refugees have fled from the region in all directions. Travel in southern Mali is still possible, but prices may escalate, and even before that **fuel** cost close to European prices.

EAST TOWARDS CHAD OR NIGERIA

From Bamako, sealed roads run via Burkina Faso to English-speaking Ghana, or directly eastwards across Niger, where beyond Zinder the bitumen breaks up and disappears altogether around Lake Chad, a tough, sandy bush track of at least two days ending at **Chad**'s expensive capital, N'Djamena, right on the border of Cameroon. On any bike that is a tough ride and lately few have gone this way, but with northern Cameroon calmer than it was while Nigeria goes the other way, it's an option to consider.

Occasionally you might hear of parties coming through the Central African Republic (CAR) or even northeastern DRC – the old overland route from the 1980s – but they're an exception. At the moment parts of CAR and the northeast of DRC are as bad as it gets in central Africa, as groups including the dregs of the maniacal Lord's Resistance Army driven out of Uganda and Sudan, periodically go on the rampage.

Nigeria

Despite **cheap fuel** (often sold watered down just over adjacent borders) and a chance to communicate in English after a few Francophone countries, **Nigeria** didn't have a great reputation even before the wave of atrocities carried out in the name of Boko Haram in recent years. Remember though, this is a country of 100 million people so as long as you keep your wits about you, a swift transit ought to pass without incident. The situation is not helped by the fact that local motorcycle taxis or 'okadas' have been banned in some cities, following their use by criminal gangs, assassins and suicide bombers, though clearly overseas riders are not affected.

GETTING SOUTHBOUND VISAS IN ACCRA, ABUJA AND CALABAR

Angola in Accra, Ghana
Liberation Road, just west of airport.
N05° 36.60' W00° 10.62'
Bank statements plus copies of everything; 30-day tourist visa for $150. Takes two weeks but could be your best bet in Africa.

Cameroon in Abuja, Nigeria
469/470 Lobito Crescent, Wuse 11 (near Hilton Hotel).
N09° 04.24' E07° 29.4'
90-day validity, 30-day visa single-entry. Normally two days, 50,000CFA or N17,500.

Congo-Brazzaville
On same road as Cameroon embassy, above. Same day N13–18,000, next day N10–12,000. Price varies depending on how you look.

No supporting documents requested.
Valid 90 days from issue for a single entry 30-day visa. Or get it at the Doussala border with Gabon: 15 days for 20,000 CFA.

DRC
Azores St.
N09° 04.9' E07° 28.1'
N17,000, similar documents to Angola, with visas required for onward country, but DRC can insist you apply in your home country.

Cameroon visa in Calabar
On the main Ididem Usang Iso Road.
N04° 58.1' E08° 20.3'
Three photos, two forms, copy of bike ownership and insurance (the ECOWAS policy will do). Same day service, 51,000CFA.

Unless you know better, make life easier on the nerves by taking a middle course across the country via Abuja (a place to get some key visas), so avoiding the big cities of the south as well the northeast states of Borno and Yobe. Up here in better times you could checkout of Niger at Diffa and head via Maiduguri (now home of Boko Haram) for Mora and Maroua in the northern tip of Cameroon. One positive development has been the scrapping of the scores of roadside **checkpoints** all over Nigeria. It was an admission that they were more effective at extortion than ensuring security, though again, foreign motorcyclists were always less prone to shakedowns compared to cars.

Abuja to Cameroon

In Abuja many take advantage of the **free camping** round the back of the Sheraton Hotel (N09 03.8' E7 29.1'). Pull up to reception, ask nicely to camp and they'll show you where to go and how to shower by the squash courts. They may refer to you as a 'tourist', as virtually none of the other foreigners in the hotel will be.

Knobby time behind the Abuja Sheraton.
© africansupertramp.blogspot.com

After collecting as many visas as you like, you need to decide if you're heading south or north into Cameroon as there are only a handful of border crossings. Heading southwards through Nigeria, it's best to aim for Makurdi. Down on the coast, **Calabar** is your last chance to get a visa, then head to Ikom and across the border to Cameroon at **Ekok**. Over the years the track over the border has earned itself a notorious reputation. Your mission is to get to Mamfe, just 70km away; not too much to ask. If you've come outside of the rains and with the right tyres you should get there intact for a late lunch. If it's wet expect the journey to take days as you, and those stuck in front of you, crawl though the mud holes. Make the most of it, it may well be sealed soon. Until then, your best bet is around December or January, otherwise try the more northern crossings away from the rain-bound coast.

GETTING SOUTHBOUND VISAS IN YAOUNDE, CAMEROON

Most of the embassies you want are located in the Quartier Bastos at the north end of town.

Gabon
Rue 1816, Bastos.
N03° 53.7' E11° 31.2'
A photo and form, 35,000CFA. Pick up next day if express fee paid, otherwise three days. Smarten up and learn some French or don't expect a warm welcome. Also said to be available at the border.

DRC
Blvd de l'URSS, Bastos.
N03° 53.65' E11° 30.96'
A photo and form, copy of passport, 45,000CFA, but they insist you get the visa in your home country.

Congo-Brazza'
Rue 1815, Bastos. N03° 53.71' E11° 31.18'
Two photos and vaccination certificates, 50,000CFA. 9.30pm–noon. Pick up noon next day.

Western Route via DRC

WITH DARRIN JOHANSEN

Once you've made it safely into Cameroon, be it via either Chad or Nigeria, you have some idea of what lies ahead and are starting to get into the swing of things. On the forecast are days of churned up mud tracks, heat, humidity, over-friendly insects, opportunistic cops and obnoxious consular staff until, slightly stunned, you pop out of Angola's or DRC's southern frontier into the Disneyland of southern Africa like a well-oiled cork.

Enjoy any **new tarmac roads** while they last. Chances are the climate, pounding cargo and lack of maintenance will see them last only a few years. The western route could be entering a golden age of all-weather accessibility before the jungle reclaims it all.

With the various **visa hassles** on this route, it's often a case of simply getting to the next country rather than cruising around whatever takes your interest, as you can do on the east side of Africa. Many will be out of their comfort zone by now, riding from dawn to dusk, and it can take some nerve to resist the 'flee' instinct. Try to slow down and have a look around as chances are you'll only be here once. Even on the easiest route, following Nigeria and with Angola or southern DRC to come, this will be the **toughest stage** of your Africa trip so as on the longer Saharan tracks, it's common to **team up** with other travellers as you may need all the support you can get.

It's also worth noting that paper or digital **maps** are hit and miss in this part of Africa. Place names won't match up and you'll pass through villages that don't exist or miss villages that do. It's all part of the fun, but having Tracks4Africa, Camping Weld and other pre-researched **waypoints** comes into its own here, allowing you to explore with some vague idea of where you are some of the time. Along with that, knowing some **French** (though not necessarily always letting on) and having a good stash of dollars is a big advantage. It's a jungle for sure but ATMs don't grow on trees.

Whichever route you take, you'll cross the equator somewhere. This sign is on the road to Lambarene. © Rob & Ally Ford

GABON TO ANGOLA

Most overlanders have an easy time in Cameroon, especially if they stick to the main drag and despite the extra visa, they end up heading south through **Gabon** on the way to Congo-Brazzaville because, as the box opposite suggests, it's much easier.

After Cameroon, Gabon is expensive and some find the people not so friendly, but like Cameroon it's no drama, depending which 'roads' you ride and your luck with the rains. Along the equator there are **no seasons**

CAMEROON TO CONGO DIRECT

If you've something against visiting Gabon (or they take against you) then it's possible to ride directly into Republic of **Congo** (or 'Congo-Brazzaville' as it is known to distinguish it from the river or DRC; the Democratic Republic of Congo). What you actually save on acquiring one less visa you'll pay back many, many times by staggering between mudholes along overgrown, waterlogged tracks and negotiating expensive ferries (where they exist), at least until you get further south towards Oyo in Congo where tarmac now runs down to Brazzaville. In this way Congo direct is comparable with the BAM track near Lake Baikal in Russia (see p230). It'll be 'rude'.

Ouesso via Socambo

The key towns for such an endeavor are the logging port of **Ouesso** in Congo-Brazza, on the Sangha river, and possibly **Pokola**, an hour or so downstream. You can get to Ouesso from Sembe in the west as described below, or by following similarly unpredictable logging tracks via Yokadouma to Socambo at the confluence of the Sangha and Ngoko rivers; passing, you'll be thrilled to learn, the birthplace of the HIV virus (as reported in 2006).

Poaching and gun-running abound in this far corner of Cameroon and the only other vehicles you'll see will be logging trucks which may not be accustomed to giving way to motos. Last told, the tarmac ends about 150km east of Yaounde and as long as the two annual wet seasons have not started or joined forces, the regularly graded dirt roads ought to be passable.

About 150km south of Yokadouma turn off southeast at Mambele and follow more logging tracks to the small border post of **Socambo** (N01° 41.66′ E16° 07.76′) in the extreme southeast corner of Cameroon.

If the river is high enough, from Socambo logging ferries come and go from the mills at Pokola which is about 60km downstream, but on the wrong side of the Sangha for Ouesso. You need to get to the west bank of the Sangha and then, either from Pokola or about 15km downstream opposite Mboko, cross back and once over, follow a 50km track via Mokelo to Ouesso for the relatively normal 800km ride to Brazzaville.

It's also said that used car traders cross directly from Socombo to Ouesso by putting vehicles on planks across two *pinasses* (large dug-out canoes), though as pictured on p257, you can get a bike in a smaller *pirogue*. The final option may be best if the rains have struck: load your bike onto a logging barge at **Pokola** and set off downstream to meet the Congo River at Mossaka, about 450km upstream from Kinshasa/Brazzaville. It's been done although this is pretty out there.

To Ouesso from Mbalam

An hour south of Yaounde, turn east at Mbalmayo onto the N9 and follow logging tracks 430km southeast to the border at **Mbalam**. On the Congolese side little used muddy tracks lead through Souanke in Sembe from where it's 200km to Ouesso. Expect tough conditions until you're well east of Sembe, though nothing that a knobbly-tyred thumper can't manage in the dry with a fuel range of up to 400km. South of Ouesso the tracks improve until after some 200km, you reach the ferry at Yengo.

From here it's 600km via Obouya (the track that's due to be road from Franceville in Gabon, see p266) and Oyo where the tarmac starts and your worries end for the moment. Next stop, Brazzaville on the Congo river and opposite the border with DRC, see p266.

to speak of, it rains pretty much all year so it's a matter of luck whether you hit a bad road during a wet spell. Rain is a mixed blessing though, it cools everything off for a while and allows a decent night's sleep. Around here you'll appreciate a tent which can be pitched inner only, like a mossie net

It's only about 270km from Yaounde via Ebolowa to the border with Gabon. Immigration is done at the police station in Bitam opposite the *Shell*, but expect the Gabonese side to be unhelpful even though some travellers have reported getting visas on arrival here. At least it's a tarmac road from the border for 400km as far as the **junction** just after the equator at S00° 04.6′ E10° 57.5′, and just before Alembé, which leads east for Lope National Park.

Here you have **three options** to get yourself to DRC and lined up for Zambia or Angola. None adds up to a precise itinerary and there are other routes; instead it's merely a trio of possibilities which between them juggle bad roads, awkward visas and intimidating or expensive borders. Whatever weather you get on the way, that comes free.

- Head east for Franceville (470km) then follow what become sandy tracks to Oyo in Congo (another 350km) where you're back on the tar down to Brazzaville (450km) for the ferry to Kinshasa. This adds up to over **1300km**, but may become the main all-weather way to Brazzaville once the Chinese roads are completed in Congo.

- Head south through Gabon any way you like and once you get to Dolisie in Congo (700km), turn east for Brazzaville (360km). In total it's over **1000km** to Kinshasa, with a very rough road west of Brazzaville, as well as the Kinshasa ferry to deal with (there are quieter outback river-crossing options, see next page).

- Assuming you have the mythical double-entry Angolan visa, at Dolisie (700km from Mevang) head west for Pointe-Noire on the coast on a super highway, and cross the Angolan enclave of **Cabinda** (220km). On entering DRC, head inland from Muanda (60km from Cabinda) to Boma – a road that can be dreadful in the rains – and cross the Congo river bridge into Matadi (220km). Rough roads, a visa for Cabinda and again, nearly **1300km** get you to the Angolan border at Songololo, but with no Kinshasa ferry ordeal.

Southeast for Oyo (Congo)

Roadwise, the rot may well set in south from Mevang in Gabon. As far as Lambarene and the Congo border at Doussala is the usual central African scenario. So strike out towards Lope National Park and **Franceville**, then eastwards out of the forest along a combination of good graded tracks then perfect tarmac from around Franceville to the border at Lekoni. **Border formalities** are said to be easy enough, with no untoward fees.

Once in Congo the party ends for a couple of hundred kilometres. Sandy roller-coaster tracks churned up by the road-building trucks lead into the grass-covered hills until you get to Obouya or Oyo, 450km north of Brazzaville. This section is not all bad as you're on a high plateau where it's slightly cooler. By 2014 they say it could all be freshly-laid Chinese tar, and when that happens this route will probably become the easiest way south from Cameroon to Brazzaville.

In **Congo** the people are friendly again and for a central African capital, **Brazzaville** actually manages to be quite a safe city – until you get too close to the ferry port, that is. Many overlanders choose to camp for free at the Hippocampe Hotel (S04° 16.4' E15° 16.7') where great Vietnamese food is served. If heading north and in need of Gabonese or Cameroonian visas, see the box on p270.

Southwest for Pointe-Noire and Cabinda

Backing up to Mevang in Gabon, most don't bother visiting expensive Libreville (though there is a slick Yamaha dealer there) and so once through Lambarene, 160km down the road, you can head southwest 700 clicks to Pointe-Noire on the coast of Congo-Brazza. From here you'll be crossing the Angolan enclave of Cabinda for DRC so make sure you have the double-entry Angolan visa sorted. Once in Congo immigration is done 50km after the border at Nyanga, where there's also a Catholic mission to stay at. An alternative route to Congo turns off at Moanda before Franceville, and take a little-used route south via Bakoumbe to the border and Mbinda for immigration.

Mila Mila (S03° 42.9′ E12° 27.1′) is a junction that doesn't appear on most maps and where a corner-cutting logging track leads through the hills to Pointe-Noire, 150km away. Otherwise continue south to Dolisie junction where the railway runs from Pointe-Noire to Brazzaville and turn west. Even if the weather is not on your side it's a beautiful day's ride from Dolisie to Point-Noire on a great road. Once there you can camp at the Yacht Club (S04° 47.31′ E11° 50.9′) but, unless

Extreme pinassing off the coast of Gabon.
© africansupertramp.blogspot.com

you're shipping out, don't come this way without a visa for the Angolan enclave of Cabinda.

Cabinda (Angola) and southwest DRC

Like a lot of the cities on this coast, **Cabinda** is not cheap. Oil, imports and ex-pats see to that, and for many travellers the place doesn't encourage extended stays, especially with visa hassles. If you've had enough you might try and find out about a ship or even a military Antonov transporter to Luanda, or just Soyo in Angola, on the south side of the Congo estuary. Otherwise, ride on through and once clear of immigration into DRC, head inland on churned up dirt towards Boma and Matadi. This road can turn into a mire after the heavens open; one Lithuanian rider rode his KLR into a puddle so deep both he and the bike disappeared. Hours later some passers-by finally offered to help fish it out and without asking for payment. If you make it to Boma, you rejoin tarmac and head north through the hills to come back down to the Congo River for the **toll bridge** into Matadi, 120km from Boma. Allow about two days to get from Cabinda to the Matadi bridge in dry conditions.

As mentioned elsewhere, assuming you have the visa, it's better not to cross into Angola at Matadi. Instead ride the 80km up to **Songololo** and head for M'banza Kongo from where better roads lead south. Among other places there are **missions** to stay at in Muanda (S05° 55.9′ E12° 20.5′), Boma (S05° 51.2′ E13° 03.4′) and Matadi (S05° 49.9′ E13° 27.7′).

Dolisie to Brazzaville, or slipping quietly over the Congo

For a while **Dolisie** was known as one of the few places to get an **Angolan visa** en route. Even then, many got refused and at $100 (or $200 for the double-entry for Cabinda) it seemed like a private enterprise, as do many visa applications at consulates hereabouts. If you missed your chance in Accra (p262), it's a small town so ask around for the building with the red-over-black Angolan flag.

East from Dolisie, the 360km to Brazzaville along the railway was once plagued by the activities of Ninja separatists. The best you can say now is the Ninjas disbanded in 2008 to pursue solo careers, but the road remains well and truly rooted up to Kinkala. You may still have the option to take the **train** (as Lois Pryce vividly described in *Red Tape and White Knuckles*), otherwise get stuck in. When dry and dusty it can take two days to cover 200km; when water-logged it's better not to ask. Expect a few official roadblocks with a set price toll.

AFRICA – ROUTE OUTLINES

ON A MISSION

Whether you're religious or not, Christian missions in Africa make great overnight havens. In some places, especially on this western route, they represent the only secure and fully functional accommodation option for overland travellers, and the priests and nuns are a great source of information on local roads and the state of security.

Finding a welcoming mission is easier than you think and many online travel blogs list them. As the weary pilgrim knocks at the gate, so shall he be rewarded. Nine times out of ten they'll put you up for a night.

The most you should expect is to be shown a place to camp and the way to the washroom. Rooms are a rarity and even camping space is improvised. In Matadi we were woken by a hundred shouting kids, and popping our heads out of the tent we discovered we'd parked in the middle of the mission school playground. A tricky position when all your clothes are in the car, a short dash away. Missions are almost always connected with schools and if you have exercise

books, text books or pens, donating them is much appreciated.

Be prepared to make a cash donation on a par with the price of a local hostel room or campsite too. Sometimes, as we found in Cabinda, there's a fee structure laid out for visitors. Don't let the dog collar put you off haggling if you're staying for a few days or if the price is just too high.

Should you be faced with a choice of missions as we were in Lamberene, go for the nuns rather than priests. Their places are cleaner, adorned with flowers and are better organised. The priests may be less strict about how the toilet seat should be left, but tend to be less friendly.

The godly effect of staying at a mission can carry through to the rest of the trip. In Calabar, confusion over our address at the local mission meant the Cameroon embassy issued us with Evangelical Missionary Visas. They certainly smoothed the route through the checkpoints later in the trip.

ANDY PAG

In recent years **alternative crossings** to the Congo river ferry between Brazzaville and Kinshasa have come to light along this road. Both involve following demanding and barely used tracks on either side of the river which could end badly if attempted in the rains. From Dolisie it's 220km to **Mindouli** where you turn right and cross into DRC to follow a gnarly track south some 100km to **Luozi** on the river. Here an inexpensive and hassle-free pontoon drops you on the far bank at **Banza Sanda** where the track continues south to the main road near **Kimpese** not far from the Songololo border post.

Or, coming from Brazzaville along the sealed road, turn southwest at Kinkala for Boko where the tarmac ends. A track leads to Manyanga where

Your typical equatorial lunch: long-life biscuits, processed cheese and spam or tuna; it's the only stuff that lasts outside a fridge.
© africansupertramp.blogspot.com

you check into DRC and where the track deteriorates to Luozi. In off-road miles the distance is about the same for both approaches to Luozi, but **if it's wet** you're better off throwing yourself on the mercy of the Brazza-Kinshasa ferry. Also, think twice about taking the alternative ferry at Pioka some 25km directly east of Luozi. The track on the south side leading southeast to Gombe Matadi has holes deeper than you are tall (and we've just read how that can end...). Allow at least two days for either route.

KINSHASA TO BRAZZA FERRY

At Kinshasa port it was the usual mob scene with stupid ferry prices being thrown about. I ended up using a guy just so the others would leave me alone. He wouldn't give a price in advance for his services but got me through customs and immigration very quickly. But then he tried to change the cost on my 'ticket' (a scrap of paper from the ticket counter) from 38,000CFA to 138,000. When I caught him and questioned the cashier she screamed at him. I paid 38,000CFA.

I rode onto the ferry, though people were yelling at me and each other the whole time. One would get in the way to try to block me, another would pull him away and the fixer kept trying to discuss his fee, but I just rode aboard.

On the ferry fixerman then asked for stupid amounts of money. I gave him my remaining CFA and kwanza and suggested he'd do much better next time by being honest. The ferry was beginning to move so he cursed at me and hopped back ashore.

On the Brazzaville side there were a few steps to negotiate before I could ride up the ramp so I needed help to get the GS off. I'd been talking to some decent guys on the boat (the joys of speaking French!) and we worked out a deal: two to lift the bike at $2 each, then $5 each to the two who arranged it, helped lift the bike, and did the whole immigration dance for me, including getting the visa! Everything worked fine and they never tried to ask for more cash.

So, for me and the GS it was: ticket $42; Kinshasa fixer $10; Brazzaville help $14 and Congo-Brazzaville visa $50.

DAVID RADFORD
🖥 www.gsguy.wordpress.com

DRC: THE CONGO FERRY TO KINSHASA

Brazzaville might be an easy-going place by regional standards, but it's time to stiffen the sinews and board the **ferry** to Kinshasa in the DRC. Start out by scouting out the costs and timings, because the regular vehicle ferry is frequently out of action, although with a bike you can make a deal for a smaller passenger boat. The Brazzaville side is easy enough with a semi-fixed tariff of inflated prices of around 20,000CFA; the crossing takes 20 minutes to an hour. Arriving on the Kinshasa side the costly whipping can take some getting used to and it can take hours to get processed.

Kinshasa

After all that, is it any surprise not everyone finds **Kinshasa** a relaxing place to spend time? The situation fluctuates, but this is one country where hanging around too long can get costly or unpleasant. Kinshasa hotels are expensive so most end up camping for free at the **Procure Sainte Anne** Catholic mission (S04° 18.03′ E15° 18.9′) next to the cathedral a short distance from the ferry terminal, and opposite the US embassy (with others close by).

The track to Lubumbashi and Zambia

Even with its visa difficulties, most travellers would still choose to continue to Angola and so Namibia and the Cape, but to do that you need a visa and as things stand you won't be getting it hereabouts.

The alternative means heading east some 2400km to Zambia via Kikwit, Kananga, Kamina and Kolwezi for Lubumbashi and on to the Zambian frontier at **Kasumbalesa**. In the 1960s this route was a road and railway with trams running in the towns, but half a century of neglect and war has seen the sort of dehumanising collapse of society for which DRC is famed. It's good tar for the 530km to Kikwit and at the other end from Kolwezi to Lubumbashi and

---

NORTHBOUND VISAS IN LUANDA AND BRAZZAVILLE

LUANDA

DRC
Largo de Joao Seca, just south of the South African embassy and near the hospital.
S08° 49.52′ E13° 13.74′

Congo
Rua de Joao de Barros, by Meridian Hotel.
S08° 48.22′ E13° 14.55′

Gabon
Near the Miramar Park and just east of the Congo embassy. S08° 48.51′ E13° 15.0′

BRAZZAVILLE
Both just south of the Meridian hotel and a ten minute walk north of the Hippocampe Hotel.

Gabon
Boulevard du Maréchal Lyautey
S04° 16.12′ E15° 16.65′
Possibly same day and about 35,000CFA

Cameroon
Rue Gouverneur Général Bayardelle
S04° 16.17′ E15° 16.54′
Next day and up to €80.

Kasumbalesa, but that still leaves well over 1500km along overgrown tracks where a relay of bicycles have become the most reliable load carriers and where they go you can squeeze through. Along the way the geniality you'll have experienced so far dries up as incessant and aggressive demands for hand-outs, as well as village 'registration' fees and other taxes add to the sustained effort in riding on what has undoubtedly become the toughest 'main' overland route in Africa. Some days you'll barely manage to cover 50km.

If you, your bike and its tyres are up for it, allow up to **two weeks** to get across without help from a truck, or investigate the Kinshasa–Lumbubashi **cargo plane**. Otherwise, for a preview track down the Al Jezeera documentary on youtube ('Risking it all – DRC') and a Belgian couple's 2011 account of travelling on XT660Zs (🖳 www.roamingafrica.be). You'll end up with bragging rights but also much less money and quite possibly some form of PTSD.

ANGOLA

It's 270km of good tar from Kinshasa to the recommended **Songololo-Luvo** crossing which leads to the least bad roads in Angola. Even then it can still take half a day to get it all done and on the road to Luanda, and at the mercy of a five- or maybe a seven-day **transit visa**, every hour counts. Coming north you might have got a 30-day tourist visa from the Angolans in Cape Town (S33° 55.2′ E18 25.4′), but as in Accra on the way south (see p262) that takes some luck and persistence. All of which is a great shame as despite the ruined roads and very high prices, like Nigeria or Sudan, the people of Angola make it a favourite amongst overland riders. Encountering delays on a five-day pass add to the pressure, but **over-staying** by a few days need not mean transportation to the local version of Devil's Island. If it's just a couple of days they may let you go, or argue over the fine, but it's best not to get caught in Luanda with an expired visa.

Fuel is a third of the price of DRC or Namibia, but make sure you have enough when you enter from the north border to N'zeto where the first reliable fuel supplies start. **Land mines** are still a big problem in Angola – don't leave the road unless you're following a recently used track and crap on the road if you have to. Because of this, **bush camping** takes some effort or risk but as always there's a network of missions.

Trans Angola

At Songololo take a turn 15km to **Luvo**. Ask to camp on the DRC side of the border and get through as soon as they open in the morning. Change your dollars on the Angolan side; you'll need some local currency for bread, tolls and possibly fuel to get you the 300km to N'zeto. With immigration done, follow the track some 50km to M'banza-Congo – it can take a while if it's wet – but from here to the coast it's all sealed or a wide track. A full day's riding should get you from the border to **N'zeto**. Brace yourself, as the 200km along the coast to Caxito is completely shot.

From Caxito it's tar to **Luanda** which manages to be one of the most rundown as well as most expensive capitals in the world, chronically congested due to the dangers in the countryside. At least a Via Expresso **ring road** can speed up your transit. As you come in from the north stay on the good sealed road that descends into a potholed mess within the city limits, until you see a motorway overpass (S08° 46.18′ E13° 23.2′) and roundabout. This is your ticket around Luanda so get on it. Otherwise, if you want to stay you can **camp for free** in the secure car park at the Clube Nautico (Yacht Club) down in the marina (S08° 48.14′ E13° 13.4′).

Leaving Luanda

South of Luanda follow the coast for 540km as far as **Benguela** as it's mainly good tar. Watch out for police with radar guns and the few road tolls to pay. The humidity finally begins to drop as you head south, the land turns to savannah and you can enjoy snuggling into your sleeping bag again at night rather than sweating and panting like a wet bat. The checkpoints, desperate scams, and the general hassle of the equatorial countries drop off too; maybe it is the climate after all.

Downtown Lubango. Is there a problem?
© metdaffieopreis.nl

From Benguela you can head inland towards Quilengues and Lubango, another 130km on, but at 1500m it can get **chilly** up here – a feeling you may have forgotten. Otherwise continue along the coast and approach Lubango via the impressive **Leba Pass**. Lubango to the border can be done in a day if you leave at dawn. Expect a mixture of new tar, torturous dirt roads or ruined tar. The main border crossing is at **Oshikango** (Namibian side), but if it's not too wet try the track from Xangongo down to Ruacana in Namibia.

As you cross the border you may wince like Steve McQueen being let out of the Cooler in *The Great Escape*. The intense strain of the previous weeks lifts and some find the adjustment quite a shock and even miss the preceding struggle as cleanliness, order and asphalt straight out of a car commercial all hit you at once. Ahead lie the fabulous desert landscapes of **Namibia**, as rich as any you've seen so don't be in a rush as the pressure's off now. The finale down to Cape Town is a piece of cake, just be wary of crime in Namibian cities. For southern Africa see p279.

The Nile route

Less of a challenge and with better organised wildlife spotting opportunities, the long-established 'Cairo to Cape' run down the east side of Africa avoids the gruelling riding, enervating climate and visa hassles of the western route. Composed largely of former British colonies, **English** is widely spoken on this side too, although the route's long overland history also means better-established scams.

South of the equator citizens with Commonwealth nationalities can usually get **visas** at the border, although Brits pay much higher prices. Instead of tread-choking mud, luggage-wrecking **corrugations** are the norm in parts of northern Sudan, Ethiopia and northern Kenya – dropping tyre pressures can soften the blows. But as few as seven English-speaking borders separate Cairo from Cape Town, and once in Kenya you can follow **sealed highways** all the way through, meaning that down here the right **season** is less critical. With the exception of Mozambique, none of the countries are in the dire straits of Angola, or as pricey as Gabon, though fees at some borders do pile up.

It's worth noting though that as you near the equator the increase in **elevation** creates a much more equable climate, as well as a lushness to the scenery which makes places like Uganda worth the diversion. Away from expensive game parks, mile-for-mile the lowland plains or *veldt* of Tanzania, Mozambique and Botswana can get rather dull.

On this side the **US dollar** is the hard currency of choice; further south the **South African rand** is acceptable in the countries which border RSA. **Hotspots** add up to the easily avoided border regions with South Sudan, eastern Ethiopia and northern Uganda (basically anywhere too close to eastern DRC or Somalia). The South African Automobile Association has a very good website; of particular value on the east side is their Crossborder Information document at 🖳 www.aa.co.za/content/2202.

Highlights include pharaonic Egypt, the desert of Sudan, Ethiopia's highlands and unique Coptic culture, Uganda and the White Nile, the game parks and chilling on the Indian Ocean coast. As you get to Zambia or Botswana, Namibia is also well worth a detour to the west before wrapping it all up.

If it's wildlife spotting you're after, be aware that motorcycles (and other exposed vehicles) are not permitted in most of East Africa's **game parks**. To get in you have to organise a rental car or join a tour – both said to be less expensive in South Africa or Namibia, compared to Kenya and Tanzania. Even then, chances are you'll encounter plenty just riding around on the less busy highways.

EGYPT

Apart from the collapse in regular tourism on which the country depended heavily, not much seems to have changed since the 2011 revolution; behind the scenes the military powerbase remains and so the upheaval may not be over. The **paperwork** on entering with a vehicle is still mind-numbingly protracted and although some claim to manage without one, you'll need an **carnet** (as do most countries on this eastern route) as well as a special driving licence, rented Arabic number plates (for which your deposit is refunded when you leave the country), plus various other documents which you'll lose track of. The oiling of even simple procedures with a little *baksheesh* helps things move along. Just remember, it's not only you who pays and it's only pocket money. The latest details are on the HUBB.

What has changed is **getting to Egypt overland**. Although Tunisia – the source of the Arab Spring protests – remains accessible by ferry from southern Europe, the same cannot be said for Libya (see p254), while immediately to the east the situation in Syria (see p197) is even more dire. Unless you choose to fly your bike in (without local help that will take days to unravel on arrival), at the time of writing overlanders are using a **ferry** service from Mersin in the south-eastern corner of Turkey to Port Said or Alexandria, or ferries from there to Cyprus and on to Israel for a land crossing at Eilat–Taba on the Gulf of Aqaba (Red Sea). Allow a fair expenditure and up to half a day to-ing and fro-ing between offices while keeping a smile going.

Once in Egypt **fuel** is cheap, and the monumental splendours are well known and not to be rushed. You're likely to need to stop in **Cairo** for onward visas anyway, in which case you may wish you'd bought that body armour. You need to get your Sudanese visa before you apply for the Ethiopian one on the west side of the Nile, unless you can leave it till Khartoum (see p276).

In the cool season with time to spare, the **Western Oases** of Bahariya, Farafra and Dakhka make a rewarding excursion. There are checkpoints in and out of every town, but you won't need an escort and can camp out in the desert. As you turn east through Kharga you can cut back to the Nile at Luxor, or even head directly down the west bank to a bridge at Aswan.

Officially you can't roam far west off the oasis route into the so-called Western Desert towards the Great Sand Sea and the Gilf Kebir; for this you need a guide, all sorts of permits and lately armed guards that take months to organise. There's more on this fabulous area in *Sahara Overland*, but most southbound riders have enough to look forward to.

AFRICA – ROUTE OUTLINES

SOUTHBOUND VISAS IN CAIRO

Sudanese embassy in Cairo
3 Ibrahim St., Garden City
(just behind a petrol station)
N29° 59.75' E31° 14.6

Ethiopian embassy in Cairo
21 Mohammed El Ghazali St.
Dokki (near Dokki metro station)
N30° 02.45' E31° 12.26'

Costs are around $30 with the usual array of passport photos as well as a letter of introduction for Brits for the Sudanese visa. The **British embassy** is a couple of minutes west of the Sudanese at 7 Ahmed Ragheb Street (N30° 00.4' E31° 13.9'). They charge about 275LE (£30) to issue it in an hour.

LAKE NASSER FERRY

The Nile Navigation Company's (NNC) ferry goes up and down the lake once a week, at the last count leaving Aswan on Monday afternoons and returning from Wadi Halfa on Wednesday evening, just in time for Friday and the weekend in Aswan when nothing can get done. Journey time is about 20 hours if all goes well. To book a place for you and your bike the NNC has an office in Cairo in the train station at Ramses Square, or try the Nile Maritime Agency, 8 Quasr el Nil. In Aswan, head for the port and follow your nose.

Unlike cars, a motorcycle can be put on the passenger ferry and a recent price from Wadi Halfa up to Aswan was just $80 at Sudanese black market exchange rates.

Should you see it in daylight, the cruise along the lake past the relocated temple at Abu Simbel may be serene, but at Wadi Halfa be ready for a full day of immigration hell. Hiring a recommended fixer to help with the paperwork is worthwhile. For the latest news, possibly including the talked about **land border**, see the HUBB's Sahara forum.

Crossing to Sudan

You might ask yourself why does crossing into Sudan require negotiating a place on a disorganised ferry from **Aswan** across the only artificial lake for miles around (the world's largest), when perfectly good road access exists? The real answer might help explain one of the causes of the 2011 uprisings, but after years of rumours, in 2012 it was announced a **land border** was due to open soon. This being Egypt, it's unlikely to be like a regular land border. Chances are you'll have to be escorted down the west bank to Abu Simbel, from where a ferry will cross Lake Nasser to a dock at Qustul on the Egyptian east bank, itself some 55km north of Wadi Halfa. Press photos and recent Google Earth imagery depicted intact infrastructure on the Egyptian side, but no sign of a road covering the key 20km Sudanese section down to Wadi Halfa. Until that happens the ferry might run from Abu Simbel the 100km directly to Wadi Halfa. Either way, it looks like a short ferry across Lake Nasser will still be necessary as the only Egyptian road is on the west side and Wadi Halfa and the newly built Sudanese roads are on the other.

SUDAN

Even if you weren't expecting Las Vegas on stilts, **Wadi Halfa** is still no oasis. The original settlement is submerged beneath Lake Nasser, but there's everything here including a bank and any number of permit-issuing government offices – including the mandatory Alien Registration Office – helping to turn dollars into documents. Keep a stash of dollars for the **black market**, you'll get around double on a good day, otherwise Sudan can get pricey.

From Wadi Halfa two routes lead south, each tracking one side of the 1000-kilometre tall 'S' bend of the Nile between the border and the capital, Khartoum. The more-commonly driven western route is now **sealed**. It meets the east bank of the Nile about a third of the way to Dongola (Candaca Nubian Guest House is recommended; N19° 11.05' E30° 28.55'). Here you can ferry to the west bank and join a sealed road all the way to Khartoum, or stick to the east bank and head south-east through the desert to the Meröe ferry in the middle of the 'S' bend.

The more isolated **eastern route** follows the **railway** and telegraph line across the Nubian Desert to Abu Hamed on the Nile (ferry) and subsequently

TRIP REPORT
SA TO EUROPE AND BACK ~ KLR 650

AFRICA – ROUTE OUTLINES

Name	Lodie de J
Year of birth	1957
Occupation	Company Director
Nationality	South African
Previous travels	Southern Africa
Bike travels	As above

This trip	SA to Russia, then back 2 years later
Trip duration	Four months up, three months back
Departure date	March 2008
Number in group	1
Distance covered	38,000km

Best day	Wadi Halfa after crossing the desert
Worst day	Hardest: Marsabit, northern Kenya
Favourite places	Senga Bay and a certain Nubian village
Biggest headache	Green Card in Europe on a weekend
Biggest mistake	Taking so much luggage and spares
Pleasant surprise	Sudan in general
Any illness	Stomach bug in Ethiopia and Egypt
Cost of trip	About $9000 up and $6000 back
Other trips planned	Would love to do it again on the KLR

Bike model	Kawasaki KLR 650
Age, mileage	2007 model, 15,000km
Modifications	All-round protection and a back shock
Wish you'd ...	Not had soft shock with heavy boxes
Tyres used	Michelin Anakee
Punctures	None
Type of baggage	Hepco & Becker panniers

Bike's weak point	Brakes!
Strong point	Fuel range, simplicity
Bike problems	Nothing
Accidents	No
Same bike again	Oh yes!
Any advice	The more speed the less travelling

Atbara at the Port Sudan junction, and from there or sooner, tarmac to Khartoum. If it's the cool season and your bike is up to it, on the initial stages of this route you can wander into the desert away from the sandy rail-side track. Depending on the duration of your visa, make the most of it; you'll miss the open desert later on, although don't expect much help from the train up here, it runs about once a week and only a couple of the stops are manned.

Southbound travellers will have done it at Wadi Halfa, but if **coming from Ethiopia** you need to park your spaceship and **register as an Alien** within three days of entering Sudan. In **Khartoum** the Alien Registration Office is close to the US Embassy. The cost is around $50, you'll need photocopies of your passport and Sudanese visa and possibly a letter from your lodgings. You may also need a Permit to Travel ($15) and are supposed to get a photography permit from the Ministry of Tourism, though you can dodge this as long as you're not caught shooting a controversial, feature-length documentary about a telegraph pole.

In **Khartoum** you can get an **Ethiopian visa** often on the same day for $20 by applying in the morning at: Plot No. 04, Block 384BC, just west of the Farouq cemetery (N15° 34.9′ E32° 32.06′). The Blue Nile Sailing Club by the main bridge has had it. Instead try the National Camping Ground (N15° 31.4′ E32° 34.2′) although location, shade and early-morning mosque proximity discourage longer stays. In that case head for the Youth Hostel (N15° 35.5′ E32° 32.4′) with aircon rooms just north of the Ethiopian embassy. Khartoum can be hotter than you expect.

With the exception of Meröe, a couple of hours north of Khartoum on the Atbara road, Sudan doesn't match the historical monuments of Egypt or Ethiopia. However, despite the tedious bureaucracy many travellers report it's all done with a wily smile, much less *baksheesh* than Egypt and the people are among the most hospitable on this route. It's something you won't necessarily be proclaiming about Ethiopia.

South Sudan looks no more accessible than before that country was formed in 2011 and the old route across **Chad** through Darfur doesn't look too promising either.

ETHIOPIA

From Khartoum most head straight down the sealed road to Gedaret and Doka and the border at Gallabat for **Metema** in northwest Ethiopia. On a good day, like a Sunday, Ethiopian immigration and customs formalities are said to be among the quickest in Africa, with insurance available down the road in Gonder. They're happy to stamp your **carnet**, but Ethiopia isn't in the carnet zone (it ought to be excluded from the list on the back of the document). If you get a carnet stamped in anywhere, you *must* get it stamped out when you leave a country otherwise there could be trouble when you decommission it at the end of your travels. But so many travellers have their carnets blithely stamped here that getting a **temporary import permit** (TIP) can take some persuasion.

A 30-day tourist **visa** obtained in Cairo is valid for three months, giving you plenty of time to get here, even if Lake Nasser freezes over and zombie pharaohs stalk the land. Or you can get it in Khartoum. Coming up from the south, you can get an **Ethiopian visa** in Nairobi or Kampala again. Or try **Harare** back down in Zimbabwe where they're issued in a day for $30.

After the barren sands of Sudan, **Ethiopia** is an exceptional looking country. Particularly in the north the greenery and vistas as you climb into the highlands can be a real tonic. The classic northern tour into the Simian Mountains for Axum, past Debre Damos monastery and the climb up to the carved rock churches of Lalibela is not to be missed, even if the roads can hammer the stuffing out of you. With bad roads and steep mountain tracks, picking the right **season** in Ethiopia is important. The months building up to June get very hot in the lowlands of the south and east, while from then to September the rains can disrupt travel anywhere. You'll also be riding as high as 3350m (11,000'), so around January expect to be cold.

Lalibela. © www.duksjourney.net

Unfortunately the welcome from the locals is not always much warmer and, as former Abyssinia got off lightly during the Scramble for Africa and was never successfully colonised for long, the language barrier doesn't help. You may get worn down by the petty aggression and incessant yells of 'You, you, you!'. It's clear from the tone that they're not cheerfully reciting Alvin Stardust's chart-topping 1974 hit. Occasional showers of sticks and stones can also make you wonder what you're doing here, although compared to further south, at least you'll find the police aren't too demanding.

This primary north–south axis through Ethiopia is relatively stable, but the south-west and more especially the Somali borders remain places to avoid. As African capitals go, **Addis Ababa** is not what you've ridden thousands of miles to see, though a Sudanese visa is now said to be easy to get again. To meet up with the gang, stay at Wim's Holland House (N09° 00.6' E38° 45.3').

Though you can tick off **Djibouti** or with much less visa difficulty, **Somaliland** (as distinct from Somali), the double entry Ethiopian visa puts people off, so from Addis drop off the highlands and head into the Rift Valley to take the sealed road south to Moyale into northern Kenya.

THE OMO VALLEY ROUTE TO KENYA

Should you want to string out your Ethiopian adventure, instead of going to Moyale, head down to the **Omo Valley**, among other things the home of Mursi tribeswomen famed for their wooden ear and lip plates. This hyper-arid corner of northwest Kenya is a hot, dusty, windy and stony stage where skirmishes between armed Samburu or Turkana cattle herders can occur. If heading this way from Ethiopia, be sure you have the **fuel range** and think twice about riding it alone. There are several ways of getting there; down to the Rastafarian enclave of Shashemene, 220km south of Addis. Here turn west and then south for Abra Minch and Kondo. If that sounds a bit tame, go southwest from Addis towards Jima, and continue to the Hamar tribal lands around Jinka (fuel), Dimeka and join the other route after Kondo.

From Turmi you pass the turn-off for the Kenyan border 18km before **Omorate** town (aka: Kelem) where you have to go to get your carnet stamped. Back at the turn-off you cross south to Lake Turkana's northeast shore in Kenya and the village of **Illeret** ('Banya Fort' on some maps) where you sign in with the police. You may need to wait till Nairobi to complete all customs and immigration procedures as there are no facilities until then. Pass through the Sibiloi National Park. As you leave, the Park charges you a fee of US$20 per day plus something for the bike. **Loyangalani**, at least 550km from Jinka, may have the first expensive fuel, then continue another 230km to Maralal (fuel), all up some **800km** from Jinka, and on to Baragoi for **Archers Post** on the main road to Nairobi.

Now back on the highway, after a thousand kilometres there's the small matter of crossing the equator and remembering to **ride on the left.** Note too that towns selling fuel will not have guaranteed supplies of petrol.

INTO KENYA VIA MARSABIT

The main route into Kenya from Ethiopia includes the notorious couple of hundred kilometres between Moyale at the Ethiopian border and Marsabit. For years the region was known for occasional raids by armed *shiftas*, Somali bandits a step or three up from squabbling cattle herders.

Talk to the local police and if they advise it, take advantage of any army convoys heading south. Otherwise, overlanders are considered to be too hot a target, inviting the attention of the Kenyan Army, so solo or in convoy, today there's little threat of being shot at or turned over by *shiftas*.

The bumpy ride to Marsabit.
© Caroline Thomas

Moyale

From Moyale the 500km run down through Kenya goes via Marsabit to Isiolo. Chinese road builders are working their way up from the south and although it's not quite a well-lit motorway with regular service stations and roadside recovery, by 2013 or so it may all be sealed and another legendary African track turns to tar.

Right now though the northern section from Marsabit is regularly shortlisted for Africa's Most Corrugated Road Award. This stretch will be taxing on both body and shocks so gird your loins and tighten your nuts – or take the Omo Valley route via Lake Turkana as detailed earlier and where you get what you asked for.

The Moyale road is a mixture of mud, sand, potholes and rocks you wouldn't expect to encounter on a main border route. Halfway along, **Marsabit** doesn't offer much in the way of first class accommodation, however er many overlanders choose to stay at the renowned Henry's Camp (ask for 'Henry the Swiss') on the west side of town (N02° 20.75′ E37° 58.0′). The final 250km from Marsabit to Isiolo eases up with the southern half now glistening tar which is inching towards Moyale year by year.

East and Southern Africa

WITH ENZO ELPHICK-POOLEY AND DAWIE DU PLESSIS

Coming from the north, or less likely, the west, most trans-African riders customarily take a breather and get repairs done in **Kenya**, sub-Saharan Africa's most visited and touristy country after South Africa.

Along with a dramatic improvement in the road and tourist infrastructure (apart from Moyale–Marsabit), you also start **riding on the left** from here all the way down to the Cape, **English** is spoken and, depending on your nationality, the worst of the itinerary-restricting **visa hassles** should be over.

But the human psyche being what it is, it can all become a bit of a parade or extended *safari* (the Swahili word for 'journey') as you hop from one superbly situated lodge to the next, while dodging rowdy backpacker haunts or overland truck groups. Suddenly, it's like Southeast Asia with endless choices and a cold beer always in the fridge. After too much easy living, some profess a nostalgia for the rough travelling in Ethiopia and Sudan, places which may have been rushed through early in your African experience for fear of something going wrong.

In East Africa most riders **carry on camping** from around $10 per person as, along with national park entry fees (where accessible), fuel prices and tempting supermarkets, things can get **expensive**. A few lodging recommendations are given in the text, but **online** is clearly the place to see what's new – including LP's Thorn Tree or even Trip Advisor.

INTO KENYA

Note that if coming up with a South African registered bike, Kenya is the first country that may be a headache to enter. It requires all vehicles from outside the East African Community (EAC) to have a **carnet** as well as a licence disc for a 'Foreign Private Vehicle' (FPV) costing $40 a month at the border, or $100 for three months from the immigration office at Nyayo House in Nairobi (S01° 17.2' E36° 49.1').

Wherever you're coming from, armed with your FPV, a carnet and your COMESA Yellow Card (or local insurance bought as you entered the country), you'll be all set to face down any bribe-extorting policeman. The **COMESA Yellow Card** programme (🖥 http://programmes.comesa.int) is similar to the Green Card issued in the EU and provides **extension** to your already obtained third party motor insurance in the following member states: Burundi, Democratic Republic of Congo, Eritrea, Ethiopia, Kenya, Malawi, Rwanda, Uganda, Tanzania, Zambia and Zimbabwe. Like a Green Card it isn't valid in the issuing country and coming from the south, Zambia is much less expensive than South Africa.

Police road blocks in Kenya concentrate around major towns and most will probably wave a foreign biker through, though not if you're caught speeding. **Reflective patches** on jackets became a new rule in 2012 to reduce the local moto death rate, though it's not clear if this gets enforced or applies

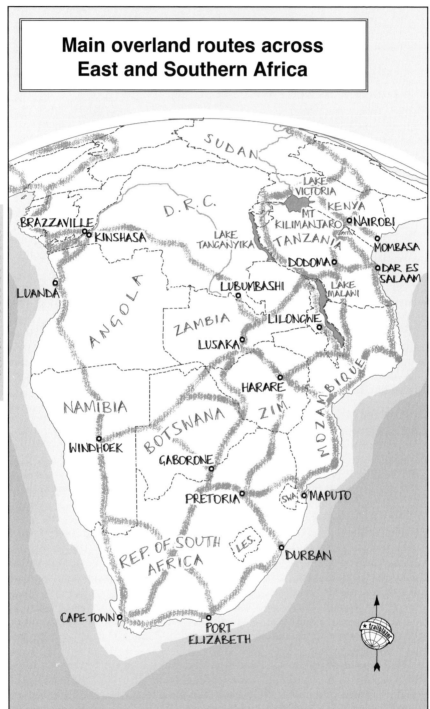

Main overland routes across East and Southern Africa

RWANDA AND BURUNDI

Entering from Uganda near the Parc des Volcans, **Rwanda** doesn't require visas for UK citizens, they'll just stamp your passport. This is a beautiful country too, but some travellers find it quite 'hard' by regional standards as the locals aren't really interested in travellers or tourism; they have their hands full with aid workers and the UN.

Camping does not exist as elsewhere in East Africa, so Presbyterian missions are your best bet, and along with near-European **fuel prices** and national parks fees, it becomes an expensive proposition. Furthermore, currently Rwandan **ATMs** only accept local bank cards so arrive with plenty of dollars to exchange, though some banks will advance cash on Visa cards.

To the south, **Burundi** may no longer issue **visas** at the border so pick them up from the embassy on Boulevard de l'Umuganda, Kigali west (S01° 56.5' E30° 05.2'). With that you can take a big loop via Makebuko to Bujumbura and then down the east shore of Lake Tanganyika to Mabanda to cross into Tanzania heading for Kigoma.

If you don't want to visit Burundi you can leave Rwanda via the border post either side of the bridge at Kagera River, however the route south alongside Lake Tanganyika is a rough and best not attempted alone. Instead, you can head east to Mwanza at the southern end of Lake Victoria and on eastwards to the Serengeti, adjacent to Kenya's Masai Mara and where the wildebeest are stamping their hooves and calling your name. Or, head south for Mbeya and so to Zambia via the Tunduma border post.

to foreign bikers (similar reflective patch regulations have been adopted in France). However, as elsewhere in sub-Saharan Africa you'll find the occasional drunk cop stationed at a roadblock looking for a cash advance. Just make sure you get into the habit of having all your paperwork handy and always ask for a receipt for all on the spot 'fines' because that'll usually put off anyone who's up to no good. Another good counter-scam is to claim your embassy insists you photograph and report all fine/receipt incidents immediately, to counter any possibility of corruption which has been known to occur in these parts.

Towards Nairobi

From **Isiolo** you'll no doubt want to stop at Nanyuki, made famous in a thousand snaps because it straddles the **equator**. There's not a lot else in Nanyuki apart from basic groceries and a few banks, although there's camping at the Somali pastoralist-styled Nanyuki River Camel Camp, 4km northwest of town on the road to Rumuruti, as well as food at the *Trout Tree Restaurant* built in a huge fig tree a few kilometres south of Nanyuki, just past an airstrip.

Watching the GPS count down and arriving at the equator will be an event you're unlikely to have to yourself, though it's a good excuse to get off and stretch your legs before you reach Mount Kenya. The road to Nairobi passes west of the mountain with another excellent campsite at Naro Moro River Lodge with good food. It's one of the base camps for those who want to have a crack at reaching the 5199-metre (17,057') summit of the mountain. From here it's a straight 200km run to Nairobi. The road starts as reasonable tar but you'll have to look out for the occasional tyre-splitting pothole.

Nairobi

As you near Nairobi, the road deteriorates, as does the quality of the driving, especially from *matatu* (minibus taxi) drivers. Passing Thika you'll be entering the city from the northeast so be prepared for several large, chaotic, round-abouts. If you brought your 'Ben Hur' wheel spikes, now's the time to fit them. One roundabout is where the A2 road filters down to Forrest Road; another is at the junction of Forrest and Ngara Roads and then there's a real bottleneck at the bottom of Museum Hill. Whatever you do, **know where you're going in Nairobi** and try to avoid the rush hours, especially on the Uhuru and Mombasa Roads.

R&R at Jungle Junction in Nairobi.
© Ken Thomas

Dealing with Nairobi

The risk of **crime** in Nairobi is overrated, especially if you're riding a battered bike (can it be anything else by now?). Overlanders are quite a common sight, so the risk of robbery is low. But as with any big city, in Nairobi you want to keep your wits about you and have a destination in mind long before you get there.

If you're entering Nairobi from the north-east and are heading towards the western side of the city where many **overlanders hang out**, when you hit the Museum Hill roundabout, get on the Waiyaki Highway (an extension of Uhuru to Mombasa Road) and head back out of town. Just after the ABC Plaza (there's a good butchers and supermarket here), turn left and take a short cut along James Gicheru Road. This will take you to either **Jungle Junction** (S01° 17.3′ E36° 45.6′) or **Upper Hill Campsite** (S01° 17.2′ E36° 46.4′), a couple of kilometres east of the junction.

WEST TO UGANDA

Depending on the season, the lush highlands and cool lakes of Uganda can also be a tonic after Sudan and Ethiopia. Many travellers are startled by this verdant upland region because there is no shortage of the more arid savannah further south.

Providing you steer clear of the South Sudan border, Uganda can be a rich experience which as yet lacks Kenya's commercialism or the prices found further south. Cost-wise, gorilla spotting in the rainforests is an exception, but there's rafting on the Nile at Jinja or you could just spin down by a lake. With the relatively inexpensive fuel, many overlanders regard Uganda as an East African favourite. **Visas** for Brits and Western Europeans are no hassle ($50), but make sure you have the COMESA Yellow Card, or buy it at the border.

The road out of Nairobi passes Lake Naivasha, 90km northwest of Nairobi as well as Lake Nakuru another 70km further on. Both are in the **Rift Valley** and offer accommodation for overlanders, such as Fisherman's Camp (S00° 49.5′ E36° 20.06′) set at a cool 1890m (6200′) on the south side of Lake Naivasha, and Kembu Campsite (S00° 17′ 59.0′, E35° 54.0′) 25km west of Lake Nakuru, and another 1000 feet higher. Crossing the **equator**, this route continues past Lake Baringo and Lake Bogoria before getting to **Eldoret** where there's another overlander-friendly campsite, New Naiberi River Campsite (N00° 26.83′ E35° 25.3′), 16km southeast of Eldoret.

Crossing into **Uganda**, the main road takes a turn towards Lake Victoria and Jinja, a popular place for white water rafting which may well have the same discolouring effect on your hair. If you decide to raft with them, Nile River Explorers at Bujagali Falls are recommended as well as offering inexpensive camping and good facilities including a bar and showers.

Travelling west, you reach **Kampala** where there's plenty of overland-friendly accommodation. If coming up from the south, not least Kenya, travellers find Kampala a relaxed and inexpensive capital. The established Red Chilli Hideaway is 5km east of the city centre (N00° 19.21, E32° 37.8'). North of Kampala, the Red Chilli folk also have a rest house at Murchison's Falls, 250km north of Kampala; a good place to base yourself if you're visiting Murchison Falls National Park.

Along with the vast **Lake Victoria**, Uganda shares several smaller lakes with its neighbours, including Lake Albert and Lake Edward. If you're travelling along the south shore of Lake Albert then you may visit the Kibale Forest National Park and the Kibale Forest Primate Reserve. Here the Original Lake Nkuruba Community Campsite offers camping right next to the best of the crater lakes on a manicured lawn, and in Kibale the Royal Supermarket (S01° 15.14' E29° 59.23') offers good exchange rates.

West of Kibale is Lake Bunyonyi lying between Kisoro and Kabale, close to the Rwandan border. East of town you'll find Lake Bunyonyi Overland Resort (S01° 16.3' E29° 56.36'), another great camp with inexpensive rates, a range of accommodation, a restaurant and a bar where the overland tour groups cut loose.

The road from Kibale to Kisoro looks due for asphalting, and as you progress southwest you're now heading towards the **Rwenzori Mountains**, Bwindi National Park, the Virunga Mountains, Rwanda's Parc des Volcans and of course, Dian Fossey's famous troop of silverback gorillas.

East to the coast

By the time most southbound overlanders reach Kenya, the idea of laying up on an **Indian Ocean beach** while a local mechanic tends to your bike is irresistible. Mombasa, Lamu or any of the other small resorts up and down the Indian Ocean coast are perfect places to recuperate before heading south to Tanzania. If you head to **Mombasa**, first make sure you survive the ride. Crashes with matatus are prevalent on this road and Athi River, 30km from Nairobi is particularly notorious.

KENYA TO TANZANIA

As travel hardships ease beyond Kenya, suitably refreshed and with your bike now running like the Swiss watch it once was, you can now entertain all sorts of ways of complicating things again. Going south into **Tanzania**, world-class game parks and natural spectacles abound, including Kilimanjaro, the Ngorongoro Crater and the Serengeti, as well as Dar es Salaam and Zanzibar on the Indian Ocean. From Nairobi there are **two main ways** to get south: either the well trodden route through Namanga, Moshi, Same and Korogwe – or from Mombasa south along the coast through the Lunga Lunga–Hora Hora border post and on to Tanga in Tanzania. Be aware that the road between Tanga and Hora Hora is dreadful and so other vehicles are rare.

284 EAST AND SOUTHERN AFRICA

Kenya-Tanzania border

Whichever you decide, at the Tanzanian **border** you'll get a 90-day tourist visa for $50 (or a transit visa for $30, although you'll need a full tourist visa to visit Zanzibar) and a **Temporary Import Permit** (TIP) for your bike for another 50 bucks. The choice is yours as to whether you use your carnet or not, but a TIP requires using a customs agent to clear the bike. No bond is required, but it takes an extra hour and of course the agent charges for the service. There is also a fuel levy or road tax of $25.

Exiting Kenya via the Namanga border post, 170km south of Nairobi, is a relatively painless business: the only irritation may be the many Maasai women who throng around, pressing their colourful wares on you.

Kenya may well have caught up by now, but in Tanzania and in many countries south of here, watch out for **speed traps** with the choice of an on-the-spot 'fine' or your day in court. One thing to note: always check that their speed guns are actually working. Quite often officers are just looking for a 'kitu kidogo' ('a little something'), although this is more prevalent in Kenya than Tanzania.

Kenya to Tanzania via Namanga

Once through the border you'll find Tanzania's main highways are well maintained, although they deteriorate quickly out bush (as does the use of English, Swahili's the lingua franca here more than in Kenya).

Expect a band of unsigned and especially acute **speed bumps** at the beginning of any village. The other thing you'll learn to love or loathe, is the Tanzanian Police department in their powder blue uniforms.

Heading south to **Arusha**, Tanzania's safari hub, there are lots of places to stay, from 1970s-style hotels in town to camping out of town at places like Meserani Snake Park, about 25km west of Arusha on the Dodoma Road. This is also the way to Lake Manyara, the Ngorongoro Crater and the Serengeti.

East leads to Moshi, the tourist hub for Kilimanjaro, and again full of places to stay, most geared up to accommodate tourists and overlanders with bars, food and secure parking. There are also **campsites** just out of town such as Maasai Camp in Arusha (noisy at weekends) or the nicer and cheaper Marungu Campsite on the way to Kilimanjaro. If you're saddle weary and serious about climbing Kili, Trailblazer has the *Kilimanjaro* guidebook for you or check out the author's informative website: 💻 www.climbmountkili manjaro.com.

The road to Dar es Salaam

Heading for Dar, if you fancy visiting historic Bagamoyo on the way – once the end of the trail for slaves heading to Arabia – then head south from Segera where, 37km north of Chalinze at Msata (S06° 20.0′ E38° 23.4′) there's a 60km long track running east to a former old trading post. From Bagamoyo to Dar is another 70 clicks down along the coast. Alternatively, if heading northward, 44km east at Chalinze on the road to Dar, at Mlandizi (S06° 43.0′ E38° 44.3′) you'll find a gravel track leading north to Bagamoyo.

Dar es Salaam is another one of those cities whose romance is these days more a sepia-tinted memory than reality, but it's a lot more agreeable than many African cities. Primarily it's the jumping off point for Zanzibar or the

Pemba islands (no bikes allowed). Traditionally overlanders stay north of Dar at Silversands, however there are many more campsites on the coast to the southeast via a ferry over the harbour mouth. They include Kipepeo Camp (S06° 51.1', E39° 21.6') right on the beach with chalets or camping, plus secure parking while you visit the islands, or the nearby Makadi Beach Resort. The YMCA in town can also look after your bike for a small fee.

SOUTH OF TANZANIA

Whether you've taken the road to Arusha, past Kilimanjaro, or down the coast, both roads meet at Segera before continuing south to **Chalinze** where you can either turn east for Dar es Salaam or west on to Morogoro. For most overlanders it's a choice between keeping inland for Malawi and Zambia, or east for Mozambique and the coast. The latter can lead you directly to the eastern border with South Africa, from where Cape Town and the end of the road is less than 2000km away. As with many such crossroads, much will depend on the state of you, your wallet and your bike, as well as your capacity for more adventure and border games.

Tanzania to Zambia

If you skipped Dar and pushed on to **Morogoro** there's plenty of accommodation here, such as the well-established New Acropol Hotel (S06° 49.5' E37° 40.4') on the old Dar road running south of town. Other than that, there's not much to the place. You're in the Mikumi National Park here, one of the few you can ride through so there's a chance to see giraffe, zebras and elephants if you've not seen any yet, as well as warnings for hippos.

Coming down from Morogoro, the next major town is **Iringa** (Iringa Farm has great camping), with access to the Ruaha National Park. From Iringa, heading on south and west it's a long trek to Mbeya. Here, many travellers overnight at Karibuni Centre mission lodge, about 2km southwest of the town centre (S08° 54.6' E33° 26.6'). The Tunduma border post with Zambia is now 100km down the road where again, all visas and other papers can be bought at the border.

Zambia

Like Uganda, Zambia delivers a surprisingly verdant country that's the home of the two Luangwa National Parks. Brits pay $50 for a visa at the border where you might also be asked to cough up for a carbon emissions tax, $30 road access fee plus motor insurance sold for one or three months ($20), if you don't have a COMESA Yellow Card. If heading south check that bikes don't require reflective stickers, as foreign cars do.

Climate-wise, you're south of the equator now so the cool dry season is from May to August; the build-up sets in with the rains letting loose from December until April when most tracks become impassable.

Slow traffic in Zambia.
© www.duksjourney.net

AFRICA – ROUTE OUTLINES

Stealthily, inch by inch, the zebras closed in.
© Ken Thomas

Taking a short cut by **crossing DRC** via Sakania is said to be OK but it's another visa; the western border crossing with Angola is very rarely used by travellers. Elsewhere the main roads are in good condition; you can shoot across Zambia in three days if the pipes are calling, or you can spend time and a whole lot of money in the national parks; even waterfalls can cost you $15 to look at. As often in sub-Saharan Africa, the capital **Lusaka** is a place to be wary after dark with tourist resorts like **Livingstone** near Victoria Falls also attracting nocturnal thieves and muggers.

The road from Tanzania enters Zambia at the Tunduma–Nakonde border post which can be particularly overwhelming due to the sheer number of trucks, money changers and touts offering to expedite your paperwork for a fee. Park up outside immigration, roll your sleeves up and get stuck in. Once you've cleared customs, had your carnet stamped and paid all the rest, they open the barrier and let you loose.

This road is known as the 'TanZam Highway' and passes the North and South Luangwa National Parks to its south and Kapishya Hot Springs to the north. Also in this area is Buffalo Camp (S11° 55.3' E32° 15.6'), popular with overland trucks visiting the North Luangwa National Park.

Between Shiwa N'Gandu and Kapiri Mposhi (the main terminal before heading north to the DRC border) there isn't much reasonable accommodation, however you can turn off the main road at Serenje and stay at Mapontela Guesthouse run by an ex-Peace Corp volunteer.

From here run west to Kapiri Mposhi where you take the main road south for Lusaka. There are lots of places to stay in Lusaka itself, otherwise 50km before you enter the city, there's helpful Fringilla Lodge.

Your choice now is either to continue south-east and enter Zimbabwe through Chirundu, or head west to Kaufe National Park 200km west of Lusaka where Mukambi Lodge on the Lunga River (S14° 58.7', E25° 59.6') is recommended. Otherwise, head past Choma to Livingstone and the **Victoria Falls,** close to where Namibia, Botswana and Zimbabwe meet Zambia.

Tanzania to Malawi

Backing up a bit, the other main route from Tanzania runs south to **Malawi**. About 10km east of Mbeya at Uyole, turn south on the B345 road and enter Malawi at the Songwe–Kasumulu border post alongside Lake Malawi. Show your COMESA or buy **insurance** and a TIP for 1200 Malawi kwatcha (MK) if your carnet needs a rest.

The road starts close to the shore and passing Karonga, it then climbs towards Mzuzu and the Viphya Mountains on the way to the capital, **Lilongwe**. Here the lakeside camping and lodge at Chintheche Inn (S11° 52.9', E34° 10.1') 4km south of that town, makes a good place to stop. You can also take the lakeside road which passes through Nkhata Bay and Senga. Both this road and the main road from Lilongwe carry on to the south end of the lake where you'll find Monkey Bay on **Cape Maclear**, another overlanders' favourite.

There are other border posts in the south of Malawi, but most are now heading for South Luangwa National Park in Zambia and so need to retrace their steps back to Lilongwe, before heading 110km west for the Mchinji crossing to Chipata in Zambia.

In Malawi

Malawi can be a place to rest up, but it can also get **expensive**, with fuel at near-European prices and 8% charged on Visa card transactions. Be aware too of the **national speed limit** of 80kph out of towns. For a place to camp in the capital, Lilongwe, the central Sanctuary Lodge on Youth Drive (S13° 58.1' E33° 47.2') has been recommended in preference to the better known Golf Course a couple of kilometres to the south.

MOZAMBIQUE

One of Africa's oldest former colonies, **Mozambique** was never the jewel in Portugal's crown and ended up more exploited and less developed than most. As elsewhere, independence led to a ruinous civil war (stirred by neighbouring countries) from which Mozambique is still recovering.

For the two-wheeled traveller the country's sole attraction is its comparatively undeveloped **coastline**. Along with a visit to Ilha de Mozambique, if you've not had your statutory week off by the Indian Ocean yet, then the resorts opposite the Bazaruto Islands near **Vilanculos** in the far south could be what you're after.

Inland you'll find not much more than a hot arid plain until you rise up into the mountains bordering the east side of Lake Nyasa (Lake Malawi). Few people venture here so it's bound to be an adventure.

Like much of the region, the **police** in Mozambique have a reputation for being a little overzealous, so observe the speed limits or pay the price. If pulled over they may want to see all the usual papers.

The infrastructure in Mozambique may not be quite as trashed as Angola's, but both of these poor countries share the menace of **landmines**. It's why most overlanders still view Mozambique as a short transit rather than a place to explore. If time, money or will are drying up, **cross into South Africa** at Ressano-Garcia (95km northwest of Maputo) for Lemombo (Kotmatipoort) south of the famous Kruger Park. Coming into Mozambique, visas are expensive here; they're cheaper coming from Swaziland.

In May 2010, 250km upriver from the coast, between Mtambatswala village in Tanzania and Negomano in Mozambique, the **Unity Bridge** across the Rovuma River was inaugurated by the respective presidents. All-weather roads to the crossing may not be complete, but the fact that there's a proper bridge at all is half the battle won.

There's another route further inland towards Lake Malawi. Head south from Makambako to Songea, and then another 100km south to cross the bridge over the Rovuma (presumably at S11° 34.7' E35° 25.7'; maps around here are pretty lean). **Border formalities** can be rather informal on both sides, but you continue south to Lupilchi (aka: Segunda Congresso or Olivença) for Cobue on Lake Nyasa (Lake Malawi), Metangula and so Lichinga, back on the main road network. You can now strike out for Malawi at Mandimba by Lake Nyasa, or cross at Milange further south, for Zimbabwe via the infamous Tete Corridor (the road from Zimbabwe to Malawi via the Zambezi bridge at Tete). Or head for the coast at Inhambane to meet the backpackers.

Moz' visa in Lilongwe, Malawi

Convention Drive, City Centre, S13° 57.7' E33° 47.3'
You'll need: two photos, one form, 5700MK (under $40). Issued same day.

For a great up-to-date source of information on overland travel in Mozambique, check out ⌨ www.mozguide.com.

AFRICA – ROUTE OUTLINES

ZAMBIA TO BOTSWANA

From Kazungula you can catch the ferry across the Zambezi to **Botswana**. As you approach the crossing, ride past the long line of trucks at the side of the road to the passenger vehicle queue.

Once there you need to pay around 20 pula for a Road Fund (about $3) which is valid till the end of the year, as well as a Road Permit of P50 for a single transit. There's no COMESA here, so insurance is about P50 for 90 days.

Reassuring sign in Namibia
© Ken Thomas

Considered a sub-Saharan success story, Botswana has taken the 'high quality, low impact' tourism route and if you're not yet 'gamed-out', a number of reserves and national parks fill nearly a fifth of the country, including Chobe close to the above border post, as well as Moremi Wildlife Reserve in the Okavango Delta, the Central Kalahari Game Reserve and the incredible Makgadikgadi Salt Pans.

If you've chosen to string out the impending end of the road, the only entry into **Namibia** outside of the Caprivi Strip is at Mamuno, west of the Central Kalahari Game Reserve.

ZIMBABWE

Following Zimbabwe's economic collapse in 2008 the US dollar is now the *de facto* currency. Food, fuel and spare parts are again available; if a Zimbabwean can make a profit out of it and it can be sourced in Botswana or South Africa, then you can buy it.

Unlike white farmers and members of the MDC, **security** for visitors has never been a problem. However, there are a lot of poor people and beggars on the streets of Harare or Victoria Falls. They aren't dangerous, just the product of Mugabe's disastrous Land Reform Programme.

Police, riding and currency

The **police** in their khaki uniforms are usually educated, polite and speak English; the paramilitary police in dark blue outfits with ZRP flashes may not be as polite but despite what you might think, you won't be robbed blind by the authorities. **Roadblocks** are plentiful and you may occasionally be asked for a little food or drink, but the outright solicitation of bribes is rare.

Take care though, **speed traps** abound and Zimbabwe has instituted a system of road tolls – usually with a police-manned toll gate just outside most towns. As a biker you'll be waved through most road blocks.

Although the US dollar is now the currency, you can also use the South African rand or Botswanan pula, especially in the west and south. US dollars come from ATMs in all major cities. You'll need lots of **small denomination** notes for the toll roads – usually one dollar. There's no currency **black market** and any such suggested transactions may be a trick.

T R I P   R E P O R T
TRANS AFRICA ~ YAMAHA XT600E

Name	Dan W
Year of birth	1971
Occupation	Writer
Nationality	British
Previous travels	Yep
Bike travels	India, Europe, Morocco and USA

This trip	UK to Togo – boat, then southern Africa
Trip duration	11 months
Departure date	December 2001
Number in group	1
Distance covered	20,000 miles

Best day	One-way ticket to Tangier & many more
Worst day	Often become the best days when over
Favourite places	Tangier, Bissau, Maputo, Pemba...
Biggest headache	My own lack of preparation
Biggest mistake	Stopping mid-way for a funeral
Pleasant surprise	Other people
Any illness	Malaria – felt like an absinthe hangover
Cost of trip	That's between me and the Tuareg
Other trips planned	The Americas came next

Bike model	Yamaha XT600E
Age, mileage	Brand new
Modifications	Kick-start, handguards, bigger tank
Wish you'd ...	thought about my luggage more
Tyres used	Pirelli MT21s, Metzeler crossers
Punctures	Yes
Type of baggage	Ortlieb throwovers

Bike's weak point	None, really – soft springs, softer power
Strong point	Soft springs/power ideal for a first-timer
Bike problems	Carb' clogged, ignition mangled by thief
Accidents	A couple but nothing to worry about
Same bike again	No, I need something sexier
Any advice	Chill out, slow down, enjoy it

Zambia to Zimbabwe via Victoria Falls

Leaving Lusaka it's a 500km ride to **Livingstone** which has picked up on the 'adrenalin' activities offered over the border at the tourist resort of Victoria Falls. Accommodation for backpackers and overlanders can be found at places like Fawlty Towers (S17° 51.3' E25° 51.3'), Jollyboys Backpackers (S17° 50.9' E25° 51.3') behind the Livingstone Museum, or Maramba River Lodge, out of town, quiet and safe.

Victoria Falls can be an easy border. After **checking out of Zambia** you cross the bridge over the Zambezi from which tourists may be hurling themselves into the abyss below. Once on the Zimbabwean side, park up and go into the little office to get your visa. Be prepared to pay $55 for a visa; $55 for your TIP (carnets aren't valid but give it a go); more for insurance if you don't have COMESA, a Road Access fee, possibly a Carbon Tax and whatever else they've come up with since.

Victoria Falls, Hwange and Bulawayo

Victoria Falls is the name of both the waterfall and the small Zimbabwean resort. Accommodation ranges from five-star hotels to basic camping at the municipal campsite (S17° 55.5' E25° 50.2') or national park lodges. There are a few fast food joints in town, but make sure you spend an evening at The Boma (S17° 55.3' E25° 49.2') to get a taste of the wildlife you couldn't eat at home without getting raided by the RSPCA.

Food and fuel are plentiful at the Falls, although for spare parts or mechanics you'll need to get to Hwange, 100km south. Hwange lends its name to Zimbabwe's largest national park. There's only one place to stay in **Hwange** town and that's the Baobab Hotel (S18° 20.65' E26° 30.2') on top of the hill to the north of the main road to Bulawayo.

Carrying on east from Hwange leads to Lake Kariba and the small resort of Mlibizi, the lake's southwestern terminal for the ferry. Passing by Mlibizi is the road to Binga where you'll find a little piece of paradise called Masumu River Lodge (S17° 35.4' E27° 25.3') right by the lake.

Bulawayo is a lovely quiet city with wide open streets and a relaxed, friendly atmosphere. There's a municipal campsite (S20° 09.5' E28° 35.6'), but a better choice might be some of the small lodges in the southeastern suburbs, such as Burkes' Paradise (S20° 12.7' E28° 35.9'). Having refreshed yourself in Bulawayo, you're ready for quite possibly your last African border crossing into South Africa.

Zambia to Zimbabwe via Chirundu

Chirundu border post is about 150km southeast of Lusaka and after passing the turn-off for Livingstone, you start your descent towards the Zambezi River and the border. Being the main trade route between Lusaka and Harare, it can be blocked for days by overturned or trapped lorries. If you look over the edge you'll see the wrecks of trucks that didn't make the bends.

Entering Zimbabwe at Chirundu finds you close to various safari and hunting areas that bound the western edge of Mana Pools National Park. This is a truly amazing wilderness area for foot and canoe safaris. The park charges at least $20 per person for campsites that really are in a wilderness, so the wildlife can be a concern, if they let you in at all. You'll need to pay in

Marangora before heading back into the park along the atrocious 70km of dirt to Nyamepi Parks Office. From Makuti you can take a ride down to Kariba where a ferry might be running to take you all the way to the lake's south-western end at Mlibizi – otherwise, carry on towards Harare.

Harare is a bland but neat city laid out in a grid fashion, rather like Bulawayo. The Rufaro Stadium is where Bob Marley and Paul Simon played during Zimbabwe's 1980 independence celebrations; there hasn't been a lot to

---

SOUTHERN AFRICA ONLINE

What some grandly call overlanding is simply recreation to many South Africans. They also benefit from minimal carnet or visa issues across southern Africa right up to DRC and Kenya. As in Australia, a huge off-road scene exists with books, DVDs, tours, detailed GPS routes and of course forums.

Although aimed at 4x4s, the **South African Overland Forum** covers six country categories plus the South African former homelands, medical and GPS chat. 🖳 www.overland.co.za.

SELLING BIKES IN OR FROM SOUTH AFRICA

Selling a foreign-registered bike in South Africa at the end of your ride will attract approximately 65% tax. This doesn't apply to SA residents returning home after more than a year with a bike in their name for that time, unless it was registered before 2000. There are also restrictions on selling it on again within two years. For the full story see 🖳 www.sars.gov.za.

Coming the other way, selling a South African-registered bike in the UK for example, will be subject to VAT of 20% plus 10% import tax, along with a not-too-stringent test of roadworthiness.

FLYING A BIKE OUT OF SOUTH AFRICA

Flying my TTR home from Cape Town after riding down through Africa was just about as easy as sending a parcel home. On arrival I contacted Air Menzies (AMI) who'd been mentioned on the HUBB. They advised me to buy my ticket home, then drop the TTR to the AMI's depot (S33° 57.7' E18° 35.6') the day before.

Here I removed the front wheel, mudguard, screen and handlebars to make the package fit on a pallet with the wheel and luggage stowed around it (see right). The tank was half full, the tyres weren't deflated but the battery was disconnected. They then nailed the forks in place with wooden blocks and strapped everything down.

The bike and gear weighed in at 131kg for which I was charged 8500 rand (£670; they take cash only from private customers) and directed to the nearby customs office for carnet stamping. They also inspected the bike, then the Air Way Bill and a Dangerous Goods certificate were issued and I got a lift back to my airport motel. Job done.

On the way home I recognised the BA flight number on the Air Way Bill was the same as my flight, but a few days later, so it was strange to be flying home thinking my bike could be in the hold.

The tracking page on BA's website confirmed my bike had landed in the UK, so I nipped off to BA Cargo in a van, where the staff assisted in the straightforward process of customs clearance (as personal effects, only the bike ownership papers were needed), and released the bike.

KEN THOMAS

TRIP REPORT
CAPE TOWN TO NAMIBIA~ KTM 950

Name	Graham B
Year of birth	1956
Occupation	Businessman
Nationality	South African
Previous travels	Many places in the world
Bike travels	Off road in southern Africa since 1978

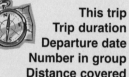

This trip	Cape Town to Namib desert
Trip duration	Ten days
Departure date	May 2010
Number in group	1
Distance covered	4000km

Best day	Exploring Ai-Ais and Richtersveld
Worst day	SA side on Richtersveld on rocky track
Favourite places	In the middle of the desert
Biggest headache	The thick sand in Kalahari
Biggest mistake	Should have taken three weeks
Pleasant surprise	No flats this time
Any illness	No
Cost of trip	R2000
Other trips planned	Karoo, and more Namibia

Bike model	KTM 950
Age, mileage	30,000km
Modifications	None really
Wish you'd ...	had a bigger fuel range
Tyres used	Pirelli Scorpions
Punctures	No
Type of baggage	Soft panniers

Bike's weak point	Fuel tank could be bigger
Strong point	Magic bike to ride
Bike problems	Nine
Accidents	None
Same bike again	Yes, or my 1978 XT500
Any advice	Make sure you have the right tools

celebrate since. From Harare you can ride south-east and enter Mozambique at Nyamapanda or go directly east to visit Mutare, Mount Nyangani and the beautiful Vumba mountains before crossing into Mozambique.

Zimbabwe to South Africa via Beitbridge

Both routes south from Harare and Bulawayo end at the hot, dusty town of **Beitbridge**, the major crossing between Zimbabwe and **South Africa**. It's well known for its crippling summer heat and the huge volume of traffic that passes through during the holiday seasons, so knowing this you may want to use a less busy border. For you the process is relatively simple but can take hours, even on the South African side.

Show your carnet if you've come from Zimbabwe or Mozambique (no need to show it or get it stamped if you've come from Botswana or Namibia). Basic **third party insurance** is now included in the price of SA fuel. If staying for a while more comprehensive insurance is available.

Once clear of Beitbridge or any other border with the adjacent countries, you'll be on some of the best roads in Africa and suddenly find yourself the slowest thing on the road whilst still being the target for every speed cop with a twitchy finger, but try as they might they can't touch you now. The struggle is over and the end (or turning point) is in sight.

TTR approaches the finishing line.
© Ken Thomas

6 **LATIN AMERICA ROUTE OUTLINES**

L ike sub-Saharan Africa, for North Americans in particular, Latin America conjures up its fair share of negative images: kidnapping, banditry and roadside police who act like petty criminals. The standard of living as well as the state of security can vary greatly from country to country or even regionally, but as usual, once you actually ride there the reality is far more benign.

Above all, compared to parts of Africa and Asia, the lack of a requirement for **carnets and most visas** in advance greatly simplifies border crossings, particularly in South America; although in Central America they still like to make a meal of it. What's notable here is that no two travellers seem to pay the same fees at a border, and some pay nothing at all to get an exit stamp or fill out a form. Clearly, some officials try it on and some riders manage to neutralise their efforts, but we're talking a couple of dollars here and there.

Right across the region a temporary vehicle import permit (TIP) is readily issued and lasts around three months. Just remember to cancel your TIP before leaving a country; it's not always demanded but if you come back your bike will still be registered and you could be in for a fine or other problems. A **Yellow Fever certificate** may also be required at some borders.

The cost of living is not always so modest and compared to the US, in most places **fuel** will be more expensive. And whatever the season (see p312), there's a decent network of sealed roads so a dual sport is not necessary, although there's as much off-road action as you can cram between the knobs of a TKC. Most will find the crazy local driving standards adventure enough, particularly in Peru.

No surprise that the **US dollar** is the most useful hard currency and is the official local currency in El Salvador, Panama and Ecuador. For other local places, wait until you're in the country and then change just enough to get you to an ATM where you'll get the regular exchange rate, although the exception is Venezuela, where currently a currency black market thrives.

Knowing **Spanish** will transform your trip outside Brazil and reduces 'gringo' taxes. Otherwise, the US-based 🖳 advrider.com will be a good resource for ride reports and information, for example the stickies in the Trip planning> Americas> forum.

Mexico and Central America

WITH GRAHAM JACKSON

Images of *banditos*, illegal immigrant tunnels and deranged drug cartel executions permeate the outsiders' view of Mexico, which has been going through a bad patch these last few years. Problems exist, but they're mainly in the north in places like Juarez, while Tijuana can also intimidate travellers facing their first visit. You have to cross the north to go south but 25 miles south of the border things ease considerably, so plan to make it well beyond this buffer zone. The crossing into Mexico is actually pretty easy and efficient, and little notice will be taken of you on the US side if you're a US citizen. Non-US nationals will have to check out at the US border and may have to track down the correct office.

South of the border

On the Mexico side immigration will issue a **tourist card** (FMT; *forma migratoria para tourista, transmigrante*; or FM3 for multiple entry) which is valid for 180 days. It can also be acquired in advance from Mexican consulates. Once in the country it's rare to be asked for your FMT, even at the frequent military checkpoints where they are mainly after drugs and weapons. Police can be a separate issue, and unlike elsewhere in the world, they may be more interested in seeing a driving licence (*licencia*) than, say, your passport.

Unless you're making an excursion to Baja, you'll need a **temporary vehicle import permit** for which you'll need to show proof of ownership (original US title) or permission from the vehicle owner, vehicle registration (not the same as title in the US), your passport, driver's licence and proof of Mexican vehicle insurance. The TIP (*Declaración de Ingreso de Vehiculo Automotivo*) costs around $18 and you'll have to post a US$400 bond (less for pre-2001 models) with the *Banjercito* bank (🖳 www.banjercito.com.mx) for your bike with a credit card to get the sticker. On leaving Mexico make sure you cancel the permit

---

CARNETS IN LATIN AMERICA

No countries in Central America, including Mexico, require a carnet. South of the Darien the situation is the same. The issuing authorities – for North America it's the Canadian Automobile Association (🖳 www.caa.ca) will happily sell you a carnet, but at over twice the price of one in the UK and with some phenomenal estimates for bank charges, it may persuade you not to bother. The website of the RAC issuing authority in the UK states a carnet is 'recommended' for South America, while the German ADAC website (with a page on carnets in English)

claims a carnet is required in the six countries bordering Brazil, from Paraguay to Venezuela.

As elsewhere, in all Latin American countries local **temporary vehicle importation permits** (TIP) are a long-established alternative and are valid from a month in Panama to three months in the rest of Central America, Bolivia, Brazil, Chile, Ecuador and Peru, and up to eight months in Argentina. As with Russia, their validity commonly exceeds the duration of your tourist visa because separate authorities are involved.

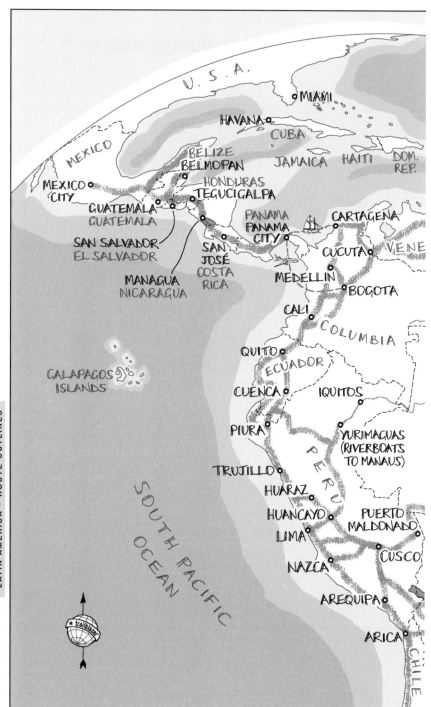

Main overland routes across Central and South America

and credit card fee with the *Banjercito* (though not every border post has a branch), otherwise you may run into trouble returning into Mexico which now has a computerised tracking system for temporary vehicle imports.

Vehicle insurance (*seguro de vehiculo*) is required and unlike further south, needs to be taken seriously; you're looking at around $130 a month or not much more for six months. Following an accident everyone's considered guilty until proven innocent, and having insurance can often be the difference between having your bike impounded, or moving on. Some US and Canadian insurance providers cover you for up to 75 miles into Mexico, but Mexican officials won't recognise this. You must have liability insurance from a Mexican provider and it can easily be obtained at the border or over the web from places like 🖥 www.mexinsure.com, 🖥 www.mexpro.com or 🖥 mex adventure.com.

If you have an accident in Mexico, immediately contact your insurance provider who usually has a legal advisor who can help you in negotiations with the police. Don't sign anything before involving your insurance company, especially settlement agreements with other parties, as they could invalidate your insurance.

The companies listed above, and doubtless many more in North America, can sell residents **vehicle recovery insurance** that's valid throughout Central America and need not cost a fortune. You won't get some guy driving down from New Mexico to collect your bike; more likely a relay of local providers will get you back up to the border if that's what you need. It's unlikely to be as seamless a transit as it would in the States, but you will be recovered.

Nationwide, **ATMs** take most credit cards but it's also possible to pay in dollars and get change in pesos at the normal rate for most services too, though this can lead to miscalculation or short-changing. You're in Mexico so pay in pesos and leave dollars as a back up, or unless they're specifically requested.

On the road in Mexico

Riding in Mexico is reasonably sane, though chaos can certainly reign in urban areas and the usual livestock and night time hazards apply everywhere. Roads often have no hard shoulder and asphalt can stop suddenly. Truck drivers also have a habit of signalling left to indicate that it's safe for you to pass – or do they plan to move out or turn left? Engage your telepathic sensors to be sure you know which one they mean before you attempt to pass.

Roads through towns will also have speed bumps (*topes*) that are often unmarked and can frighten suspension if ridden over too fast. In rural areas here and elsewhere in Central America, delays can occur when **militant locals** set up road blocks in response to some injustice or complaint; a frequent Latino way of expressing grudges with authorities. If you handle yourself correctly, as a foreigner you might be allowed to ride round these, but don't count on it. Just because the people hampering your progress are not state officials doesn't mean they're inconsequential. If they were, then the police would clear them as soon as they appeared.

Fuel is available in Mexico at the state-run Pemex stations. Make sure you check your change as attendants have been known to miscalculate, especially if you pay in US dollars.

In Mexico **police checkpoints** are more of a problem than the military equivalent. Heading north towards the US, they're looking for drugs, so a sniffer dog may make the rounds. Police are less professional, especially around Mexico City. To avoid them use the national road atlas, the **Guia Roji** (🖳 www.guiaroji.com.mx) at around $20. It gets updated annually.

AN AMERICAN IN MEXICO

I lived in Mexico for a year and found it to be safe. Yes petty theft occurs, and yes drug smugglers are being killed in all sorts of horrible ways, but the average tourist will feel safe and welcomed. You won't be shot at while riding your bike in Mexico. Has it ever happened? Sure; same can be said for the US.

Now the important stuff! Smiles, *holas, buenos dias, buenas tardes, buenas noches, por favors* and *gracias* go a long way to having a great experience with the locals. Bring LP's Mexican Spanish Phrasebook and practice the basics. If nothing else say *hola*, smile and look people in the eye. Americans tend to not do this as much but Mexicans will find it rude if

© thedarienplan.com

you don't look them in the eye. Mexico is a slower paced society too, so it's rude to rush into things or be too direct. Start a question with salutations or pleasantries then fire away, you'll get a better response.

If you're lost, asking for the next location is best. Mexicans think it rude to not have an answer, even if it's the wrong one, plus many haven't travelled more than a village or two away. In cities I ask for the next biggest city and often ask someone again just to verify (see p135 for more). For **GPS** I use routeable bicimaps (🖳 www.bicimapas.com.mx), plus the Guia Roji paper atlas mentioned above. For the big picture get National Geographic's double-sided, plastic paper 1:2.4m-scale (1" to 38 miles) 'Adventure **Map**'.

Mexico is a cash society. If businesses accept cards they're probably over-priced tourist joints. The easiest and safest way to get cash is from an ATM (see p121); let your bank know you'll be in Mexico. You might pay between $2-7 for the transaction so take out maximum pesos each time.

If you offer a gift to a Mexican and they say no, they expect you to offer it again and they will accept it. Works the same if you're offered a gift.

Expect to pay for a public toilet too and bring your own tissues or use a restaurant toilet when you have the opportunity.

Fuel station attendants are paid with tips; they'll let you pump but give them a few pesos or stop shy of a round figure and let them keep the change. Food store baggers also survive on tips and as in the US, 15% is normal at restaurants. Street vendors and taxi drivers don't expect a tip but negotiate a taxi fare before the ride.

Almost anything can be bargained for except at stores, fuel and tolls. At a market it's expected, in a store give it a try. For a cheap hotel, ask for *habatacion mas barato* or *economico*.

Accept that the boundaries of personal space are smaller than in the US, so when lines form be assertive or they'll pass you by.

Photocopy your important papers and show them to the cops if stopped. After that give a copy of your driving licence. By law they can't keep your passport so never even show it. If you've done nothing wrong wait it out; insist they write a ticket or let you go. They're waiting for a bribe. I resisted a transit cop in Puerto Vallarta for ten minutes, then he gave up and only transit cops tend to give tickets. Federal police and military are looking for drugs. On the road Mexican drivers are fast but alert and compared to the US traffic rules are far less rigid which can be very liberating once you get the hang of it.

And try as many types of foods as possible. The variety will blow you away. The best meals and prices come from street vendors.
BILL EAKINS 🖳 www.butlermaps.com

LATIN AMERICA – ROUTE OUTLINES

BAJA

Baja is an off-roaders' paradise that can be regarded as a recreational extension of California and also happens to be an easy introduction into Mexico. Ride south through Baja and catch a ferry to the mainland before carrying on south. Bush camping is easy and safe, beaches are easily accessible and remote deserts and mountains make for great adventures. There's even a wine region in the north in the Guadalupe Valley, as well as pine forests in the mountains around Laguna Hanson and ancient rock art sites in Baja Sur. South through the peninsula, beaches abound and parts of the Baja 1000 race-course can be run to spice up your ride.

Crossing into Baja is easier at the smaller border posts like Tecate or Mexicali in the east, rather than the main crossing at Tijuana. Make sure you do the full tourist card/insurance/TIP deal here as detailed earlier; it's easier than at La Paz where you catch the ferry to the mainland.

Ferries leave daily from the Pichilingue terminal in La Paz. One docks at Mazatlan after a 12-hour crossing; the other at Topolobampo after about 6 hours. Bikes cost from $US75 or $160 for Mazatlan, plus $75 for you (if looking at ferry tariffs you'll notice the Mexican peso also uses '$' but is worth about 8 cents US). For planning and route finding, the Baja Almanac (🖥 www.baja-almanac.com) offers a topographic map book for all of Baja.

MAINLAND MEXICO

Mainland Mexico is not like Baja. While remote areas can certainly still be found, it's harder to locate discreet **bush camps** as towns and private fenced land becomes more common.

One of the foremost destinations in northern Mexico is **Copper Canyon**, a system of canyons in the State of Chihuahua, south of Juarez. If you end up here the towns of Creel and Batopilas should not be missed. Road improvements are fast encroaching on Copper Canyon and security from the on-going drug cartel problems can make it dicey, so check on travel forums before heading in.

Picturesque beaches can be found all the way down the mainland side of the Gulf of California which also allows exploring of the Sonoran Desert. On the other coast Mayan ruins in the south offer some of the finest archeological sites in North America. Palenque is considered one of the best, but travelling into the **Yucatán**, you'll have no end of great choices.

Tolls and more checkpoints

On the way south another big mainland feature are the **toll roads**. Main highways have toll booths and can end up being pretty expensive. Again, watch your change from the toll attendants. However, good time can be made on the toll roads if you're on a mission to get south fast.

There are **military checkpoints** all over mainland Mexico, but especially along the coast directly west of Mexico City and in the state of Chiapas on the Pacific border with Guatemala. Just as in Baja, the main reason for these posts is to limit drug and illegal immigrant traffic. The soldiers are often pleasant and may want to see your paperwork as well as to perform a cursory search but asking for *mordidas* (bribes) is extremely unusual. The police are not quite the same.

BELIZE

Crossing from Mexico to Belize you pass from a Latino to a Caribbean culture which itself has diverse origins and influences. As the former colony of British Honduras, **English** is the official language here which can make things easier except when you need to act dumb. There's great **diving** and snorkelling on the coast, and inland the jungle offers more Mayan ruins.

Bringing a bike into Belize involves nothing more than showing proof of vehicle ownership along with passport and a driving licence. Your domestic licence will be accepted for visits under three months; for longer stays an IDP (see p23) is required, but on any ride a 'disposable' IDP is handy anyway. They'll also require three copies of all your documents (title, registration, passport and licence) as well local **insurance** which costs about $50 for three months; you'll get an ICB insurance sticker. As with much of Latin America, the **temporary import permit** can last up to 90 days. On leaving the country you may be charged a departure tax, though this is more usual at airports.

Belize is not heavily populated, with only 18,000 or so residents in the capital, **Belmopan**. Roads between the few cities aren't busy, though very few are paved. **Driving standards** are consistent with developing countries and vehicles are often in bad shape – the two seem to go hand in hand. In the **rainy season** from June to November, it's common to come across trucks and buses bogged down in the jungle tracks as downpours transform the top layer into a greasy mire. For **fuel,** fill on leaving Mexico and before entering Guatemala and you'll save a bit.

Travel is easy until you close in on the border with Guatemala. You'll consistently hear Belizeans speak badly of Guatemalans – just like most neighbouring countries. **Police** tend to keep a low profile and in rural areas are virtually non-existent, although Belize City has a bad reputation.

Inglewood Camping Grounds (N17° 08.43' W89° 05.05') is a favourite on the way out of San Ignacio, also on the Western Highway heading for the Guatemala border. Wi-fi is free and the grounds are clean and quiet with hot showers available. For chalet accommodation, just south of Georgeville Gumbo Limbo (N17° 10.15' W88° 58.18') offers comfortable surroundings and a great bar. Just south of Belize City, Cucumber Beach Marina (N17° 28.44' W88° 15.01') is recommended, with laundry, a beach nearby and good security.

Bush camping can be difficult in Belize mainly due to the amount of private land or the density of the jungle. When on jungle tracks it can be very hard to find enough space to camp, though traffic is sparse in many areas, so camping by the road itself may be possible.

LATIN AMERICA – ROUTE OUTLINES

MEXICO & CENTRAL AMERICA: RELATIVE FUEL PRICES

Outside of Mexico, the countries of Central America are small and distances modest, but everywhere except Mexico, gasoline or petrol is more expensive than in the US. In Mexico prices are about 80% of the US, but Belize is 35% more, and through Honduras and the other four countries it ranges from 50% up to 80% in Costa Rica.

Shipping out of Panama to Colombia, gasoline costs 50% more there. Of course, one currency crash or a fuel crisis will make a mess of these 2012 figures, but it's a start.

GUATEMALA

Guatemala can get a bad rap from neighbouring countries, and on initial impression the border experience can support this. Mexico and Belize are all very well, but in poorer Guatemala border officials can be surly and make heavy demands on your paperwork.

As elsewhere you'll need proof of vehicle ownership along with passport and driving licence. Three copies of each document are required and can be made at the main border posts. Things might start with a fumigation for a few quetzals, and if entering from Mexico you may be asked to show your receipt for cancellation of your Mexican TIP. A passport stamp comes next and may cost a few pesos or quetzals, but no motor **insurance** is required. Show a US driving licence or an IDP and buy a tourist permit for some 40 quetzals.

Temporary vehicle importation permits are issued for another 40 quetzals ($5) and last for 90 days with extensions available. Since Guatemala is part of the 2006 Central America Four Border Control Agreement (CA4) with Honduras, El Salvador and Nicaragua, you should be covered for 90 days for all of these countries on immigration, but in practice there seems to be no reciprocity on vehicle imports, at least for foreigners, so you'll have to repeat the procedure in each country. Just like in Mexico you'll be issued a sticker which needs to be surrendered on export. All up the border experience comes to around $15.

On the road

The CA13 highway heading north to south is in good shape, and the Western Highway from Belize may be as good by now. **Guatemala City** is the largest city in Central America and the traffic is as you'd expect, horrendous. To add to the torment, just as in Mexico, large and often unmarked **speed bumps** (*topes* or *tumulos*) are ready to catch the unwary. Guatemalan drivers in the capital are aggressive, but elsewhere driving is no worse than usual.

Once away from the border and Guatemala City, **police** tend to keep a low profile and checkpoints are not too common. **Fuel** is easy to come by with branded stations from Shell and Texaco provide most of the service.

Attractions in Guatemala centre on the **Mayan ruins** and ancient sites, Tikal being best known. There's camping here in a non-fenced site with a night watchman. North of Tikal, Uaxactun can prove a challenge to reach, but offers entry into the Mayan Biosphere Reserve as well as the ruins of Peten. Finca Ixobel, just south of Poptún near the Belize border, offers nice camping, good food, wi-fi and tour services.

HONDURAS

Entry is the same story except they might want four copies of each of your documents, as well as four copies of each of the import permit documents issued at the border and the stamps in your passport. Facilities for money changing and copies are available at the borders, as are pushy fixers. No proof of **insurance** is required to leave the border and the 90-day vehicle *temporal* costs some 235 lempira (around $13).

Some riders report bribes being demanded at various Honduran borders, especially El Florido east of Guatemala City where you may also pay a foreign licence plate fee of L435 (around $22) and another few dollars to the customs.

HONDURAS ~ YAMAHA XT600E

Name	Jakob A
Year of birth	1970
Occupation	Bureaucrat
Nationality	Danish
Previous travels	Middle East, North Africa, Asia
Bike travels	None

This trip	Honduras
Trip duration	Two weeks
Departure date	July 2006
Number in group	1
Distance covered	1500km

Best day	Riding insane rainstorm near Gracias
Worst day	Ill while riding from La Ceiba to Tela
Favourite places	Parque Nacional Calaque
Biggest headache	None really
Biggest mistake	No real mistakes that I can think of
Pleasant surprise	The laidback and friendly countryfolk
Any illness	Yes – bad stomach thing
Cost of trip	Didn't count – Honduras is cheap
Other trips planned	No but plenty of ideas

Bike model	Yamaha XT600E
Age, mileage	Late Nineties? 29,000km
Modifications	None
Wish you'd ...	It was a rental
Tyres used	Some sort of knobblies
Punctures	No
Type of baggage	Backpack strapped on the back

Bike's weak point	Weight!
Strong point	Simple and easy to ride
Bike problems	Died briefly in a storm
Accidents	No, but a few low-speed falls
Same bike again	Yes, or the Ténéré I got me afterwards
Any advice	Don't video handheld while riding

Out of the frying pan... © Nick Taylor

Membership of CA-4 makes little odds and the usual vehicle import hoops still have to be cleared with space-consuming stamps in your passport on entering and leaving the country. Total border costs are around $35 for vehicle import fees.

There'll often be a police checkpoint shortly after the border, watching for infractions and demanding a copy of your TIP. Making extra copies at the border can alleviate hassle here. Leaving the country, some travellers end up paying a couple of dollars for a passport stamp and a few dollars more to fill out a customs form, others pay nothing which you assume is the norm.

Honduras is very mountainous in the west where roads are narrow and the going slow, especially behind heavy trucks. Overland travel is more difficult in the lowlands to the east of the country as there are few roads.

Police checkpoints are frequent, especially along the Pan-American highway approaching borders. Usually you'll just be asked for your papers, but some officers will go further or just be a pain. On the CA-3 highway from Choluteca to the Nicaraguan border at Guasaule I've been stopped half-a-dozen times.

Because of these well known hassles in Honduras, some travellers cross from Guatemala into El Salvador and from there try to nip across Honduras to Nicaragua in a couple of hours. It's less than 200km but El Amatillo border can be a pain and the Honduran police are on to you; a lot of shakedowns occur on this section. In the pine forests in Honduras **bush camping** spots can easily be found, but near towns it gets difficult and security can be a concern.

EL SALVADOR

With well-paved roads for the main arteries, El Salvador can be crossed quickly and navigated easily. Along with many familiar US fast food franchises and the US dollar currency, **beaches** are the major draw here, with every beach running six-foot plus surf between March and October.

At the border it's the same story as before, but with only two copies of everything required. Proof of **insurance** is not required, but is a good idea to have, as is an IDP. Entry permits are good for 90 days and extensions may be applied for. Fumigation costs a couple of bucks but only happens at some crossings. Otherwise, there's a $5 road use fee. Fixers or *tramitadores* inhabit all border posts and can be helpful, especially if you don't know where to go for immigration or customs (*aduana*) or if you don't speak Spanish. **Police** do set up checkpoints, but any shady business seems to be less common than in other Central American countries.

El Salvador is the most densely populated country in Central America so **bush camping** can be quite a challenge. Beach camping is possible in certain areas, but check with the locals. Since the beaches are the main tourist attraction, there are many hotels along the coast.

NICARAGUA

These days Nicaragua has good roads, especially in the west, and travel is easy. As in El Salvador and Panama, you'll find the familiar American fast food joints and a much more developed feel than in Honduras or Guatemala.

© paddytyson.com

At the border it's another Xerox party with three copies of everything. Buy **insurance** for around $12 a month and a TIP which lasts 90 days once you've shown them a *boleta de revision turismo* or **tourist card** that's surrendered on exit. **Fuel** is everywhere, at familiar fuel stations like Shell.

Police hassle is less common here and experiences vary greatly from polite hellos to full shakedowns. Nicaragua seems to be split down the middle; the west is mainly Spanish-speaking with a well maintained infrastructure and some charming colonial towns, while the English-speaking east is a wild and remote jungle, once the stronghold of the Sandinistas and with less intact infrastructure. With not so many ancient ruins in Nicaragua, most of the interesting historical sites are old cities like León and Grenada. Both are well worth exploring, with a wonderful colonial ambience as well as great restaurants and charming (if expensive) hotels. **Volcanoes** start to dominate the skyline especially between lakes Managua and Nicaragua.

There was a spate of so called 'express kidnappings' in Managua, where tourists were briefly abducted (usually from unauthorised taxis) and led to an ATM. On a bike you ought to be immune to that but even on a good day Managua itself can be difficult to get around. Protests are frequent and roads get closed by the police.

Bush camping is possible away from cities and towns, especially in the highlands and the eastern jungle. Otherwise, overlander stopovers include Hospeje Nuestre Casa on Calle la Libertad in Granada by Lake Nicaragua (N11° 55.79' W85° 57.43') and Luna Hostel just north of the cathedral in Esteli (N13° 05.65' W86° 21.30'), itself north of Managua and right on the Pan-Am.

COSTA RICA

By Central American standards Costa Rica is a mainstream tourist destination, and as such might offer a bit of a respite if you're finding the going hard. People fly here for holidays they wouldn't consider taking in the neighbouring countries. It has great places to see, but with the usual tourist-related issues and expense. There are several biosphere reserves, zip line canopy tours, volcano hikes and fabulous sandy beaches.

To get in it's the usual procedure: they want to see vehicle ownership (original US title) and registration along with your passport and driving licence; three copies of all documents are required. **Insurance** costs around $14 a month. Where it's required, fumigation costs $2 so if there were any bugs in your nooks and crannies when you left Mexico, by now they're extinct. The

LATIN AMERICA – ROUTE OUTLINES

borders teem with fixers and as elsewhere, before you hire anyone agree on a price, set some conditions under which they will not be paid (if extra costs are incurred, for instance) and don't pay them until the border transaction is complete. Also don't hand over any of your documentation; often they'll try to get things going in a second line while you're waiting in the first. A little patience here can be invaluable and avoid situations where your documents are held to ransom. On leaving fill in a form to cancel your vehicle import permit.

PANAMA

For much of the last century the US controlled the **Panama Canal**, and these days Panama feels like a state of the USA. The **US dollar** is the currency, highways abound, ex-pats roam the streets and there's a lot of construction.

Vehicle import, you know the drill by now: **insurance** is bought at the border for $15 a month, while temporary vehicle importation permits (TIP) are good for just 30 days, but can be extended at customs. If you're freighting out of Panama it's vital that this document is completed correctly and that they know the difference between your licence plate (registration number) and your VIN (chassis ID plate). As mentioned at the start of the book, it helps to highlight the long VIN on your vehicle ownership documents (or copies) with a marker pen so it's clearly distinguishable from your licence plate. Fumigation costs at least a dollar and individuals buy a $10 tourist card plus a $1 sticker for the passport. These stickers are sometimes offered by bystanders, probably looking for a tip.

Once on the way, checkpoints tend to be staged closer to the border with Costa Rica so watch your speed within the first few miles of the border. It's possible to store bikes at Panama customs in both David and Panama City for around $1 a day, though some have had mixed results with the security in Panama City.

The famous canal is the main attraction here, offering impressive views of huge ships gliding past. **Panama City** itself is a bit schizophrenic; there are modern high-rises with the feel of Dubai in some places, but in the old town squatters live in bombed-out buildings with no roofs.

The Pan-American highway is in pretty good condition. Road signs are not common though and finding your way can mean asking the locals. The ride from David north to Boquete is well worth the scenic views and visiting Parque Nacional Volcán Barú makes a great end to that ride. For somewhere to camp, in Santa Clara on the Pacific the American-owned XS Memories RV Park (N08° 23.26' W80° 06.61') is along the north side of the Pan-Am, about 130km before Panama City and has a pool, wi-fi and a American restaurant plus a couple of cabins; a good place to sort out the bike before preparing to ship out or turn round.

AROUND THE DARIEN GAP

La Panamericana comes to a stop at Yaviza on the Rio Chucunaque alongside the so-called Darien Gap. The next nearest town is Turbo in Colombia, 300km north of Medellín. It may seem absurd that over 27,000 kilometres of road is separated by less than 90 kilometres of jungle and swamp, when just up the road a canal nearly as long was built a century ago to link two oceans.

Colombia being the world's biggest producer of cocaine is why the world's biggest consumer of that narcotic – the US – is happy for any crossing to remain plugged.

Since ferry services were suspended in the late 1990s, most bikers end up either air freighting their bikes between Panama and Bogota, or putting them and themselves aboard a private boat across the Caribbean to or from **Cartagena** in Colombia, often enjoying a mini cruise through of the San Blas islands making a voyage of

Motorcycle departure lounge at Girag cargo.
© oneworld2explore.blogspot.co.uk

some four days. You can also ship your bike in a container, but for such a short stretch this is the worst of both worlds; use air freight or take the cruise.

In 2012 a new ferry service between the two Caribbean ports was boldly announced, but it soon transpired that the Panamanian government was completely unprepared to deal with the expected traffic from Colombia, not least because of the heavy searches required. Meanwhile the proposed vessel remained docked in an Aegean port and deposits were refunded. If it ever happens you'll hear about it on the usual forums

So you're either flying to Bogota or sailing to Cartagena. **Air freighting** with Girag can be organised in a few hours, no reservations required. Ride out to the cargo area of Tocumen airport, east of the city and at the gate the guard will know what you're after and direct you towards Girag's offices. Leave your bike there early in the morning without a full tank and it might be in Bogota next day, though two to three days seems more usual. At the cargo warehouse shrink wrap your luggage for security and make sure you take a photo of your bike; you'll read occasional complaints about damage due to poor handling. The total price is $900 whatever the bike's weight, a taxi back to town is $25 and a flight for yourself with Copa might be another $500. At Bogota's international cargo terminal allow half a day to get through the customs clearance. Flying north *from* Bogota it's said the staff are a bit more tuned in, while arriving in Panama the immigration is less so.

Do your research with the **boat options**. It's a few days at sea which can get rough and some boats are overloaded, ill-equipped and poorly maintained. In 2012 a well-known catamaran used by motorcyclists was abandoned 50km offshore with a dozen backpackers aboard.

Conversely, the *Stahlratte*, a reassuringly spacious converted old schooner, gets few complaints from riders. With room for twenty two passengers and probably as many bikes, it

San Blas stopover. © thedarienplan.com

LATIN AMERICA – ROUTE OUTLINES

Hoisting off a canoe onto the Stahlratte
© jamminglobal.com

uses a jetty just east of **Carti** airstrip (N09° 27.38' W78° 58.75') which is visible on Google satellite and is some 140km and two and a half hours northeast of Panama City. Head down the Pan-Am past Chepo and after El Llano and three steel bridges, turn north at the sign. It's all sealed but hilly and at one point you cough up $9 for you and the bike to enter the autonomous Kuna Indian reservation. At Carti airstrip head for a concrete pier a hundred metres left of the airstrip hut. If the ship's there and expecting you, it'll come in and winch your bike on deck.

Once aboard you're expected to help out with food preparation and other duties, but chilling off the palm-capped desert islands straight out of a cartoon has its rewards. Your bike gets stowed on deck and may be covered against the spray, though greasing the chain and a liberal squirt of GT85 or any thin oil won't hurt any bare metal surfaces.

At the other end you berth at the Club Nautico de Manga marina in **Cartagena** (N10° 24.72' W75° 32.48') where the crew help sort out immigration for you. Other boats may be cheaper but currently the Stahlratte costs just over $900 which perhaps not coincidentally is the same as Girag air freight. But you save on your flight and the snorkelling comes free.

NOT RIDING BUT DROWNING

Back in 2006 yacht owners were just getting into taking bikers over to Panama. With my visa about to expire, in haste I accepted a lift from a 60-year-old Italian skipper, let's call him Alberto. It's ironic that having spent three wonderful months in supposedly 'dangerous' Colombia, I should have my most terrifying experience leaving. It still makes me shudder.

I'd ignored a fellow yachtsman's warnings about Alberto's people-smuggling activities, incompetence and hostility, putting it down to rivalry. But shortly after we set sail, with my trusty Enfield lashed to the foredeck, things started to worry me. The compass light didn't work. Neither did the autopilot. The torch batteries were exhausted and the anchor was inadequate. A faulty alternator disabled access to computerised sea charts and freshly pumped water and dirty diesel was clogging the injectors. These were not my observations – what do I know about ocean yachts – but Alberto's! Then the weather turned, snorkelling was off and we spent two days sitting out a Force 7 gale. Alberto started behaving like a caged animal, snarling abusively, and during a lull late one afternoon made a desperate break for Porvenir island, just opposite Carti.

I still recall the terror of the prospect of drowning that night as the storm intensified and the boat drifted towards a reef when the anchor wouldn't hold. When he wasn't either wailing with despair or rigid with panic, Alberto screamed abuse at me for getting him in this mess. Luckily, some islanders appeared on the jetty and waved torches to guide us in, but it took three hours to get safely ashore.

The next morning, still far from the agreed drop-off point, Alberto ordered me off his boat. I didn't hesitate. A deal was made with some fishermen and $30 later, I was dropped at a Kuna village on the Panamanian mainland from where I chugged up to Panama City, thrilled to be safely back on two wheels.

JACQUI FURNEAUX

South America

WITH ORIGINAL RESEARCH BY MARK HARFENIST

Riding around Central America is not so difficult if you're based in North America and a great way of dipping your toe into the overland experience. For the experienced it can be a bit of a holiday on a par with a European's visit to Morocco or Turkey.

Approaching Cartagena. © jamminglobal.com

In South America you're overlanding for real, if for no other reason than you can't skip home inexpensively if a metaphorical pterodactyl lands in your soup. But when you add it all up South America is among the best adventure motorcycling destinations on the planet. An extreme range of environments await you, from barely-penetrable jungle, hyper-arid deserts, wildlife-rich wetlands and fern-clad mesas, the shimmering volcano-dotted altiplano and the snowbound passes across the Andes. Did I miss anything out? Yes, a rich pre-Conquest heritage, nearly a single language, fewer tedious borders than Central America and no visa issues except for Americans.

That leaves only **crazy drivers** on steep Andean roads, shaky infrastructure in the poorer Andean countries, and the **fear of crime** in some cities, all of which can either be avoided or taken on with your wits about you.

Costs will average out at around $70/day, less in the Andean countries and more down south or in Brazil.

ROUTES IN SOUTH AMERICA

There are thirteen countries in South America, but most overlanders visiting the region for the first time are satisfied ticking off about half. They follow the **Pan-American Highway** along the Andean-Pacific spine where Colombia leads to Ecuador, Peru and Bolivia, and with some criss-crossing of the Chile-Argentine border, roll on down to Ushuaia and **Tierra del Fuego**. That done, it's common to head up to **Buenos Aires** and ship out.

In taking that ride of 10,000 miles or more, it's not impossible to rise 13,000 feet or four kilometres in a single day and these variations in **altitude** can play havoc with comfort levels and fuelling. But mile for mile this route delivers spectacle with little interruption and if time, funds or will are limited, you'll certainly see the best of South America following La Panamericana.

> In South America you're overlanding for real, if for no other reason than you can't skip home inexpensively if a metaphorical pterodactyl lands in your soup.

From the **inland borders** of Colombia, Ecuador and Peru no reliable roads lead down into the Amazon basin. Linked to each other by an hour's ride, Nauta and **Iquitos** are in the heart of this area in eastern Peru, but both are only accessible by boat or air. And so in Colombia or Venezuela you have to decide on the Pacific side, the Caribbean-Atlantic route via the Guyanas, or if you're feeling sporty, straight down the middle across the central Amazon.

COLOMBIA

Despite its once notorious reputation Colombia has become a hit with riders. The idyllic beaches, jagged mountains and verdant jungles were always an attraction and the people are welcoming. Roads are sometimes superb, not least when twisting through the Andean sub-ranges, though on occasion riders find themselves tailing long lines of belching trucks crawling up winding grades. Main roads will be paved and may include tolls unless you go out of your way to look for gravel or dirt. There's also at least one bike-friendly hostel, a thriving local riding scene, relatively easy availability of parts and an upbeat air in a country only recently emerged from a long civil war. Expect to spend longer in Colombia than you may have planned.

Although most areas in Colombia are considered safe, there's an element of street crime in the cities, and it's still a good idea to ask locally before venturing off the main highways to some of the standard tourist destinations. In some cities the front line between safe and unsafe *barrios* may not be apparent to outsiders. Certain rural routes are still known for banditry which may or may not relate to FARC or other revolutionary activities – particularly in the south.

After Central America, Colombia is a big country but unless you're an amphibious tapir of some kind, you can write off the eastern Amazonian provinces. That leaves the two lofty eastern and western cordilleras which converge to the point of a 'V' at the Ecuadorian border. How you get there is up to you.

Insurance is mandatory in Colombia, and chances are you'll be checked at some point, so either buy a month's worth or be ready with a convincing 'self-generated' document of some sort. In theory this compulsory traffic accident insurance (Seguro Obligatorio de Accidentes Tráfico' or just SOAT) can be bought in fuel stations, shopping malls and bike shops, but usually for a minimum of one year. But in Cartagena there's a Sura seguros office doing three months insurance for around $50. It's located on the crossroads of Calle 25 and Carrera 17 or 17A (blue and white sign; aim for N10° 24.94' W75° 32.51'), a ten

---

SHIPPING FROM US TO SOUTH AMERICA DIRECT

Not everyone is inspired to tackle the many small countries and the multiple borders of Central America, only to find they have to pay up to a grand if they're intent on continuing to South America.

If you want to head straight to the main event, from the US **Miami** is the best port to organise shipping to Cartagena, Rio, Buenos Aires (BA) or even Santiago. No need to ride

there, they can pick up your bike from anywhere in the US; budget on at least $1200 to get the job done and see what bike freighting specialist SamericaXplorer has to offer on the usual forums. Coming from Europe see p330.

On the way back, see what Dakar Motors in BA (🖳 www.dakarmotos.com) can do for you and check out the shipping database on the HUBB.

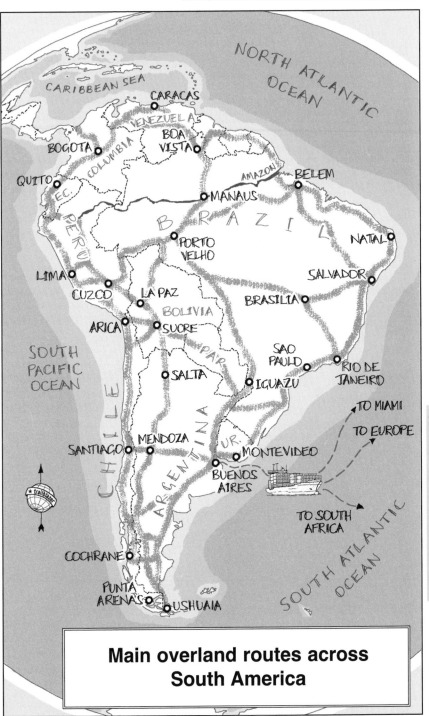

Main overland routes across South America

SOUTH AMERICA: CLIMATE AND SEASONS

The immense size of the continent, along with its extreme variations in landforms and altitude tend to render generalisations rather difficult. The only certainty is that you'll experience a certain amount of uncomfortable weather. With this in mind, let's make a few generalisations.

During the **southern summer** (November to March) storms in southern Brazil, northern Argentina and the altiplano of Bolivia, Peru and Chile are largely thunderstorms rather than unbroken periods of rain. By their nature they're intense and in places may temporarily disrupt travel, but they're localised; you'll often spy black clouds stalking the altiplano without feeling a drop.

Summer temperatures in the altiplano often slip below freezing at night but during winter (May to September) it gets brutally cold, although this is also dry season, and the sun quickly warms the thin air. Take this into account if you expect to camp or use budget lodgings.

At lower elevations throughout southern Brazil, Paraguay, Uruguay and northern Argentina summers tend to be hot and humid. This area can more comfortably be visited during March and April. During winter it gets surprisingly chilly and a damp 10°C/50°F is not uncommon.

Down in Patagonia moisture-laden air runs up along the western slopes of the Andes from Tierra del Fuego through the ice fields and rain forests to the Lakes District of Chile and Argentina before petering out completely around the latitude of Santiago. If trying to pinpoint your own scheduling, this storm track shifts markedly between seasons, hovering between 45 and 55 degrees latitude in summer and 35 to 45 degrees in winter. This produces gorgeous weather in the Chilean Lakes District during summer,

after which winter storms roll in. At the same time, areas on the western side of the range south of 45 degrees latitude tend to have damp, chilly summers until the storm track shifts northward. Shielded by the heights of the southern Andes, Patagonia is generally dry, if famously windy. Note the abrupt change as you transit from steppes to mountains just before reaching Ushuaia; the winds die, you're suddenly surrounded by forest, and almost instantly it begins to rain and snow, particularly during summer.

North of the equator, you'll find that there's no real dry season in the Amazon, although there are 'less wet' periods. December to March is generally rainiest; April to November slightly cooler, June to August a bit drier. In Colombia the dry season is most pronounced from January to March; in Andean regions of Ecuador it's June to September, while the rest of the year can be cloudy and cool, obscuring views of the volcanoes. In the Guianas and Venezuela, two rainy seasons prevail: one from October to February with a peak from December onwards, the other April to July. However, with August to October even hotter than the rest of the year, the best travel window is February and March.

These guidelines should be taken with a grain of salt and the influence of altitude; while Cartagena boils, Bogotá can be chilly. No one's managed to come up with an itinerary that visits everywhere in the best season. Crossing the Guianas might be ideal in March, but Angel Falls in neighbouring Venezuela are best in June when the falls are at full tilt. Similarly, no single trip can see the best conditions in Colombia, Ecuador and the Peruvian altiplano.

MARK HARFENIST

minute walk north of the Manga marina on the Calle 24 esplanade where you may have arrived from Panama. After Central America, it'll feel pleasantly reassuring to be insured again.

Most motorcycle brands are sold in Colombia and **parts** will be readily available in Bogotá, so if you've been nursing your rig this is your best opportunity to service it. For routeable **GPS maps** for your satnav, Gisco (www.gisconavigation.com) is recommended.

SOUTH AMERICA: RELATIVE FUEL PRICES AND CURRENCY

Taking US fuel prices as a benchmark with 95-octane gasoline costing 80 cents a litre there, as things stand now in South America, you're paying about two or three cents in Venezuela. In Ecuador it's about two-thirds of the US price and the same as the US in Bolivia to foreigners (or half at local prices where you can pay it, see p321). In Colombia it's about the same as the US or half as much again up north, same as in Guyana. Gasoline is up to double or more in Surinam, Chile, north Argentina, Peru, Uruguay and Brazil. In French Guiana you pay around $1.70 a litre, or about the same as western Europe.

In Ecuador, Bolivia and Peru gasoline at octanes above 90 can be hard to find in rural areas and what you do get in the mid-80s can be hard on lean-burning, high-compression engines. As long as the fuel is clean and unadulterated, when compared to carburettors, modern computerised electronic fuel injection can compensate for low octane fuel as well as very high altitude.

In Brazil most light vehicles run on E25 'gasohol', composed of 25% cane-based anhydrous ethanol; pure gasoline costs nearly as much as in Guiana. Fuel pumps in Brazil are marked: A for alcohol; D for diesel and G for gasoline. 'Gas' refers to CNG, also widely used. Running a bike on E25 ought not ruin it, but E100 (100% hydrated ethanol) costing around 60% of E25 won't go down so well at the plug.

As mentioned elsewhere, fuel prices in remote, roadless states like Amazonas (the far west) can be double those of heavily agricultural or urban states like Mato Grosso, Panara or Sao Paulo.

Exchange rates per US dollar

Argentine peso	4.5
Boliviano	7
Brazilian real	2
Chilean peso	500
Colombian peso	1800
Ecuador	US dollar
Guyanese dollar	203
Fr. Guiana euro	0.81
Paraguayan guarani	4550
Peruvian nuevo sol	2.7
Suriname dollar	3.25
Uruguayan peso	22
Venezuelan bolivar fuerte	4.3

Riding around Colombia

For many riders **Cartagena** is their first sight of South America which is a good start as it's said to be one of the continent's most beautiful colonial cities. Not so inspiring is the humid climate and relatively drab hinterland which doesn't greatly reward riding. Just up the road from Manga marina, past the Texaco and over the bridge, is the renovated old walled town of Getsamani where most of the ambient lodgings, bars and cafés are to be found. Note that many budget lodgings don't provide off street parking. Upgrades may pay off in terms of security, air-con, privacy and a respite from partying backpackers.

Air arrivals will be some 1000km down the road in the capital **Bogotá,** where the feeling in the safer, upscale barios is of a vibrant and energetic European city, but with a heavy police, military and security guard presence. Situated at around 2600m/8500', the climate is comfortable after the torpor of Panama or Cartagena. Most riders establish themselves at a hotel before taxiing to the airport's cargo zone on the northwest edge of the city where it won't be any kind of Delhi scenario getting your bike released from Girag. There'll be some fees to pay and as usual, speaking some Spanish helps before riding back down Calle 26 into the city. Heading up to Panama, expect arrangements to be as simple; give it half a day.

As is happening elsewhere in the world, to discourage moto-mounted assassins and robbers, local riders must wear **dayglo vests** and helmets bearing license plate numbers matching their bikes. It's said tourists are exempt, but expect to be stopped if not riding in full overland regalia.

TRIP REPORT
CANADA TO ARGENTINA ~ CB450

Name	Michael S
Year of birth	1943
Occupation	Teacher
Nationality	Canadian
Previous travels	Cycling in England, climbing in Canada
Bike travels	None

This trip	Ottawa to BA, then Barcelona–London
Trip duration	Seven months
Departure date	November 1967
Number in group	Just me
Distance covered	14,000 miles

Best day	In Mexico most days were good
Worst day	Quito, Ecuador
Favourite places	I liked Argentina
Biggest headache	Lack of money
Biggest mistake	Should have taken more money
Pleasant surprise	The bike was eating better than I was
Any illness	Amoebic dysentery
Cost of trip	CAN$1000
Other trips planned	Would like to do it again with money

Bike model	Honda CB 450 (Black Bomber)
Age, mileage	No idea
Modifications	None
Wish you'd ...	Windscreen would have been good
Tyres used	Black, round
Punctures	None
Type of baggage	Rope saddlebags from Costa Rica

Bike's weak point	Torque too high!
Strong point	It didn't break down
Bike problems	Nothing
Accidents	No
Same bike again	Don't make 'em! Maybe a Suzuki single
Any advice	Hammock

Leaving Bogotá by road, all directions are enticing. Routes north toward Bucaramanga and northwest 450km to Medellín are fun, while the same distance over the mountains towards Cali is obvious but clogged with slow trucks. The less direct and even more scenic route southwest through the Neiva valley has had a reputation for FARC activity so ask around first.

Formerly the home of drug cartels, **Medellín** is a common stopover when heading down from the Caribbean coast. The surrounding area is rugged, with ranches and coffee plantations scattered between small villages and colonial towns so the riding is correspondingly rewarding no matter which way you go.

Cali is another stop for many riders. The well-known riders' hang-out, Casablanca Hostel (🖳 www.casablancahostel.com, N03° 28.14' W76° 31.79') manages to combine repair services, long-term parking, help with shipping, bike rentals, guided tours and even a micro-brewery into one well-run operation. The owner can also give reliable advice about local roads and routes, and riding partnerships are often formed here.

South from Cali, most make a 140-km beeline to beautiful **Popoyán** from where rough roads loop through the mountains to San Agustín and Tierradentro, both also well worth the effort. Bear in mind that these routes get muddy during rain, and the surrounding countryside can harbour bandits. Enquire locally, but in any case allow at least a couple of days to go exploring. Outside Tierradentro is the location of the precarious swing bridge made famous by Graham Styles' 2009 youtube video (search user 'easyg1409').

The day's ride south towards the Ecuadorian border is a cracker: huge, gorge-cut mountains on all sides, deep slot canyons carrying roiling rivers far below, and always the magical light in which the distant grassy hillsides glow unearthly green. A left off the Pan-Am just before the border at Ipiales takes you to Santuario Del Las Lajas, a short but worthwhile side trip.

ECUADOR, PERU AND BOLIVIA

Between them these three countries also boast some of the most spectacular mountain riding and highest passes in the continent, unfortunately shared with the craziest drivers and treacherous conditions.

In between grand colonial cities like Quito and Sucre, Inca ruins and puffing volcanoes, you get a well-developed tourist infrastructure which adds up to easy travelling and a rich experience on the road through the cordilleras. Heading east for Venezuela and the Guianas? You should be on p334.

Colombia-Ecuador border

The main Colombia–Ecuador crossing at Ipiales–Tulcán is open daily from early till 9pm. It may be your first internal border in South America so compared to what went on in Central America, you'll be thrilled by the speed and efficiency. Only single copies of the usual documents are required: passport, vehicle ownership and driving licence. On leaving Colombia you need to cancel your vehicle TIP as you do in most countries here, and in Ecuador fill out a *Tarjeta Andina de Migraciones* (TAM) immigration card, making sure to keep and not lose the half they return to you to re-present on leaving the country. You can stay for 90 days in any 12-month period, though you may get only a month on arrival. If they ask, say you want 90 days.

In Ecuador the **US dollar** is the currency which simplifies things a bit. Getting some SOAT **insurance** is less so. For foreigners staying less than a month it's said not to be mandatory and some manage to cross the country without it while others won't get away from a border without buying a month's worth for about $8, so buy some if the office is open and obliging. You may not be asked to present it at checkpoints but if you have an accident you may well go to jail before it's sorted out. It's possible for North Americans to buy third party only motor insurance for Latin America for around $700 for a 600cc-plus bike from someone like ⌨ motorcycleexpress.com. Collision cover is another $500 or so.

Heading for Quito © Ken Thomas

Ecuador

For such a relatively small country Ecuador has a lot going on; beach and mangrove seacoasts, glaciated volcanoes, pristine island ecosystems, rainforest jungles and cities with yet more colonial splendour. Border formalities are relaxed, services are cheap, and as the American dollar is the currency you can stock up on cash for the weeks or months ahead at any ATM.

Coming from Colombia, the scenery in northern Ecuador resembles what you just left: looming volcanoes and pretty upland farms and villages all around. A 100km from the border, Ibarra and Otavalo (another 25km) have services; the later has a Saturday market famed for its indigenous crafts.

Another 100 clicks down the Panamericana takes you over **the equator** just south of Cayambe to **Quito** (2800m/9300′) where you can reasonably expect to get completely lost and if you're very careless or unlucky, robbed too. Local streets are clogged with traffic, but there's a bypass through the hills to the west of town or, once you find it, exploring Quito's old town will have been worth the effort. For inexpensive SOAT **insurance** in Quito try Panamericana Seguros (⌨ www.panamericana.com.ec; S00° 10.92′ W78° 28.55′).

Having fought your way back out of Quito, the Parque Nacional Cotopaxi has a road which, though it deteriorates markedly as you follow it uphill, ends at a parking area at about 4800m/15,800′. From here try and stagger another kilometre to the refuge from where, on a clear day, the views over the ash- and snowscapes can be impressive indeed.

Often described as one of Ecuador's highlights, at Latacunga, some 30km south of the Cotopaxi turnoff you'll find the beginning of the famous **Quilatoa Loop** to the west, a day's dirt roading at around 4000m through small highland towns alongside a crater lake. The scenery is otherworldly and there are ample places to eat and sleep should you decide to spend more than a day up here. Be prepared for cold temperatures and problems with the thin air (guidelines on p163).

That said, on a heavy road bike the scenery on the Pan-Am down to Cuenca won't exactly give you nightmares. A couple of hours south of Quito, a left turn in Ambato leads to **Baños** set in a deep canyon at the foot of the

5000m Tungurahua volcano which has lived up to its name – 'Throat of Fire' – since the turn of the century. The surrounding area is well worth exploring, despite the necessary closure of some back roads, and the town itself is attractive, cheap and friendly. If you've an urge to go rafting, climbing, mountain biking, trekking or just soaking in the hot springs which give the town its name, this is your spot.

An interesting alternative to returning to the Pan-Am for Cuenca heads downhill through the canyon, stopping to view waterfalls along the way, then takes a right in Puyo onto the E45, a smoothly paved road to Macas and a little beyond. This is newly felled jungle on the edge of the vast Amazon basin, offering hints of the primeval forest beyond. Even here in the lowlands you're at 600m, so it gets warm but not blindingly hot.

From **Macas** a splendid road winds back up through disparate landscapes of the Sangay NP over to Guamote, where you rejoin the Pan-Am. Otherwise, continue south on the E45 for 100km to Limon (not on web maps) and turn west through deep, jungle-clad valleys over a high pass to Cuenca. As long as it's not pouring the route's not too difficult.

Back north on the Pan-Am, most will stop in **Cuenca** to admire the picturesque cobblestone, whitewash and red tile Old Town before dropping down to **Loja** and deciding on meeting the Peru border at Macará (180km), up on the coast at Huaquillas (210km), or the less reported dirt route south-east to **San Ignatio** down in the jungle. The tar resumes at Jaen so in good weather allow a couple of days and enough fuel for that one.

Ecuador–Peru border

Depending on what time of day or the week you arrive, the coastal border crossing at Huaquillas/Aguas Verdes near **Tumbez**, Peru can be a little chaotic and intimidating, with the Aduana done a few miles before at Chacras. Low-level smuggling goes on here and with the 'gringo' element, on a bad day there can be a fair amount of scammery going down with the local entrepreneurs as you make your way to the bridge over the frontier creek (S03° 28.88' W80° 14.59'). The **Peruvian formalities** are done a couple of kilometres down the road. Coming from Peru to Huaquillas, it's said $8 for a month's SOAT is obtainable. To buy it, less than 500m from the border, turn north into Santa Rosa past the park; the SOAT office is just after the Banco de Machala (around S03° 28.81' W80° 14.33').

Knowing all this and depending on your destination and the weather, you will find the inland border crossing at **Macara** more relaxed. It's said to be open round the clock and involves crossing the new Puente International bridge at S04° 23.58' W79° 57.83', a couple of kilometres southwest of town. (Coming north from Peru, no one mentions insurance and there are no costs.) The first Peruvian town of Suyo is 16km on. In most cases you'll be given 90 days on entry to Peru and even if you don't visit the well known sites at Machu Picchu and Nazca, it's easy to spend a month exploring this country.

Wherever you cross, fill out the usual forms and get a SUNAT (*Superintendencia Nacional de Administración Tributaria*) temporary import permit and a two-part form; hand your section back on leaving Peru. You'll need SOAT **insurance** in Peru from a Mapfre bureau (🖥 www.mapfreperu.com, or try 🖥 www.soat.com.pe). A month can cost you $30. Coming from Ecuador, La

Positiva Seguros in Piura has been recommended – it's on Lima #544, east of the main cathedral and towards the river (aim for S05° 11.82' W80° 37.52'). Otherwise, you may want to avoid Trujillo where the cops have been known to take an earnest concern in correct paperwork. If starting out from Buenos Aires and looking for insurance to cover Argentina, Chile, Ecuador, Paraguay, Brazil, Bolivia and Peru, see p329.

Without a GPS-equipped bike the best **maps** are a set of three sold by the Touring y Automóvil Club del Peru (🖳 www.touringperu.com.pe). They have offices in major cities, including Piura on Ave. Sánchez Cerro #1237, the Pan-Am main road in the town centre. For your routeable satnavs 🖳 www.perut.org gets the nod.

Peru

Improbable though it seems, Peru has it all: the deepest canyons; some of the tallest peaks; uncounted miles of desolate coastal deserts close to a substantial chunk of Amazon jungle; fantastic biking roads and moderate prices.

It's over a thousand kilometres to Lima, and from the north initially at least, it's tempting to follow the arid Pan-Am across the coastal desert before cutting east over to Cusco by whichever route you fancy. Don't make the mistake of proceeding directly into northern Chile, unless you're on some record-breaking high-speed caper to Ushuaia. Do the right thing and pay your respects to Machu Picchu before carrying on from Cusco into Bolivia, or over into southern Brazil (see p320). A glance at a map of Peru will show roads resembling so much over-boiled spaghetti thrown against a wall; it's why the folding footrest was invented.

Where sealed Peruvian roads are usually in good shape; the Pan-Am is entirely paved while secondary roads are usually good gravel (outside in the Amazon), and many are being upgraded. In the mountains there are countless dirt tracks to pursue.

Tyres and many other **parts** are cheap in Peru; postponing repairs until Bolivia may be tempting fate and waiting till Chile, Argentina or Brazil may cost you double. Lima has the best selection, but parts are also found in Cusco or even Ica because avoiding Lima's notorious traffic is another one of Peru's highlights.

Entering Peru from Ecuador, there is no apparent lodging along the Pan-Am for a couple of hours, so time things with that in mind. Having temporarily forsaken the scenic Andean plateau it's likely you'll be in a mild state of sensory under-stimulation, surfing arrow-straight highways over barren, trash-strewn scrub. Furthermore, the instant you cross into Peru **driving standards** collapse. Pedestrians don't stroll across the roads here; they get their heads down and sprint. Other hazards lie down this coast too: ferocious crosswinds and drifting sand that's more dangerous than it looks when hit at speed.

A glance at a map will show roads resembling so much over-boiled spaghetti thrown against a wall; it's why the folding footrest was invented.

So stay alert or get off the Pan-Am; it's the Andes roads you want, from smooth *pavimento* to dirt tracks

LATIN AMERICA – ROUTE OUTLINES

through boulder fields with stream crossings and gaping washouts, though the construction zones which upgrade the latter into the former aren't much fun. Just remember, passes reach well above 4500m or 15,000 feet so swift climbs from near sea level may give you a headache if you rush it.

Perusing Peru
Assuming you've not set off for Tarapaco and the road's end at **Yurimaguas** for a river boat down the Amazon to otherwise inaccessible **Iquitos** and western Brazil (in which case, *hasta la vista*, baby), from the north the first obvious side trip leads into the peaks of the Cordilleras Blanca and Huayhuash rising to over 6500m/21,500'. **Huaráz**, 430km north of Lima is a favourite base hereabouts and at only 3000m or 10,000', too. There are a variety of approaches, including coming inland from Santa on the coast (just before Chimbote) into the **Cañon de Pato** for Carza on Ruta 3 north of Huaráz. The unmade road follows a former rail grade through nearly three dozen car-wide tunnels as well as a few airy bridges over the churning Rio Santa below. Another access road is the 14A leaving the Pan-Am at Casma and ascending more precipitous slopes before dropping directly into Huaráz.

Cruising the cordillera to Cusco
Take it from me, the roads from Huaráz through the **cordillera** are world class and the possibilities numerous, including following the paved Ruta 3 south and turning west onto 14 for a superbly-twisting descent to Paramonga on the coast. Or take any number of single lane dirt tracks up into the Cordillera Blanca for glaciers, lakes and ancient ruins. Careful study of maps, blogs and forums will reveal one- to three-day loops past remote villages, over high passes and through deep canyons. By now you're understanding why you left the Panamericana to the crows, but inquire locally before venturing too far afield, as security can be a concern.

Heading inland, at Ruta 3 junction south of Huaráz continue over narrow gravel roads and through construction zones down to Huánuco over the vast and infinitely variable altiplano ringed by spectacular mountain views and lined with hardscrabble Quechua villages. It can be a rough 330km so allow a full day, if not two. Pushing on from Huánuco, if not dropping back down to Lima for some good reason, keep going to Huancayo. You can make no bad choices here: the two routes reaching south-east from Cerro de Pasco are equally stunning. Down in Huancayo more superb roads extend to Ayacucho where you can bail onto the paved Ruta 24 to the coast at Pisco.

Ayacucho is a splendid colonial-era town set deep in the Andes and well off the popular routes to Cusco, yet easily accessed by the paved highway from Pisco on the coast. This was a prime battleground during the Sendero Luminoso (Shining Path) years, and there's a moving museum and memorial to the victims of this struggle who were subjected to atrocities by both sides. The road over to Abancay is wonderfully scenic gravel so allow a full day from Ayacucho. On the way you'll join the main route from Nazca to Cuzco, now fully paved (more below).

Back on the coast, **Lima** is one of the largest cities on the continent, but transiting on the main highway is actually surprisingly painless. With composure and a degree of blind faith you'll be through almost before you notice.

The shrewd overland rider will skip breakfast and be airborne over Nazca early in the day to avoid afternoon breezes and the risk of hurling over that girl they fancy once in the confines of the cabin.

To the south, the desert tightens its grip and brings you to Nazca, passing the huge dunes in Huacachina just out of **Ica**, where dune buggies, sandboarding and the backpacking throng is to be found. Ica may make a better stopover, along with moto-related parts and services.

Nazca itself is pleasant enough, although the job here is to cough up for a flight over the enigmatic Nazca Lines. Prices have increased dramatically following long overdue inspections after a fatal crash. The shrewd overland rider will skip breakfast and be airborne over Nazca early in the day to avoid afternoon breezes and the risk of hurling over that girl they fancy once in the confines of the cabin. Aside from the lines themselves, Nazca has ruins, mummies, graveyards and the sandboarders' 'Everest' of Cerro Blanco; five hours up, two minutes down…

Leaving Nazca, some riders strike out south-east to Arequipa before backtracking north to Cusco. **Arequipa** is a spectacular town in a spectacular setting, flanked by picture-perfect volcanoes and surrounded by wild high country cut by a canyon twice as deep as Arizona's famed example. Although it's possible to continue to the Chile border, most choose to follow a winding road north to Cusco.

An alternative route to Cusco – formerly a long, dusty haul but now paved – is Ruta 26 from Nazca through Puquio to Abancay. You may be getting blasé about Peru but listen up; this is a stellar route with two highland sections teeming with comely vicuñas and split by a deep river valley awash in the shifting light and colours of the afternoon. Allow at least twelve hours, so start early or take a break in Abancay. Don't underestimate the distance; temperatures drop quicker than your keys over a drain and sudden summer storms will flush you back to the Pacific before you can say '*Qué bonitos ojos tienes, mi querida vicuñita*'.

Cusco

Cusco may be touristy and therefore pricey, but it was the former capital of the Incas empire so it's a destination in its own right, even without the nearby splendours of Machu Picchu. Off-street parking is not the norm with budget lodging so many riders park in the courtyard at the Casa Grande (S13° 31.01' W71° 58.58'), just east of the Plaza de Armas. Another option is the Hostal Estrellita, on Avenida Tullumayo 445 (S13° 31.12' W71° 58.44'). Once installed, unpacked and gelled up to the nines, roaming motards set off to swap yarns at the famous Norton Rats tavern on the southeast corner of the Plaza.

And once they've had their fill, the overland gang swings out the kickstarter and lights out towards Bolivia down Ruta 3, perhaps stopping after nearly 400km in Puno on Lake Titicaca, before reaching the border crossings another 150km on for Copacabana or La Paz.

Others might choose leave the Cusco–Puno highway before **Urcos** and ride over the passes and down to **Puerto Maldonado** (430km) and so to Brazil.

THE WAY TO MACHU PICCHU

Machu Picchu can be done as a long daytrip from Cusco or by overnighting in Aguas Calientes below the ruins. But you're on a bike so can leave the herd and ride into the Sacred Valley to spend some time exploring the numerous ruins in the area.

Ollantaytambo makes a good base; you can catch the train to Machu Picchu from here – buy your train- and entry ticket in Cusco online.

The back way into Machu Picchu, which climbs on pavement to a high pass past Ollantaytambo, then turns to dirt and descends to river level, has become increasingly travelled since the floods of 2010 washed out the railroad. It may not be possible to actually ride all the way to Aguas Calientes yet, but you might get to a town

© Bingham Thomas

called Hydroelectrica, where you can park by the police station and walk along the seldom-used railroad tracks to Aguas. A small tip will ensure continued access for bikes.

However, if the landslide hasn't yet been cleared you may get only as far as Santa Theresa, 10km from Aguas. Walking is still an option, as is the occasional train.

You'll find basic lodgings in Santa Theresa, which is also a base for exploring the tracks into the highland jungles beyond. It should go without saying that inquiries should be made locally before pinning your hopes on any of these roads; all are prone to storm damage.

MARK HARFENIST

Bearing the grand name of the Carretera Interoceanica, this road is being upgraded in the hope of living up to its name by linking Lima with Santos near Rio, over 5000km away on the Atlantic, although your stake in the Panama Canal is probably secure for a few years yet. If you're a gritty gnarletarian, it's also the way across the Amazon basin north towards Venezuela (more on p339). Cusco to Caracas, how hard can it be?

Over the border into Bolivia

Whichever way you get into Bolivia from the five bordering countries, Canadian and most EU nationals can enter without a **visa**, getting from 30 to 90 days. South Africans need a visa and US citizens can buy one at the border for a hefty $135 with a passport photo. On top of that you'll need to fill out a tourist card, possibly show an international vaccination certificate and get a TIP for the bike.

It's said foreigners don't need motor **insurance** (SOAT) for stays of less than a month, because like Peru you can only buy a policy for a year. Other overlanders just try and pass off their IDP or similar document, manage to buy an international policy covering Bolivia, or have a document which says as much. See p329 for an Argentinian policy which could get you out of a fix if involved in an accident.

At the moment the locals' price for **petrol** is 3.74 bolivianos a litre, about 50 cents. Those with foreign licence plates must pay just over 9. This isn't necessarily intended as a tourist-gouging measure, more of a way of stopping those from neighbouring countries taking advantage. On major highways the stations sell at the high rate or aren't allowed to sell to foreigners. In smaller towns fuel goes for local price. The local *tienda* or store may have jerricans of fuel where you pay midway, but selling from jerries got outlawed too so you may now have a hard time scoring cheap fuel. You might try and stress that valued foreign tourists to Bolivia are exempt from the high price.

In Bolivia

Most sources list Bolivia as South America's poorest country and as having the highest percentage of indigenous inhabitants. To most riders it's also one of the best rides on the continent, the least expensive and where the thin air gives the sky a deep cerulean hue matched by brightly dressed locals, impressive colonial-era cities and dense jungle lowlands. Oh, and don't forget the refreshing green leaves sold by the bushel in local markets right across the country.

Roads in Bolivia are said to be undergoing long-overdue upgrades which means being braced for gruelling sections of mud, gravel and sand before slithering onto steaming fresh asphalt. You might try and catch up with the state of play on the official **map** at ▣ www.abc.gob.bo/Mapa-interactivo, while Geogroup (▣ www.geogroup-online.com) produces a Garmin satnav-compatible routeable **GPS map**. On top of road issues, never forget that like Peru, rural Bolivians will mount roadblocks at a moment's notice in the name of political expression. As a consequence nowhere in South America are you more likely to be trapped by the resultant fuel and commodity shortages or complete shutdowns of major highways. However, these evaporate as quickly as they arrive, so park up, hang the lid on the mirror and meet the locals.

At 3700m **La Paz** is by far the highest capital in the world. The city fills a winding canyon and is divided into neighbourhoods which knowledgeable residents refer to frequently. However, most of the obvious sights and lodgings are in central district within walking distance of the Plaza San Francisco. The main thoroughfare, which follows the canyon bottom, has various names but is generally referred to as The Prado.

Streets in La Paz are steep, and with the altitude's effects you may wonder if that Chinese 125 that looked so tempting on ▣ alibaba.com was such a smart idea after all. Motorcycle parts and repairs are available here, although not in the quantity and quality found elsewhere, so don't pass up tyres and other necessary items when in Peru or Argentina. If arriving during the summer watch out for torrential afternoon storms which briefly turn the steep streets into torrents.

The Road of Death and other fun rides

A popular day trip from La Paz is along the North Yungas Road or 'Road of Death' (left) which over 70km takes a stomach-lifting 3500m drop to the pleasant lowland town of Coroico and Bolivia's steamy **Yungas** region where the anacondas grow thicker than a redwood pine. It's not just a

La Muerte. © darienplan.com

TRIP REPORT
LATIN AMERICA ~ SUZUKI DR650

Name	Jay K
Year of birth	1981
Occupation	Mechanical Engineer
Nationality	Indian
Previous travels	RSA, India, SE Asia, China, US
Bike travels	Mexico and USA

This trip	Latin America
Trip duration	Nearly one year
Departure date	March 2010
Number in group	One
Distance covered	36,000 miles

Best day	Riding & camping the Carretera Austral
Worst day	Shunt in Bolivian fog @ 4200m
Favourite places	Couchsurfing in Picinguaba, Brazil
Biggest headache	Visas with an Indian passport
Biggest mistake	Initially, not taking a good SLR camera
Pleasant surprise	Generosity of the poor in rural areas
Any illness	One day stomach in Peru
Cost of trip	About $10,000
Other trips planned	Continued to Africa and India

Bike model	Suzuki DR650
Age, mileage	1998, 26,000 miles
Modifications	Tank, shock, screen, brace, Trail Tech
Wish you'd ...	Fitted a bigger alternator
Tyres used	Kenda K761 and Metzeler Tourance
Punctures	Four
Type of baggage	Happy Trails panniers and top box

Bike's weak point	Small alternator for touring!
Strong point	Simple and strong design
Bike problems	Fried a clutch in sand – my fault
Accidents	Two
Same bike again	Yes!
Any advice	Know bike repairs before leaving

nickname. Before they built the less dangerous bypass, the mist-shrouded Carretera de la Muerte annually saw off hundreds when it served as one of the main access roads to the capital. It now attracts thrill-seeking mountain bikers as well as a smattering of overland motorcyclists and even quad riders – some of whom continue to sustain La Muerte's deadly appetite.

But as long as you have brakes, hands and eyes the Road of Death isn't a difficult ride. The roadway is just one lane of mostly dirt, and features some spectacular drop-offs from eroded soft shoulders. It traverses some gorgeous terrain too, but must have been terrifying when clogged by hundreds of trucks, buses and crazed taxis shoving in both directions.

As elsewhere in Bolivia, local custom dictates that the driver's side of a vehicle hugs the **outside edge** of the road along the abyss so they can better judge if space remains when squeezing past oncoming vehicles. This may mean they drive on the wrong side of the road so be prepared for this in the unlikely event that you encounter oncoming traffic. Now the main hazard is more likely a panic-stricken mountain biker who's cooked his brakes. Pay attention and stop for photos near the top where the drop-offs are most impressive. And don't overlook the new highway to La Paz which is spectacular in itself, cresting at 4700m/15,400ft and featuring plenty of satisfyingly banked sweepers on both sides of the pass.

Elsewhere in Bolivia

How about leaving La Paz north for the 1000-km ride down through the misty Yungas and along corrugated lowland tracks via Rurrenabaque to the **Brazilian border** over the Rio Guapore (outboard canoe, $10) at **Guajara Mirim** for Porto Velho (p339) or the Pantanal (p342). Or cross the altiplano to Oruro then Potosi, before deciding whether to head for Uyuni or turn east towards Sucre, Santa Cruz and beyond. Another option is to access Sucre directly from Oruro via Ruta 6, which mixes pavement with gravel and dirt.

All routes in this area traverse the lonely altiplano, with towns and cities located at 3000–4000m (10,000–13,200ft) and separated by higher passes. In summer be prepared for storms which come on suddenly, then dissipate after clobbering you with cold rain, hail or snow.

Each of the cities in this part of Bolivia has its own unique character – Potosi with its gritty remnants of vast colonial wealth and jarring mine tours; **Sucre** far more conventionally pretty, surrounded by indigenous towns and endless back road adventures; tropical Santa Cruz, staging point for tours into sweaty lowland jungles impossibly remote from the nearby altiplano. If you've got this far you'll want to try and see it all. From Sucre few riders continue to **Santa Cruz**, and fewer still continue all the way into the Brazilian Pantanal on the paved road via Quijarro to **Corumbá**. Most prefer to double back towards the mind-bending shapes and colours surrounding the fabulous **Salar de Uyuni** – rightly regarded as the best dual sport touring around.

The Salar salt flat often floods during the winter rains, usually by just a few inches. While this is undeniably photogenic, the corrosive briny spray you kick up will eat your bike's electric and electronic components quicker than a shoal of munchy-crazed piranhas, possibly causing problems for months. Leave the bike in Uyuni and let a tour's 4x4 feed the salt while you shoot rainbows in the spray. Despite the scammers don't be tempted to just skip the entire thing.

During the dry season, it's easy enough to shoot straight across the Salar de Uyuni itself directly to Chile or as an excursion from town – riding the glaring pan is surreal and exhilarating. Other tracks trace the northern edge of the Salar, with many other possibilities for exploration. Ask around but try to leave some margin for error in your planning if venturing too far alone.

Descent into Chile

Two major routes head from Uyuni towards Chile, skirting the southern edge of the Salar. One which can be completed in a long day follows actual roads to the border at **Ollagüe**, then on to Calama, transiting high valleys rimmed with psychedelic shades, the shoulders of perfectly formed volcanoes and the edges of smaller salars incongruously choked with flamingos on diamox.

The tougher route takes a series of roads mixed with true off-road riding and tracks, passing Laguna Colorado and Laguna Verde before intersecting the Paso de Jama road and dropping like a fragmented clay pigeon to San Pedro de Atacama. Riders do manage this route with neither GPS or a guide, but most will prefer to obtain a GPS track online as there's risk of getting lost or of minor problems having major consequences. A group of riders might hire a 4x4 to carry the baggage and a guide. The fast-and-light can knock it out in a day, but it's more commonly done over two or more.

Note that in all cases it's easier to have **passports** stamped out of Bolivia at the migración office in Uyuni, since the more remote border posts are sometimes unmanned. Aduana offices remain at, or near border crossings. Bolivian fuel is cheaper than Chile so smuggling is rife and fuel is scarce. You'd want a range of 500km, otherwise ask in Ollagüe or one of the small mining camps on the Bolivian side of the border. Whatever your route, remember that summer or winter, it gets pretty chilly after sundown.

Other great roads in Bolivia include the spectacular ride from Oruro off the altiplano down to Arica in Chile; the mostly unsurfaced routes south from Uyuni to Tupiza, Oruro to Tarija and Sucre to Yacuiba for Argentina, as well as the routes east and north from Oruro or La Paz which descend to the Yungas jungles of the Amazon basin.

CHILE

Chile! Twenty times longer than it is wide, it slices through climates, seasons, expectations and landforms like lava through a glacier, and appropriately throws everything at you from temperate rainforests, tidewater glaciers, hyper-arid deserts and a chain of active volcanoes with some of the world's highest peaks looming over lakes and forests. Oil the chain and kick the tyres, the party's not over yet!

On the list are more eye-popping landscapes surrounding San Pedro de Atacama, the novelty of the modern, Europeanised cities of Santiago or Valparaiso, but above all it's the picturesque Lakes District around Puerto

© Duncan Hughes

CHILE TO PERU ON THE PAM-AM

On the Pan-Am some 20km north of Arica you get to the Chilean border post with parking right by the immigration and Aduana.

Remember to pick up a *Relacion de Pasajeros* form for 500 pesos before you leave Arica. I understand you can buy them at the bus station; it's a requirement to enter Peru. There may be different versions depending on your next country.

For Chilean departures, join a line and wait for your number and go to the window to get your passport *Relacion de Pasajeros* form stamped. Nearby you'll find a couple of Aduana windows to cancel your TIP.

Back on the bike for a few hundred metres and you arrive at the Peruvian post, another new complex with parking opposite booths with barriers. Fill out an immigration form, get it stamped with your passport and keep the bottom bit.

Aduana is in the same building, signed CIF. Sign a declaration and get a TIP, half of which they keep. They may ask for a drivers licence and copies of your documents.

Then go out and get two stamps on your Relacion de Pasajeros form and answer questions about football and the quality of Argentine wine. They may check through your gear.

Back to Aduanas, collect your documents and ride to the last barrier, show your stamped *Relacion* forms – they keep one – and you're away.

The post is open from 8am to midnight, it took me an hour to get through. There are small charges on weekends and holidays – something like $2. I saw no money changing facilities but I got a poor rate in Arequipa offloading my Chilean pesos.

PAT McCARTHY ✉ patonabike.blogspot.co.uk

Montt, the relatively untravelled Carretera Austral south of there, and way down in the southern latitudes, the incomparable Torres del Paine. After weeks or months in the tropics, you're back in temperate lands where good roads and summer days last longer.

Infrastructure in Chile is of a high standard and for the most part a road on a map will correspond to a well-constructed and maintained highway. For a **map**, Copec's Rutas de Chile and the atlases produced by Telefonica CTC Chile are recommended.

At the borders

You're unlikely to need a **visa** in advance or at the border. Instead, fill out an immigration form or *tarjeta* of which you keep a copy for you to get stamped when you leave the country and indeed to show to Argentinian immigration. Next you get your *temporal* for the bike and maybe fill out an SAG (Agriculture and Livestock Service) form declaring what foodstuffs you're bringing into the country. Chile has strict laws on this so declare everything and don't bring any fresh produce or meat into the country. They might then inspect your bike and once that's done, you pay the immigration fee of about $7 and ride on. If you're planning on crossing the border with Argentina a few times you'll have to go through this all again each time. Unlike in Central America 'helpers' (*tramitadores*) are absent and blatant scams are rare. And as an overlander you're not required to pay the fees paid by international air arrivals – US$140 for Americans arriving in either country.

Insurance isn't asked for at the border and is said not to be required or available to non-residents. The driving is at least recognisably saner than up north, and with perseverance cover can be bought locally for a minimum of three months for around $50. They may also sell you a regional policy for all neighbouring countries for a few months but as elsewhere this can take some effort; among others check out 🖳 www.svs.cl or 🖳 www.bciseguros.cl.

Hitting the road

San Pedro de Atacama is an easy jaunt from the copper mines at Calama and is worth a look if you missed out Uyuni in Bolivia. You could spend a day to a full week exploring the area. And where the Pan-Am ducks inland away from the coast there are alterna- tive unpaved routes, mainly along the

© Duncan Hughes

seaside through parks and small towns, allowing a bit of off highway explo- ration without giving up onward progress entirely.

North of Santiago a dozen or so roads, mostly gravel, penetrate the Andes to Argentina via high, arid passes skirting brooding 6000m volcanoes. The eas- iest is certainly the southernmost, on the main route to Mendoza, which fea- tures high-speed switchbacks, heavy traffic, glimpses of Aconcagua (6962m, 22,841′) and a notoriously busy border crossing. This route also features a gravel alternative which follows the original road far above the modern high- way; see p331. In the far north, Paso de Jama is also paved but don't overlook exit formalities at the customs on the outskirts of San Pedro de Atacama or you'll be refused entry to Argentina, two or three hours down the road. Between these two stretches of pavement are a series of 4500-5000m passes transected by gravel roads, each with its own character. Even further north, a few passes lead into Bolivia: one paved road from Arica to Oruro, plus a cou- ple of high, sand and washboard routes to Uyuni (see p325).

Southbound riders had better have a pretty good excuse to cross into Argentina at **Santiago** or earlier – most probably the onset of winter. From Santiago highways lead south through fertile valleys full of farms and vine- yards. Then multiple routes diverge to the mountains or the coast and the ter- rain gets wilder as you enter the Lakes District – here, as in adjacent Argentina, a region of lakes, mountains and statuesque volcanoes. From Puerto Montt a right turn leads to pretty Chiloé island, while a left takes you onto the initial stretches of the **Carretera Austral** which ends at **Cochrane** among majestic forests.

The Carretera, Chile's Ruta 7, was only completed a few years ago, link- ing formerly isolated towns, parks and wilderness areas over 1200km south from Puerto Montt. In good weather it makes for a fabulous ride, but after some 9000 years, in 2008 the eponymous volcano erupted, buried the town of Chaitén and severed the Carretera near its northern terminus. There is no indication this section will be repaired anytime soon, so coming from the north you need to **ferry** to Chaitén from Puerto Montt or from Quellón on Chiloé.

With its ghost town ambience and half buried in muddy ash, Chaitén is definitely worth a visit. The volcano remains active but there are several houses renting rooms, as well as a hotel, some bungalows plus a few restaurants and bars. There's also beach camping north of the ferry terminal, and the road con- tinues north to remoter spots near the airfield, before dwindling rapidly.

CATCHING THE DAKAR AND BECOMING A RALLY GOD

For some, crossing paths with the Dakar Rally is a high point of their travels; for others, staying as far as possible from all the commotion is a goal.

Whatever your preference, it's worth studying the Dakar schedule if you find yourself in Chile or Argentina in January. The race stages are amazing to watch, and the energy and enthusiasm demonstrated by racers, crews, media onlookers and locals alike is a splendid thing.

On the other hand, with thousands of participants and spectators milling around, lodging becomes scarce or expensive and other services get stretched thin – and this is true the week before and for several days after the race passes.

My favourite part of being around the Dakar was how excited the local kids would get when they'd see me trundling into town. After a couple of weeks of amped-up television coverage, a KLR covered with stickers looks much like a rally racer to a 12-year old, so kids would ask for autographs or get ridiculously gleeful upon merely saying hello.

Explaining I had nothing to do with the Dakar, wasn't famous, and had never been on TV didn't dampen their enthusiasm.

MARK HARFENIST

South of Chaitén, the Carretera consists of a mix of pavement and gravel – generally of a higher standard than the Argentine alternative, Ruta 40 and without the lashing gales. Services are available mainly in Coyhoique, the largest town, and to a lesser extent in Cochrane. Small hotels and campgrounds are widely scattered and wild camping is possible. The route is spectacular enough in its own right, but there are even more impressive side roads to explore, including toward the coast at Puerto Aisén and Puerto Cisnes. The easiest exit to Argentina hereabouts is via Chile Chico after riding around Lago General Carrera (or ferrying across to shorten the journey). A few other routes will be obvious on your map. One notable possibility probably not on your map runs from the southern tip of the Carratera Austral in Villa O'Higgins. There's a track to roads near El Chaltén in Argentina. It is rarely done by motorbike, see p331.

Riders heading north along the Carretera Austral will exit via Futaleufú or carry on to Chaiten and one of the ferries. From Quellón or Puerto Montt, you can explore Chile's Lake Country and onward up to Santiago and Valparaiso, or cut back into Argentina near Bariloche and make the long trek across to Buenos Aires on the back roads.

Allow a few weeks between Ushuaia and Santiago or Buenos Aires if following any of the Carretera Austral, but note that it would be easy to spend twice that time here. The weather is most tolerable during summer; it begins to get stormy and oppressive during the autumn as the jet stream and its storm track shift. As you'd expect, the winters are brutal.

One more option bears a mention; Navimag (🖥 www.navimag.com) runs cruises down the 'inside passage' from Puerto Montt to Punta Natales over three nights. Riders who catch good weather give glowing reports about the stunning scenery. Pay from a seasonal US$450 to $650 for yourself and bike.

ARGENTINA

Like Brazil, Argentina can be a bit too big for its own good at times, but if you pick your spots you'll find still more eye-popping natural spectacle and riding adventures, plus cosmopolitan Buenos Aires and the best beef steaks or *asado* on the planet. Those interminable grass-covered Pampas do have their uses.

Argentina has the highest per capita income in South America, although wide economic disparities mean that half live at a poverty level. After the 2001 financial collapse the country became a cheap destination, but **prices** are now almost equivalent to Chile, and the remote south can be downright expensive. Standards for food and accommodation are fine and roads, bridges and ferries are as good as it gets down here. Motorcycles are well-supported too, with parts for most brands available in the major cities.

Argentine enforcement of **insurance** has been stepped up recently and you may not get past a border without it, particularly coming from Bolivia. Insurance may be available at border towns and is certainly available from bike insurance spacialist ATM in BA (🖳 www.atmseguros.com.ar) to cover Argentina, Bolivia, Brazil, Chile, Ecuador, Paraguay, Peru and Uruguay for around $20 a month. Another broker to try is 🖳 speiserseguros.com.ar

Buenos Aires is a grand city sometimes compared to Paris for its expansive boulevards and café culture. It also features a lively and accessible motorcycle culture. **Dakar Motors** (🖳 www.dakarmotors.com; S34° 32.47' W58° 31.01') is a good address to know, combining repairs, storage, a basic hostel and advice in onward shipping and insurance. The shop is also a contact point to buy or sell an overland-ready bike from other riders but isn't involved.

To those making the 5600km round trip (yes, 3500 miles!) to Ushuaia from Buenos Aires, Argentina will feel unnecessarily vast and uncharacteristically dull. Days will pass with little change in terrain which was pretty boring to begin with. Instead, head west for the action: the mountains along the Chilean border. In the north are volcanic peaks and desert; the central regions have vineyards, lakes and forests; further south, glaciers and ice fields are pierced by jagged peaks. You may find 🖳 www.ruta0.com useful in your planning

North to Brazil

The falls at **Iguazú** on the Argentinian border are one of the continent's premier attractions, and worth seeing even if you think you've seen enough waterfalls elsewhere in the world. The most direct routes between BA and Iguazú follow Argentina's Rutas 14 or 12, but on these highways the famously corrupt **cops** have had a habit of flagging down foreign bikers and issuing tickets for offences real or imagined. Despite the officious-looking paperwork – which can even include documents purporting to enable customs to seize bikes or forbid their export – pay nothing if you weren't actually doing anything wrong. Just watch your speed and make sure all your paperwork is spick and span.

Iguazú is a decision point: east leads to the Brazilian coast's sandy beaches, north goes to the vast inland wetlands and wildlife habitats of the Pantanal and eventually **Prudhoe Bay**. Or hop over into Paraguay on your way to north-western Argentina and the Andes, or take the Trans-Chaco highway north to Bolivia (p322). If you've just arrived in BA you're already being tormented by the continent's mouth-watering options.

Coming from the altiplano

Swooping over from Chile like a windsurfing condor, you'll enter by one of the couple of dozen passes through the Andes. These vary greatly in character,

CRUISING THE ATLANTIC TO BUENOS AIRES

Faced with the discouraging reports surrounding crating and freighting our bikes to South America, we decided to travel with them in some form or other and eventually took a container ship from London to Buenos Aires. We found the process relatively straightforward.

We made our booking through Safemariner (🖳 www.safemariner.co.uk) who were very helpful, and to top it off there was the prospect of a day ashore in Antwerp, Le Havre, Bilbao, Dakar, Freetown, Rio, Santos, Montevideo, and Zarate up the Rio Parana before disembarking in Buenos Aires (BA). The cost was $1800 per person and bike.

There is only one word of caution, you need to be very flexible with your departure date. Our reservation was made in November 2010 and at this time the estimated sailing date was July 29 2011. We eventually sailed on the September 3rd. Grimaldi (the freight company) and Safemariner were keen to stress that sailing times were estimates and the ports of call likely to change. Our sailing eventually took six weeks (instead of the scheduled four) due to delays in Freetown, Sierra Leone. It just meant we had two more weeks of food and sunbathing to enjoy at no extra cost!

On arrival in BA the Grimaldi agent came aboard to carry out the formalities which the country may or may not require. In the case of BA, we handed over our bike ownership documents (V5) and passports which were taken to the customs office while we prepared the bikes.

We were then escorted from the ship with the other overlanders to the customs and immigration car park where a brief inspection was carried out. We were then issued with the nine-month TIP for the bikes and our stamped passports.

We were assured by the customs officer that our bikes were fully compliant with Argentine legislation and we should ignore any attempts by an unscrupulous police (see p329) who may suggest otherwise. We were also told never to surrender the TIP to anyone other than the customs officer at the border on exit. In other words don't lose it.

With a quick pat on the back, a hand shake and a fond farewell to the other passengers we had spent the last six weeks with, we threw ourselves into the melée of BA traffic.

For photos and a details of life on the ocean waves read the appropriate dates on our blog: 🖳 ccgadventures.wordpress.com.

CHRIS & CHLOE GRANGER

FLYING A BIKE FROM UK TO BA

I'd read that Buenos Aires docks can get expensive so I got James Cargo to air freight my XTZ to BA for just under £1800.

I found flights cheapest with Alitalia from Barcelona and on arrival in Argentina got a free 90-day tourist visa. There were some questions about the bike parts in my luggage but in the end the nice chap was more interested in my plans.

To pick up the bike I needed a copy of my passport's visa stamp and Argentinean bike insurance, plus copies and originals of the bike's registration document, my IDP and passport. I was walked through the process by Sandra from Dakar Motos, so it was pretty easy, really.

At the airport south of town I paid about £85 at the freight office. They prepared my file, then we walked over to the customs building opposite. I showed my passport and the file and was given a security slip.

When the office opened around 10am we took a number from the machine and joined those already there. It was an hour's wait to be seen, but in the meantime they brought the Yamaha in its box to the entrance. My bike was here!

I must confess that I then got a little lost with the series of visits to various desks, but that included authorising the opening of the box so we could take the bike out – inside all was OK.

Then back to customs to check the bike. More stamps and £167 storage paid over a holiday weekend. More stamps, back to the customs chap, more paperwork, and I was finally handed a slip which enabled me to ride out of the compound. Thanks to Sandra's help we were back in Dakar Motos in time for lunch.

PAT MCCARTHY

🖳 www.patonabike.blogspot.co.uk

WHAT ABOUT URUGUAY AND PARAGUAY?

Although both are undoubtably great places to live, most travellers' closest contact with Uruguay is gazing across the River Plate estuary from BA – and with Paraguay from visiting Iguazú Falls. You could say these two countries are the opposite of the equally obscure Guianas (see p336) which are harder to get to but, by and large, reward the effort.

Paraguay's Ciudad del Este lies just across the bridge from Foz do Iguaçu (Brazil), a decrepit border town with a smattering of lowlife and corrupt officials surviving off contraband.

Paraguay's long been a regional haven for smugglers and their wares, and a wide variety of grey- or black-market goods, including bike parts, can be found in Ciudad del Este or Asunción, 330km to the west.

A foreigner can easily **buy a bike** here too. It's not legal, but then neither is smuggling so ask around in either town. Just remember that such transactions are dodgy so use your wits.

The remainder of Paraguay is not entirely without interest. **Asunción** has attractive colonial barrios, more shopping plus bike dealers and parts. Elsewhere there are the remains of Jesuit monasteries and prosperous Mennonite towns adrift in the Chaco which fills the barely populated north.

Across this prairie stretches Ruta 9, El Transchaco, running 1400km from Asunción to **Sucre** in Bolivia on rapidly deteriorating pavement. Get here in late September and you have a chance of being run over by the Transchaco Rally.

If that makes **Uruguay** sound all the more tempting then a ferry (💻 www.buquebus.com) crosses the estuary to Colonia, 160km west of Montevideo, costing from $35 and taking from three hours.

with MARK HARFENIST

scenery and difficulty: in the far north the Paso de Jama is paved all the way from **San Pedro de Atacama** to **Salta** and is the easiest Andes crossing north of Mendoza. Just to the south of Jama is the more remote, unpaved Paso de Sico winding past multi-coloured lakes and soaring volcanoes. Between Jama and Ruta 7 near Mendoza, half a dozen gravel roads cross less used passes of varying difficulty. Paso de San Francisco is a favourite, requiring a 500-km fuel range and frequent stops to record the epic landscapes. Others are harder still, and all top out around 4000 or 5000 metres (13,100-16,500'). Always enquire about food and fuel because for the most part there isn't much of either.

The 360km route between Santiago and **Mendoza** (Argentina Ruta 7/Chile Ruta 60) is fun too, and during the summer you can avoid the tunnel by taking the old unpaved 'Road of Curves' up and over the pass. Start looking for the signed turn-offs from the main highway on either side of the tunnel. Be aware that this Argentinian border station is renowned for lengthy queues, although these won't faze anyone recently arrived from Turkmenistan.

South of Mendoza another dozen roads cross lower passes, such as the fully paved Osorno to Bariloche (240km); others include the crossing near Futaleufú and another outside Los Antiguos. The most rugged is certainly the 140km track that connects **Villa O'Higgins** (Chile) with **El Chaltén** (Argentina) used by trekkers, hardcore mountain bikers and very rarely by demented overland riders. Midway your passage must be timed to coincide with the small ferry across the windy expanse of Lago San Martin.

Southbound riders also enter Argentina directly from Bolivia, usually via La Quiaca or Aguas Blancas. These border roads are scenic and fun, but forgo the distinct appeal of the arid Andean crossings from Chile.

LATIN AMERICA – ROUTE OUTLINES

A ripio- and gale-free section of Ruta 40.
© Duncan Hughes

Ruta 40 – the road south

Argentina's **Ruta 40** has long held iconic stature among adventure riders. Che Guevara came this way in the early 1950s and since then countless riders, both local and gringo, have followed in his Norton's tracks. Other great rides in this area include some 190 kilometres of twisty Ruta 68 between Cafayate and **Salta**, the mix of *ripio* (see below) and tar on Ruta 33 from Cachi to Salta (160km), and Ruta 9 north from Salta. This is just the tip of the ripio iceberg.

Mendoza is a popular stopping place for those hankering after spares, repairs and winery tours. If heading south, this is the last place to feature whole blocks crammed with bike dealers and mechanics, so get ahead of the maintenance curve while you can. Lodgings can fill up here but La Casa de Mhayl (S32° 53.38' W68° 49.96') has secure parking and the Bolivian consulate is just down the road, if you have any Ferrero Rocher to spare.

West of Mendoza, Ruta 7 crosses into Chile with stunning views of Aconcagua on cloud-free days. Watch your neck, it's the highest mountain in the Americas. Conversely, eastwards Ruta 7 traverses nothing much at all for 12 hours or more to Buenos Aires. Knowing this, most discerning adventurists continue on Ruta 40 or parallel roads south toward the Lakes District. This section of 40 is paved and the riding is not so thrilling; hugging the Andes on parallel routes is more like it if you don't mind long hours on gravel roads.

The Lakes District comes with snow-capped mountains framing pretty lakes, cosy cabins, forests and cute towns brimming with adventure tourism opportunities. Hereabouts your satnav is trying to show you the 200km Ruta de Siete Lagos following Ruta 234 from San Martín de los Andes to **Bariloche**.

During the summer season, streets in the major Lakes towns are full of brightly clothed tourists so lodgings can get lean, though most towns have campgrounds. Just don't expect privacy and quiet – as in Spain, camping for the Argentines is a gregarious affair.

After a day or two wandering south through the lakes and forests, subtle changes are noticed. Your bike labours more than it should and you meet northbound riders carrying a thousand-yard stare, cradling armfuls of crumpled plastic. Yes, it's **windy**; Patagonian windy. Somewhere south of El Bolsón the famed *ventarrón del diablo* manifests itself, usually blowing out of the south or off the peaks. Many riders fight gales at a steady 100kph/60mph with gusts up to 160kph and once you're out in the steppes, a fallen bike and a crumpled Zega is your only shelter.

The round stones or *ripio* with which Patagonian roads are often surfaced doesn't help at all, and may well be named after the effect it has on plastic bodywork and jeans. Tracks often consist of half-metre wide ruts with 8-inch high ripio berms to either side. When the roads get muddy more ripio is tipped on with only cursory attempts at compaction. Catch a front wheel in one of these berms while bracing against a 120kph gust and be ready for a ripio faceplant. This can happen many times daily for days on end

Start early as the wind takes a while to warm up, giving you a good six hours of riding before things get scary. If you've had enough, the sealed Ruta 3 runs from BA to Tierra del Fuego and is connected to Ruta 40 by several paved connections.

The problem with dodging Ruta 40 is that much of Patagonia's epic scenery lies at its foot, notably El

Ushuaia this way please.
© thedarienplan.com

Chaltén and the Fitzroy range, El Calafate and the Perito Moreno glacier, plus Torres del Paine National Park. Stay on Ruta 3 and you'll miss it all, so unless you can cook up a believable excuse, soldier on through the winds and ripio before crossing over to the Atlantic coast and Ruta 3 at Rio Gallegos.

You probably know this already but **Tierra del Fuego** is an island divided between Chile and Argentina. To get there you take one of the two **ferries** back in Chile: from either **Punta Arenas** ($20; 2–3 hours) or further east from **Punta Delgada** off the end of Ruta 3 (20 mins). Keep your receipt as you might get a discount on boat trips out of Ushuaia.

Once on the island lodging options become increasingly scarce and pricey so unless equipped with a Whillans Box tent you may find yourself pushing onward into the crepuscular austral twilight in search of a bed. There's a road-house in Paso San Sebastián, just before the crossing back into Argentina, and a hostel in the centre of Rio Grande, but both fill up during high season.

From either ferry it's about 100km of gravel to the Argentine border with no fuel stations, so fill up in Punta or Rio Gallegos, or at Rio Grande 230km north of Ushuaia. In Argentina the road is sealed and it's about three hours over the mountains to Ushuaia. Expect snow and rain.

Ushuaia is a surprisingly bustling place, with a lively pub scene and a sur-feit of penguin-themed souvenirage. There are quite a few hostels, hotels and vast numbers of guest houses, but only the crowded hostels come cheap. The Campground Rio Pipio or the Rugby Club, on the western edge of town (S54° 49.90' W68° 21.56') are favoured among riders, the latter with a bar, internet and secure parking.

Your obligatory end-of-the-road shot is waiting another 10km west, at the end of Ruta 3 and within the Parque Nacional Tierra del Fuego. You'll have to pay a park entrance fee to get there, but few begrudge that after all those miles. Wherever you've come from, it's been a long ride getting here and it's not over yet.

All aboard for the Straits of Magellan.
© Chris Granger

LATIN AMERICA – ROUTE OUTLINES

VENEZUELA AND THE GUIANAS

Most riders stay west and keep to the high roads and cooler temperatures through the Andean countries, partly because eastward, Venezuela and the three countries known collectively as **Guianas** have a reputation for high prices, uncertain security and an uninspiring coastline of mud flats. From Georgetown in Guyana to Macapa in Brazil you're stuck on a single transit route which even then isn't entirely sealed and so prone to the weather. Add the low elevation and it's always **hot and muggy**, year round.

Plus even with a dual sport, inland exploration in the Guianas takes some commitment, and there's no way into Brazil. So once you do get to Belem you'd better hope you're a fan of Brazil because you're about as far from any-where else in South America as it gets.

Venezuela

You may get tired of reading this but to the roaming motard Venezuela has plenty to offer: great scenery, reasonable food and lodgings, and of course the world's cheapest gasoline. Eighty dollars of fuel in Brazil costs a buck in Venezuela and even by South American standards you'll find unique land-scapes among the tepui mesas, Caribbean beaches and islands, lowland jun-gles where cocoa evolved, serrated peaks draped with remnant glaciers, and inland wetlands teeming with bizarre wildlife which, if you've been in the jungle a little too long, may well include yourself.

Now for the small print. If you credit the US State Department warnings on Venezuela you'll be tempted to give the place a miss. After all, it's not like there's a shortage of great destinations in the region where you don't risk rob-bery, scams, kidnapping, carjacking and other forms of mayhem. As always, a generous helping of salt is in order as the travel advice might have as much to do with politics as your journey.

There's no doubt that life in Venezuela has been deteriorating. Disenchanted businessmen describe with great gusto the crisis that has befall-en them. However, while this might not bode well for the country as a whole, it doesn't mean Venezuela is a bad country to ride in or that you'll have a rough time there. The few gringo motorcyclists who pass through each year report great riding, spectacular sights and friendly people who go out of their way to be helpful and kind, as is often the case in places with a bad rap. In fact, the main problem with Venezuela is that it tends to fall at the beginning or end of a big South American journey when riders are either fired up for the charge south or running low on funds and will.

There's no doubt your **security** requires attention here, as it does in parts of Colombia. **Caracas** in particular is famously corrupt and sometimes violent; most riders don't bother because, like many big cities, the stress/relaxation ratio is against you. You need to know which barrios not to blunder into and at what time the informal curfew starts. Cops can fish for bribes too, but it's said they're not particularly persistent or intimidating about it. Shipping a bike into or out of Caracas is not recommended; do it in Colombia.

On top of cheap fuel, Venezuelan currency is subject to a robust **black mar-ket**. According to the government you're allotted four bolívars per US dollar. If you use a credit card, ATM, or change money at a bank, this is the rate you'll get at which point the country gets nearly as expensive as Argentina. Change your dollars informally and you'll double your bolívars. You'll get about twice the official rate for Colombian pesos or Brazilian reais too, provided you change them near the relevant borders. There's obviously a furtive aspect to these exchanges and getting ripped of or plain mugged is a risk; guest houses and hotels owned by Europeans are a good bet. Rates will be better in border towns if not just across the border in Colombia or Brazil, since currency exchange is not illegal there. Obviously you don't want these bolívars declared or found on entering Venezuela.

At the borders

Coming from Colombia exit procedures at **Maicao** are easy and the Venezuelan entry is also quickly processed, with vehicle paperwork completed a few kilometres on at Guarero. However, the main crossing point is at **Cucuta** for San Antonio del Tachira or **San Cristobal**. The DIAN customs office is in Cucuta back at N07° 55.1' W72 30.1' where you need to check your bike out; the DAS immigration is at the border. On the Venezuelan side, Onidex (immigration N07° 48.85' W72° 26.65') is a kilometre from the bridge in the border town of **San Antonio del Tachira**. You'll also need to visit SENIAT (customs N07° 49.05' W72° 26.87') right opposite the border post for your TIP. At the first fuel stop expect to be shocked and if heading into Colombia expect long queues for petrol and that Colombian insurance may take some organising before applying for your temporary import permit

The country's main attractions lie in the Paramo cordillera around Mérida and many national parks, as well as an excursion to Angel Falls or Salto Angel. Good timing is required to ensure full flow over the Falls (June) while beating the onset of rains in the Amazon. Ciudad Bolívar is the starting point for flights to Angel Falls from where you travel up-river by motorised canoe to the base of the world's tallest waterfall, a real jungle adventure. You have to stash your bike for the few days you'll spend upcountry; it's easily done.

South of here is the Gran Sabana, a vast flatland on a plateau dotted with table-top mesas or tepuis emerging Lost World-like from the mists. You'll have some spectacular wild camps, refreshing waterfalls and rivers and all-round gorgeous scenery.

If coming up from Manaus it's an easy two day ride into southern Venezuela and the gradual rise in elevation is refreshing after the long run through the tropics. From Guyana you'll join the road from Manaus in Boa Vista, where ATMs offer your last chance to stock up on Brazilian currency to exchange at the border.

It's best to arrive at **Santa Elena Uairén** during regular business hours on a weekday, failing which there's basic accommodation just short of the border in Brazil. From Santa Elena, trekking tours set off to the nearby tepui of Roraima, but most riders are keen to start burning that cheap fuel on the road to Ciudad Bolivar. After Ciudad Bolivar red-blooded motorcyclists head for the terminal peaks of the Andean range which even here still manage to scale 5000m/16,500' near **Merida**, a rather uninspiring long day's ride to the west. Merida is a centre for adventure travel of all sorts, as well as tours to Los Llanos, a huge inland savannah wetland to the south. Roads in all directions are supple as a whip and steep, with pockets of Andean villages to explore.

THE GUIANAS

Like Belize, Guyana, Suriname and French Guiana – the Guianas – have a Caribbean rather than Latino culture, and like Belize, few riders make the diversion so for those that do there's a sense of pioneering rather than following the hordes. The route is obvious; in fact from one end to the other there's no choice. Once there, fly-in tourists may wonder how on earth you got here.

The colonial history of the Guianas saw the rice and sugar plantations helped along with immigration from the former British and Dutch territories in India and Indonesia as well as Hmong refugees from Laos and Maroons, descendants of African slaves. The less accessible and developed inland regions not suited to cattle ranching remains largely pristine, unlogged jungle populated by indigenous and protected Amerindian tribes.

A few years ago, bandits were the scourge of roads in the Guianas, but like Colombia, the worst seems to have passed so now only the usual vigilance is required, especially in the cities. Rain and muddy roads will be much more significant impediments to travel. August to November is the main **dry season**, with a dry pause in February, although tropical deluges hit at any time.

Guyana

Though it gets discussed, there's **no road link** between Venezuela and Guyana. Access from the west is along the sealed road from **Boa Vista** in Brazil, itself some 200km south of the Venezuelan border. From here head northwest 140km to **Lethem** (hotels) on the Guyanese border where a bridge now crosses the Takutu River – a ride you can do from Venezuela in a day if your ducks line up. Coming from Guyana the Brazilians can be tedious.

As you cross the bridge start **riding on the left** and speaking **English**. An IDP may not be accepted, so along with **insurance** you may need to acquire a local driving permit if you're here as well as in Suriname for more than a month. Note that if coming from Suriname to Guyana at Moleson Creek (see opposite), you'll have to get insurance at Corriverton, 12km up the road.

Nearly three-quarters of Guyana remains as it was in the Jurassic period and it's thought the Roraima plateau (actually more easily reached from Santa Elena in Venezuela) gave Conan Doyle the idea for his 1912 book, *The Lost World*, where dinosaurs survive in isolation.

Still known as 'The Trail', the once notorious dirt road 460km to **Georgetown** is fine even during the rainy season, with a couple of mudholes on the northern section. Note that **maps** of this route are inaccurate – not least Google based on a satellite image from the 1970s! Realistically, it's a two-day ride so take a break halfway at the Iwokrama Lodge rainforest centre just before the Essequibo ferry crossing (N05° 18.71' W58° 54.11'). Full board is about $130 but this area is famous for jaguar sightings so you may get lucky.

Guyana's government runs more red tape than the infant Khrushchev's birthday presents; as in India, another Brit legacy. In **Georgetown** ordinary folks are friendly, polite, helpful though at night a cautious person might not stagger around drunk with pocketfuls of cash and singing like Freddie Mercury. Scotia Bank's offices have possibly the only international **ATM** in the land. Food, lodging and services are a notch or two below Suriname, but so are prices. The Melbourne Hotel on Sheriff Street is in a good neighbourhood and has secure parking. To get there aim for N06° 48.95' W58° 8.15'.

Suriname

Suriname has an odd mixture of British and Dutch names befitting its colonial past. Towns called Glasgow or Manchester are a few kilometres from Europlodder, while Bombay is just down the road and Hindu temples dot the countryside. It's also one of the few South American countries where you'll probably need a **visa in advance** (check 🖳 www.surinameembassy.org). They're available in Georgetown at 171 Peter St (near Rose & Crown St; N06° 48.76' W58° 08.88'). In Cayenne you may get it next day for a hefty €100, from the consulate on rue Madame Payee, just off rue Mole on the north side of the street, or from the nearby address more commonly given: 3 Avenue Leopold Helder (near N04° 56.39', W52° 20.06').

The link with Guyana is a daily **ferry** at around 11am from **Moleson Creek** (N05° 46.75' W57° 10.21'), some 12km south of Corriverton over the Corentyne River to South Drain (N05° 44.56' W57° 08.18'). This brings you in 40km south of **Nieuw Nickerie** where you'll need to buy **insurance** (🖳 www.assuria.sr).

Riding is still **on the left** and it's a rough metalled road from Nieuw Nickerie 230km to the **Paramaribo** which is said to be less edgy after dark than Georgetown or Cayenne. Suriname does have a few roads which penetrate the interior, offering glimpses of primeval forest without resorting to river or air travel. Take yourself out to the Brownsberg Nature Reserve, 130km south of Paramaribo.

Freighting bikes by air or sea to the Netherlands is easy and surprisingly cheap – sea shipping without crating costs as little as 500 euros. Track down N.V. Global Expedition in Paramaribo just south of the bridge (aim for N05° 47.85' W55° 10.45'; 🖳 www.nvglobalexpedition.com/en) for sea shipments or Surinam Air Cargo (🖳 www.surinamaircargo.nl) at the airport 50km south of town. From Paramaribo the road runs in good shape through uncut jungle some 140km to Albina on the Maroni River to St Laurent with several daily ferry runs to French Guiana.

French Guiana

French Guiana is a former penal colony that's still an overseas province or *département* of France (there are three others, all islands in the Caribbean and off Madagascar). As such EU nationals can scoot right on in as if they were riding off a ferry at Calais; others have to do the usual police and customs dance. Just as in France you **ride on the right**, the currency is the **euro**, the food ought to be to your liking, but the **prices** probably won't be. French is the dominant language; Portuguese may see you through but Spanish is rarely spoken. Customs will hint that you need to arrange **insurance**, but coming from Brazil you can't buy it until **Cayenne** anyway. Often enough, insurance papers aren't checked until you leave, but at that point they seem to be essential.

Fuel is probably the most expensive in South America, though at about 450km from border to border, you won't need much more than a tank's worth and at least some of this expense is reflected in roads you could take home to meet the parents, complete with white lines down the middle. Remember those?

With 5.5 million square kilometres of jungle at your disposal in the Amazon basin, most take more notice of Guiana's man-made attractions, namely the **space centre** at Kourou, located here not because the labour's cheap, but because gravity is moderately less strong near the equator and, as with Cape Canaveral in Florida, an aborted satellite launch can fall harmlessly into the Caribbean, and not on somewhere like Dusseldorf were it launched from metropolitan France. The other attraction in Guiana is the former prison at Devil's Island just off the coast, made famous in the book and film, *Papillon*.

The ferry from Brazil. With a good run-up you'll make the far bank. © Graham Styles

On to northeast Brazil

The good road continues to the border with Brazil at Saint Georges. A bridge is under construction but don't hold your breath; they don't build themselves. Pay around $40 for the ferry based over the river in **Oiapoque**.

Once over, get stamped at the police station, then your TIP at the *aduana* (customs) in the north end of town (N03° 51.0' E51° 49.9', closed Saturday afternoon and Sunday).

From here to Macapá is nearly 600km, but 60km out of town the tarmac deserts you again, leaving around 190km of dirt and possibly mud until Calcoene, 250km from Macapá. If it's been pouring and you're two-up on an FJ Twelve you may want to wait a day or two, and whatever you're riding, make sure you fill up before you leave; fuel stations are stretched out in the middle.

Located on the 400km-wide Amazon estuary and strung right across the equator, expect to perspire in **Macapá**. For a hotel with parking try the Hotel America Novo Mundo on Ave. Coaracy Nunes 333 (N00° 01.94' W51° 03.23').

To get the pontoon ferry to Belém, track down Sanave (⌨ www.gruposanave.com.br). They're based by the river in Porto Santana, west of Macapá (S00° 00.88' W51° 12.17'). Expect nothing more than a **barge** pulled by a tug and a bill of a couple of hundred dollars for the duration of what may be a two day trip. It's no pleasure cruise, but if you've just got here from Colombia, you'll probably need the rest. Lash your bike down well – as the pontoon nears Belem the tidal swell gets a bit choppy.

BRAZIL

Spreading across nearly half the continent and accounting for over half its population, Brazil borders every other South American country except Ecuador and Chile.

You'd think you can't avoid it, but as the Pan-Am slips down the west side, many riders skim this vast country or don't bother, citing language and visa issues, vast distances and the fact that mile for mile Brazil is scenically less diverse than some of its smaller but more spectacular neighbours. In the south, sugar cane plantations stretch for hours and arrow-straight highways are clogged with trucks. The northern interior is a semi-arid scrub broken by occasional mesas where again the hours turn to days without appreciable changes to the scenery. The vast Amazon basin is fascinating to see up close, but rideable roadways are few and surrounding jungles have often been levelled for timber or grazing.

TRANS AMAZON NORTH TO SOUTH

The Andes offer spectacular and lively mountain roads, but the Amazon basin is the other definitive South American habitat; a humid, partially-depleted rainforest that spreads across at least half a dozen countries creating an untameable obstacle to overland travel. New roads are boldly carved to snatch resources, but one good 'Wet' (which in some places *is* the climate) and a few overloaded trucks soon churn up an unnavigable mire which gets reclaimed by the jungle as soon as you turn your back.

Up or down the Amazon, the smartest way of travelling (and west of Manaus, the only way) is on a series of river boats. Few formal ferries exist, it's more of a freight barge scene, especially over longer distances; see where companies like Sanave (🖳 www.gruposanave.com.br) are operating.

Top down though, you can ride across Amazonia. Start at **Santa Elena de Uairen** on the Venezuela–Brazil border. It depends on your nationality, but most bar Americans get into Brazil without a visa in advance, though you may need to show an international vaccination certificate. From there to Manaus is just over 1000km all sealed, via Boa Vista and the turn off to Guyana (see p336).

In **Manaus** the Amazon is already three kilometres wide. Locals take the boat up the Rio Madeira to **Humaita** but with a bike they'll try and stiff you for up to 1500 reais when it's worth a third of that.

© dwq.com.br

Anyway, improvements are underway on the once notorious **BR319**, with the more dilapidated of the 200-plus bridges repaired. And like on the BAM, bikes can cross what cars dare not. Overnight you can crawl behind the fenced-off telecom mast stations to avoid the marauding pumas.

Once ferried to the south side of the Amazon the first couple of hundred kilometres are paved and include three short ferry crossings. Thereafter, it's broken tarmac with short stretches of mud and wooden bridges which may be reaching their cross-by date. The next two days will be tough if it's been

raining and you're on the wrong tyres, but after that the track is interspersed with stretches of tarmac again, and some 650km from the Amazon you get to a point 30km north of Humaita where Brazil's network of sealed roads resumes. I now pronounce the ordeal on hold, you may stop and kiss the tar. Just remember this isn't a tourist area but an isolated beef and logging region with drugs smuggled in from Peru and Bolivia, so in places like **Porto Velho**, 215km down the road, keep your wits about you.

From Porto Velho you can stay in Brazil and fight it out with the truck traffic southeast towards the Mato Grosso, the Pantanal wetlands, eastern Bolivia and Iguazu Falls on the Argentina-Paraguay border, some 1400km from Buenos Aires (see p342).

Or in the dry season from April to November head for Peru via **Rio Branco**, 540km from Porto Velho with a one-hour time change on the way. Another 220km gets you to Brasileia (check out with the police) and a final 100km or so to Assis Brazil opposite the Peruvian **border** at a corner with Bolivia. A bridge here crosses the river to Inapari; left after the bridge is immigration and customs.

It's said to be sealed from here at least halfway to **Puerto Maldonado**, 240km to the south. At a lowly 200m or 650 feet, once you ferry over the Rio Madre de Dios you're in the hot humid epicentre of Peru's Amazonian tourism scene with plenty of places to stay, eat, rest and get healed in the hands of shamen and their mind-altering potions

With that done, straighten your tie and brush down your hair; it's 430km along nothing less than the **Interoceanic highway** to **Cusco** up in the Andes at a cool 3500m (11,600'), with the 4950m (16,000') Hualla Hualla pass on the way and Machu Picchu nearby (see p321). They're working on making the road live up to its name, but until that happy day, expect the ride to take a couple of days to Cusco. Once in Cusco grab a cold one at the Norton Rats tavern, you've earned it.

TRIP REPORT
SOUTH AMERICA ~ KTM950

Name	Peter B
Year of birth	1973
Occupation	IT
Nationality	Kiwi & Brit
Previous travels	A fair bit
Bike travels	London to India with an Africa Twin

This trip	BA to Ushuaia then up to Colombia
Trip duration	Ten months
Departure date	November 2006
Number in group	Two
Distance covered	30,000km

Best day	Dude, they're all good
Worst day	...still can't come up with one
Favourite places	How long you got? Bol, Arg, Chile, Peru
Biggest headache	At altitude, but soon abates
Biggest mistake	Should have free camped more
Pleasant surprise	Anything is fixable – but I knew this
Any illness	Solamente hangovers
Cost of trip	About £1000 a month
Other trips planned	Of course

Bike model	KTM 950
Age, mileage	2004 model, 16,000km
Modifications	Nothing major. It's bloody good as is
Wish you'd ...	Used 16T front sprocket from the start
Tyres used	Pirelli Scorpion ATs
Punctures	Three or four
Type of baggage	Alu panniers with Ortlieb on the back

Bike's weak point	Some might argue but for me: none
Strong point	Suspension, engine, easy to service
Bike problems	Water pump seal, oil light sender unit
Accidents	One
Same bike again	Yes!
Any advice	KTM 950 is THE most fun bike (for me)

Having said that, there are a few worthwhile destinations: for birds and wildlife there's the famous Pantanal in the south; Rio de Janeiro for all the well-known reasons; the pretty colonial towns of Minas Gerais 500km northeast of Rio; the Afro-Brazilian vibe in Salvador and the adjacent beaches of Bahia; the epic Foz do Iguaçu waterfalls (see p342) and of course the Amazon Basin. If only these sights were more geographically condensed.

There are mountains too – notably around Curitiba in the south, between Sao Paulo and Rio along the coast, throughout Minas Gerais province and in the Chapada Diamantina further north. These highlands are full of winding roads, ranging from tiny dirt tracks to smooth ribbons of *asfalto*. There are also stately colonial towns and Brazil features thousands of miles of stunning coastline lapped by perfectly formed waves from the southern border to the Amazon delta. Riding Brazilian back roads can be confusing, but you're never too far from somewhere and most small towns will have some form of lodging, food and mechanical services.

Most fortunate of all, wherever you go Brazilians are remarkably friendly and welcoming. This spirit is the country's core appeal and because overland riders are less common here, every gas or food stop will attract interest and invitations, and it'll be difficult to spend any length of time here without making local friends. There are also riding clubs throughout the country, and emailed invitations from local riders are frequent if you have any sort of internet presence.

Not only is Brazil huge but it's comparatively expensive. Tyres, for example, are more expensive than elsewhere, despite the fact that most are manufactured in Brazil where rubber was invented. Expect to pay more for lodging and fuel, about US$1.50 per litre ($5.70 a US gallon, more on fuel on p313).

EU nationals get visas for up to 90 days, for others they can be expensive, slow and require documentation and appointments. The consulate in Puerto Iguazú (Argentina) is said to have an overnight turnaround. Coming from Venezuela a US citizen might get just a week. You might be asked for a handwritten note promising to export your bike but motor **insurance** isn't required.

Unlike elsewhere down here, they speak **Portuguese** and English speakers tend to be thin on the ground. Most Brazilians see no reason to speak even Spanish (not as similar to Portuguese as you might think) so learning a few words will greatly enhance any trip. Of course it's possible to eat, drink, take a leak and book a hotel (usually in that order) without speaking too much Portuguese, but where's the fun in that?

Routes

Coming from Buenos Aires, riders usually enter along the coastal route from Uruguay where roads are good but riding and scenery somewhat uninspired until mountains appear near **Florianópolis**. At 1800m they offer some relief from the heat as well as good roads and colonial-era towns in various states of decay. Parque Nacional de Aparados da Serra and Canela are recommended points of interest and riders often gather at the well-known Residencial Holandês (⌨ www.pousadadoholandes.com/en; S27° 08.08' W48° 30.97') in Bombas, 60km north of Florianopolis. There is a small workshop here, and one of the owners is a former mechanic.

Continuing along the coast the mountains get more rugged, the colonial towns more beautiful and the beaches more soul stirring between São Paulo and Rio and onwards into Espirito Santo and Minas Gerais. Note that neither Rio or São Paulo are relaxed motorcycling destinations; better to locate secure parking and explore by other means. Smaller cities like Petrópolis, Saquarema, Buzios and Paraty are more amenable.

Rio aside, the biggest tourist draw in southern Brazil is **Foz do Iguaçu** at the borders of Paraguay and Argentina. Quite a few riders make their way here from Buenos Aires along Ruta 14 for the ease with which Brazilian visas are issued in Puerto Iguazú. Although this inland route misses some nice beaches and winding roads through the hills, you'll get your fill further north.

A solid day's ride north from Iguaçu is the **Pantanal**, the world's largest savannah wetland. Reports differ on the best season for visits; some say rainy season floods concentrate the animals on high ground; others that the dry concentrates wildlife at the remaining water sources and you don't need a boat to get around. It's easy to ride the dirt roads into the Pantanal, stopping at whatever lodge looks interesting and negotiating the services you want (food, lodging, guided tours, boat rides), otherwise you might depart wondering what all the fuss was about. Contrary to what some maps show, the Trans-Pantanal highway doesn't connect the northern and southern sections and probably never will.

From the Pantanal, one paved route stretches northwest. At Ariquemes turn west for **Guajará-Mirim** (310km) and a crossing to Bolivia (see p324). Otherwise carry on for **Porto Velho**, with a sealed road to Humaitá from where river boats head down the Rio Madeira to **Manaus**. Expect to pay a couple of hundred dollars and stay about three days. Or from Humaitá you can set off along the infamous but recently improved BR319 track – more on p339 – as well as the route to Peru or Bolivia. From Manaus you can reach Iquitos in Peru by riverboat, or spend days on the red dirt BR230 Trans-Amazonian Highway all the way back west. Riding in this area, often your view will be over the acres of deforestation you've been hearing about all these years.

Another option from Iguaçu Falls is to cut east across the country, via the flawed modernist capital of **Brasilia** to Minas Gerais province, where you might find more great riding and pretty sights than the rest of Brazil put together. Head for Ouro Prêto or Tiradentes among the crags. Virtually any route will deliver villages tucked into steep valleys along endlessly entertaining roads, paved and unpaved, a huge relief from the interminable truck-clogged highways further west and south.

North of Rio, beaches stretch for thousands of kilometres and larger cities like **Recife** (Olinda), **Salvador da Bahia**, São Luís and **Belém** all throb with energy, while Itacaré, Porto Seguro, Arraial d'Adjuda, Jericoacoara and others offer smaller-scale charms and all the relaxation you can handle. Throughout Bahia the ethnic and cultural connections originating from the West African slave trade are very pronounced.

Although everyone owes themselves at least a quick look at Salvador and the Bahia coast, inland roads from Rio are the quicker way to Belém. A half-day's ride west of Salvador, the Chapada Diamantina offers a bit of highland relief and tracks diverge from Lençóis out to mesas, waterfalls and swimming holes. These and other inland parks offer relief in the midst of thousands of square miles of dreary, semi-arid *sertão* (but don't tell BMW that).

Belém is a hustling waterfront city with a picturesque old town, but like many big South American cities, has a reputation for thievery. Ferry yourself over the huge Amazon delta to Macapá for the Guyanas (see p338), or boat upstream to Manaus (3 to 5 days and from $250-500 depending on your negotiating skills). Head down to the marine terminal; brokers will find you and offer to secure whatever tickets you need. Prices are negotiable; you'll pay separately for bike and rider, with a reasonable surcharge if you want a cabin (as do most riders for security and comfort).

All these trips are on riverboats or even more basic barges, not lavish ferries equipped with casinos and cinemas, so come prepared for crowds, noise, unsanitary conditions and limited food. Loading, unloading and stowage are subject to the tides and the whims of baggage handlers who'll demand tips. The precarious loading process involves narrow, wooden ramps and a couple of sweaty guys in flip-flops so carry baggage separately.

Manaus itself is a remarkable place of a million inhabitants in the midst of the jungle, and teeming with half-decayed grandeur from its 19th-century rubber boom. Or you may find it merely grimy and depressing. The city is the focal point for tours into the Amazon hinterland, but scammers are on the prowl so exercise caution.

The sealed BR174 runs north to Boa Vista, entering Venezuela at Santa Elena de Uairén (see p335). Allow two easy days from Manaus. When planning this section note the 'less wet' season in the Amazon (April to November) corresponds with the wet in Venezuela. You'll get rained upon no matter what you do or when you do it. More on p312. On occasions riders set forth to traverse the entire Amazon Basin north to south, reporting that roads are fine when dry, and with little traffic. But be sure to enquire locally and prepare thoroughly; heading south there's a reason most take to the river.

TALES FROM THE SADDLE

Early adventures with motorcycles

Lois Pryce delves into the archives of the first motorcycle explorers to discover that once the 'motor-bicycle' became established, brave individuals soon saw the appeal of continent-spanning adventures.

With the recent arrival of adventure motorcycling into the mainstream, you might be forgiven for thinking that this two-wheeled globe-trotting is a 21st century phenomenon. Far from it. The irresistible combination of motorcycle plus wanderlust has been inspiring men and women to hit the road since the first machines appeared in the early 20th century. As far back as 1913 and certainly by the 1920s there are records of Europeans and Americans making long-distance, international journeys by 'motor-bicycle' or in sidecar combinations. But as is the nature of unrecorded adventures, many of these expeditions have slipped into obscurity, existing only as a faded newspaper clipping or a tattered sepia photo that crops up occasionally on the internet.

The savvier of these early motorcycle travellers had the good sense to record their adventures, usually in a book, but occasionally on grainy black-and-white film too. Luckily for us their stories live on and show us not only how different the experience was all those years ago, but often how similar too.

Here's my selection of a few of the greatest adventure motorcycling pioneers, in whose tyre treads we follow…

Robert Fulton Junior – Around the world 1932-34

To motorcycle solo around the world aged twenty-three would be a major achievement for anyone today, But back in the 1930s, for American, Robert Fulton Jnr., his eighteen-month odyssey through twenty-two countries was merely the springboard for a remarkable life as an inventor, writer, photographer, painter and sculptor.

In 1932 Fulton was a young man fresh out of college, and like most chaps of his age, keen to make an impression with the ladies. Finding himself at a dinner party in London, when asked by an

attractive female guest about his plans to sail back home to New York, he announced, somewhat rashly 'Oh no! I'm going around the world on a motorcycle!' This was probably not the first testosterone-fuelled declaration in the history of motorcycling and it certainly wasn't the last, and if it hadn't been overheard by a fellow dinner guest it may well have gone no further. Little did Fulton know that he was sharing the table with the head of Douglas Motor Works who interjected, 'I say old chap, that sounds grand! We can furnish you with a machine for your journey.'

Fulton's fate was sealed there and then, for as any budding adventurer knows, once you've mouthed off to all your friends, you have to go.

It was thus that Fulton found himself setting off on his very own *One Man Caravan*, the title of his marvellously enter-

> **As any budding adventurer knows, once you've mouthed off to all your friends, you have to go'.**

taining book about his 40,000-mile ride. His route took him through a pre-war Europe, a Middle East still firmly under British control, an India seemingly destined to be British forever, the (then) Dutch East Indies, into pre-communist China, and finally to Japan before taking a steamship back to his native USA.

He makes it clear from the beginning that he wasn't entirely sure how he got swept up in the whole plan, but his bluff having been called, he had no choice but to go along with it. However, the spirit of adventure was obviously smouldering in him somewhere, as he describes how the idea of this grand expedition began to gradually fire his imagination, 'the lure of travel; a different road ever day, a different fireside every evening, beneath a different star every night.'

His romantic visions will resonate with anyone who's pored over a map and dreamed of getting away from it all on their bike; these are the same urges that have inspired travellers through the ages and will continue to do so. Unfortunately for Robert Fulton, the same annoyances and obstructions were also just as prevalent then as they are today, most notably the finger-wagging pessimist who enjoys nothing more than to pour water on the sparks of a young buck's dreams.

'How does one go around the world from London, heading east?' enquired Fulton to a 'beefy-faced, hearty attaché' of the Royal Automobile Club in London.

'Too easy, my dear fellow' came the reply, 'One simply doesn't!'

Fulton's response illustrates the practical, can-do attitude that would serve him well on his adventure: 'But surely, wherever there is man, there must be some sort of route?' he countered.

It's this approach to his journey, and to his frequent crashes, arrests and various other scrapes along the way that make Fulton's story so engaging. His tribulations with both man and machine are treated with a warmth and wisdom and he's not afraid to admit to his own weaknesses and misgivings. The book captures perfectly the agonies and ecstasies of what we now call adventure motorcycling while transporting the reader to a bygone age of colonial-era travel – exotic Baghdad, wild Waziristan, steamy Sumatra and primitive China. But for all the ups and downs of overland travel, it's Fulton's intense curiosity, insightfulness and humane approach to his fellow man that makes *One Man Caravan* such a refreshing read and the accompanying film, *Twice Upon a Caravan*, such a joy to watch.

Theresa Wallach – London to Cape Town 1934-35

While Robert Fulton was making his way home to New York another ground-breaking expedition was preparing to depart from London. On the 11th December 1934 two adventurous motorcyclists were waved off by a cheering crowd, embarking on a venture that had never before been attempted – to ride a motorcycle the length of the African continent. It was a remarkable ambition in itself, but the fact that these motorcyclists were two young women in their twenties made it all the more incredible, and one can't help but wonder why Theresa Wallach and Florence Blenkiron aren't more famous. Their 14,000-mile journey to Cape Town, as told in Theresa Wallach's book *The Rugged Road*, took them almost eight months and saw the two women tackling gruelling conditions, incredible hardships and mechanical calamities that would defeat many of today's machines and riders!

As keen trials riders and racers, Theresa and 'Blenk' were not averse to bucking trends, but when they tried to drum up sponsorship for the expedition no motorcycle manufacturer wanted to get involved in backing these two unlikely explorers. 'Preposterous, my dear!', 'You're going WHERE?', 'You'll never make it' declared their detractors. No company wanted to be associated with a project that was so obviously doomed. But as you'll no doubt have gathered by now, Theresa and Blenk were no ordinary ladies, and not to be put off by a bunch of nay-saying men in suits.

> **Theresa and Blenk were no ordinary ladies, and not to be put off by a bunch of nay-saying men in suits.**

Eventually they managed to secure the sponsorship of a pioneering British motorcycle manufacturer of the day, Phelon & Moore, who produced the 600cc single-cylinder Panther. It was this bike, named The Venture, complete with sidecar and pulling a trailer, that would take the two women from London to Cape Town, although not without plenty of drama along the way.

Unsurprisingly, it was the crossing of the Sahara that proved to be the most demanding section of their trip. The sheer physical effort involved in motoring their five-wheeled rig across sand dunes, rocky plateaus and the steep tracks of the Hoggar mountains is exhausting just to read about. They became stuck on an alarmingly regular basis, resorting to hauling the trailer and sidecar out of endless sand drifts with a block and tackle, making progress of just fifteen feet at a time, and all of this in lead-lined pith helmets under a scorching 120°F sun! As their rig fell apart they routinely came up with ingenious fixes, raiding wrecked cars for parts as they worked through the night fuelled only by a bottle of smuggled Cognac. Emerging from the Sahara the drama continued with endless breakdowns, crashes and exciting forays into the central African jungle where they mingled with pygmy tribes and witch-doctors before finally rolling into Cape Town, weary but triumphant.

Reading their story, it's obvious that modern-day adventure motorcyclists have the advantage when it comes to equipment and the machine itself. But from a cultural and logistical point of view, African travel actually seemed an easier business back in the colonial era of the 1930s. Their route through the European-controlled continent where safari-suited colonels saluted them at every border post, is a far cry from the interminable delays, intimidation and palm-greasing we know today. The fact they were two women travelling alone appears to be more a source of pleasant surprise to the people they encountered rather than a cause for concern, although they did have to argue long and hard with the French colonial authorities for permission to cross the Sahara. On the whole, their female novelty value barely gets a mention and Theresa's story is full of tales of assistance, kindness and generosity from colonialists and natives alike, something female travellers will still attest to today.

It really is a staggering tale of true grit, sheer bravery and lashings of British stiff upper lip. Theresa Wallach however, is remarkably self-effacing about the expedition. 'Our exploit was not intended to be a geographical expedition,' she states in the book, 'nor did we pretend to be geologists, photographers or journalists. Blenk and I, with a bit of true-life reality, were simply going to see Africa'. If you think you have ever done anything even slightly hardcore, read *The Rugged Road* and prepare to be humbled!

If you think you have ever done anything even slightly hardcore, read *The Rugged Road* and prepare to be humbled!

Danny Liska – Alaska to Tierra del Fuego 1959-61

While Robert Fulton Jnr. was born into a privileged family, Danny Liska's humble background was entirely opposite. He is the everyman's motorcycle adventurer, son of a Czech immigrant, brought up on a farm and driven by a thirst for the unknown and the exotic. Liska's story is an inspiration for every

small-town boy who's ever watched a motorcycle roar past his bedroom window and longed to take off for faraway lands. And indeed for any middle-aged man who longs to skip out on his wife and do the same.

In 1959, aged thirty, Danny Liska did just that. He left his wife and farm in Nebraska and set off on his BMW R60 to become the first person to ride a motorcycle the length of the Americas. In the style of the true purist, he went first to Arctic Circle City (then the most northerly town in Alaska) to begin his epic journey. Two years and 65,000 miles later he arrived in Ushuaia, at the tip of Argentina. But most significantly he eschewed the idea of skipping over the still unrideable Darien Gap between Panama and Colombia, and instead tackled this notorious jungle on foot and by canoe.

Liska's book about his journey *Two Wheels to Adventure* has become a classic of motorcycle literature. Written in the 1960s, it wasn't published until the '80s, and the original now sells for hundreds of dollars. It's a great, rip-roaring read accompanied by fabulous photos, illustrations and maps. A frankly written account, the book tells of his adventures along the Pan-American Highway which was still under construction in many of the countries he passed through, but the real highlight is the detailed account of his

Liska's book about his journey *Two Wheels to Adventure* has become a classic of motorcycle literature.

incredible trek through the jungles of the Darien. Along his journey he's attacked by Indian tribesmen, has his blood sucked by vampire bats, contracts malaria, and even ends up working as a stunt double for the actor Yul Brynner on the shoot of the little known Cossack revenge epic, *Taras Bulba*! Like all grand adventures, *Two Wheels to Adventure* has a cast of fantastically inglorious characters, a handful of loose women, some hard times, high jinks, a dash of desperation and a very complicated love-life!

Written in the 60s, Liska's tale verges on the comical in its lack of political correctness. He admits an excessive interest in the workings of Latin American brothels, visiting them for research purposes to provide detailed reports on the shape, size and quality of every pair of breasts he encounters and concludes that the finest prostitutes are to be found in El Salvador (you won't find that kind of travel tip in a Rough Guide). In keeping with the spirit of the age and his nationality, he's also openly disdainful of the Latinos, making scathing observations about their poor timekeeping, insincerity and deceitful nature. The spectre of Communism also runs through the book, a reminder of how in this era the Latin American countries were ripe for a leftwing revolution as had recently occurred in Cuba. The fear comes across as slightly hysterical now, but it's easy to forget how seriously the threat was considered at the time, and the parallels to the current 'War on Terror' are painfully obvious.

Although he can come over as the typical brash American, Danny Liska was no mindless oaf, more a product of his time. His human curiosity was insatiable, his grasp of cultural and political situations intelligent and, like the best travel writers, he relished nothing more than to immerse himself in the heart of every culture he encountered. He was drawn to the mysterious, the exotic and the supernatural, and his nose for a good story outweighs any fear or discomfort that might have hampered a less brave or inquisitive traveller.

> He admits an excessive interest in the workings of Latin American brothels, visiting them for research purposes...

TALES FROM THE SADDLE

Ted Simon – Around the world 1973-77

Ted Simon will be well known to many readers of *AMH*. His 64,000 mile journey around the world in 1973 on a 500cc Triumph Tiger was impressive by anyone standards but above all, he deserves a place in this pantheon for the fact that his four-year odyssey resulted in him writing *Jupiter's Travels*, the book that is responsible for bringing the notion of 'adventure motorcycling' to the wider public. It's become one of the classics of travel literature and more than any other motorcycle travel book, has inspired others to hit the road. As Ted states early on, 'It was going to be the journey of a lifetime, a journey that millions dream of and never make, and I wanted to do justice to all those dreams.'

In 1973 Ted was working in London as a journalist at *The Sunday Times* when he set off as a forty-year old novice rider to explore the world. The resulting story is a beautifully written tale of what happens when a curious, enquiring mind meets a 1970s British motorcycle. It is full of humour and insights into the human condition as well as all the escapades one would expect from such a grand adventure. *Jupiter's Travels* is a book that changes lives and the 400,000 copies it has sold is a testament to its lasting influence. In 2003 Ted Simon set off again to retrace his route, resulting in the book, *Dreaming of Jupiter*, a fascinating if sometimes melancholic view of how the world has changed in the thirty years since his original trip.

Jupiter's Travels **is the book that launched a thousand trips.**

Although *Jupiter's Travels* is the book that launched a thousand trips, Ted is always keen to make the point: 'It's not about the motorcycle'. Robert Fulton had a similar sentiment regarding his choice of transport: 'The motorcycle wasn't the reason for taking the trip' he writes, 'rather the trip was the reason for the motorcycle.' Interestingly, this is a common theme among successful motorcycle travellers – they're often travellers first, motorcyclists second. As Ted would be the first to point out, it's all about the journey…

They Also Served…

There have been many other great pioneering motorcycle journeys, but they often remain unknown due to the fact that they hailed from outside the English-speaking world. Here are a few of the non-Anglo heroes…

Robert Sexe was a French reporter and photographer who rode around the world, including a brutal crossing of Siberia, on an obscure Belgian prototype motorcycle in the mid-1920s. He is reputed to be the inspiration for Hergé's character, Tintin.

The **Omidvar Brothers** were two Iranians who in 1957 acquired a pair of Matchless motorcycles and travelled the world for seven years, living with remote tribes and filming their adventures.

Adbab Husni Tello was a famous Syrian adventurer who rode the world in the 1950s on a BSA and reputedly visited 5000 cities and towns on four continents, and wrote eleven books about his travels. He makes an appearance in Danny Liska's book as a fellow traveller and successful lothario!

Zoltan Sulkowsky was a 25-year old Hungarian who set off with a friend on an eight-year ride around the world on a Harley Davidson outfit. His book, *Around the World on a Motorcycle: 1928 to 1936*, is now available in English.

Asking the audience

On the road from the UK to Australia on a KTM 990, **James and Cat Rix** *suggest that breaking down need not be so bad.*

Before you set out on a big trip you have a million things you think you need to know or worry about. This includes the assumption that you need to be a master mechanic. But if you're like me you might set out with a hope, a prayer (and a couple of screwdrivers) that if you're really lucky things won't go too wrong. Well I'm here to tell you I hope they do. Not in a sinister way of course, but enough of a problem that you need help from others, because that's where your stories will come from.

The culture shock hits you hard the first couple of days, but we were finally getting the knack of India. For so many reasons this isn't something you're going to be able to comprehend until you get there, but that's half the reason you should go. We were scooting along on a nice stretch of road headed to Jagdalpur in the south. Our plan was to see the waterfalls nearby before cutting across towards Goa for a bit of a Christmas treat.

The road was potholed and dusty, in other words pretty good going for India. I'd just passed over an unexpectedly large railway crossing with two big lurches and up ahead a lorry crawled along, bouncing side to side over the potholes. As I put the power down to overtake it, the KTM felt odd and quickly got odder so I pulled over quickly, thinking my wheel was collapsing. Cat jumped off and I looked down; sure enough we had a flat, our first since leaving England a few months ago.

No problem I thought, I'll get the tyre off and replace the tube using my snazzy, untried titanium tyre levers, all the while trying to think back to the videos I'd watched showing how to break the tyre's bead by the roadside. For once in India, there was nothing really around; the next village was about 10km away. We slowly unpacked the 990 and I spun the wheel to see if there was a nail or something, but to my horror found a three-inch split in the TKC.

Cat, the usual optimist, was trying to reassure me it would be OK, even though it was she who'd suggested we leave our spare tyres in Nepal – we could get them sent out if needed. Scratching my head for a minute, I knew one thing, the wheel and tyre had to come off so I got to work.

As we progressed, one by one people began to stop, until there were push-bikes, tuk-tuks, cars, bikes and even a bus parked nearby while onlookers and helpers gathered round. It was hot and I was sweating, but soon the questions about the bike began, the same questions we always got. So once the wheel was off, I paused for a minute to go over the bike with the curious crowd.

'OK folks, listen up. What we have here is a KTM 990S v-twin with two discs up front and three fuel tanks giving us 30 litres so at about 12kpl that's about three-fifty clicks between fill ups. This baby's got 105 horsepower with a top speed of about 200kph. She cost us about £4000, and yes, we've ridden it all the way from England, give or take'. I then used my Garmin to zoom out and show them our route. This was something I always tried to do with big crowds as it got us all talking. It might have been the twentieth time that day, but it was the first time for this lot.

Enough chat; I needed to get the tyre off the wheel. I got Cat to stand on one side of the tyre and I on the other – weighing 115kg (me, that is) can be handy for popping tyres off rims. But once both beads were off, not having done this before, I found removing the actual tyre nearly impossible. Many of the onlookers tried to help but they were as clueless as me, until suddenly a voice piped up from the crowd:

'Hello my friend.' I looked up and saw a well-dressed Indian gent.

'Goodness gracious, what has happened to your motor bicycle?'

'Goodness gracious, what has happened to your motor bicycle?'

I pointed at the big split in the tyre.

'Oh not good, not good at all. Come with me. Next village is tyres shop.' I checked Cat would be OK on her own for a few minutes and left her to continue hosting Question Time while I hopped on the back of a tiny moped. We talked all the way into town. This guy turned put to be a local phone shop owner who'd heard there was a mysterious bike broken down and had come out to take a look. He took me to the tyre guy who, with a smile quickly got the tyre off the rim, showing me how to do it in the process. Little did I know that I was soon to become an arch exponent of the dark art. He looked at the big split and shook his head. My new Indian friend explained the tyre couldn't be fixed. I suggested a temporary fix so he shrugged his shoulders and fitted a few

pieces of tyre liner and the new tube I'd given him. 'Go very slow,' he advised. 'Slowly, slowly.'

My Indian help kindly declined any payment so we headed back to the bike. As we got close we both laughed as the crowd had doubled and in the middle was poor Cat trying to let everyone have their say in the finest Dimblebonian tradition:

'Yes, lady at the back there in the red sari?"

The throng parted as we rode up and even though he was wearing his nice suit trousers and a clean shirt, my new friend got straight on the dirt to help me. Soon we had the KTM back together and waved goodbye to our admiring audience. Our moped-mounted benefactor asked us to stop by for some chow but it was getting late. We had at least an hour's slowly-slowly ride to Jagdalpur and didn't want to arrive in the dark. He was very understanding so we gave him our website and email and he was very pleased with this.

We crawled into the small town of Jagdalpur but after two days sniffing around it was clear we had no chance of getting a fat 18-inch tyre to fit the 990. After some thought we decided for the third time on this trip to hire a truck to take us back to the city of Raipur 400 kilometres back where we'd stopped a few days ago.

We woke nice and early and wandered into the town market where we'd spotted truck drivers hanging out, and set about negotiating our ride and after a small bit of haggling we were on our way. Once back in Raipur the owner of our previous hotel immediately offered us help to find the tyre. One of his cousins made some calls and located a 120/80. The KTM ran a 150/80 and at £150 the replacement came a with a four-day delay. I decided to shop around and the owner gave me the use of his jeep and two of his hotel staff.

Eventually I came across a small shack where a scruffy guy was fixing flats. He asked me what the wheel was for as he'd not seen one that size before. The guy then insisted I could get a tyre nearly that size and pointed us to a Sikh guy on the other side of the street. As soon as we met I got a great vibe from him. He was a big guy like me with a full beard, wearing a Sikh turban. He smiled and asked how he could help me. I explained my situation and straight away he dug up another 120/80 for just £40. He smiled and laughed when I told him what I'd been offered so far. He pointed at my skin and said 'That's an expensive colour you're wearing' with a big smile.

He said he was sure he could get a bigger one and before we knew it, he was shutting his shop and telling my hotel aides to follow him. In the car he explained he was passionate about travel and listed about fifteen countries he'd visited, telling me about time he had spent in Dubai, China and Japan. We drove around and stopped at what looked like a fruit and veg shop with a sideline in fan belts and oils. He advised me to wait in the car so he could negotiate a local rate. If they had anything and saw me the price would shoot up. My Sikh chum reappeared with what looked like a pretty big tyre, and after a five-minute conversation with the shop owner, he waved me over and introduced me. The tyre was a 130/90, much bigger than anything else I'd seen, although they still only wanted £35.

I was still hopeful of finding something the right size and pointed to a tyre shop across the road.

'Oh no, they are Chinese tyres, you don't want them.' Said the Sikh.

When I asked why he explained, 'Those Chinese, they make poor quality products.' I took a risk and cracked a joke, suggesting, 'It's funny you say that, in England that's what we say about Indian made products!' Both big men fell about laughing and the big Sikh high-fived me, saying I was a very funny chap and then proceeded to explain my joke for the others standing nearby.

I bought the oversized tyre and we jumped in his car and returned to the small shack to get it fitted to the wheel. We chatted some more over coffee and dhal and I promised to return later that afternoon with Cat and the mighty KTM which ended up drawing a huge crowd around his shop.

As you might expect, this was not the end of the problem. The side effect of sticking the oversized tyre on the 990 was not just odd handling, but also the amount of heat that must be generated (well, that's my assumption). Our replacement, heavy duty inner tube burned up after two days after which we had to make do with skinny local tubes for front tyres – and they popped every 100km or so.

This meant we had to cut short our India excursion and Christmas in Goa, and instead head straight out for Nepal and our stash of spare tyres. Doing so, we got through about nine tubes in three days but every time without fail, people came to watch or offer help. During one of our stops, a guy even rode me to a town 50 kilometres away on his moped to buy five new tubes.

You're never on your own – certainly not in India. Riding a big bike around the world invites curiosity and exposes you to the people, and one of the best ways to see how friendly and helpful they can be is to need their help. I promise they'll be far more helpful than you'd ever expect and there's not a single problem that's ever going to leave you stranded by the road next to your bike.

A tale of two bridges

Tony Pettie *recalls a couple of moments while negotiating the scores of bridges, fair and foul, along the BAM track in Far Eastern Russia during the now-legendary Sibirsky Extreme Project.*

As often, I was riding a little way behind Walter and Terry. Rounding a bend, through some trees I spotted a great expanse of what looked like a turbulent lake, but as I approached saw it was in fact a very wide river. Soon I was confronted by the chilling sight of a very, very long bridge with no sides, just an elevated causeway of old wooden railway sleepers a little wider than a car stretching into the far distance. Not only was the river nearly half-a-mile wide here, it was in full flow, a swirling mass of turbid water some fifteen metres below.

I was too late for the team discussion we usually had when confronted with the latest obstacle; the other two had decided better not to think about this one too long and had set off. I learned later without so much as a shared word or a look that the sight had similarly fazed them. They were already more than fifty metres into it, Terry some way ahead of Colebatch. I had little choice but to work out for myself how I was going to tackle it. I felt it was too far and narrow to ride straight – evidently something the others had each already decided, as they were 'power walking' their bikes.

I was fully aware that my accursed alloy panniers would make walking awkward, but before starting I had two other problems to overcome. Firstly, my right boot sole was falling apart, catching the ground on every footfall. Duct tape wouldn't stick so I decided to let it flap and lift my foot higher than normal. The other problem was the side stand had lost its spring weeks earlier and was kept up with elastic straps. This made deploying it on a narrow bridge rather difficult. Thinking I'd need to take rests, I opted to let it drag along the uneven bridge surface. This proved to have probably been a life saving decision. Having also decided to power-walk the bike under engine power, there was only one thing left to do: get on with it.

The initial hundred metres or so were particularly awkward as there were some lateral 'running' planks of wood for four-wheeled vehicles and a further centre plank fixed over the sleepers. All very inconvenient as it made judging where to position the bike and myself midway between the exposed edges rather difficult. I was acutely aware I had to keep control of the XT at all times. If it fell, depending on direction either it or me with it would certainly be in the river below. Hopefully the fall would knock me out as with the weight of my riding gear the frigid, fast-flowing river would have done for me.

I walked the bike forward at tick over, letting the clutch from time to time to gain a little surge. My right thumb rested on the kill button as I focused intently on the bridge's surface immediately ahead. Approaching midway there was a series of loose, rotten sleepers either side of a strange, flat topped

metal ridge raised some 15cm above the sleepers. I wrongly assumed this would be my biggest problem.

I went about it slowly so as to remain stable, particularly when applying extra power to get over the step and then holding it steady as it dropped off the far side. After a couple of minutes I was safely over and back on sleepers.

By now I was sweating profusely from the effort and tension. Perspiration was dripping onto my glasses which steamed up and blurred. I kicked the dangling side stand forward, pulled the gear lever into neutral with my right hand and rested my arms, wrists and my twisted back and neck.

While doing this I glanced away from the planks for the first time and was alarmed at the mass of dense black clouds building up to the right. Just as soon as I clocked them, a rush of wind swept over the bridge, followed by the crackle and hiss of nearby lightening and a deafening clap of thunder which shook me, the bike and the bridge. Colebatch later told me he'd watched the bolt strike the adjacent rail bridge about a hundred metres to my left. A heavy downpour followed with more thunder and lightning.

Mindful that I was clinging to the only metal object above the wooden bridge, I didn't really know what to do. I thought about moving away and lying on the sleepers, but the wind was picking up and gusting from all directions. As it was I had difficulty standing and thought the bike might get blown over. I decided walking home to Moscow with no bike was only slightly worse than being struck by lightning and so I draped myself sideways across the bike to weigh it down.

I decided walking home to Moscow with no bike was only slightly worse than being struck by lightning

As I hung on, hoping the side stand would support the additional weight, I soon realised I'd stopped just in time. The winds were now reaching gale force gusts and constantly changing direction. There's no chance I'd have been

able to hold the bike while removing the elastic side stand strap in such conditions. To make matters worse, as the gusts increased the rain turned into pelting hailstones bigger than peas. What had I done to deserve this! Although stinging my skin, seeing an opportunity for refreshment, I twisted my face upwards and opened my mouth to grab a few hailstones.

Cold water seeped up my arms and ran down my neck. The storm was so low over the river that cloud obscured all vision beyond a few metres. I couldn't see either bank, nor even the river below and hung on, suspended in limbo like some mythical Greek hero enduring his latest torment thrown down by the gods. I couldn't see my mates and hoped they'd made it safely across. There was as much possibility that they could have gone over the edge as me.

I hung on, suspended in limbo like some mythical Greek hero enduring his latest torment ...

After ten minutes the storm abated to steady rain and the cloud lifted a little. Shivering with cold and in clothes soaked inside and out (a feeling I was getting used to on this trip), I resumed walking the bike over slippery oil-coated sleepers. As I progressed the other two bikes emerged through my rain-flecked glasses at the end of the bridge and with ten metres to go I heard English voices from below. I was so, so relieved I was no longer alone out on that bridge!

We said nothing. Nothing needed to be said. After a couple of minutes recovering I got on the bike and we all continued, each silently wondering what the BAM would throw at us next.

Throughout the trip I was eternally grateful to everyone we met along the way and to my riding buddies for the help without which I'd not have reached the Vitim River Bridge – but that half mile was me, just me. For the first time in months I had no need to thank anyone.

The first time we first took to riding the BAM's railway embankments and track to get around impassable sections, we watched several trains pass. By standing sticks upright in the ballast and seeing which ones got knocked over we worked out the train body width was no greater than the sleepers. So, in theory, if we kept bikes, luggage and ourselves out of 'sleeper range' all should be fine. Except the bridges.

On most BAM rail bridges, including the one we were about to tackle, there wouldn't be sufficient space between the train and the bridge's structure to get a bike through. Longer bridges had short rectangular refuge balconies every 20 metres, each slightly longer than a bike, but no wider.

Having hauled my luggage to the other side first (those metal boxes were my biggest mistake of the whole trip) and watched my buddies ride across, I gaffered up my boot and set off. But within a short distance I saw Colebatch and Terry jump out, waving their arms. Unsure if it was another wind-up we occasionally pulled to keep spirits up, I waved back and plodded on.

... a heart stopping sight and sound that'll live with me forever.

Then, about a third the way across came a heart stopping sight and sound that'll live with me forever. A huge locomotive hurtling round the bend, entirely filling the bridge's metalwork box sections and blasting its horns and sirens – at me! The next refuge was about three metres ahead. I dumped the clutch and rammed the front wheel into the far corner, leant the bike away from the train and steadied myself for an impact.

Of all the many rail bridge refuges we'd seen along the 2700 miles of BAM road, this was only one with something blocking it. An oil drum stood at the back of the balcony, right by my roll bag preventing the bike from leaning away from the oncoming train. If the train clipped the roll bag it would take the bike and me with it. I had to get clear of the bike but I only half dismounted with my right leg half way over the seat when the train loomed over me and started thundering past.

The whole bridge trembled and on the smooth metal surface, with my weight off balance, the bike slowly slid away from under me with the vibration. The wheels slid towards the track as the rest fell sideways, pushing the upper parts further away from the train. I was held there, left leg under the bike, body pinned against the refuge railing and my other leg on the rear roll-bag. I dared not move but thought, 'Colebatch! You filming this?'

It was a long train of oil tanks with locos at both ends and although travelling at 40mph, it took two or three agonising minutes to pass. It was only during this time I realised the peril I was in. Until that point, in the few seconds from seeing the train coming at me, I had felt no panic, just an urgent need to quickly reassess the possibilities and act accordingly. It was all calmly done – until I stopped to think about it. Even now I get a cold sweat realising what so nearly could have been.

Twice in my life I've knowingly been close enough to my probable end to reach out and touch it. Both occasions were on bridges on the BAM road in Far Eastern Russia.

Surviving Morocco

Ural-eulogising **Carla King** *confronts the myth of Moroccan mayhem*

I ride the motorcycle off the ferry in Tangiers, steeling myself for the hours-long ordeal I've been promised by friends who have travelled here before. I hand over my passport, resolving to be calm and patient while fending off corrupt officials demanding bribes. I have two weeks before I meet friends in Marrakech for a luxurious week in a private villa with swimming pool, a chef, servants, and tour guides, and I give the officials that address thinking that if anything horrible happens to me, at least my friends will know. Until then, I'm on my own with camping gear and a tight budget.

The police and the customs officials and several men who don't seem to have any official purpose at all take my documents on separate journeys. My registration card, green card, and insurance forms are boring, but my just-renewed American passport is a fascination. The police examine it between sips of espresso and conversations with their friends. I am invited to sit, but I just smile and stand while they hold the hologram up to the light, then flip through the visa pages with their soft images of American icons: The eagle, a grizzly bear, cowboys, saguaro cacti, a totem pole, the Statue of Liberty.

Half an hour later I'm shocked to be dismissed with all the required stamps, signatures and receipts.

Half an hour later I'm shocked to be dismissed with all the required stamps, signatures, and receipts. Riding on a few hundred feet I see a cash point. How convenient! But do I dare? What if it eats my card. Diligently scanning for potential muggers, I stick my card in the slot, enter my code and it spits out 1000 dirhams. This also seems a miracle. I won't have to negotiate with unscrupulous money-changers. Whatever the bank charges, it's worth it.

The whitewashed gates to the city stand beyond the still empty and expansive black asphalt parking lot and I start up the hill into the city, leaving the sparkling Mediterranean behind me. Where are the Arabs demanding bribes? The clamouring hordes, touts, pickpockets, and mobs of dirty children selling trinkets?

According to my map the central square is at the top of the hill, but all the roads look like mere alleyways, so I hesitate. A cab jumps in front of me and I quickly follow in his slipstream as he blasts his horn through streams of pedestrians wrapped in bright cloth, streetside stalls piled with colourful spices and racks of knockoff purses, dresses, belts, wallets, watches. Suddenly we are in the main square.

Startled, I pull over and find myself at a Maroc Telecom stall, which is really just a card table with a sign and a pile of used cell phones attended by a teenage boy. He helps me replace the Spanish SIM in my cell with a prepaid

THE OPEN ROAD

Moroc SIM, and voila! For less than five dollars I have a Moroccan phone number.

With the help of a young man I find at McDonald's, I find my hotel, which turns out to be a thirty-second ride from the port. I get a basic room with hot shower, toilet and secure parking. I wash up and go wandering the streets, still on guard against touts and pickpockets and mobs of dirty children, steering clear of carpet shops notorious for holding tourists as virtual hostages, while drowning them in sugared mint tea, until they purchase a rug whether they want it or not.

At the souk, European tourists scurry about in shorts and backpacks, clutching their cameras and staying close to their guides. I've taken care to dress modestly in light brown slacks, a long-sleeved shirt, hiking sandals, and a hand-woven straw hat acquired in Spain. I carry a large purse slung over my shoulder and, with the addition of a henna-patterned scarf, I figure I blend in with the expats.

Nobody tries to sell me anything, much less lock me in a shop until I buy a carpet. And the next day there are no police barriers on the road to the coast, or later, on the road to Marrakech, or Fez, or to the Sahara. There is no black-mailing, demand for bribes, or planting of hashish in my panniers or, to my great relief, the lewd sexual overtures I'd been told to expect as a solo female traveller, 'especially a blonde'.

My friends had visited over a decade ago, but big changes came with King Mohammed VI who inherited the throne when his father died in 1999. He implemented an aggressive program to attract more tourism (already

Morocco's second-biggest income generator after phosphates), programs to attack poverty and corruption and human rights issues and, to further piss off the fundamentalists, a family code that gives women more freedom. Burkas are in the minority, and though bellies and breasts are never, ever visible (except on tourists), young women usually wear headscarves but sport fashionable jeans and blouses.

This is not to say that I pass unnoticed; I'm riding an outfit after all. I ride into town, park next to a fruit vendor or small shop. The rumble of the big Ural attracts attention and onlookers understandably gather. I remove my helmet and smile, enjoying the collective dropping of jaws as my blonde braids tumble down my back, and then there's laughter and a rush to shake my hand. The circus has come to town.

The rumble of the big Ural attracts attention ... I remove my helmet and smile, enjoying the collective dropping of jaws as my blonde braids tumble down my back ...

It's a win-win situation. I buy some apricots and pears from the vendor and chat with him a while. He shoos off the irritating young man who wants to guide me through town and I'm free to wander while he keeps an eye on the bike and enjoys the increased business that comes from curious passers by.

Today you can travel much of Morocco on paved roads and an expanding network of toll highways, but I prefer the back roads. A dirt track veering off into the unknown sucks me in like a magnet. Results vary: stunning views, positively Alpine landscapes, tea with a Berber family, a hundred goats blocking the path, wildflowers, a beekeeper who offers me a honeycomb, women in bright fabrics tending fields, a creek crossing that's deeper than expected. It's only a lack of fuel that sends me back to the main route.

I underestimate the Atlas mountains. Winding my way through a cedar forest I'm surprised by a large baboon who scurries into the road to jump on a female preening herself in the middle of an intersection. Climbing higher onto a bare plateau, a storm suddenly attacks and I'm caught in dark, almost night sky, with high winds, hail, and snow. I'd not experienced this much weather even in the European Alps, which I'd crossed a few weeks earlier after picking up the Ural outfit from friends in Austria. When bolts of lightning zigzag horizontally across the road I park the bike and crouch in a ditch until I see a large truck coming. My plan is to catch up with it and stay close, believing that lightning always strikes the bigger or higher object. Hail pummels my helmet and finds its way into my summer-weight gear to soak my clothes. My gloves are wet and fingers numb.

Not even an hour later it's baking at over 40°C with the dunes beckoning down a sand track marked with painted yellow rocks leading to a hotel. The man at the last fuel station recommended it as cheap, clean, and air conditioned, with excellent food and a swimming pool at the foot of the dunes.

Hobbled camels startle at the sound of the engine, rock clumsily up in their see-saw way, and stumble off the road. Ten miles later the auberge welcomes me into its gates. The man was right, it was lovely and I couldn't tear myself away for three days enjoying the pool, the black starry night from the rooftop, early morning walks in the golden rose dunes, mint tea, and cold sliced oranges marinated with salty black olives. As I'm not experienced riding in sand, I appreciated being able to practice safely within walking distance of the auberge, and my confidence grows.

On departure I finally get a taste of the trouble I've been warned about – the hotel owner tries to overcharge me by double. Thank goodness. Now I can warn my friends of the dangers of Morocco. It isn't completely unwarranted I find, once I join my friends in Marrakech. As seven well-dressed women touring the city we are absolutely bombarded by touts, dirty children pressing trinkets upon us, and the object of lewd comments by Arab men peering down the substantial cleavage of one of us who's dressed as if she was at home. Don't get me wrong. I loved vacationing with the girls at the villa. I could get used to having a chef, and servants who know how to make my favourite drink and when I like it, and to keep a fresh supply of cold watermelon by my side at the pool. But when I really want to get to know a country, I'll rough it solo on a bike anytime.

Tea with Bin Laden's brother

Reeling from the shock of a personal tragedy, graphic artist, **Simon Roberts** *set off on a life-affirming road trip from Bristol to Kathmandu.*

Quetta, Pakistan. 'A meeting point for numerous tribal groups. Unlike most other Pakistani cities, it exudes the air of a wild frontier town. Although the main township is safe for tourists, occasional tribal clashes do spill out onto the street'.

I'd read this the previous night as I lay in my tent while camped in the police compound at Notkundi, a small settlement half way across the Baluchistan desert in western Pakistan. I had hoped to camp out under the stars on this stretch but at dusk I was flagged down by the police. 'Sir, it is not safe on this road after dark', he informed me, 'There are bandits in this area – you must stay here tonight'. I turned into the dusty compound and metal gates were locked behind me. I unpacked, set up my small tent and was invited to join the other men for a meal. I slept uneasily contemplating my ride along the Afghan border the next day.

Quetta lay spread out beneath me. I bungeed the guidebook onto my tank bag, open at the relevant page, clicked the bike into gear and cautiously rejoined the early evening traffic descending into the town.

I slept uneasily contemplating my ride along the Afghan border the next day.

Sunset was always a difficult time to arrive in a town. The streets invariably seethed with traffic and people. Trucks, buses, tuk-tuks, bicycles, mopeds and of course, overloaded horses and carts all fighting for space along already overcrowded roads. People spilled out of busy markets, smoke from food stands and thick diesel fumes filled the air. Try riding through this with one eye on your map, looking for street names and asking directions with a full-face helmet. Eventually I wrestled the bike onto the forecourt of the Hotel Bloom Star which promised an oasis of calm within. I unloaded the bike, checked in and ordered tea in the tranquil courtyard garden. Perfect. After a tough day on the road I was always thrilled to track down these havens; such a contrast to the mayhem left outside the gates.

'So, what is your job, sir?' asked the man at reception, having talked of his dream of running his own hotel. I explained I was a freelance graphic artist and added how I also drew caricatures at parties and weddings. 'Maybe you draw me later?' he added, excitedly. I nodded and went in search of a meal.

I stepped out onto the now deserted street – transformed from the chaos of a few hours before – and picked my way along the broken pavement avoiding open drains, smouldering fires and wild-eyed dogs. Coming across a brightly lit café, I stepped inside. Men looked up, nodded and resumed eating. I ordered what seemed to be that night's speciality and made a note. In future, avoid eating out on Mondays. The mood seemed tense, not the kind of place to get out my photos and journal or try and strike up a conversation.

The mood seemed tense, not the kind of place to get out my photos and journal and try to strike up a conversation.

I'd been keeping a visual record of my trip in the form of drawings and paintings in a journal which I often used to introduce myself when I met people. These were eventually to form the basis of my illustrated book of the trip. But that night my journal remained in my backpack. I ate quickly and scurried back to the hotel.

'Ah… now a cartoon, sir?' the young receptionist suggested as I walked past. I looked around and immediately regretted having put the idea into his head. The once empty foyer was now full of surly looking men in scruffy turbans engaged in deep conversation with the owner. These did not look like the kind of happy, drunken wedding guests I normally caricatured. I reluctantly pulled out my sketchpad and sat in the chair that had been thrust towards me.

The man sat opposite me could have been Osama Bin Laden's brother. Thick beard, hooked nose and piercing eyes under a mono brow. Normally this would have been perfect material for a caricaturist, but this was not a normal situation. A drop of sweat trickled down my temple.

I sketched feverishly trying to work up a drawing that would not offend my subject resulting in me being dragged naked through the streets of Quetta tied to the back of a Hilux. I feared he was expecting a proud portrait of himself with a hooded falcon on his arm, attentive women at his feet and a white stallion rearing in the background. I concentrated on doing a close-up of his head and shoulders, while hoping to keep mine attached. I finished the sketch, turned it round to show him and braced myself.

'Huh?' was his initial response. Was that the sound of a pickup backing up? He frowned and showed the other assembled men. Silence. Headlines flashed in my head: 'Tourist's body found mutilated in Pakistan'. Then one started laughing. Then another. Then they all guffawed with in merriment.

'Ha! Now you draw ALL of us!' exclaimed the man nearest to me, grabbing my shoulder. I rubbed my still-intact neck, laughed nervously and moved round the group. I slept poorly that night, fearing what might have been.

Next morning the day was already baking as I fought my way out of Quetta heading south over the Bolam Pass on the road to Sukkur, a route '…not recommended to those travelling independently'.

The tarmac shimmered as I gained speed along the deserted road. All was quiet. Quiet that is except for the nagging rumble coming through my foot pegs. I'd felt it in third gear over the previous days and had optimistically changed the gearbox oil in Quetta hoping for a smoother ride. It was not to be. The sensation was coming through in all gears now, louder and LOUDER. I stopped and let the engine cool down. I checked the oil. All OK. I started the engine and engaged first gear. KKERRUNCHHH!!! I'm no mechanic but it sounded terminal. It's over, I thought. I slumped to the ground and lit a cigarette. It should have been a Hamlet cigar with a bit of Bach in the background.

I felt surprisingly calm. Ted Simon had assured his readers that a breakdown is where adventures begin. But this desert road seemed completely, well, deserted. Eventually I made out a shimmering speck on the horizon. Two men on a moped. I'm saved! It was only as they got nearer I realised they were heavily armed.

> I felt surprisingly calm. Ted Simon had assured his readers that a breakdown is where adventures begin.

Find out the rest of the story at ⌨ www.teawithbinladensbrother.com

South America on a plate

Jay Kannaiyan *takes his taste buds to South America for a ride of their lifetime.*

One good thing about life on the road is that it boils down to the simpler things. When I'm travelling on my motorcycle I'm not fretting about my next utilities bill or how I'll be rated against my co-workers. In the saddle my concerns extend no further than 'how far till the next fill up' and 'what's for lunch?' Travelling like this becomes a way to clear the mind and feel comfortable with my place in this world. And with an inquisitive appetite, exploring the markets and roadside food stalls was a conduit for expanding my palate while experiencing the local culture. Being an aspiring cook back in Chicago, it was interesting to see what foods locals considered to be staples.

I rode south through Central America then crossed to Colombia and made my way down the Andes to Bolivia. From La Paz I headed down into the Amazon and crossed Brazil before coming down the Atlantic coast and then turning inland to see the rest of the Andes all the way down to Tierra del Fuego. I'd prepared many years for this journey and knowing that my budget wasn't infinite I sought out the cheapest meals along the way. They ranged from steaming fish tacos in Mexico to lumps of quivering pork fat in Ecuador and in Argentina steaks as tender as a new-born calf.

Mexican food is perhaps the best-known Latin American cuisine, but what Mexicans eat isn't what you'll get served in your local Tex-Mex joint by waiters dressed as cartoon *mariachis*. Chilli con carne, fajitas and nachos are all creations cooked up by Mexican migrants in the US. In Mexico the most common food was soft corn tacos with grilled meat, rice and beans. I spent some time in a remote Mayan village in southern Mexico where the villagers ate corn tortillas for every meal. They said they got stomach aches if they ever ate anything else. It can be tough for the stomach to change its habits, but for the adventure rider adapting to change is the name of the game. My intestines gamely volunteered to become willing martyrs in the search for exotic new dishes.

Cuy (guinea pig)... is served disembowelled and splayed out on your plate like a fireside bearskin rug.

In Ecuador I was introduced to *cuy* (guinea pig). Raised as pets by Europeans and North Americans, eating them might be considered bad form but cuy first hit the pan thousands of years ago as a viable source or protein. In Cuenca, my biker hosts took me to a market where we ate *cuy al horno* ('roasted'). It tasted great, like rabbit or the dark meat of chicken, although the presentation can be unnerving as it's served disembowelled and splayed out on your plate like a fireside bearskin rug; head and feet still attached. My hosts joked that it was customary for the guest of honour to eat the brain, which I duly did, prompting chuckles from all around.

Ecuador sits mostly at high altitude. I rode up to Laguna Quilotoa, a crater lake that sits at over 3900m (12,800'). Up there even on a sunny day it was extremely chilly, and I stopped in the small town of Zumbahua, numbed by the freezing winds. A few roadside stalls were open and for a dollar I got two pieces of pork fat attached to a few strands of meat and some oily plantains. It's not my first choice; I'd normally have picked a couple of boiled eggs but up here in the cold pork fat was a good source of calories to sustain body heat.

Along the highways in Ecuador I saw complete pigs (the regular, curly-tailed variety) swinging from hooks and occasionally grilled with a blowtorch, like a South London doner kebab. The stall vendors told me that each pig cost about $100 and they got through several in a day. As truckers stopped for a bite, meat was carved from the carcass, grilled and served with sauces. I admired how close and pragmatic these Andean folk were to their food; not turned-off by seeing the entire dead animal that they were going to eat. This aspect of food production has become lost to us. School kids don't even know that chicken nuggets come from chickens. Send them to the Ecuadorian Andes!

Riding in the bracing Andes, what's better than a steaming bowl of heartening soup. I had all sorts of soups as I traversed Peru and one morning in the town of Celendin on the Cloud Forest Route in northern Peru, I chose what everyone else was having for breakfast – a bright green soup. It was appropriately named Caldo Verde, a broth made from kale, potatoes and eggs. It had a strong mint flavour, too, perfect for awakening the senses in the biting morning air. Another great Peruvian dish was *papa rellena* (stuffed potatoes). On my ride up to nearly 5000m to admire the snow peaks of Parque Nacional Huascarán, I passed another stall where a little lady swathed in blankets was frying up fresh papas, a potato patty stuffed with meat, deep fried and then topped with a green chilli sauce. Up there where the air was as thin as a dime, that was just what my stomach demanded.

Peruvians love their potatoes and many confided how they didn't feel they'd eaten properly until they've had their daily serving of papas. Introduced to the Old World by the Spanish, it's just a shame that they get processed out of all recognition. Of the 4000 or more varieties found in Peru, only a few are known to the outside world, depriving us of the biodiversity that the descendent of the Incas continue to enjoy today.

On the other side of Lake Titicaca lies Bolivia, the land of the coca leaf. Coca is grown in the lowlands of all the Andean countries, but Bolivia's largely indigenous population has an established relationship with the coca plant. Long before Europeans discovered how to isolate the coca alkaloid to make cocaine, the people of the Andes were chewing coca leaves to benefit from its mild stimulant properties. Along with helping to cope with the thin air, chewing coca is locally considered medicinal and nutritional.

I was taught how to chew coca by some friends I made in Oruro. The small green leaves are inserted into one side of the mouth where after half an hour a green ball of masticated leaves forms in your cheek. It tastes a little bitter but now comes the key ingredient, a small piece of ash is added to the ball to release the alkaloids. The immediate effect is a numbing sensation of the cheek although I didn't get a rush, more a lack of tiredness and a suppressed appetite. I chewed coca all through my high altitude stages in Bolivia and during my long crossing of the savannahs of northern Bolivia to the TransAmazonica in Brazil. Fatigue was kept at bay and hunger didn't distract me when riding miles of slimy mud, soft sand and eyeball-frothing corrugations across the Amazon basin. In small quantities the alkaloids in coca are just fine for the body and not addictive, but I guess too much of anything isn't good for you.

I think the people of Argentina would say that there's no such thing as too much beef. The reputation of succulent Argentine steaks is well deserved – the meat is unlike anything you'll eat elsewhere. I had a delicious strip steak, grilled on the streets of Buenos Aires and served on the traditional wooden platter for just $3. It came ladled with spicy *chimichurri*, a sauce made with olive oil, parsley, garlic, vinegar and a variety of other condiments. The excessive consumption of red meat in the Western world is associated with ill health because cows are fed grain in controlled environments while being pumped with antibiotics against the diseases that come from living in such conditions. In Argentine the vast amount of pasture available allows cattle to live and eat naturally, out on the range chewing on Pampas grass. The result is higher quality beef than we're used to with less saturated fat as well as higher levels of omega-3 fatty acids that keep brains pin sharp. Next time you see a gaucho win Mastermind you'll know why.

Grilling meat is an essential part of the Argentine experience and I was treated to countless *asados* (barbecues) whenever I stayed with local bikers and other hosts. Steaks are cooked over a wood or coal fire on a smoky grill called a *parrilla*, along with beef ribs, chorizo and some hearty *morcilla* (blood sausage). I also enjoyed some creative vegetable grilling: sweet peppers cut in half with an egg broken into the pepper cup and then slow-cooked.

From tacos to arepas, chichi, mate de coca, Colombian bandeja de paisa, asados and churrascos, a motorcycle ride through Latin America is guaranteed to be a feast as grand as the Andes and as vast as the Amazon. *Vamonos moto-quieros*!

AMH CONTRIBUTORS

Walter Colebatch is a leading adventure motorcyclist and Russia/Mongolia/Siberia specialist. From the first unescorted crossing of China to a world record for motorcycle altitude, Colebatch has been at the forefront of adventure motorcycle travel for 20 years. Born in Australia, he's now based in London.

Chris & Chloe Granger, both architects from the UK, stressed out and desperate for an adventure, set off for South America having only six months riding experience between them. Armed with two 650s, they are leisurely making their way from Ushuaia to Vancouver, learning the ropes on the way. How difficult can it be...?!

Australian **Ken Duval** started riding at 15 and in 1985 travelled around Australia and New Zealand with Carol on a CX650. Between 1997-2001 they completed their first RTW on a BMW R80G/S covering 57 countries. Their second RTW on same bike continues to this day.

Duncan Hughes is a 44-year-old former IT contractor from Manchester on his first big ride outside of Europe. He's currently residing in a Santiago backpackers hostel waiting for a new rear shock.

Mark Harfenist lives in Bellingham, WA where he dabbles in mountain biking, ski mountaineering, sea kayaking and world travel when not complaining loudly to anyone within earshot about his inexorable decline into plump, undignified, decrepit old age. He took up motorcycling only recently, in a rare moment of clarity.

Jay Kannaiyan sold up in Chicago and set off on his Suzuki DR650 in March, 2010 with the intention of exploring the countries of the Global South on his way back to his homeland of India. After Latin America, Jay is currently riding through Africa.

Valerio De Simoni, **Jamie Kenyon** and Ted Davant are the Quad Squad, three young Australian riders who set the Guinness World Record for the longest journey on a Quad. Doubling the previous record, they rode over 56,000km through 38 countries to raise $100,000 for Oxfam.

Gaurav Jani films documentaries about remote places and indigenous people. Riding *Solo to the Top of the World* and *One Crazy Ride* have won awards at film festivals worldwide. Gaurav also founded the 60kph.com motorcycle travel club and is part of Ride of My Life which conducts motorcycle tours in India.

Pat McCarthy (aka Barcelona Pat), a Spanish based Welshman of Irish decent and lifelong motorcyclist has ridden in Europe extensively over many years. A new challenge for 2012 was a solo charity ride from Tierra del Fuego to Alaska. His story can be found at 🖳 www.patonabike.blogspot.com

Lois Pryce is a British travel writer who left her job at the BBC to hit the road and has never looked back. Her books about her motorcycle journeys have been published around the world in several languages and have inspired many female (and male!) riders to launch their own adventures.
🖳 www.loisontheloose.com

Tony Pettie has been riding since 1958, first rode in Russia in 2004 and now lives in Moscow. When invited to join of the SibirskyExtreme Project it seemed a natural and proved to be the most demanding, exhilarating, and satisfying journey of his life. 'Age is no barrier, if the attitude is right'.

With little experience, in May 2009 **David Radford** set off on his first big ride from Edmonton, Canada. Nearly 200,000km and ninety countries later he finds himself in Chiang Mai, Thailand, still on the road. 'I guess I might as well admit, I'm trying to go around the world'. 🖳 gsguy.wordpress.com.

London-based 20-somethings, **James & Cat Rix** decided to take a year out and left the UK in June 2011 to ride to Australia via thirty countries or more on a KTM 990 Adventure S. 🖳 www.jamesandcat.com

Dr Paul Rowe is a Cornishman who spends his time between biking and working as an anaesthetist in Western Australia. He and wife Jenni are taking a brief break from the longer trips until their three little bikers are old enough to get addicted too.

After spending many hours in detention for drawing caricatures of his teachers, **Simon Roberts** now works successfully as a freelance graphic artist. The British climate has driven him to the south of France where he now lives with his wife Monica. Next trip/book? South East Asia – with backpack and drawing pad.

Ken Thomas started riding and racing in 1964. Thirty years later he rode a Ducati to Ukraine with daughter Caroline as pillion followed by backpacking around the world then cycling from Canada to Mexico along the Rockies. Recently he again rode with Caroline, this time to Cape Town. 🖳 www. horizonsunlimited.com/tstories/thomas

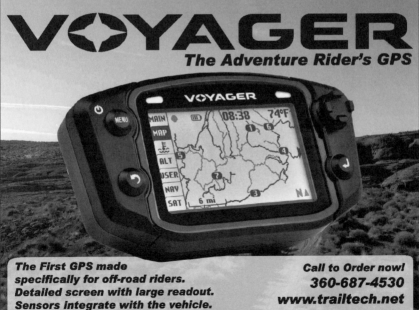

Index

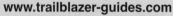